ACCOUNTING AND FINANCE INNOVATIONS

ACCOUNTING AND FINANCE INNOVATIONS

Howard Bethe
Gerty Bialik

Kruger Brentt
Publishers
2024

Kruger Brentt Publishers UK. LTD.
Company Number 9728962

Regd. Office: 68 St Margarets Road, Edgware, Middlesex HA8 9UU

ISBN: 978-1-78715-246-5

For information on all our publications visit our website at http://krugerbrentt.com/

Preface

In today's fast-paced and ever-evolving world, the realms of accounting and finance have undergone a profound transformation. Traditional practices that once shaped the financial landscape have given way to a new era of innovation, driven by technological advancements, changing regulatory landscapes, and shifting global economic paradigms. This surge of innovation has unleashed a wave of opportunities and challenges, prompting financial professionals to rethink and revolutionize the way they approach accounting and finance. The introduction of cutting-edge technologies such as artificial intelligence, blockchain, and data analytics has revolutionized the financial sector, streamlining processes, enhancing efficiency, and providing unparalleled insights into financial data. This influx of disruptive technologies has not only optimized day-to-day operations but has also empowered financial decision-makers to make more informed, data-driven choices, thereby shaping the strategic direction of businesses in unprecedented ways.

As the lines between accounting and finance continue to blur, these once distinct disciplines now find themselves intertwined, with professionals needing to possess a diverse skill set to navigate the complexities of this new era. A forward-thinking approach and a willingness to embrace innovation have become essential for businesses to remain competitive and agile in a rapidly changing landscape. This comprehensive exploration of "Accounting and Finance Innovations" delves into the latest trends, breakthroughs, and best practices that are reshaping the financial world. From embracing cloud-based accounting platforms to leverage real-time data access, to exploring the potential of decentralized finance (DeFi) and cryptocurrencies, this book seeks to equip readers with a thorough understanding of the transformative potential that waits within the financial sector.

Finance innovations leverage advanced technologies and streamlined processes to automate routine tasks, reduce manual errors, and accelerate financial operations. This increased efficiency allows finance professionals to focus on more strategic initiatives and value-added activities, ultimately boosting productivity across organizations. The integration of data analytics and artificial intelligence in finance enables better data-driven decision-making. Real-time insights and predictive analytics empower financial leaders to make informed choices, identify growth opportunities, and mitigate risks effectively. Finance innovations often extend to customer-facing aspects, such as digital payment solutions, mobile banking, and personalized financial advice. These improvements lead to a better customer experience, increasing customer satisfaction and loyalty.

The present book contains 15 chapters covering all related disciplines. It explores the dynamic and transformative landscape of modern finance, shedding light on the latest trends, breakthroughs, and best practices. It examines how these innovations are revolutionizing financial processes, decision-making, risk and also explores the integration of Environmental, Social, and Governance (ESG) considerations in finance, emphasizing the growing importance of responsible investing and sustainable business practices. Understanding the rapidly changing regulatory environment is crucial, and the book discusses how finance innovations interact with existing and evolving financial regulations and exploring how finance innovations facilitate global connectivity, the book discusses cross-border payments, foreign exchange, and their impact on international trade and investment.

We are grateful to all those persons as well as various books, manuals, periodicals, magazines, journals etc. that helped in the preparation of this book. In spite of the best efforts, it is possible that some errors may have occurred into the compilation and editing of the book. Further queries, constructive suggestions and criticisms for the improvement of the book are always welcome and shall be thankfully acknowledged.

Howard Bethe

Gerty Bialik

Contents

SECTION-1

MANAGEMENT ACCOUNTING AND E-BUSINESS MODEL

01 Management Accounting Practices and E-Business Model in the US Walmart Corporation

1. INTRODUCTION

Walmart is one of the world's largest global retailers, operating discounted, departmental, and warehouse stores across various jurisdictions. Walmart stores have been grown rapidly as they become very popular as a retail giant. In 2017, the total number of stores had 11,695 stores, of which 5,332 were located in the United States, and 6,363 were located overseas. The majority of Walmart stores outside the US are placed in Mexico as it has 2,411 Stores. Besides, the UK had 631, Canada 410, and Brazil 498 Walmart stores operated in 2017 [1]. Walmart has also increased its existence in China, where there were 439 stores in 2017. The Asian economy is proliferating, making China and India significant markets for Walmart (*ibid.*).

As a retail corporation, Walmart collects information on its stores, sales, and purchases through a centralized accounting information system connected to all stores. The system contains the details of daily transactions from every store. Walmart's Accounting System enables the company to make accurate projections of its stores' financial sales and purchases. This factor aids the company's decision-making process at the operational level [2]. The paper analyzes Walmart's management accounting system by discussing its inventory control and accounting practices, including its budgeting, costing, and capital decision making as presented in the capital structure to establish the strengths and weaknesses of its accounting system.

Gilbertson and Lehman [3] noted that Walmart has, specifically, installed the vision-suite accounting management software, composed of different financial management functions that include the general ledger, financial reporting, and integration of external accounting systems. Vision suite software automatically generates accounting documents for use within the company's accounting system. This helps the management access vital reports used in the decision-making process [4, 5]. Gilbertson and Lehman [3] observed that the main limitation to the vision suite software is its vulnerability to hacking and computer viruses. This means that gaps in control and security mechanisms could affect the company's financial information confidentiality. Such risks affect the reliability of an accounting system and its ability to ensure operational efficiency.

This chapter is divided after the introduction as follows. Section 2 presents the literature review. Section 3 provides the research methodology and US case study. Section 4 explains the analysis and discussion of the chapter, and Section 5 introduces the SWOT analysis of Walmart's business. The final section is the main conclusions and recommendations.

2. LITERATURE REVIEW

Contemporary accounting studies have shed light on how accounting is practiced in social activities and arrangements [6, 7, 8, 9, 10, 11, 12, 13]. Walmart's retail business has no exception as 'the social, or the environment passes through accounting. Conversely, accounting ramifies, extends and shapes the social' [14, 15]. One of the management accounting practices that can influence social activities is operating cost or overhead cost. According to Alsharari [16], there is no problem if all cost items could be directly traced to each cost center, so accurately calculating the product cost and profitability would be very easy. However, overhead costs are becoming prominent, and these might arrive at more than half of total manufacturing costs.

On the contrary, Walmart has reduced its operating expenses or overhead costs through implementing an advanced accounting information system, including management accounting practices. Walmart uses online accounting systems and software programs to automate business and accounting functions, online grocery, payments and receipts, and virtual communication. Advance accounting information systems led to the high efficiency of Walmart assets. This helped Walmart to reduce the operating costs to satisfy the social arrangements. Walmart has lowered the highest overhead expenses in labor costs as they can only get the minimum wages consistent with local laws.

2.1 Management Accounting Practices

Management accounting practices are systems that enable firms to generate information for budgeting, reporting and controlling, measuring performance, and costing products and services that in turn assists in managerial decision making [8, 17, 18, 19]. Management accounting information systems are structured differently across organizations and employ different techniques for collecting, processing, storing, and reporting financial information, in tandem with the agency theory. The significance of accounting systems has grown with increases in consumer demands, market competition, and market unpredictability, where proven scientific methods and reliable data is a prerequisite for managerial decision-making [20]. The significant new approaches that are relevant to management accounting systems; include the Just in Time (JIT) for inventory management, overhead costs management, capital budgeting techniques, and Activity Based Costing (ABC) method [14, 15, 21, 22, 23, 24, 25].

JIT is an inventory management technique where goods within the supply chain innovation are produced or delivered on a need or demand basis. JIT inventory management measures consist of stock-out rate, inventory turnover, and storage costs. According to Agrawal and Smith [26], inventory management reflects the average time inventory is sold out and refilled. The key objective of this technique is to ensure the constant supply of goods while minimizing inventories and storage costs [27]. On the other hand, the ABC system allows for the accurate costing of goods to enhance decision-making. In the ABC system, major products classified as category A items in the inventory are outputs sold in stores, supported by an effective accounting information system at the supply chain and inventory management [16, 28, 29]. Alternatively, the category B items symbolize other materials used to support operations, such as maintenance and office equipment. Finally, the last category of C items reflects the minimum monitored and registered inventory items, just like toiletries and other materials [26].

Walmart has reduced the operating and overhead costs and the costing system, but the burden was on the employees and suppliers. It has changed different accounting practices in response to external pressures, and several improvements have been emerged to improve its image in the market and among its customers. At the same time, it has also increased the hourly labor rate with a new work atmosphere. At the center of Walmart's business model is cost leadership. Walmart's brand has controlled the US retail market through reduced costs [30]. Accordingly, Walmart uses its strategy to achieve a competitive advantage based on low overhead costs and correspondingly low selling prices. Porter's [31] model shows that the organization effectively uses a competitive system to compete against other organizations in the same industry. In the case of Walmart, the competitive advantage is maintained through various accounting strategies and practices. Although the entire system used in Walmart's business depends on reducing overhead costs, this strategy enables Walmart to change its selling prices accordingly. In this regard, selling price reduction is a strength that helps Walmart compete against other organizations operating in the retail market.

2.2 Walmart's Business Model, Business Strategy, and Competitive Advantage

Brea-Solis *et al.* [32] defined a business model as a description of how an organization works, stating how the organization creates value for consumers and harnesses part of the value as profit. Walmart's complex accounting system, which integrates all its stores and business channels, reflects its Omni-channel business operation model. The Omni-channel retail model relates to a business framework based on the retailer's need to provide goods and services and communicate with consumers seamlessly across multiple business channels. These channels may include physical stores, websites, mobile applications, call centers, and so on. The Omnichannel retailing model is founded on the pressure to meet the consumer's need for convenience and availability in the backdrop of market competition. Many retailers are increasing their business channels by incorporating online stores, mobile channels, or opening physical stores to improve their market presence and availability [33, 34].

Brea-Solis *et al.* [32] noted that two main components operationalize a business model: the first one is leadership choices, and the second is related to policy choices. Leadership choices are usually relying on policies, corporate assets, and corporate governance. Ulrich et al. [35] described the policy choices as a strategy that each organization should develop for each part of its operations. The asset choices comprise tangible resources such as manufacturing assets, satellite communication systems between offices, or using a specific airline. For instance, where the choice element revolves around a company's use of trucks, the governance choice is to lease or own a fleet. Making decisions in such scenarios has consequences on the firm that mainly affect its competitive advantage. Bromiley and Rau [2] noted that governance choices at Walmart incorporate the organizational structure employed to develop contractual plans.

Business strategy is defined as a contingent action plan through which a given objective is realized through the use of a set of activities that focus on uniqueness and valuable positioning [32]. Contrary to a business model, an activity system, a strategy dwells more on how the system is created. A strategy determines the business model used, the logic and manner in which a firm operates, and the way through which value is created. Walmart thrives on the strategies of differentiation, cost leadership, and technology to achieve a competitive advantage. The use of technology in demand forecasting and inventory management has been crucial in boosting the company's competitiveness [36]. Brea-Solis *et al.*, [32] framework bridges the industrial organization and resource-based approach to competitive advantage. Gagnon [37] noted that firms are more profitable to adopt the resource-based approach to operations strategy. In the current market in which the competition is high, product market positioning is an unsustainable strategy, and firms should, instead, develop and leverage their essential resources and abilities to realize long-term profitability [38, 39].

The emphasis of Walmart is currently on creating a unified accounting practice for its customers whether they are shopping online or physically at the stores. Walmart contributes highly to the global economy as it hires around 2.2 million employees, of which 1.5 million are inside the US. This discussion of Walmart's E-business model and business strategy shows how it has helped them achieve a completive advantage and strong growth [30].

3. US CASE STUDY: WALMART CORPORATION AND RESEARCH METHODOLOGY

This study uses qualitative research and depends on the online and website methodological underpinnings. The case study, Walmart, adopted in this study has limited previous literature and database. This study has collected all essential data from the Walmart database, websites, Walmart annual reports, accounting data, and secondary data. A systematic literature analysis was conducted to collect data and develop an understanding of management accounting practices in Walmart. The analysis was made within the limits of a case study where the data collection and analysis were narrowed down to the example of Walmart's accounting management, budgeting, inventory cost measurement system, and capital structure [40]. The SWOT analysis has been introduced in this study to consider as a basis for future research and decision-makers.

Walmart is the largest US-based retailer among the physical retail brands in the US. It was founded in 1962 initially at Rogers, Arkansas, US. Since 2021, Walmart has owned more than 11400 stores; and it has served more than 240 million customers each week at different retail stores and e-commerce websites under 54 banners in 26 international regions. Walmart employs more than two million people who are named as Walmart associates. Walmart is not just a brick-and-mortar company. Over the last decade, it has invested in e-commerce and made acquisitions to grow its e-commerce capabilities. By 2020, it will have earned about $36 billion from e-commerce.

Walmart drives different businesses, retail, wholesale and other stories in the US, Canada, UK, Japan, Africa, Argentina, Brazil, Central America, Chile, China, India, and Mexico. It builds its business in three popular segments: Walmart US, Walmart International, and Sam's Club. The prevalent of these segments is Walmart US, with operations in all 50 states in the U.S., Washington DC, and Puerto Rico. Walmart International has functions in 27 international regions outside the USA. Sam's club is a group of warehouse store clubs with a membership.

4. THE ANALYSIS AND DISCUSSION

4.1 Walmart's Corporate Structure and Culture

Walmart's organizational structure regulates the company's business activities. These activities are largely in the retail industry, comprising operations in the e-commerce market and online accounting. The corporate structure determines how the business addresses corporate problems. It helps to facilitate the corporate strategy implementation in capturing a retail market share. Walmart's organizational culture regulates the way of doing that the people respond to challenges in work. The flexibility of Walmart's human resources comparatively depends on the mindset reinforced by the corporate culture. Cultural qualities aid the retail business adapt to changes and emerging changes in the international market based on IFRS [41]. The history of Walmart displays that the corporate structure and culture support to bring competitive advantages and success. Walmart's structure interrelates with the corporate culture to sustain the major competitive advantage against other competitors, such as Amazon, Kroger, Apple, Google, and other technology corporations, with the same online digital content of the distribution operations.

Walmart takes a leadership position in the retail industry. Such position and long-term success are connected with the valuable combination of the corporate structure and culture. The qualities and implications of Walmart culture are affected by how the corporate accounting system supports HR development and other parts of Walmart's business operations, for instance, supply chain, accounting practices, marketing, and business strategy.

Walmart has a hierarchical functional corporate structure. This structure has two sides: hierarchy and function. The hierarchy side relates to the vertical lines of authority among the corporate structure. On the other side, the function feature involves groups of employees achieving positive functions. The key influence of Walmart's structure is the ability of Walmart managers to inspire the whole corporation.

On the other hand, Walmart's culture has four key elements. These elements direct Walmart's staff behaviors, which govern managerial capacities to add value in delivering the services to customers. The cultural elements as influenced by Walmart's structure can include: (1) service to customers; (2) respect for the individual; (3) strive for excellence; and (4) action with integrity.

4.2 Walmart's Accounting System

An effective accounting system used by Walmart highlights a combination of accounting information and digital accounting that includes past performance, future information, actual risks, costs, and prices. Walmart also uses cost–benefit analysis, IRR, and NPV to evaluate the feasibility of any project or region. Walmart continually evaluates its investment appraisal methods to make better capital decisions through the combination of financial and strategic project elements. Capital investment decisions rely on economic features that include income growth, returns on investment, global expansion, and profitability [42].

Walmart recently used a new accounting system to develop accounting practices for traditional and online customers. It has changed the framework to value inventory using the retail inventory accounting structure. The new accounting system has focused on cloud computing options and online accounting for different areas, such as costing, budgeting, inventory management, and management accounting.

Walmart's accounting system focuses on inventory and cost management, used to measure its liquidity and profitability. Walmart uses different costing methods in order to reduce inventory costs and providing accurate product costs. These costing methods are "Last In First Out" (LIFO) and "First In First Out" (FIFO). Walmart's annual report [43] shows how the company uses LIFO to calculate the average weighting cost for US products. However, it uses FIFO on the other side at international operations inventories [44, 45]. Walmart uses retail accounting to evaluate sales at low cost or market value [46]. This is necessary to reinforce the operation's effectiveness and competitive advantage. Walmart's leadership uses the ABC system to realize the total cost view; therefore, the ability to reduce overhead costs by eliminating cost determinants.

According to Brigham and Daves [47], Walmart uses capital budgeting techniques, which comprise 'discounted cash flow' (DCF), NPV and IRR methodology to evaluate different global investments and opportunities [48, 49].

4.3 Walmart's Competitive Advantage and Business Model

Walmart's competitive advantage is located in different factors, but the leading driver is pricing strategy. This strategy draws customers from the lower-income and middle-income segments in huge numbers. Besides, Walmart's supply chain strategy has also facilitated prices reduction. The corporation sources buy directly from the producers. Since Walmart buys in bulk, the producers sell their products at lower prices to Walmart, and in turn, Walmart sells its products at lower prices than other competitors. Walmart has continued a large fleet of trucks in the US market. Managing its logistics has enabled Walmart to control operating expenses and save cash. Since its establishment, Walmart adopted cost-saving accounting practices and continued to develop these practices. Consequently, its competitive advantage has continued to build up over time.

Walmart's general strategy is cost leadership. Porter's model describes cost leadership as a general competitive strategy that focuses on attaining low costs. Walmart as a low-cost producer of retail products, compete with others in the retail market. Low prices are the major strategic objective used in Walmart's pricing strategy and key selling target of the retail business. Walmart uses different approaches to continue low costs and, therefore, low prices. As Walmart continues to automate its technologies and minimize HR spending, they achieve low costs in operations. Cost leadership comprises low product differentiation. With a focus on low prices as a selling point, Walmart's services and products are standard and, therefore, poorly differentiated from retail services from other companies in the market.

4.4 Walmart Revenues from Domestic and International Operations 2011–2021

Walmart was started in Delaware in 1969. It extended its international operations in 1991. E-commerce initiative was first introduced in 2000 and was extended internationally among 27 countries by 2020. The following table shows Walmart's domestic and international Revenues over time (Table 1).

Table 1. Walmart's domestic and the international revenues over time.

Year	US operations (Mil)	Non US operations (Mil)	Total (Mil)
2021	$436,649	$122,502	$559,151
2020	$402,532	$121,432	$523,964
2019	$392,265	$122,140	$514,405
2018	$380,580	$119,763	$500,343
2017	$367,784	$118,089	$485,873
2016	$357,559	$124,571	$482,130
2015	$348,227	$137,424	$485,651
2014	$338,681	$137,613	$476,294
2013	$332,788	$135,863	$468,651
2012	$319,800	$126,709	$446,509
2011	$311,591	$110,258	$421,849

Walmart generated $436.65 billion in net revenues from its US operations in fiscal 2021, compared to $402.5 billion in fiscal 2020. The company generated $122.5 billion from its overseas operations in fiscal 2021 compared to $121.4 billion in fiscal 2020. The company's total net revenues for fiscal 2021 jumped to $559.15 billion from $524 billion in fiscal 2020. In fiscal 2020 (ended Jan 31, 2020), Walmart generated $402.5 billion from its US operations and $121.4 billion from non-US operations. The company's total revenue climbed to $524 billion in fiscal 2020 from $514.4 billion in fiscal 2019.

5. WALMART'S SWOT ANALYSIS AND RESULTS

The SWOT analysis shows that the corporate's leading position in the international retail market is based on Walmart's strengths and competitive advantages. These advantages are used in contradicting the influences of competing retailers and digital content distribution companies especially, Amazon, Kroger, Apple, and Google. According to Walmart, the SWOT analysis provides insights into the internal and external factors important in Walmart's strategy development in the retail market. Whereas these factors fluctuate over time, its growth underpins its ability to exploit its retail effectiveness and strengths. Although it has weaknesses, its strengths are far more major considerations. Walmart can employ these strengths to capitalize on its opportunities in the retail industry as Walmart uses its strengths to counteract the threats to its retail business, particularly its e-commerce procedures (Table 2).

Table 2. Walmart's SWOT analysis. Source: Adapted by the Author.

Strengths (Internal Forces)	**Weaknesses (Internal Forces)**
1. Global organizational size 2. Global supply chain 3. High efficiency of supply chain	1. Thin profit margins 2. Easily copied business model 3. Competitive disadvantage against high-end specialty sellers
Opportunities (External Forces)	**Threats (External Forces)**
1. Expansion in developing countries 2. Improvement in human resource practices to develop competitiveness in the labor market 3. Improvement in quality standards	1. Healthy lifestyle trend 2. Aggressive competition 3. Online retailers of various sizes

As clarified in the above table, the SWOT analysis of Walmart shows how Walmart can have higher long-term success potential over aggressive global expansion, particularly in retail markets in developing countries. Walmart's internal factors (strengths and weaknesses) represent capabilities for this type of expansion. Nevertheless, Walmart's external factors (opportunities and threats) need to create more value through the retail service value chain to overwhelm the hindering force of competitors and influential local and regional incumbents.

6. CONCLUSIONS AND RECOMMENDATIONS

Conclusion This study concludes that there are different justifications that Walmart has proved good for the US market and international market. One of these is how it has been assisting people to buy at low prices and save money. Scale, technology, size and shopping accessibility have assisted Walmart in developing the competitive advantage of brand loyalty. However, accomplishing this advantage is not an easy job because Walmart needs to reduce overhead costs. Currently, it is working even aggressively to implement business growth and keeping low prices. This study also concludes that Walmart's international expansion has taken place rapidly, and the most critical factor is that Walmart is concerned with competition. The retail market of the US has reserved growing hyper-competitive. Numerous non-U.S. brands have also accessed the market, but some are equipped with a price advantage.

This study concludes that Walmart's management accounting practices have helped them conduct relevent forecasts and predictions, allowing for evaluating the retail inventory industry. It also recognizes that Walmart's costing methods and cost allocation helped reinforce its current position as a leader in the international retail market. The study found that management accounting practices at Walmart have been implemented to support their global operations, including the e-business model. The Walmart accounting system supports the vendor-management inventory model essential in minimizing costs and capacity to sell products at low prices. With the allocation of the costs, Walmart implements a cost leadership strategy by minimizing costs, thus supporting corporate profitability and financial stability.

The study recognizes that Walmart has also concentrated on using advanced technology for better results from its business. Inventory and cost management is a key driver of managing a great retail system. Walmart has used a more efficient supply chain system by handling a direct relationship with the producers. This leads to greater cost-effectiveness and better savings which can be transmitted to the customers through low product prices.

Based on SWOT analysis, Walmart should prioritize using its strengths to exploit opportunities in the international retail market. Walmart's weaknesses and threats can be secondary priorities. Walmart can develop its HR management and product quality standards to increase corporate performance. At the same time, Walmart must continue extending its business to capitalize on economic opportunities in developing markets. Walmart's strengths are based on its global corporate size and international supply chain, supporting aggressive international expansion in foreign markets. However, Walmart must implement strategic changes based on the weaknesses and threats introduced in the SWOT analysis to prepare the business for the longstanding developments of a globalized and gradually online retail market.

REFERENCES

1. Walmart Report, 2017. Retrieved from: https://cdn.corporate.walmart.com/3a/73/1a181d66407686dd9bd6d1a4b0ae/wmt-2017-ar.pdf
2. Bromiley, P., & Rau, D. (2016). Missing the point of the practice-based view. Strategic Organization, 14(3), 260-269.
3. Gilbertson, C. B. & Lehman, M. W. (2008). "Fundamentals of Accounting: Course 1". USA: Cengage Learning.
4. Alsharari, N. M. (2017a). Institutional logics and ERP implementation in public sector agency. The Journal of Developing Areas, 51(2), 417-425.
5. Alsharari, N. M. (2017b). The development of accounting education and practice in an environment of socio-economic transformation in the Middle East: The case of Jordan. International Journal of Educational Management, 31(6), 736-751.

6. Abou Samra, R., AlSharari, N., & AlTunaiji, S. (2020). Conceptual model for challenges and succession opportunities for virtual project teams in the GCC. In *Future of Information and Communication Conference* (pp. 328-340). Springer, Cham.

7. Alsharari, N. M., & Alhmoud, T. R. (2019). The Determinants of Profitability in Sharia-Compliant Corporations: Evidence from Jordan. Journal of Islamic Accounting and Business Research, (just-accepted).

8. Alsharari, N.M., Al-Shboul, M. and Alteneiji, S. (2020), "Implementation of cloud ERP in the SME: evidence from UAE," Journal of Small Business and Enterprise Development, Vol. 27 No. 2, pp. 299-327. https://doi.org/10.1108/JSBED-01-2019-0007.

9. Alsharari, N. M., Alomari, A., & Alnesafi, A. (2020). Costs allocation practices and operations management in the hotels' industry: evidence from UAE. International Journal of Innovation, Creativity, and Change, 14(5), 512-545.

10. De Souza, C., Pesserl, F., & Merry, S. (2002). US Patent Application No. 09/730,383.

11. Fishman, C. (2007). "The Wal-Mart Effect: How an Out-of-town Superstore Became a Super Power," Penguin Books Limited, 01-Feb-2007.

12. Roberts, B., & Berg, N. (2012). *Walmart: Key Insights and practical lessons from the world's largest retailer*. Kogan Page Publishers.

13. Walmart Annual report 2010 to 2012. Retrieved from: http://stock.walmart.com/annual-reports Accessed on Oct 25, 2012

14. Alsharari, N. M. (2019a). Management accounting and organizational change: alternative perspectives. International Journal of Organizational Analysis, (Accepted Manuscript).

15. Alsharari, N. M. (2019b). A comparative analysis of taxation and revenue trends in the Middle East and North Africa (MENA) Region. Pacific Accounting Review, (just-accepted).

16. Alsharari, N. M. (2016a). Results-Based Costing (RBC) System: Questioning the Unit of Analysis in ABC. Corporate Ownership and Control, 13(2), 587-603.

17. Alsharari, N.M. (2021a), "Institutional change of cloud ERP implementation in the public sector: A transformation of strategy," International Journal of Disruptive Innovation in Government, Vol. 1 No. 1, pp. 2-14. https://doi.org/10.1108/IJDIG-03-2019-0002

18. Alsharari, N.M. (2021b), "Risk management practices and trade facilitation as influenced by public sector reforms: institutional isomorphism," Journal of

Accounting & Organizational Change, Vol. ahead-of-print No. ahead-of-print. https://doi.org/10.1108/JAOC-11-2018-0117

19. Langfield-Smith K, Thome H, Hilton RW (1995). Management Accounting: An Australian Perspective, McGraw-Hill, Sydney.
20. Adesina, O. T., Ikhu – Omoregbe, S., & Aboaba, K. O. (2015). Accounting information and profit planning: The case of Nigeria listed manufacturing companies. European Journal of Accounting Auditing and Finance Research, 3(4), 86-97
21. Alsharari, N. M. (2018a). Internationalization of the higher education system: an interpretive analysis. International Journal of Educational Management, 32(3), 359-381.
22. Alsharari, N. M., Eid, R., & Assiri, A. (2019). Institutional contradiction and BSC implementation: comparative organizational analysis. International Journal of Organizational Analysis. (Accepted Manuscript).
23. Alsharari, N. M. (2019c). Accounting changes and beyond budgeting principles (BBP) in the public sector. International Journal of Public Sector Management, (just-accepted).
24. Alsharari, N. M. (2019d). Internationalization market and higher education field: institutional perspectives. International Journal of Educational Management, (just-accepted).
25. Alsharari, N. M. (2018b). Multilevel institutional analysis of accounting change in public management. International Journal of Organizational Analysis, 26(1), 91-106.
26. Agrawal, N., & Smith, S. A. (2013). Optimal inventory management for a retail chain with diverse store demands. European Journal of Operational Research, 225(3), 393-403.
27. Huge, EC, 1988, The Spirit of Manufacturing Excellence, Irwin, U.S.
28. Alsharari, N. M. (2016b). The Diffusion of Accounting Innovations in the New Public Sector as Influenced by IMF Reforms: Actor-Network-Theory. International Journal of Actor-Network Theory and Technological Innovation (IJANTTI), 8(4), 26-51.
29. Alsharari, N. M. (2016c). Management Accounting Relevance: Practice, Variance and Current Research Agenda, UOS JOURNAL FOR HUMANITIES AND SOCIAL SCIENCES, University of Sharjah.
30. Walmart 2018 Annual Report. (2019). Retrieved Aug 21, 2019, from https://s2.q4cdn.com/056532643/files/doc_financials/2018/annual/WMT-2

31. Porter, M. E. (2008). Competitive advantage: Creating and sustaining superior performance. Simon and Schuster.

32. Brea-Solis, H., Casadesus-Masanell, R., & Grifell-Tatje, E. (2012). Business Model Evaluation: Quantifying Walmart's Sources of Advantage. Harvard Business School.

33. Frazer, M. & Stiehler, B. E. (2014).Omnichannel retailing: The merging of the online and offline environment. Global Conference on Business and Financial Proceedings,9(1), 655-657.

34. Klosek, N., (2012). Creating the Omni-Channel. Dealerscope, 54(11), 1-4.

35. Ulrich, R. B., Jones, N. A., Lewis, J. C., Todd, J., Webb, T., & Cox, R. (2011). US Patent No. 7,997,486. Washington, DC: US Patent and Trademark Office.

36. Fearne, A., Garcia Martinez, M., & Dent, B. (2012). Dimensions of sustainable value chains: implications for value chain analysis. Supply Chain Management: An International Journal, 17(6), 575-581.

37. Gagnon, S. (1999). Resource-based competition and the new operations strategy. International Journal of Operations & Production Management, 19 (2), pp. 125-138.

38. Hayes, R. H. & Pisano, G. P. (1996). Manufacturing Strategy: At The Intersection Of Two Paradigm Shifts. Production and Operations Management, 5(1), pp. 25-40

39. Wernerfelt, B. (1984). A Resource-based View of the Firm. Strategic Management Journal, 5, pp.171-180.

40. Alsharari, N. M. & Al-Shboul, M. (2019). Evaluating qualitative research in management accounting using the criteria of "convincingness." Pacific Accounting Review, (Accepted Manuscript).

41. Almasarwah, A., AM Omoush, Nizar Alsharari (2018). IFRS compliance and stock prices influence evidence from Jordanian banks, Banks and Bank Systems.

42. Walmart Homepage 2012. Retrieved from: http://corporate.walmart.com/our-story/our-stores Accessed on: Oct 25, 2012

43. Walmart annual report, 2020. Retrieved from: https://corporate.walmart.com/media-library/document/2020-walmart-annual-report/_proxyDocument?id=00000171-a3ea-dfc0-af71-b3fea8490000

44. Alsharari, NM and AA Lasyoud (2019), Is Traditional Management Accounting Still in Use? Contemporary Issues, Journal of Accounting Dynamics and Business.

45. Alsharari, NM and R Abousamra (2019), Financial Crisis, Bad Debt and Uncollectible Receivables: Evidence from UAE, Indonesian Management and Accounting Research.

46. Drury, C. (2006). "Cost and Management Accounting: An Introduction." USA: Cengage Learning EMEA.

47. Brigham & Daves, P. R. (2012). "Intermediate Financial Management." USA: Cengage Learning.

48. Al-Shboul, M., & Alsharari, N. (2018). The dynamic behavior of evolving efficiency: evidence from the UAE stock markets. The Quarterly Review of Economics and Finance, (Accepted Manuscript).

49. Ailworth, E. (2012). "Walmart to install solar panels on 27 stores in Mass." Retrieved from: http://bostonglobe.com/business/2012/05/14/walmart-install-solar-panels-stores-mass/kxHjt9sQrPxSvN5sPWTjsN/story.html Accessed on Oct 25, 2012

SECTION-2

MANAGEMENT ACCOUNTING AND DATA ANALYTICS

02 Accounting in a Social Context

1. INTRODUCTION

Accountants operate within a complex web of business practices involving a wide range of actors and clusters of actors performing a variety of activities. Accounting itself is not as prescriptive or normative as conventional wisdom would suggest. It is embedded in the every-day interactions taking place throughout the organization [1] and is best understood by taking a broad view over the organization's social system in order to develop a complete picture of the clusters of actors involved. Exploring the work of the accountant as a social phenomenon reveals it to have a complex relationship with those who use it. Critical, multidisciplinary research facilitates a depth of insight into the sociological implications of accounting information use, and in turn the role of the accountant.

Accounting and the practice of accounting permeates all of society. It influences how people behave, it is used to exert power, legitimize action and signify intent. Sociologically informed research helps us to understand why accounting is practiced in the way that it is and how these practices might evolve. Accounting research, and we are focusing here on management accounting research, was not always viewed through this broad, societal lens. Section 2 in this chapter sets out how management accounting research has evolved over the past three decades enroute to its current pluralistic 'boundaryless' management accounting research landscape. Sections 3 and 4 examines the increasing scope and complexity of the accountant's role resulting from Big Data and Artificial Intelligence (AI) respectively, while the growing sustainability agenda is discussed in Section 5. Section 6 concludes the chapter by exploring opportunities for future research in management accounting.

2. THE ROAD TO A SOCIOLOGICAL RESEARCH AGENDA

Johnson and Kaplan [2] initiated concerns in their seminal text 'Relevance Lost: The Rise and Fall of Management Accounting' as to the continued relevance of management accounting techniques in light of then changes in the business environment. This was followed by a decade of criticisms of the management accounting discipline coupled with suggestions for improvement in the form of new and improved techniques such as Activity Based Costing [ABC] and the Balanced

Scorecard [3, 4, 5, 6, 7]. Subsequent, empirical research suggested that traditional techniques such as budgets, variance analysis and standard costing were as popular as ever, while more contemporary tools were enjoying only modest application [8, 9]. Changes occurring in the accounting profession were not necessarily in the tools and techniques which the accountants were using but more in who was performing these tasks and how they were being performed [10]. Accountants were being required to provide non-financial data [11] and 'softer', more strategically relevant information [12]. The 1990s also witnessed vast improvements in field-based research methods, resulting in more studies being conducted, addressing issues not previously focused on in the management accounting literature [13]. Topics such as the accountant's skills and competencies, management accounting practices and the impact of change on the accountant all became key areas for analysis [14, 15, 16]. Increasingly the literature was presenting an accountant who interpreted information so as to facilitate control in a contemporary business environment and contribute to decision-making in a more useful manner. The term 'hybrid accountant' [17] was coined to encapsulate this dual role of the modern accountant.

A large body of literature emerged which explored this evolution of the accountant's role from a bean-counter to a type of business advisor [18, 19]. Developments in advanced manufacturing technology [20], information technology [21] and Enterprise Resource Planning (ERP) [22] facilitated the decentralization of accounting information which discharged the accountant of much of their traditional scorekeeping duties [23], and the proliferation of an array of contemporary strategic management accounting (SMA) techniques enabled the accountant to play a key role in the development and execution of organizational strategy [24]. This 'business partner' placed greater emphasis on communication, people skills and general business acumen [25]. Their expanding role incorporated newer and wider dimensions such as consultant, advisor and change agent, but alongside the traditional function of financial monitoring and scorekeeping. Here we begin to observe the accountant influencing organizational behavior. As opposed to just retrospectively reporting results, accounting is being used to exert power, legitimize action and signify intent [26].

In unearthing an accountant who supports the organization in responding to changes in technology, product innovation, organizational structures and consumer markets we began examining accounting in a social and institutional context [27, 28, 29, 30] and it is through this critical, multi-disciplinary lens we must look to the future of accounting. Technology substantially changed the nature of work for accountants intensifying the evolution of the accountant's role from a bean-counter to a type of business advisor [19]. Today, digital technology is impacting how organizations process information, make decisions and formulate strategy. Digital technology blurs the boundary between inside and outside the organization, reshaping organizational relationships through enhanced connectivity and ever-growing interactions. The sociological map surrounding the accountant is growing. It has never been more important to explore the sociological implications of these organizational changes so as to understand the existing and potential relationships between individuals, groups and organizations in the context of accounting information use.

The work of accountants will undergo major changes in the future as a result of technological advancement. Some roles and tasks will remain under the remit of the accountant but will evolve in nature, some will not be performed by humans at all and new roles will emerge as accountants increasingly collaborate with digital technologies. The next two sections examine the changing role of accounting in this complex and evolving business environment as it transforms in the wake of data and AI. In addition, as the growing research agenda around sustainability accounting acknowledges the increasing interaction between accounting and the society around them, section five looks at some of the information flows emerging from organizations' interactions with their physical and social environment and how this too has implications for the future role of accountants (Figure 1).

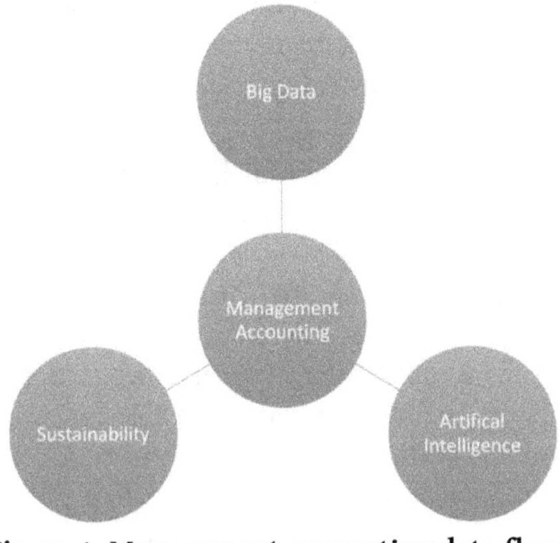

Figure 1. Management accounting data flows.

3. BIG DATA

Data plays a central role in all aspect of society, from business to government to individuals' everyday lives. Data is behind everything we see, hear and do in the world. The term Big Data reflects the voluminous information flows emerging from today's data driven environment. It provides new ways of 'making sense of, doing work in, managing, or imposing control upon different aspects of the social world ([31], p. 1)'.

The term itself is difficult to define but it is best understood in terms of the four Vs- huge volume, high velocity, broad variety and uncertain veracity [32]. The volume, velocity, and variety of this data simply means that vast amounts of transactions are quickly created and captured from a wide variety of sources [33]. Veracity refers to the accuracy and reliability of the data [34]. Ultimately, big data refers to enormous data sets which cannot be managed or analyzed using traditional software programs [35]. Automatic sensor devices, machine to machine communication, web site traffic, email and social media postings are continuously generating data [36]. This creates various technical challenges in terms of data access, storage and processing but the real challenge is in determining how to effectively use this data to make organizations better. Data is a corporate asset now [37] and effectively managing data has become critical to establishing and maintaining competitive advantage [38]. Organizations have been forced to expand the scope of their information system from traditional internal data processing to automated data capture connecting businesses to suppliers, affiliates and consumers on a real time basis. Critically, the organizations's data ecosystem is expanding [32] and this significantly affects how data are accumulated and recorded, how reports are processed and assembled and ultimately how management uses data to achieve its objectives. As a result, in addition to being more commercially focused and strategically aware, the accountant's scope of analysis has broadened.

Let us be clear, accumulating data is relatively easy. For it to be useful in a management accounting context it must be understood, mined, analyzed and incorporated into control and decision-making. Accounting, in a broad sense, provides a set of techniques, rationales and practices for doing this kind of work relatively efficiently. And indeed several scholars have suggested how big data ought to be successfully integrated into accounting and control systems [32, 36], decision-making processes [39, 40]; operational and strategic planning [41, 42] and management control [32]. For instance, traditional budgeting has been criticized for its inward focus, preventing rapid reactions to changes in the business environment and stifling creativity and innovation [43, 44, 45, 46, 47, 48]. The Beyond Budgeting model developed in response to these criticisms reflects a more agile and people oriented organization which ties organizational goals to peers, competitors and global benchmarks [49]. Big Data is poised to enhance Beyond Budgeting methodologies by incorporating a broad array of data streams enabling the development of new and alternative ways of analyzing and controlling organizational performance.

We are, however, lacking empirical insight as to whether this is actually happening, and if it is, how. Big data can offer accountants opportunity for further re-invention. They are experienced at gathering and analyzing financial data and this experience can be applied to a variety of non-financial and other data sets, but for this data to have a management accounting application, the accountant will need to upskill- to bridge the gap between themselves and the IT department, specifically, the data scientist who traditionally manages data [50]. Again, accumulating data is easy. Arguably, analyzing data is also relatively easy. But effectively incorporating this data into management accounting procedures and practices requires a proactive effort on the part of the management accountant and this requires education at a professional level- developing a stronger skillset in the techniques and technologies of big data in combination with the accountant's natural analytical skills [51].

A consistent feature of the literature relating to management accounting and big data is its prevalence of largely normative assertions suggesting how big data ought to enhance accounting processes and information and the role the accountant ought to play in facilitating this. Empirical reviews testing these assertions are scarce and so we are left with a limited understanding of where the accountant sits in this new organizational map. Future research in this area must explore how big data and accounting interact within a social and institutional context. A critical view should be used to explore how the varying motivations and objectives of different users and groups of users are implicated in this evolving relationship. Big data is more than a technical phenomena and to understand it in an accounting context requires an exploration of its social origins.

4. ARTIFICIAL INTELLIGENCE

Artificial Intelligence [AI] and related technologies were initially prevalent in more process-oriented activities but have now progressed into the knowledge sector, creating a unique opportunity for professionals to rethink how they engage with their role in an organizational context [52]. While some suggest that a variety of accounting roles will be replaced by AI-related technologies [53] there is a growing recognition that accounting can in fact harness AI's potential to add value to organizations [54, 55].

AI systemizes activities which are associated with human intelligence including planning, learning, reasoning, problem solving, knowledge representation, perception, manipulation, and to a lesser extent, social intelligence and creativity [56, 57, 58]. The key difference between an AI and a non AI application is that AI tools learn to do their job and advance based on experience without being explicitly programmed [59].

AI methods such as data mining and machine learning extract knowledge and learn how to act and interact with their environments. Data mining extracts knowledge from large volumes of data using techniques such as regression, classification, association rules, pattern recognition, outlier detection, anomaly detection, and clustering [60]. Data mining techniques used in machine learning predict future outcomes by identifying patterns in clusters of data and building models of what is happening in the data. Machine learning is an application of AI that enables systems to learn and advance based on experience. Deep learning is a specialized form of machine learning that emulates the way the human brain works by processing information and building patterns for making decisions. It uses computational models involving several processing layers to learn representations and patterns of data with multiple levels of abstraction [61]. Essentially computers are teaching themselves to write software to solve problems and make decisions [62].

While AI presents a number of opportunities and challenges for the discipline, it is not an entirely new phenomenon in an accounting context. First generation artificial intelligence in the form of expert systems, knowledge based systems and intelligent systems have existed for decades. Expert systems developed in the 1980s attempted to replicate human expertise and transform it into rules to perform accounting tasks [63]. They arguably did not live up to their potential [64], probably because they were based on 'if-then' rules and decision-trees which frequently codified flawed logic facilitating the same mistakes to be made over and over again [65]. However, with artificial intelligence supporting these knowledge-based systems, together with more emphasis on data analytics and the associated use of machine learning techniques, increased use of artificial intelligence in accounting seems inevitable [66].

The ability of AI technology to automate work, combined with the availability of big data as discussed earlier [32] together with the use of smart big data analytics [67, 68] elevate the true potential of AI to replace human endeavor [69]. With AI-based technologies, as people use and communicate with these tools, they are creating new routines while simultaneously facilitating the programming of autonomous working tools to take over certain areas of activity [70].

This raises questions as to which aspects of human work in accounting will be transferred to AI software. Prior research has focused on accounting and the automation of data processing and transaction based activities [71, 72, 73]. However, the digitisation of the accounting function using AI and big data analytics appears only to increase the network of people and software, both within and outside the organization, creating more data pools and, dare we say, more decisions [74]. It is as though the accounting function will be responsible for handling and using even more data [75] and the real value of digital technology will be in enhanced planning, control and forecasting in this significantly broader information ecosystem [76, 77].

It has been suggested that, societally, tasks requiring medium qualification levels are more likely to be digitized, meaning that individuals with low, or indeed high, qualification levels will still be required in the workforce [56]. In accounting, we have seen how the automation of more procedural tasks have freed the accountant up for more complex work [75, 78]. It is expected that digital technologies will continue this trend. AI and data analytics will increase the quantity and complexity of data and information flows increasing the demand for well qualified accounting professionals to use this information to good effect [79]. This suggests that the qualification level demanded of accounting professionals will continue to increase even when accounting systems increasingly incorporate AI technologies [74, 75]. Accountants themselves can play a key role in the implementation and operation of digital technologies in increasingly complex organizational settings. However, to achieve what is characterized in the literature as a 'human-machine symbioses' accountants must develop competencies in digital technologies and analytics [80].

Again, research in this area, despite our enlightened sociological research agenda, is largely normative consisting mainly of assertions as to how accountants can engage with AI, or more alarmingly, how accountants will ultimately be replaced by AI! The reality is much more nuanced. The role of the accountant will indeed be subject to major change in the coming ten years in keeping with the broader digital transformation of society. Key accounting roles and tasks are set to stay- some will not be performed by humans but by AI. New accounting roles and tasks will emerge and will perhaps be performed by humans in collaboration with AI. It is clear that organizational structures, networks and boundaries are likely to shift as AI and human accounting functions interact with the similarly mixed accounting functions of external partners and third parties. This is where we see a real expansion in the sociological map surrounding the accountant. Understanding these phenomena in a social context will allow us to understand why accounting is evolving in response to AI in the way that it is and how things might be done differently.

5. ACCOUNTING AND SUSTAINABILITY

In 1987, the United Nations (UN) World Commission on Environment and Development described sustainable development as meeting 'the needs of the present without compromising the ability of future generations to meet their own needs' [81]. The UN's agenda for sustainable development centers around 17 sustainable development goals (SDGs) which have a variety of objectives including eradicating poverty and hunger, encouraging well-being, education and gender equality and promoting responsible consumption, climate change and environmental sustainability (see Figure 2). In 2019, Heads of State and Government gathered at the United Nations Headquarters in New York to comprehensively review progress in the agenda for sustainable development. This resulted in world leaders and leading sustainability activists collectively calling on governments, economies and the business sector to gear up for a decade of action and delivery on issues of sustainable development [83].

Figure 2. The United Nation's 17 SDGs [82].

Businesses are becoming increasingly compelled to manage their social and environmental performance alongside their financial performance. The extent to which they do this will depend on the organization's core values, business strategy, external stakeholders, and regulatory environment but it is important to recognize that companies do not need to be 'in the business of sustainability' to ensure that sustainability objectives are integrated into their management accounting systems. A lot of what organsations do in their day to day activities and operations, is already subscribing to a sustainability agenda but there is now a growing recognition that prioritizing sustainability in areas like supply chain transparency, staff health and well-being and climate resilience creates organsational value, through brand recognition, conscious consumerism and even government support.

'Sustainability' has grown in prominence within the accounting literature [80, 84, 85, 86, 87]. Research in the area covers broad territory, e.g. linking sustainability initiatives to company strategy [88], examining the efficacy of sustainability control systems [89], exploring accounting and sustainable development goals [90], examining carbon accounting [91] and investigating how management accounting can improve the organization's environmental performance [92] – but ultimately it recognizes that organizational decision making must be based on a combination of financial, ecological, and social data. Accounting, as a discipline, has leadership potential in this area. Accountants can help managers to understand the environmental and social impacts of business operations and benchmark their corporate, social and environmental performance. This requires further expansion of their role and some adaption of their management accounting toolkit, but accountants have proven adept at evolving in response to changes both within and around the organization – this simply represents the next stage in that evolution.

When discussing big data and AI we acknowledged the organization's expanding data eco-system. The growing sustainability accounting agenda reveals how organizations are also operating within a larger biophysical and social environment than ever before [88]. Accounting in this context is complex – crossing organizational boundaries, impacting a broadening range of stakeholders resulting in a variety of implications for different aspects of the accounting sphere. However, academics have a moral imperative to move this topic even higher up the research agenda. We need to better understand what motivates corporations to pursue different sustainability strategies, and how managers implement effective management accounting and control systems to achieve improved sustainability outcomes.

6. CONCLUSIONS: FUTURE DIRECTIONS FOR MANAGEMENT ACCOUNTING RESEARCH

It is clear that the continued development of accounting will be subject to technological change in the form of big data and AI which will place new demands on the accountant. The lack of necessary skills and competencies to handle these technologies is still a major barrier to a fully successful partnership between digital technology and accounting. The accounting profession has traditionally lagged general business adoption of emerging technologies [93] so the professional bodies as well as educators at university level have a role to play in improving the technical preparedness of future generations of accountants. As well as an upgrading of qualifications, these technologies demand new forms of collaborations and interactions. Accountants must play a key role in bridging the gap between the business functions and the data scientist, the current custodian of the big data treasure chest [32]. With all of this in mind it is not possible to fully assess the effect these technologies will have on the role of accounting as a whole, but it is clear that some form of human–machine symbiosis is on the horizon and this requires critical and continuous attention from researchers [94, 95].

Accounting and the practice of accounting permeates society and nowhere is this more evident than in the continued quest to incorporate management accounting and calculative mechanisms into societal and environmental matters [96]. Organizations are under increasing pressure to behave in an environmentally sustainable and socially responsible manner whilst still maintaining profitability. Big data and AI facilitate the expansion of the organizations data ecosystem, the growing sustainability imperative broadens the organizations biophysical landscape creating even more data flows.

Let us be clear, the goal of management accounting remains unchanged. Its primary function is to support planning, control and decision-making, but accounting cannot simply be understood in terms of its functional properties. Yes, accounting is about measuring, calculating and reporting but, ultimately, it is a socially constructed set of actions in which organizational individuals construct, reconstruct, and interpret accounting information depending on how they personally interact with the management accounting system as well as their exposure to other systems throughout these interactions [97]. Management accounting has proven its capacity to adapt and evolve in response to an increasingly unpredictable and innovative environment [98], and accountants have already demonstrated their ability to mediate between internal and external parties with regard to expectations and deliverables [99]. But this chapter demonstrates the extent to which future developments in accounting, and the research which explores these phenomena, must have big data, AI and sustainability at its core.

This chapter calls for a deeper understanding of the relationship between accounting and big data, AI and sustainability, which moves beyond normative assertions and suggestions of how things ought to be. Future research in accounting must acknowledge that boundaries shift and alter in time and space [100]. According to Quattrone ([101], p. 120) 'the realm of the measurable' is expanding with the result that research approaches characterized by epistemological diversity, framed in psychology, sociology or organizational theory will provide a fresh perspective in examining the evolution of accounting in a less static way.

REFERENCES

1. Feeney, O. and Pierce, B. Accounting and new product development: The importance of interactions within social and technical structures. Qualitative Research in Accounting and Management. 2018: 15: 2: 251-279

2. Johnson, H. T. and Kaplan, R. S. Relevance lost: the rise and fall of management accounting. Boston: Harvard Business School Press. 1987

3. Cooper, R. and Kaplan, R. S. How cost accounting systematically distorts products costs. In Bruns, W Jnr and R.S. Kaplan, R. S., editors. Accounting and Management: Field Study Perspectives. Boston: Harvard Business School Press. 1987

4. Cooper, R. and Kaplan, R. S. Measure costs right: make the right decisions. Harvard Business Review: 1988: 88:5:96-10.

5. Cooper, R. and Kaplan, R. S. The design of cost management systems: texts, cases and readings. New Jersey: Prentice Hall. 1991

6. Kato, Y. Target costing support systems: lessons from leading Japanese companies. Management Accounting Research. 1993: 4: 1: 33-48

7. Bromwich, M. and Bhimani, A. Management Accounting: Pathways to Progress. 1994. London: CIMA

8. Pierce, B. and O'Dea, T. An empirical study of management accounting practices in Ireland. The Irish Accounting Review. 1998: 5: 2: 35-65

9. Burns, J. and Yazdifar, H. Tricks or Treats. Financial Management. 2001. March: 32-35

10. Scapens, R. Turley, S., Burns, J., Joseph, N., Lewis, L. and Southworth, A. External financial reporting and management information: A survey of UK management accountants. Management Accounting Research. 1996: 7: 1: 73-93

11. Drury, C., Braund, S., Osborne, P. and Tayles, M. A survey of management accounting practices in UK manufacturing companies. London: CIMA Publishing. 1993

12. Roslender, R. Relevance lost and found: critical perspectives on the promise of management accounting. Critical Perspectives on Accounting. 1996: 7: 5: 533-561

13. Scapens, R. W. and Bromwich, M. Management accounting research: the first decade. Management Accounting Research. 2001: 12:1/2:245-254

14. Brignall, S., Fitzgerald, I., Johnson, R. and Markou, E. Improving service performance: A step change towards continuous improvement. 1999. London: CIMA Reseearch Publishing

15. Granlund, M. and Lukka, K., Toward increasing business orientation: Finish Mas in a changing cultural context. Management Accounting Research. 1998: 9

16. Friedman, A. L. and Lyne, S. R. Activity based techniques and the death of the beancounter. European Accounting Review. 1997: 6:1:19-44

17. Burns, J., Ezzamel, R. and Scapens, R. Management Accounting Change in the UK. Management Accounting. 1999. March:28-30

18. Scapens, R. W., Ezzamel, M., Burns, J. and Bolvinsdottir , G. The future direction of UK management accounting practice. London: Elseview CIMA Publications, 2003

19. Jarvenpaa, M. Making business partners: A case study on how management accounting culture was changed. European Accounting Review. 2007: 16: 1: 99-142

20. Bhimani, A. and Bromwich, M. Prospect and retrospect. 2010. London: CIMA

21. Pierce, B. and O'Dea, T. Management accounting information and the needs of managers: Perceptions of managers and accountants compared. The British Accounting Review. 2003: 35: 3: 257-290

22. Scapens, R.W. and Jazayeri, M. ERP systems and management accounting change: opportunities or impacts? A research note. European Accounting Review. 2003: 12: 201-233

23. Siegal, G. and Sorensen, J. E. The 1999 practice analysis of management accounting: USA: Institute of Management Accountant

24. Yazdifar, H. and Tsamenyi, M. Management accounting change and the changing roles of management accountants: a comparative analysis between dependent and independent organizations. Journal of Accounting & Organizational Change, 2005:1: 2: 180-198

25. Frezatti, F., Carter, D. B. and Barroso, M. F.G. Accounting without accounting: Informational proxies and the construction of organisational discourses. Accounting, Audit & Accountability. 2014: 27: 3

26. Hopwood, A. G. The archeology of accounting systems. Accounting, Organization and Society. 1987: 12: 3: 207-234

27. Hopwood, A. G. Accounting and organization change. Accounting, Audit and Accountability Journal. 1990: 3: 1: 7-17

28. Roslender, R. and Dillard, J. Reflections on the interdisciplinary perspectives on accounting project. Critical Perspectives on Accounting. 2003: 14: 3: 325-335

29. Baker R. A genealogical history of positivist and critical accounting research. Accounting History. 2011: 16: 2: 207-221

30. Broadbent, J. and Laughlin, R. Accounting Control and Controlling Accounting: Interdisciplinary and Critical Perspectives. Bradford: Emerald. 2013

31. Van der Flist, F. Accounting for the social: Investigating commensuration and big data practices at Facebook. Big Data and Society. 2016: Jan-Jun: 1-16

32. Vasarhelyi, M.A., Kogan, A. and Tuttle, B.M. Big data in accounting: an overview. Accounting Horizons. 2015: 29: 2: 381-396

33. Merritt-Holmes, M. [2016]. Big Data & analytics: The DNA to a successful implementation in 2016, Whitepaper, The Data Analytics Report. 2016

34. Zhang, J., Yang, X., & Appelbaum, D. Toward effective Big Data analysis in continuous auditing. Accounting Horizons. 2015: 29: 2: 469-476

35. Syed, A., Gillela, K and Venugopal.C. The future revolution on Big Data. International Journal of Advanced Research in Computer and Communication Engineering. 2013: 2: 6: 2446-2451

36. Warren, D.J., Moffitt, K. C. and Byrnes, P. How Big Data Will Change Accounting. Accounting Horizons, 2015: 29: 2: 397-407

37. Brown, B., M. Chui, and J. Manyika. Are you ready for the era of 'Big Data?'. McKinsey Quarterly. 2011: Oct: 24-35

38. Bughin, J., Livingston, J. and Marwaha, S. Seizing the potential of 'Big Data'. McKinsey Quarterly. 2011: Oct: 103-109

39. McAfee, A., & Brynjolfsson, E. Big data: The management revolution. Harvard Business Review. 2012: 90, 61-68

40. Côrte-Real, N., Oliveira, T., & Ruivo, P. Assessing business value of Big Data Analytics in European firms. Journal of Business Research. 2017: 70: 379-390

41. Davenport, T. H. How strategists use 'Big Data' to support internal business decisions, discovery and production. Strategy & Leadership. 2014: 42: 4: 45-50

42. Wang, G. Gunasekaran, A. Ngai, E. W. and Papadopoulos, T. Big data analytics in logistics and supply chain management: Certain investigations for research and applications. International Journal of Production Economics. 2016: 176: 98-110

43. Neely, A., Sutcliff, M.R. and Heyns, H.R. Driving value through strategic planning and budgeting. New York: Accenture. 2001

44. Hope, J. and Fraser, R. Beyond Budgeting – How Managers Can Break Free from the Annual Performance Trap, Boston: Harvard Business School Press. 2003

45. Hansen, S., Otley, D. and Van Der Stede, W. Practice Developments in Budgeting: An Overview and Research Perspective. Journal of Management Accounting Research. 2003: 15: 95-116

46. Horvath P., and Sauter R. Why budgeting fails: one management system is not enough? Balanced Scorecard Report. 2004: 6: 5: 8-11

47. Pietrzak, Z. Traditional versus activity-based budgeting in non-manufacturing companies, Social Sciences. 2013: 82: 4: 26-37

48. Zeller, T. L. and Metzger, L.M. Good by traditional budgeting, hello rolling forecast: Has the time come?', American journal of Business Education. 2013:6:3: 299 – 310

49. Goode, M. and Malik, A. Beyond budgeting: the way forward? Pakistan Journal of Social Sciences. 2011:31: 2: 207-214

50. Drew, J. Merging accounting with 'big data' science. Journal of Accountancy: 2018: July

51. Chua, F. and Lawson, R. The data revolution. The Association of Chartered Certified Accountants and Institute of Management Accountants, 2015: November

52. Chiu, M., Manyika, J. and Miremadi, M. Where machines could replace humans—and where they can't [yet]. McKinsey Quarterly. 2016: Jul

53. Frey, C.B. and Osborne, M.A. The future of employment: how susceptible are jobs to computerisation? Technological Forecasting and Social Change, 2017: 114: 254-280.

54. Issa, H., Sun, T. and Vasarhelyi, M. A. Research ideas for artificial intelligence in auditing: the formalization of audit and workforce supplementation. Journal of Emerging Technologies in Accounting. 2016: 13: 2: 1-20

55. Issa, H., and Kogan. A. A predictive ordered logistic regression model as a tool for quality review of control risk assessments. Journal of Information Systems. 2014: 28: 2

56. Autor D.H. and Dorn, D. The growth of low-skill service jobs and the polarization of the US labor market. The American Economic Review. 2013: 103:5: 1553-1597

57. Autor, D.H., Levy, F. and Murnane, R.J. The skill content of recent technological change: an empirical exploration. The Quarterly Journal of Economics. 2003: 118: 4: 1279-1333

58. Bolton, C., Machova, V., Kovacova, M., and Valaskova, K. The power of human-machine collaboration: Artificial intelligence, business automation, and the smart economy. Economics, Management and Financial Markets. 2018: 4: 51-56

59. Burstrom, T., Parida, V., Lahti, T. and Wincent, J. AI-enabled business-model innovation and transformation in industrial ecosystems: A framework, model and outline for further research. Journal of Business Research. 2021: 127: 85-95

60. Gepp, A., Linnenluecke, M. A., O'Neill, T J and Smith, T. Big data techniques in auditing research and practice: Current trends and future opportunities. Journal of Accounting Literature. 2018: 40: 102-115

61. LeCunY., Bengio, Y. and Hinton, G. Deep Learning. Nature. 2015: 521: 436-444

62. Parloff, R. Why deep learning is suddenly changing your life. Fortune: 2016: 28 September

63. Gregor, S. and Benbasat, I. Explanations from intelligent systems: theoretical foundations and implications for practice. MIS Quarterly. 1999: 23: 4:497-453

64. O'Leary, D. E. Building and evolving data warehousing and business intelligence artefacts: The case of Sysco. Intelligent Systems in Accounting, Finance and Management, 2011: 18: 4: 195-213

65. Makridakis, S. The forthcoming Artificial Intelligence [AI] revolution: Its impact on society and firms. Futures. 2017: 90:46-46

66. Sutton, S, Holt, M and Arnold, V. The reports of my death are greatly exaggerated- artificial intelligence research in accounting. International Journal of Accounting Information Systems. 2016:22-60-73

67. Cockcroft, S. and Russell, M. Big data opportunities for accounting and finance practice and Research. Australian Accounting Review. 2018: 28: 3: 323-333.

68. Green, S., McKinney, E., Jr, Heppard, K. and Garcia, L. [2018], Big data, digital demand and decision-making. International Journal of Accounting and Information Management. 2018: 26: 4: 541-555

69. Loebbecke, C. and Picot, A. Reflections on societal and business model transformation arising from digitization and big data analytics: a research agenda. The Journal of Strategic Information Systems. 2015: 24: 3: 149-157

70. Leitner-Hanetseder, S., Lehner, O. M., Eisl, C and Forstenlechner, C. A profession in transition: actors, tasks and roles in AI-based accounting. Journal of Applied Accounting Research. In Press.

71. Ghasemi, M., Shafeiepour, V., Aslani, M. and Barvayeh, E., The impact of information technology [IT] on modern accounting systems. Procedia – Social and Behavioral Science. 2011: 28: 112-116

72. Guney, A. Role of technology in accounting and e-accounting. Procedia – Social and Behavioral Science. 2014: 152: 852-855

73. Taipaleenmaki, J. and Seppo, I. On the convergence of management accounting and financial accounting – the role of information technology in accounting change. International Journal of Accounting Information Systems. 2013:14: 321-348

74. Marrone, M. and Hazelton, J. The disruptive and transformative potential of new technologies for accounting, accountants and accountability, Meditari Accountancy Research, 2019: 27: 5: 677-694

75. Oesterreich, T.D., Teuteberg, F., Bensberg, F. and Buscher, G. The controlling profession in the digital age: understanding the impact of digitisation on the controller's job roles, skills and competences

76. Brynjolfsson, E. and McAfee, A. Race Against the Machine: How the Digital Revolution Is Accelerating Innovation, Driving Productivity, and Irreversibly Transforming Employment and the Economy. Lexington Massachusettes: Digital Frontier Press, 2011

77. Vial, G. Understanding digital transformation: a review and a research agenda. The Journal of Strategic Information Systems. 2019:28:2:118-144

78. Zuboff, S. In the Age of the Smart Machine. The Future of Work and Power. 2011: New York: Basic Books, New York

79. Hirsch-Kreinsen, H. [2015]. Digitalisierung von Arbeit: Folgen, Grenzen und Perspektiven. Soziologisches Arbeitspapier. 2015: 43

80. Bebbington, J. and Larrinaga, C. Accounting and sustainable development: an exploration. Accounting, Organizations and Society. 2014: 39: 6: 395-341.

81. United Nations. Our Common Future: Report of the World Commission on Environment and Development, Chapter 2 'Towards a Sustainable Development'. 1987. https://sustainabledevelopment.un.org/content/documents/5987our-common-future.pdf [Accessed: 2021-04-26]

82. Transforming our world: the 2030 Agenda for Sustainable Development. https://sdgs.un.org/2030agenda [Accessed: 2021-05-25]

83. United Nations. Report of the SG on SDG Progress. 2019. https://www.un.org/sustainabledevelopment/progress-report [Accessed: 2021-04-26]

84. Bebbington, J. and Gray, R. An account of sustainability: failure, success and a reconceptualization. Critical Perspectives on Accounting, 2001:12: 5: 557-588

85. Unerman, J. and Chapman, C. Academic contributions to enhancing accounting for sustainable development. Accounting, Organizations and Society. 2014: 39: 6: 385-394.

86. Hall, M., Millo, Y. and Barman, E. Who and what really counts?: stakeholder prioritization and accounting for social value. Journal of Management Studies. 2015: 52: 7: 907-934

87. O'Dwyer, B. and Unerman, J. Fostering rigour in accounting for social sustainability. Accounting, Organizations and Society. 2016: 49: 32-40

88. Joshi, S. and Li, Y. What Is Corporate Sustainability and How Do Firms Practice It? A Management Accounting Research Perspective. Journal of Management Accounting Research. 2016: 28: 1-11

89. Ditillo, A., and I. E. Lisi, I. E. Exploring sustainability control systems' integration: The relevance of sustainability orientation. Journal of Management Accounting Research. 2016: 28: 2: 125-148

90. Bebbington, J. and Unerman, J. Achieving the united nations sustainable development goals: An enabling role for accounting research. Accounting, Auditing and Accountability Journal. 2018: 31: 1: 2-24

91. Gibassier, D. and Schaltegger, S. Carbon management accounting and reporting in practice: A case study on converging emergent approaches. Sustainability Accounting, Management and Policy Journal. 2015: 6: 3: 340-365

92. Schaltegger, S. and Zvezdov, D. Gatekeepers of sustainability information: exploring the roles of accountants. Journal of Accounting & Organisational Change. 2014: 11: 3: 333-361

93. Dai, J. and Vasarhelyi, M. Imagineering Audit 4.0. Journal of Emerging Technologies. 2016: 13: 1: 1-15

94. Gendron, Y., On the elusive nature of critical [accounting] research. Critical Perspectives on Accounting. 2018: 50: 1-12

95. Palea, V. Whither accounting research? A European view. Critical Perspectives on Accounting. 2017: 42: 59-73

96. Hopwood, A. G. Accounting and the environment? Accounting, Organizations and Society. 2009: 34: 3-4: 433-43

97. Feeney, O. and Pierce, B. Strong structuration theory and accounting information: an empirical study. Accounting, Audit & Accountability Journal. 2016: 29: 7: 1152-1176

98. Davila, A., Foster, G. and Li, M., Reasons for management control systems adoption: insights from product development systems choice by early stage entrepreneurial companies. Accounting, Organizations and Society. 2009: 34: 3-4: 322-347

99. Carlsson-Wall, M., Kraus, K. and Lind, J. Strategic management accounting in close inter-organisational relationships, Accounting and Business Research. 2015: 45:1:27-54

100. Jack, L. Accounting and social theory: an introduction. Abingdon Oxon: Routhledge; 2017

101. Quattrone, P. Management accounting goes digital: will the move make it wiser? Management Accounting Research. 2016: 31: 118-122

SECTION-3

BLOCKCHAIN AND ARTIFICIAL INTELLIGENCE IN ACCOUNTING AND FINANCE

03 Survey on Blockchain Based Accounting and Finance Algorithms Using Bibliometric Approach

1. INTRODUCTION

One of the fast-paced innovations in accounting and finance is based on applications that have recently focused on blockchain. The major advantage of blockchain technology is that it offers a way to structure data without the need for any central authority [1, 2, 3]. In this context, the meaning of a blockchain in terms of accounting and finance function is to have a distributed ledger based on database structure that contains an ever-increasing number of accounting records [3, 4, 5, 6]. In such a blockchain-based database, all records are in blocks, rather than being combined in a single file. Each block is chained to the next one in linear and chronological order using cryptographic infrastructure and signature [1, 2, 7]. Thus, if a change is attempted in the records, it can be seen by all participants within a predefined verification in governance structure [8, 9, 10]. This approach refers to a situation where future businesses especially financial and accounting processes thereof are affected and forced to change [5, 11, 12]. In this context, future accounting and finance functions will be carried out based on algorithms [5, 11].

The organization of this chapter is as follows: Firstly, the impacts of blockchain on accounting and finance functions are explained. In this context, the effects of blockchain applications that change the "balance of power" between stakeholders are examined [9]. At the same time, areas of change regarding the future strategic position of CFOs and the restructuring process of accounting and finance functions come up for discussion. Secondly, blockchain algorithm samples in the field of accounting, finance, and auditing are presented by using bibliometric methods, i.e., "VOSviewer" [13] and "Bibliometrix" via R Program [14]. "VOSviewer" is a software tool based on web of science (WOS), and this tool is mainly used for constructing and visualizing bibliometric networks [13]. In conclusion, policy recommendations are made based on the survey results for the professionals and academics to contribute to the literature.

2. THE IMPACTS OF BLOCKCHAIN ON ACCOUNTING AND FINANCE FUNCTIONS

Blockchain is a creative response to replace a trusted intermediary position in various fields and processes of accounting and finance functions [1, 2]. In the literature, Yermack [15] first demonstrated the advantages offered by the blockchain-based accounting system. Accordingly, Yermack states that a company that has an accounting and finance function based on blockchain algorithms, offers an infrastructure for both the internal and external stakeholders to access financial statements at any time [15]. Such an infrastructure eliminates the need to wait for the announcement of periodic financial reports. In this respect, the impact of blockchain on accounting and finance functions is directly related to the transformation in governance structure of organizations and hence, this important event is a cutting edge since the Securities Exchange Act in 1934 [16].

Whatever sector you take into consideration, the common feature of them all is that they have an accounting and finance function. Therefore, the effect of blockchain technology is observed in all sectors and economic units all around the world [8, 17]. When it comes to accounting and finance function, the first thing that comes to mind is the book recording system and the management of monetary movements. It is generally accepted that companies, that perform these two functions effectively, efficiently, and economically, will gain competitive advantage. Recently, blockchain-based algorithm has been defined as a new turning point for this competition. The main reason for this is that it reduces costs and improves the corporate functioning thanks to its distributed ledger structure that eliminates intermediaries and provides accuracy in transactions [3, 4, 6].

The benefits of blockchain technology go well beyond the cost advantage, transparency, and increased efficiency [8]. It transforms organizational culture as a fundamental tool of digital governance, especially with a perspective that forms the subject of this study. In this respect, the most important contribution of this transformation is that it changes the balance of power and promotes trust among stakeholders [9]. It is a fact that with the blockchain technology, the elements of double entry system such as debit and credit transactions, recording systems, and the balance sheet structure, which form the basis of accounting and auditing standards, become redundant [18, 19].

According to Yermack [10] and Byström [20], if a company performs all their transactions through the blockchain-based infrastructure, there will be a permanent time stamp in every transaction. This means that the entire ledger of the company will be instantly accessible for the authorized stakeholders. Therefore, considering the accounting and finance function of such a company, the purpose, scope, and frequency of implementation of processes and transactions, and the controls and audits performed for them will need to be changed. Although digitalization and automation are being used in every field of business environment, there will always be a need for human in decision-making processes [21]. In this context, there is a similar situation for CFOs who are the top managers of the digitalized accounting and finance functions.

2.1 The Strategic Role of CFOs

One of the priorities of the CFO, which plays a strategic role in the corporate structure, is to create the fundamental building blocks of a strong, stable, and reliable financial functioning for a company [22]. In general, what is expected from a CFO is to perform an accurate and secure analysis of financial data by providing data reliability with an approach that adopts an advanced level of security.

It is important to have clean, reliable, and consistent data required for financial analysis and financial reporting, which are among the main responsibilities of accounting and finance functions. A great deal of effort is put to ensure that the data is accurate and reliable. This great effort put is considered a significant cost item for businesses as well as a risk factor that has the power to affect reputation [23].

Blockchain technologies for reliable financial analysis and reporting through effective and efficient, as well as transparent and consistent data are recognized as a revolutionary contribution to the accounting and finance functions [5, 11]. In this context, the use of smart contracts offered by the blockchain-based infrastructure, can be expressed as an example of how technology can provide more reliability, assurance, and efficiency for CFOs [22].

There are various examples of blockchain applications in finance field which are discussed in detail in the relevant literature. Each of these are practices that strengthen the strategic role of the CFO and shape its agenda [4, 8]. In the Figure 1, based on the main articles of this survey, the areas where the block chain is used for improving the strategic role of CFO and the accounting and finance function are summarized.

Firstly, blockchain ensures the end-to-end visibility in the supply chain management process [8, 21]. With the help of blockchain, it increases the quality of record keeping and reduces costs by ensuring the reliability and consistency of the data of all units that are related to finance. In this way, all business units are integrated via blockchain as considering "single source of true data" [24].

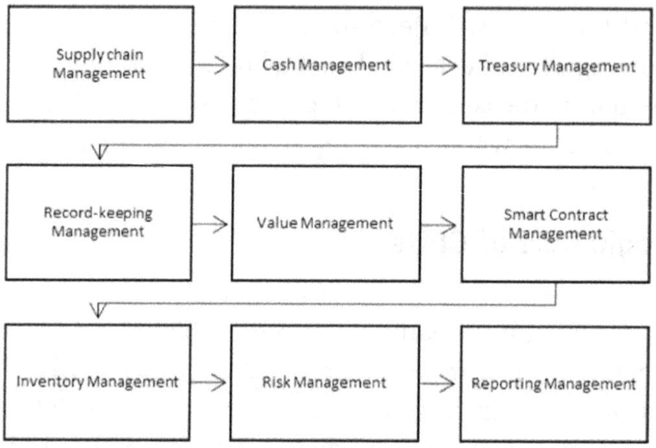

Figure 1. Use-cases of blockchain in accounting and finance functions. Source: Compiled by the authors.

With untouched transactions and money transfers, the cash flow management of a company is realized with low cost and protected against misuse and fraud risks [5, 17, 24]. It should be noted that blockchain is the genesis of trust, which is not rely on any central party and distributed to the participants in a network. However, effective results are obtained when blockchain applications are supported by artificial intelligence in a wide variety of areas such as smart contract management, inventory management and treasury management [17, 25]. Thus, a solid reporting management supported by above mentioned process management and controls starting with reliable data entry based on the blockchain is achieved [24, 25]. This is the guide for the entire board of directors, and stakeholders of the company under the strategic leadership of the CFOs.

2.2 The Restructuring Process of Accounting and Finance Functions

The most basic feature of a blockchain is that it simplifies the way people or businesses transact [2, 7, 11]. For this, there is an online general ledger that uses data in the blockchain infrastructure. It helps users to manage the trading book of all transactions made securely and without the contribution or intervention of a third party [1, 5]. The implementation of the innovative structure of the blockchain that simplifies the system, makes it transparent and reduces costs, means the restructuring of businesses using this type of infrastructure. In order for this restructuring to be effective and efficient i.e., "business process optimization (BPO)" [23], the business model [12] must be transformed, depending on blockchain technologies [7].

It is a fact that the blockchain-based algorithms contain a complete history of every transaction. Notwithstanding there are important advantages of blockchain technology, there are also issues that still await research [23, 26]. For example, although sensor data received in a blockchain application can be verified, it is not possible to identify data that has been manipulated in the "off-chain environment" [5, 7], that is, previously corrupted. Therefore, the way to reliably process blockchain algorithms is to determine the techniques to detect corrupted data incoming to the ledger before processing and posting [27].

3. BLOCKCHAIN ALGORITHM SAMPLES IN THE FIELD OF ACCOUNTING, FINANCE, AND AUDITING

In this section, the data, methodology and the key findings are explained respectively as follows. Although the main subject of this study is to investigate the impact of blockchain on accounting and finance, an approach that includes the auditing of these areas, constitutes a more appropriate scope. In particular, the primary field of internal audit, internal control, and risk management in the literature is mostly based on analysis of the effectiveness of accounting and finance functions [9, 18, 28]. Therefore, digital transformation process necessitates the use of digital auditing and monitoring techniques in the governance of these functions. In this respect, expanding the scope by including auditing in the survey, becomes a common intersection point for our work to make more accurate policy recommendations.

3.1 Data and Methodology

In this study, bibliometric method is used for executing the survey on blockchain algorithms in the field of accounting, finance, and auditing. In this respect, both VOSviewer [13] and R programs [14] are used, respectively. Bibliometric methods help to examine scientific studies from a diverse perspective by applying statistical analysis for books, articles, and other publications [29]. With this method, researchers are given the opportunity to move from "micro focus" to "macro focus" [30]. Thus, the researchers could examine and interpret the dynamics of the field they are studying with a broad perspective. As a result of the bibliometric network analysis made, inferences are obtained regarding various patterns of authors, documents, and countries [31]. The basic work steps of this analysis are shown in the Figure 2 below:

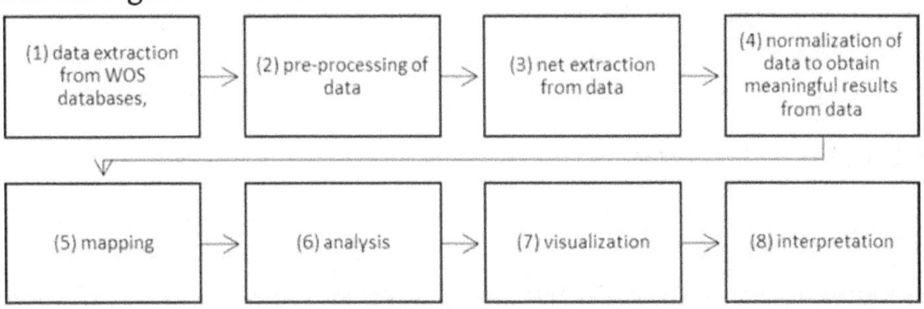

Figure 2. The basic steps of bibliometric network analysis. Source: [31, 32].

The filtering words used to find relevant publications from the web of science (WOS) database are as follows: "Blockchain", "Algorithms", "Accounting", "Finance", "Digital Auditing", "Auditing", and "Artificial Intelligence". There are (435) relevant articles obtained from the WOS. Since the discovery of blockchain has been a recent event, the survey period is intentionally chosen for the period 2005–2021. In this respect, after applying the basic steps in Figure 2, the mapping is formed by VOSviewer which is shown in Figure 3. The bibliometric network analysis findings are explained and discussed in the below section.

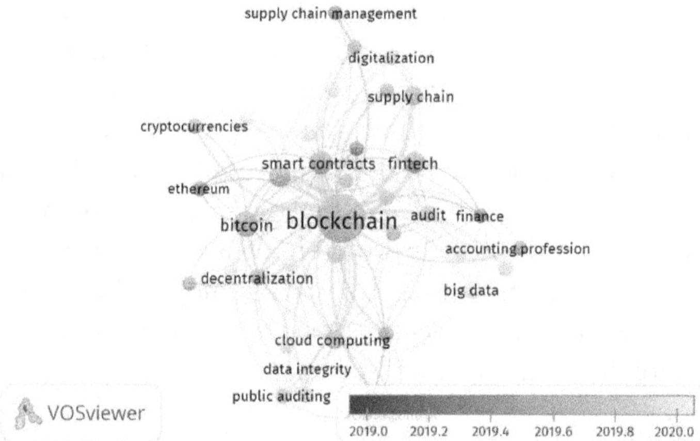

Figure 3. Bibliometric network of Blockchain, accounting, auditing and finance. Source: [13].

When the filtering area on the web of science is set as "blockchain" only, over a million articles are listed. However, when other keywords are added together with the blockchain by making the field specific and analyzed at the same time, the number decreases considerably as shown in Figure 3. Accordingly, the findings are obtained and discussed as follows.

3.2 Discussion on The Bibliometric Findings

The findings of the bibliometric network analysis are summarized based on "Co-citation" aspects for the period 2005–2021 considering the SSCI indexed articles. In bibliometric network analysis, a total of (6) basic clustering structures have emerged. Hence, there are basically (39) items, (6) clusters, (200) links and (469) strength of the "Co-citation" mapping. The keywords that make up these clusters are presented in Appendix A and findings are discussed as follows:

3.2.1 Cluster 1: Finance

The first set of bibliometric network analysis reveals a strong interaction between blockchain and finance. In the literature, it has been determined that the other keywords, that are mainly considered together with finance and blockchain, are "accounting profession", "artificial intelligence", "audit", "big data", "internet of things" and "machine learning". This means, it can be stated that the perspective of the "accounting profession" has changed with "fintech" in the financial sector. In addition, "machine learning", "big data", "internet of things", and "artificial intelligence" are shown as the main source of this change. The point to note here is that the keyword "audit" has been processed in terms of the private sector within this cluster. However, the scope of "public auditing" in Cluster 2 within the context of auditing, mainly deals with compliance auditing and tax regulations relevant for public sector.

3.2.2 Cluster 2: Public Auditing

In bibliometric network analysis of the Cluster 2, the keywords are presented as "access control", "cloud computing", "cloud storage", "data integrity", "data privacy", and "privacy" respectively. Hence, it is understood that the scope and purpose of blockchain applications in the public sector differ from those of the private sector. Here, it can be stated that especially prominent keywords give priority to the purpose of making the legislative harmonization process in public business processes safe and confidential. At the same time, it is observed that data security and data storage conditions are the main areas of discussion to reveal the social benefit in the digitalization process.

3.2.3 Cluster 3: Blockchain

In Cluster 3, there are keywords such as "digitalization", "distributed ledger technology" and "traceability", which are directly related to the blockchain implementation process and can be considered an integral part of the technical characteristics of blockchain. On the other hand, the key words defining the "supply chain management", "supply chain finance", and "smart contracts" applications that stand out among the sectoral best practices, are also included in the list.

3.2.4 Cluster 4: Accounting

Keywords in this cluster, which are closely related to accounting, can be expressed as "auditing", "blockchain technology", "permissioned blockchain" and "security" respectively. Accounting and "auditing" are generally regarded as intertwined practices. One of the primary audit areas in auditing in the literature is financial statements and financial management processes. Therefore, the keywords given in this cluster as "blockchain technology", "permissioned blockchain" and "security" are also supportive of the current situation of accounting profession and related findings in the literature.

3.2.5 Cluster 5: Bitcoin

When it comes to blockchain, "bitcoin" comes to mind first. The keywords associated with bitcoin such as "crowd funding", "cryptocurrency" and "Ethereum" are clearly monitored in this cluster. In the literature, developments that are closely related to accounting and finance, especially covering these keywords, are discussed. "Crowd funding", which has the potential to change the corporate functioning of accounting and finance, can be given as an important example among these clusters.

3.2.6 Cluster 6: Consensus Algorithm

The consensus algorithm is a concept that is closely related to the blockchain. This concept is considered widespread as to be mapped under a separate cluster within this bibliometric network analysis. In addition, there are other important and related keywords which are as follows: "decentralization", "distributed ledger", "peer to peer computing", and "smart contract".

The "Conceptual Structure Map" based on the correspondence analysis method is performed by using R program and the findings are presented in Figure 4. This analysis is performed by using R code, namely "bibliometrix" package with BiblioShiny App which is used for "performing bibliometric analysis and building data matrices for co-citation, coupling, scientific collaboration analysis and co-word analysis" [14]. In this respect, Figure 4 can be seen as the big picture concerning the blockchain in the literature and hence, based on the block chain and related concepts that are the subject of bibliometric network analysis, it is stated in the literature that there will be considerable technological developments that deeply affect accounting, finance, and audit processes.

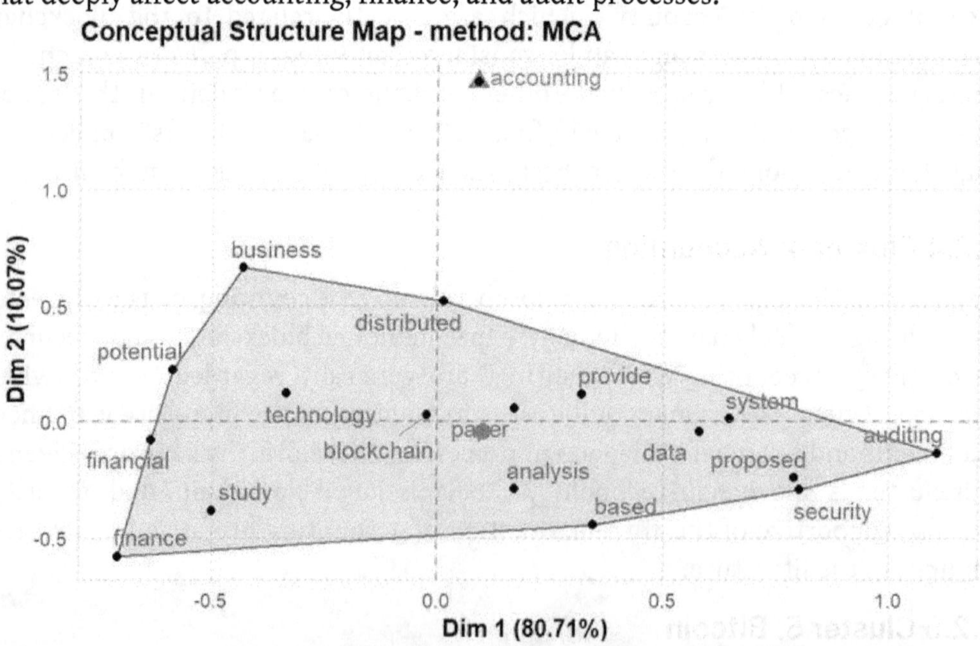

Figure 4. Conceptual structure map of Blockchain, accounting, auditing and finance. Source: [14].

The prominent and top (10) journals, in which these studies were conducted, are given below in Figure 5. For instance, the first journal in the list is "COMPUTER SCIENCE INFORMATION SYSTEMS" and the second is "BUSINESS FINANCE". Accordingly, it is seen that journal structures are interdisciplinary and the whole list is presented in Appendix B.

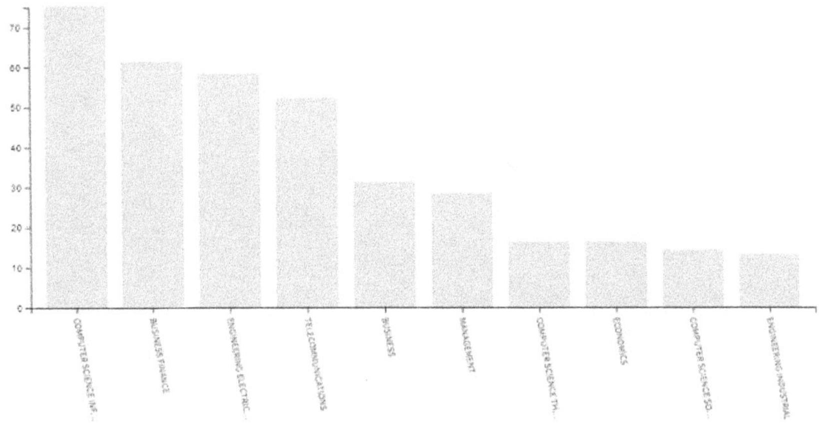

Figure 5. Top 10 journals related to the bibliometric network survey. Source: [13].

Looking at the development of the literature on blockchain over the years, it is predicted that a significant acceleration has been observed in 2020 and this will increase further in the coming years. This situation is clearly monitored in the Figure 6.

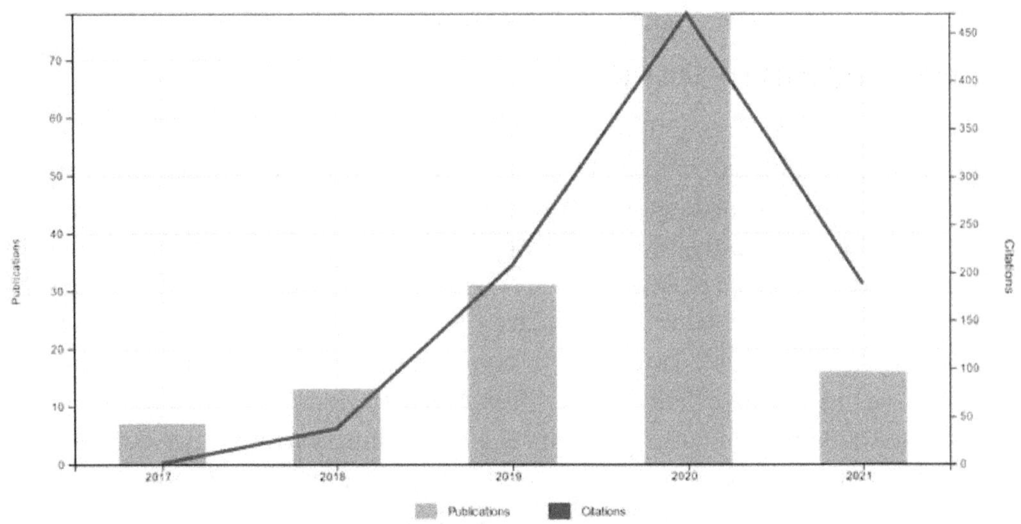

Figure 6. Publications and citations related to Blockchain (2005–2021). Source: [13].

In addition, it has been determined that China is by far the first among the contributing countries among the top (20) countries. This is true for China in the case of both single and multiple country publications. This is presented in Figure

7. The countries included here are generally similar to the G20 countries. However, it can be stated that there is no ranking proportional to their economic size. China is by far the top three, followed by the USA and the UK. This situation indicates that China, the USA and the UK will be the countries producing technology and determining innovation policies in the future.

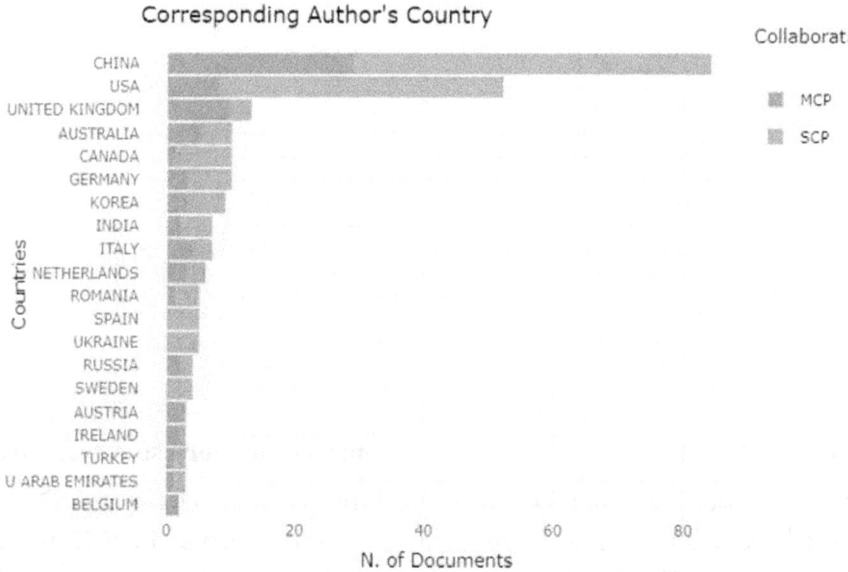

Figure 7. The list of top 20 corresponding Author's country. SCP: Single country publications (intra country collaboration); MCP: Multiple country publications (inter country collaboration). Source: [14].

4. CONCLUDING REMARKS

In this study, the developments in the literature in the field of accounting, finance and auditing with block chain algorithms were investigated through bibliometric network analysis. According to the findings obtained by using VOSviewer and R program for this analysis, the development areas seen in the literature are collected under six basic clusters. When the interaction areas within these clusters are examined, the first is; It can be stated that private sector and public sector distinction has emerged. Latter, it is concluded that finance, blockchain and auditing are intertwined. Third, it has been revealed that the interaction of public auditing with the blockchain differs and the data security perspective comes to the fore. Fourth, it has been determined that there is an important literature dealing with accounting, finance, auditing, and blockchain interaction. Fifth, it is revealed that a separate literature on the blockchain and bitcoin and cryptocurrencies in general has developed. This cluster gives a significant clue for the emergence of new financial instruments in the near future. Sixth, since the blockchain is based on algorithms, it has been demonstrated that algorithmic applications have evolved significantly to the extent of being located in a separate cluster.

In this context, it is concluded that the three countries, that contribute the most to the literature, have the power to determine the areas of change in the fields of accounting, finance, and audit in the future. These countries are China, USA, and the UK respectively, and the ranking is evaluated in accordance with the expectations within the framework of general economic standards and approaches.

While this survey is a pioneering work, the limitations arising from the current state of the blockchain are also worth mentioning. There is a need for standardization of the blockchain. When this structure is standardized, it may be possible for it to become widespread and to be more accepted in the field of finance. Since the blockchain is not yet subject to generally accepted legal regulations, it may cause difficulties in registration and valuation processes in the financial field. Difficulties may also arise if the consensus lead time on the blockchain is prolonged. Therefore, it would be appropriate to cooperate at international level on blockchain-related issues in order to use resources effectively.

Appendix A. Bibliometric Network Analysis-Mapping of Co-Citations Clusters (2005–2021)

Cluster 1 (8 items)	Cluster 2 (8 items)	Cluster 3 (8 items)	Cluster 4 (5 items)	Cluster 5 (4 items)	Cluster 6 (5 items)
Finance	Public auditing	Blockchain	Accounting	Bitcoin	Consensus algorithm
Accounting profession	Access control	Digitalization	Auditing	Crowd funding	Decentralization
Artificial intelligence	Cloud computing	Distributed ledger technology	Block chain technology	Cryptocurrency	Distributed ledger
Audit	Cloud storage	Smart contracts	Permissioned blockchain	Ethereum	Peer to peer computing
Big data	Data integrity	Supply chain finance	Security		Smart contract
Fintech	Data privacy	Supply chain management			
Internet of things	Data sharing	Traceability			
Machine learning	Privacy				

REFERENCES

1. Potekhina A, Riumkin I, Blockchain – a new accounting paradigm Implications for credit risk management: Umeå School of Business and Economics, 2017, [Master degree thesis].

2. Nakamoto, S. Bitcoin: A Peer-To-Peer Electronic Cash System; CoinDesk: New York, NY, USA, 2008, . 1-9.

3. Kokina, J., Mancha, R. and Pachamanova, D., Blockchain: emergent industry adoption and implications for accounting: Journal of Emerging Technologies in Accounting, 2017, Vol. 14 No. 2, pp. 91-100.

4. Calderon, M., Lawrence, S. and Churchil, S. Distributed ledgers: a future in financial services? : Journal of International Banking Law and Regulation, 2016, Vol. 31 No. 5, 246-247.

5. Dai, J., Vasarhelyi, M.A., Toward blockchain-based accounting and assurance: Journal of Information System, 2017, 31, 5-21.

6. Alarcon, J.L. and Ng, C., Blockchain and the future of accounting: Pensylvania CPA Journal, 2018, Vol. 88 No. 4, pp. 26-29.

7. I.-C. Lin and T.-C. Liao, A survey of blockchain security issues and challenges: International Journal of Network Security, 19, 2017, 653-659.

8. Avdzha A. K. The Coming Age of Blockchain Technology in Corporate Governance: LLM International Business Law, [Master's Thesis], 2017, Under the supervision of Ivona Skultetyova, Available from: http://arno.uvt.nl/show.cgi?fid=143457

9. Singh, H., Jain, G., Munjal, A. and Rakesh, S. Blockchain technology in corporate governance: disrupting chain reaction or not?: Corporate Governance, 2019 Vol. 20 No. 1, 67-86. https://doi.org/10.1108/CG-07-2018-0261

10. Yermack, D., Corporate governance and blockchains: National Bureau of Economic Research, Working Paper No. w21802, 2015, available at: www.nber.org

11. Fanning, K.; Centers, D.P., Blockchain and its coming impact on financial services: Journal of Corporate Accounting and Finance, 2016, 27, 53-57.

12. Morkunas, V.J. Paschen, J. Boon, E. How blockchain technologies impact your business model: Business Horizon, 2019, 62, 295-306.

13. VOSviewer 1.6.16 program, 2021: available at: https://www.vosviewer.com/

14. R program, 2021: available at : https://www.bibliometrix.org/ and https://rdrr.io/cran/bibliometrix/man/conceptualStructure.html

15. Yermack D, Corporate Governance and Blockchains: Review of Finance, Volume 21, Issue 1, March 2017, 7-31, doi/10.1093/rof/rfw074

16. New York Stock Exchange (NYSE), Securities Exchange Act of 1934, Available from: https://www.nyse.com/publicdocs/nyse/regulation/nyse/sea34.pdf

17. Bozkus Kahyaoglu, S., An Analysis on the Implementation of New Approaches and Techniques in the Auditing of Business Processes Based on Blockchain Technologies: Cryptocurrencies in all aspects, Editors, Ayhan, F. and Darıcı, B. 2018, Peterlang Publications, ISBN: 978-3-631-78387-0.

18. Westland, J. C. Audit Analytics-Data Science for the Accounting Profession: Springer Publications, 2020, ISBN: 978-3-030-49091-1, https://doi.org/10.1007/978-3-030-49091-1

19. Makhdoom, I. Abolhasan, M. Abbas, H. Ni, W. Blockchain's adoption in IoT: The challenges, and a way forward: Journal of Network Computer Applications. 2019, 125, 251-279.

20. Byström H., Blockchains, Real-Time Accounting and the Future of Credit Risk Modeling: Lund University Working Paper, 2016, 43-5.

21. Wang, Huaiqing, Kun Chen, and Dongming Xu., A Maturity Model for Blockchain Adoption: Financial Innovation, 2016, 2, 12.

22. KPMG, Blockchain and the future of finance, A potential new world for CFOs—and how to prepare, 2019, available at: https://assets.kpmg/content/dam/kpmg/ca/pdf/2019/05/blockchain-and-the-future-of-finance.pdf

23. Sandner P., Lange A., and Schulden P., The Role of the CFO of an Industrial Company: An Analysis of the Impact of Blockchain Technology: Future Internet 2020, 12, 128; doi:10.3390/fi12080128

24. Deloitte, How CFOs Can Use Blockchain to Drive Value for Finance: CFO Journal, 2018, with contribution of Terence Lam, a consultant in Deliotte: available at: https://deloitte.wsj.com/cfo/2018/09/18/how-cfos-can-use-blockchain-to-drive-value-for-finance/

25. Singh, M., Blockchain Technology for Corporate Reporting: An Investor Perspective: CFA Institute Position Paper, available at: https://www.cfainstitute.org/-/media/documents/article/position-paper/cfa-blockchain-wp_text.ashx

26. Hughes, L., Dwivedi, Y.K. Misra, S.K. Rana, N.P. Raghavan, V. Akella, V., Blockchain research, practice and policy: Applications, benefits, limitations, emerging research themes and research agenda: International Journal of Information Management, 2019, 49, 114-129.

27. Risius, M. Spohrer, K., A blockchain research framework: What we (don't) know, where we go from here, and how we will get there: Business Information System Engineering, 2017, 59, 385-409.

28. Zhang Yingying, Xiong Feng, Yi Xie, Fan Xuan, And Haifeng Gu, The Impact of Artificial Intelligence and Blockchain on the Accounting Profession: IEEE Access, 2020, Volume 8, available at: https://ieeexplore.ieee.org/stamp/stamp.jsp?arnumber=9110603

29. Oxford Dictionary, 2021, available at: https://www.lexico.com/definition/bibliometrics

30. Zupic, I., Bibliometric methods in management and organization: Organizational Research Methods, 2015, 18, 3, 429-472.

31. Martinez M. A., Cobo, M. J., Herrera, M., Enrique Herrera-Viedma, Analyzing the scientific evolution of social work using science mapping: Research on Social Work Practice, 2015, 25, 257-77.

32. Chen, C., Science mapping: a systematic review of the literature: Journal of Data and Information Science, 2017, 2, 2, 1-40.

SECTION-4

BITCOIN AND CRYPTOCURRENCY: DIGITAL ASSETS

04 Analysis of Return and Risk of Cryptocurrency Bitcoin Asset as Investment Instrument

1. INTRODUCTION

As cryptocurrencies become popular and market places for cryptocurrencies are growing rapidly. Understanding the rate of return can support cryptocurrency world is and how design choices affect investors. One threat to cryptocurrencies is high fluctuations in traders' willingness to buy or sell [1]. The adoption of crypto assets has been a great concern for policy makers ever since Facebook announced its cryptocurrency, Libra, in June 2019 [2].

The technology behind these cryptocurrencies, a decentralized and open-source system named "blockchain" is often presented as one of the most innovative technology offering several many disruptive innovations in the next years [3, 4, 5, 6]. The crypto-currencies trading volume also has a granger-causality to energy consumption [7]. A crypto asset is an intangible digital asset whose issuance, sale or transfer are secured by cryptographic technology and shared electronically via a distributed ledger [8].

The era of digitalization of technology has given birth to the cryptocurrency Bitcoin (BTC) as a new exciting currency for the world community, including Indonesia. BTC is an alternative to complement the needs of global financial transactions that want convenience, efficiency and security. Use of the digital computing tools to process scientific, economic, and social information has changed the human capacity, considerably. Virtual space is being activated year over year being the result of efficient application of information resources [9].

The development of BTC is very rapid in Indonesia. Indonesia, which has a total population of 271,349 889 people in 2020 (BPS, 2021). The population of Indonesia is very potential for the growth of the investment climate for BTC.

Almost all countries in the world experienced a decline in economic growth in 2020 due to the 19 virus pandemic. However, BTC price growth showed a very significant increase in 2020. BTC prices recorded the best performance since 2013 amounting to 260 USD / BTC. The price of BTC is USD 12,310 in 2020 or an increase of 68.04% compared to 2019 amounting to USD 7,326 / BTC (investing, 2021). Table 1 shows the development of the value of BTC (USD / BTC) in 2020–2010.

Table 1. Operational variable.

Variable	Indicator	Measurement	Type of data	Source
Stock	Indonesia Composite Index	Average Stock Price/ Baseline*	Ratio	www.investing.com
Exchange Rate	Convert from USD to IDR currency	IDR/USD	Ratio	www.investing.com
Gold	Gold price in USD per 1 Troy Ounce	USD/Troy Ounce	Ratio	www.harga-emas.org
Bitcoin	Bitcoin price in USD per Bitcoin	USD/BTC	Ratio	www.investing.com

*Source: various sources, 2021. * The baseline used to calculate the composite stock price index is the average price of the shares on August 10, 1982.*

Indonesians who start investing in bitcoin currency can change the existing financial asset structure. The development of bitcoin currency in Indonesia can disturb the stability of the rupiah as the only valid currency for domestic transactions. Therefore, Bank Indonesia as the determinant of monetary policy has not or has not legalized bitcoin currency as a virtual currency in Indonesia.

This research aims to examine bitcoin cryptocurrency as an investment instrument opportunity compared to other investment instruments, namely stocks, gold and the rupiah exchange rate. For the government as policy makers, this research is expected to be an input for the development of digital currency in the era of information technology. In addition, for investors, this research is expected to illustrate the returns and risks faced when investing in bitcoin (Figure 1).

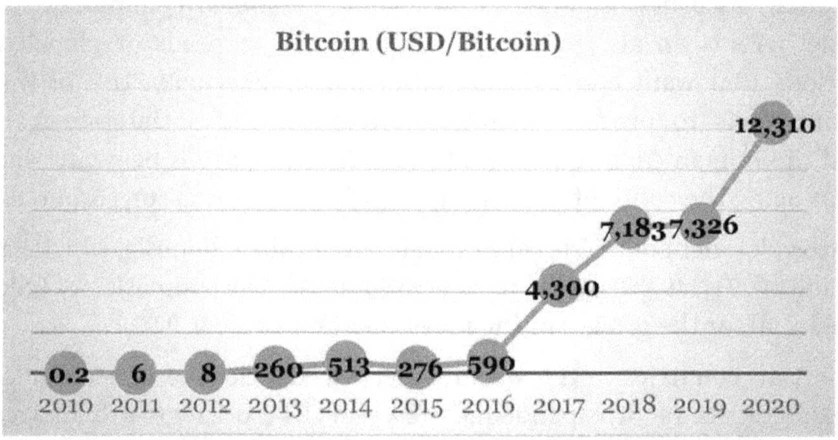

Figure 1. Bitcoin cryptocurrency graph 2010–2020 (USD/BTC). Source: www.investing.com, 2021.

2. LITERATURE REVIEW AND HYPOTHESIS DEVELOPMENT

The study and analysis of the cryptocurrency market is a relatively new area. A few works published in recent years have had the potential interest in this topic. Many scientists have been studying Bitcoin from different angles ever since it appeared. Cryptocurrency is a digital currency, whose creation and control is based on cryptographic methods. Some researchers claim that Bitcoin is just a bubble. The fundamental value of Bitcoin is difficult to reveal, and history shows that innovative assets are indeed more prone to bubbles [10].

Bitcoin is the first decentralized peer-to-peer payment network that is fully controlled by its users without any central authority or intermediary. Bitcoin is a digital currency residing in an open source P2P (peer-to-peer) payment network. P2P is a computer network model that consists of two or more computers, where each computer in the network environment can share. This network makes it easy for users to transact directly without the need for services from third parties.

The elements of Bitcoin are the existence of a peer-to-peer network, blocks, blockchain, and miners. The peer-to-peer network in Bitcoin allows users to transfer a certain amount of Bitcoin value, these transactions are stored in files called blocks, these blocks are intertwined with each other to form a block chain called the blockchain, and miners solve complex mathematical formulas. to prove ownership of Bitcoin.

Bank Indonesia responds to the existence of Bitcoin if it can be used, traded, or stored as an asset or a form of digital commodity by the people of Indonesia, but it cannot be used as a means of payment because only the Rupiah currency is the only legal means of payment in Indonesia.

Bitcoin is the first implementation of the concept of cryptocurrency, which was first described by Wei Dai in 1998. The proposes of cryptocurrency is a new form of money that uses cryptography to control creation and transactions rather than using a centralized authority.

Cryptocurrency is a digital asset designed to function as a medium of exchange that uses strong cryptography to secure financial transactions, control the creation of additional units, and verify asset transfers.19 Cryptocurrency is a type of alternative currency and digital currency. Cryptocurrencies use decentralized controls compared to centralized digital currencies and central banking systems.

Cryptocurrency is a virtual currency that circulates without being regulated by a particular central bank, is not "backed up" with gold as currency, and is not protected by any particular country. Distribution and use through the internet network media. With this crypto many benefits are obtained without exchanging it for real money, the value of crypto prices has international standards so that the value is the same everywhere, the transfer time is very fast, and crypto is not owned by a particular company. Crypto is a digital asset where transactions are carried out using an online network. Crypto assets are virtual so if one wants to see what the physical form of this currency is, then the answer is no. The form is not like a physical currency issued by a bank and also not the currency of a country.

Investors can maximize asset allocation through a combination of risky assets to reduce high risk. Investors who have an aversion to risk tend to reject investments that are more likely to have speculative content. Investors who do not like risk consider risk-free investments or speculate on investments that have a positive premium.

Research related to virtual currency, especially bitcoin cryptocurrency, is still rarely done in Indonesia. However, the development of bitcoin cryptocurrency has recently begun so that further studies are needed to provide an overview to the public and policy makers regarding bitcoin cryptocurrency investment. Some of the research results that have been carried out both domestically and globally can be summarized as follows:

Voskobojnikov et al. [11] identified and qualitatively analyzed 6,859 reviews pertaining to the user experience with top five mobile cryptocurrency wallets. They suggested that both new and experienced users struggle with general and domain-specific user experience issues that, aside from frustration and disengagement, might lead to dangerous errors and irreversible monetary losses. They reveal shortcomings of current wallet user experience as well as users' misconceptions, some of which can be traced back to a reliance on their understanding of conventional payment systems. Based on their findings, they provide recommendations on how to design cryptocurrency wallets that both alleviate the identified issues and counteract some of the misconceptions in order to better support newcomers.

Hachicha and Hachicha [12] proved the efficiency of Markov Chain for our sample and the convergence and stability for all parameters to a certain level. On the whole, it seems that permanent shocks have an effect on the volatility of the price of the bitcoin and also on the other stock market. Our results will help investors better diversify their portfolio by adding this cryptocurrency.

Mikhaylov, A. [10] conclude that the cryptocurrency market has entered a new stage of development, which means a reduced possibility to have excess profits when investing in the most liquid cryptocurrencies in the future. However, buying new high-risk tools provides opportunities for speculative income.

Igoni et al. [13] concluded that market capitalization and volume of digital currency did not constitute the significant variables of policy to influence the monetary policies in the South African economy, hence they operate independently. A decision to adopt and regulate digital currency operation or not in Nigeria does not affect. They recommend the Nigerian to embrace the digital environment in terms of regulations for tax advantage.

Le Tran and Leirvik [14] shown that the level of market-efficiency in the five largest cryptocurrencies is highly time-varying. Specifically, before 2017, cryptocurrency-markets are mostly inefficient. This corrobo-rates recent results on the matter. However, the cryptocurrency-markets become more efficient over time in the period 2017–2019. This contradicts other, more recent, results on the matter. The reason is that they apply a longer sample than previous studies. Another important reason is that they apply a robust measure of efficiency, being directly able to determine if the efficiency is significant or not. On average, Litecoin is the most efficient cryptocurrency, and Ripple being the least efficient cryptocurrency.

Agosto and Cafferata [15] found that extremely rapid price accelerations, often referred to as explosive behaviors, followed by drastic drops pose high risks to investors. From a risk management perspective, testing the explosiveness of individual cryptocurrency time series is not the only crucial issue.

Rabbani et al. [16] identified that the sharia compliance related to the cryptocurrency/Blockchain is the biggest challenge which Islamic Financial Technology organizations are facing. During our review we also find that Islamic Financial Technology organizations are to be considered as partners by the Islamic Financial Institutions (IFI's) than the competitors. If Islamic Financial institutions want to increase efficiency, transparency and customer satisfaction they have to adopt Financial Technology and become partners with the Financial Tech companies.

Hairudin et al. [17] indicated that public embrace of cryptocurrencies continues to lag as the masses currently show reluctance in embracing cryptocurrencies as a complement, let alone a substitute to fiat counterparts. Governments have also successfully defended their sovereignty in preserving legal tender status, structural seignior age and exclusivity. Market-based studies hint at consistent inefficiencies across the spectrum. The most promising areas of research for crypto-financial intelligentsia would be delving into establishing trial runs for central bank-backed cryptocurrencies.

Grobys et al. [18] indicated that a variable moving average strategy is successful when using the 20 days moving average trading strategy. Specifically, excluding Bitcoin the technical trading rule generates an excess return of 8.76% p.a. after controlling for the average market return. The results suggest that cryptocurrency markets are inefficient.

Amsyar et al. [19] concluded that cryptocurrency has the disadvantage of not having the authority responsible for dealing with all problems that occur in all transactions, and money laundering crimes also often occur, this is a challenge for how to utilize cryptocurrency and blockchain technology in the current era of globalization.

Vaz de Melo and Fluminense [20] indicated that indicate that the strength of dependence among the crypto-currencies has increased over the recent years in the cointegrated crypto-market. The conclusions reached will help investors to manage risk while identifying opportunities for alternative diversified and profitable investments.

Tu et al. [21] detected two sudden jumps in the standard deviation, in the second quarter of 2017 and at the beginning of 2018, which could have served as the early warning signals of two major price collapses that have happened in the following periods. They propose a mean-field phenomenological model for the price of cryptocurrency to show how the use of the standard deviation of the residuals is a better leading indicator of the collapse in price than the time-series' autocorrelation. Their findings represent a first step towards a better diagnostic of the risk of critical transition in the price and/or volume of crypto-currencies.

Fang et al. [22] summarized the existing research papers and results on cryptocurrency trading, including available trading platforms, trading signals, trading strategy research and risk management. This paper provides a comprehensive survey of cryptocurrency trading research, by covering 126 research papers on various aspects of cryptocurrency trading (e.g., cryptocurrency trading systems, bubble and extreme condition, prediction of volatility and return, crypto-assets portfolio construction and crypto-assets, technical trading and others). This paper also analyses datasets, research trends and distribution among research objects (contents/properties) and technologies, concluding with some promising opportunities that remain open in cryptocurrency trading.

Drożdż et al. [23] found that A particularly significant result is that the measures applied for detecting cross-correlations between the dynamics of the BTC/ETH and EUR/USD exchange rates do not show any noticeable relationships. This could be taken as an indication that the cryptocurrency market has begun decoupling itself from the Forex.

Panagiotidis et al. [24] found that a significant interaction between bitcoin and traditional stock market. The increased impact of Asian markets on Bitcoin compared to other geographically-defined markets. Two years after the Chinese regulatory interventions and the sudden construction of CNY's share in bitcoin trading volume.

Aysan et al. [25] found that bitcoin can be considered as a hedging tool against global geopolitical risk. Krafft et al. [1] found that individual "buy" actions led to short-term increases in subsequent buy-side activity hundreds of times the size of our interventions. From a design perspective, we note that the design choices of the exchange we study may have promoted this and other peer influence effects, which highlights the potential social and economic impact of HCI in the design of digital institutions.

Panagiotidis et al. [26] found that search intensity and gold returns emerge as the most important variables for bitcoin returns.

Koutmos [27] found that the contribution of return shocks to transaction activity is quantitatively larger in magnitude.

Demir et al. [28] found that bitcoin can serve as a hedging tools again uncertainty.

Balcilar et al. [29] found that non-linear relationship between bitcoin returns and trading volume. The trading volume cannot help to predict the volatility of returns at any point of the conditional distribution.

Urquhart [30] found that bitcoin return significantly inefficient but in the process of moving towards an efficient market.

Based on the research objectives, the researcher wants to compare the returns obtained from bitcoin currency and others investment instrument, namely stocks, exchange rates and gold to see how rate of return behavior on bitcoin currency. Besides measure rate of return on bitcoin currency, the researcher also measures the risk of bitcoin currency investment. Standard deviation of bitcoin currency employee to measure the risk of the investment. Thus, the statistical hypotheses and research hypotheses used in this study are as follows:

Ho1: $\mu_1 = \mu_2$.

Ha1: $\mu 1 \neq \mu 2$.

Ho2: $\mu 1 = \mu 3$.

Ha2: $\mu 1 \neq \mu 3$.

Ho3: $\mu 1 = \mu 4$.

Ha3: $\mu 1 \neq \mu 4$.

Ho4: $\mu_1 = \mu 2 = \mu 3 = \mu 4$.

Ha4: At least one of the average returns are not equal.

where:

$\mu 1$ = average bitcoin returns.

$\mu 2$ = average exchange rate returns.

$\mu 3$ = average gold returns.

$\mu 4$ = average stock returns.

While the research hypothesis developed in this study is as follows:

H01: There is no difference between the bitcoin returns and the exchange rate returns.

Ha1: There is a difference between the bitcoin returns and the exchange rate returns.

H02: There is no difference between the bitcoin returns stock and the gold returns gold.

Ha2: There is a difference between the bitcoin returns and the gold returns.

H03: There is no difference between the bitcoin returns and the stock returns.

Ha3: There is a difference between the bitcoin returns and the stock returns.

H04: There is no difference between the bitcoin returns and the others investment instrument.

Ha4: There is a difference between the bitcoin returns and the others investment instrument.

3. METHODOLOGY

This study compares the return and risk of bitcoin, stocks, gold and the rupiah exchange rate. This research is a type of quantitative research using secondary data. Secondary data used in the study were obtained from www.investing.com [31]; for bitcoin and share prices. Gold prices were obtained from www.harga-emas.org [32]; Rupiah exchange rate is obtained from www.bi.go.id [33]. The research period from 2010 to 2020 used monthly data or 132 observed data.

The return calculation uses the formula for the difference from the current value to the previous value divided by the value in the previous period. In general, the return formula can be written as follows:

$$\text{Return} = \frac{R_{t-}R_{t-1}}{R_{t-1}} \quad (1)$$

where:

R_t = the return at period t.

R_{t-1} = the return at period t1-.

In this study also measure risk of each investment instruments. Standard deviation is employed to measure the risk of investments. Standard deviation to measure how far the deviation from the average of each investment instruments. The higher standard deviation value means the higher risk of the investment. Here the formula to measure standard deviation (σ):

$$\sigma = \sqrt{\frac{1}{n-1}\sum_{s=1}^{n}\left[r(s)-r\right]^2} \quad (2)$$

where:

σ = standard deviation of investment.

n = number of observation.

r (s) = return of investment.

r = average of investment.

Table 1 shows the operational variables used in this study include investment instruments, namely bitcoin, exchange rates, gold and stock.

4. RESEARCH RESULTS

Statistical descriptions include the average, minimum value, maximum value and standard deviation of each investment instrument, namely bitcoin, exchange rate returns, gold returns and stock returns during the study period 2011–2020. Bitcoin's return has the largest average of 18% compared with returns from other investment instruments. In addition, the standard deviation of bitcoin returns has the largest value of 61.08% compared to other investment instruments. The range of bitcoin returns between -38.87% till 470.88%. Table 2 shows the descriptive statistics of the investment instruments studied.

Table 2. Descriptive statistic.

Instrument	N	Min	Max	Mean	Std. dev.
Bitcoin (μ1)	120	-0.3887	4.7088	0.1800	0.6108
Exchange Rate (μ2)	120	-0.0905	0.1367	0.0040	0.0258
Gold (μ3)	120	-0.1212	0.1363	0.0035	0.0472
Stock (μ4)	120	-0.1676	0.0944	0.0049	0.0415

Source: data processing, 2021.

The correlation matrix between investment instruments can be found in Table 3. The highest correlation is obtained from the return stock and return exchange rate (–0.602). The more the stock return increases, the lower the return exchange rate will be. In other words, the stronger the rupiah exchange rate, the more the composite stock price index will increase. The strengthening of the rupiah exchange rate had an impact on increasing domestic economic growth so that investors invested heavily in stocks. Therefore, stock returns also increase when there is an increase in the rupiah exchange rate. Meanwhile, bitcoin does not show a correlation with other investment instruments which is indicated by a correlation matrix value below 5%. This figure shows that the bitcoin returns are not affected by the others instruments investments returns namely exchange rate, gold and stock returns.

Table 3. Correlation matrix.

Instrument	Stock	Exchange Rate	Gold	Bitcoin
Stock	1			
Exchange Rate	-0.602	1		
Gold	0.218	-0.258	1	
Bitcoin	0.042	0.023	-0.018	1

Source: data processing, 2021.

An overview of the return fluctuations obtained from each investment instrument of stock return, exchange rate return, gold return and bitcoin return can be seen in Figures 2–5. Each investment instrument shows different return fluctuations. The lowest standard deviation is the exchange rate 2.58%, while the highest standard deviation is Bitcoin 61.08%. In other words, investment in bitcoin have the highest risk compared to the alternative investment instruments. The others investment instruments have low risk between 2.6% till 4.7%. Investment in foreign exchange rate has the lowest risk compared to the others alternative investments. Investment on gold and stock have similar risks around 4.2% to 4.7%.

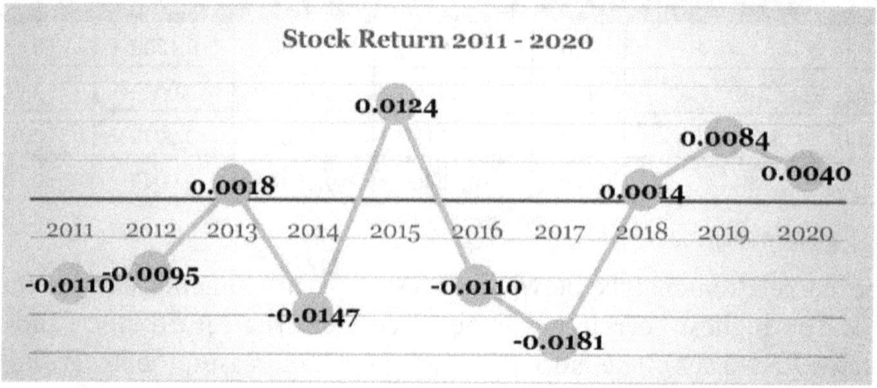

Figure 2. The return stock 2011–2020. Source: data processing, 2021.

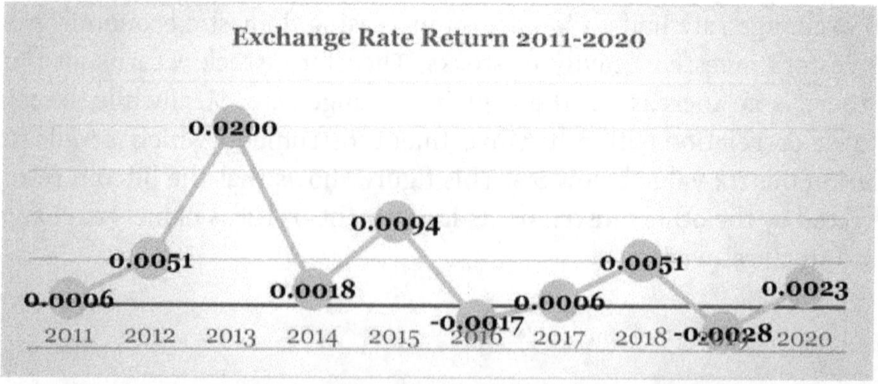

Figure 3. The return exchange rate 2011–2020. Source: data processing, 2021.

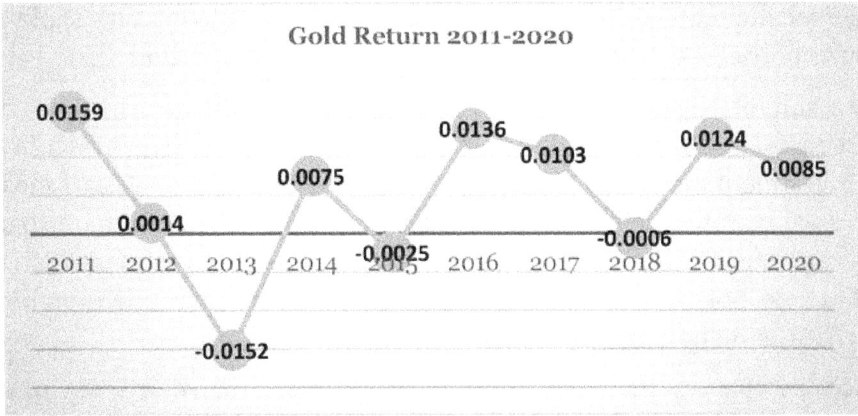

Figure 4. The return gold 2011–2020. Source: data processing, 2021.

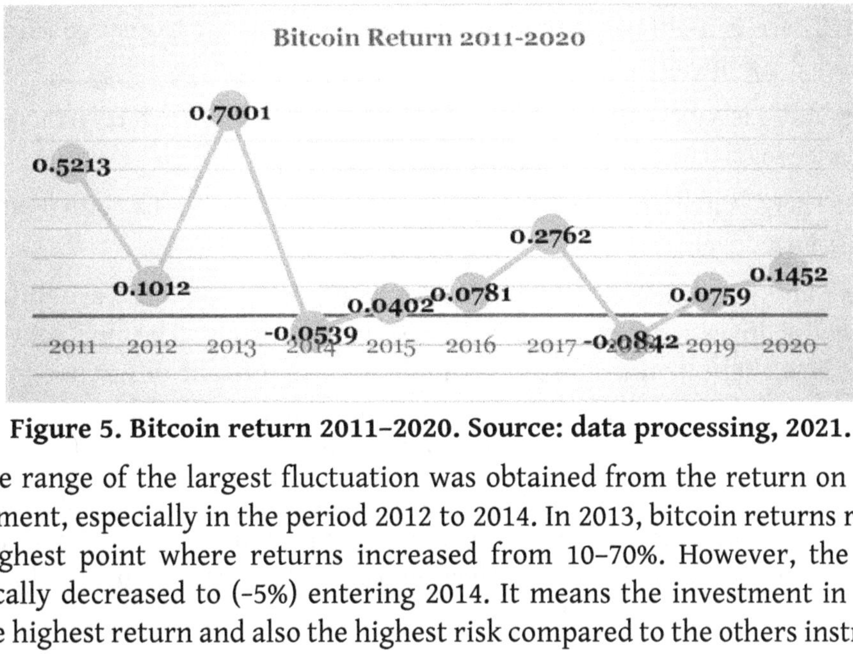

Figure 5. Bitcoin return 2011–2020. Source: data processing, 2021.

The range of the largest fluctuation was obtained from the return on bitcoin investment, especially in the period 2012 to 2014. In 2013, bitcoin returns reached the highest point where returns increased from 10–70%. However, the return drastically decreased to (-5%) entering 2014. It means the investment in bitcoin get the highest return and also the highest risk compared to the others instrument of investment.

Table 4. Paired samples test.

Instrument	Mean	Std. dev.	Std. error mean	t	df	Sig.
Bitcoin - Ex. Rate	-0.1760	0.6108	0.0558	-3.156	119	0.002
Bitcoin - Gold	-0.1765	0.6135	0.0560	-3.151	119	0.002
Bitcoin - Stock	-0.1751	0.6105	0.0557	-3.143	119	0.002

Source: data processing, 2021.

The next test was to compare the returns between each investment instrument through paired sample tests, namely stock-exchange rate, stock-gold, stock-bitcoin, exchange rate-gold, exchange rate-bitcoin and gold bitcoin. Table 4 shows the results of the paired sample test of each investment instrument.

The results of the paired samples test of returns between investment instruments can be seen in Table 4. The results of the paired sample test between bitcoin and the others investment instruments shows significant level less than 0.01. It means that is difference of return between bitcoin and the others investment instruments. The average means difference of bitcoin and the others investment instruments around −17.6%. Standard deviations show around 61% of investment on bitcoin. It means that the highest risk of bitcoin investments.

Based on the results of testing paired samples test return on investment between investment instruments and the explanation above, it can be concluded that the research hypothesis is as follows:

Ha1: There is a difference between the bitcoin and the exchange rate return (accepted at significance level 0.01).

Ha2: There is a difference between the bitcoin and the gold return (accepted at significance level 0.01).

Ha3: There is a difference between the bitcoin and the stock return (accepted at significance level 0.01).

One sample test is conducted to prove whether or not there are differences between the investment instruments used in this study. The one sample test results show that bitcoin returns provide a very significant difference ($\alpha < 0.01$) compared to other investment instruments: exchange rate, gold and stock. The average return of stock, exchange and gold investment instruments.

Table 5 shows analysis of variance single factor for each investment instruments. The variance of bitcoin the highest (0.37) if compared to stock, exchange rate and gold returns (0.002–0.001). It means there us a big different between bitcoin returns and the others investment instruments.

Table 5. Anova single factor summary.

Groups	Count	Sum	Average	Variance
Stock return	120	0.585183	0.004877	0.001723
Ex-Rate return	120	0.483912	0.004033	0.000663
Gold Return	120	0.422361	0.00352	0.002228
Bitcoin return	120	21.60168	0.180014	0.373122

Source: data processing, 2021.

Table 6 shows analysis of variance to test hypothesis 4 whether there is significant level of the return. The result indicates that F calculation (0.9826) is higher than F critical value (2,624). It means there is significant different between bitcoin and the others investment instruments.

Table 6. Anova single factor test.

Source of variation	SS	df	MS	F	P-value	F crit
Between Groups	2.783868	3	0.927956	9.826513	0.00000	2.623637
Within Groups	44.95054	476	0.094434			
Total	47.73441	479				

Source: data processing, 2021.

Based on the results of the analysis of variance single factor test shows that there is a difference between the average return of all investment instruments. Thus, the statistical hypothesis and research hypothesis (Ha4) is accepted at significant level 0.01 or can be written down as follows:

Ha4: There is a difference between the investment instruments (accepted at significance level 0.01).

Based on the average test between the research instruments used, bitcoin has a very significant difference in return compared to other investment instruments. Meanwhile, stock investment instruments, exchange rate and gold have the same average return.

5. CONCLUSIONS

Based on the research results discussed in the previous chapter indicate that the investment in bitcoin still promising. The price of bitcoin rapidly increase during the study 2011–2020. The rate of return of bitcoin investment is the highest compared to the other investment instruments: stock, exchange rate and gold. Meanwhile, the bitcoin investment also has the highest risk compared the others investment instruments.

It can be concluded that bitcoin investment provides the highest return (18%) compared to other investment instrument returns. However, the very high return on bitcoin comes with high risk investment. The risk of investing in bitcoin is indicated by a standard deviation of 61%, while the standard deviation of other instruments: stock, exchange rate and gold less than 5%.

Based on the results of the paired sample test, it shows that the average return on bitcoin shows a very significant difference compared to the others instrument. Meanwhile, the return on the others instrument: stock, exchange rate and gold show the same return.

For the investors who love risk, then the investment in bitcoin could be an alternative for an investment. The investment on bitcoin promise higher return compare to the other investment instruments. For the investors who are risk aversion, an investment on bitcoin doesn't fit since this investment have the highest risk. This research has practical implication for the investors who require high return. In the same time, the investors also have to understand the risk along the investment on bitcoin.

The other implication for government of Indonesia as policy maker on crypto currency. The crypto currency quite develops rapidly in this crypto world era. The role and regulation on crypto currency are needed to secure investors and economic growth.

REFERENCES

1. Krafft, P. M., Della Penna, N., & Pentland, A. S. (2018, April). An experimental study of cryptocurrency market dynamics. In Proceedings of the 2018 CHI Conference on Human Factors in Computing Systems (pp. 1-13).
2. Taskinsoy, J. (2019). Facebook's Libra: Why Does US Government Fear Price Stable Cryptocurrency? Available at SSRN 3482441.
3. Casino, F., Dasaklis, T. K., & Patsakis, C. (2019). A systematic literature review of blockchain-based applications: current status, classification and open issues. Telematics and informatics, 36, 55-81.
4. Macrinici, D., Cartofeanu, C., & Gao, S. (2018). Smart contract applications within blockchain technology: A systematic mapping study. Telematics and Informatics, 35(8), 2337-2354.
5. Underwood, S. (2016). Blockchain beyond bitcoin. Communications of the ACM, 59(11), 15-17.
6. Yli-Huumo, J., Ko, D., Choi, S., Park, S., & Smolander, K. (2016). Where is current research on blockchain technology? —a systematic review. PloS one, 11(10), e0163477.
7. Schinckus, C., Nguyen, C. P., & Ling, F. C. H. (2020). Crypto-currencies trading and energy consumption. International Journal of Energy Economics and Policy, 10(3), 355.
8. Bartolucci, S., & Kirilenko, A. (2020). A model of the optimal selection of crypto assets. Royal Society open science, 7(8), 191863.
9. Tarasova, T., Usatenko, O., Makurin, A., Ivanenko, V., & Cherchata, A. (2020). Accounting and features of mathematical modeling of the system to forecast cryptocurrency exchange rate. Accounting, 6(3), 357-364.
10. Mikhaylov, A. (2020). Cryptocurrency market development: Hurst method. Finance: Theory and Practice, 24(3), 81-91.

11. Voskobojnikov, A., Wiese, O., Mehrabi Koushki, M., Roth, V., & Beznosov, K. (2021, May). The U in Crypto Stands for Usable: An Empirical Study of User Experience with Mobile Cryptocurrency Wallets. In Proceedings of the 2021 CHI Conference on Human Factors in Computing Systems (pp. 1-14).

12. Hachicha, A., & Hachicha, F. (2021). Analysis of the bitcoin stock market indexes using comparative study of two models SV with MCMC algorithm. Review of Quantitative Finance and Accounting, 56(2), 647-673.

13. Igoni, S., Onwumere, J. U. J., & Amaewhule, P. W. (2020). Digital currency and monetary policy in the South African economy: Praxis of financial dualism and suggestion for Nigerians. Asian Journal of Economics, Finance and Management, 49-57.

14. Le Tran, V., & Leirvik, T. (2020). Efficiency in the markets of crypto-currencies. Finance Research Letters, 35, 101382.

15. Agosto, A., & Cafferata, A. (2020). Financial bubbles: a study of co-explosivity in the cryptocurrency market. Risks, 8(2), 34.

16. Rabbani, M. R., Khan, S., & Thalassinos, E. I. (2020). FinTech, blockchain and Islamic finance: An extensive literature review.

17. Hairudin, A., Sifat, I. M., Mohamad, A., & Yusof, Y. (2020). Cryptocurrencies: A survey on acceptance, governance and market dynamics. International Journal of Finance & Economics.

18. Grobys, K., Ahmed, S., & Sapkota, N. (2020). Technical trading rules in the cryptocurrency market. Finance Research Letters, 32, 101396.

19. Amsyar, I., Christopher, E., Dithi, A., Khan, A. N., & Maulana, S. (2020). The Challenge of Cryptocurrency in the Era of the Digital Revolution: A Review of Systematic Literature. Aptisi Transactions on Technopreneurship (ATT), 2(2), 153-159.

20. Vaz de Melo Mendes, B., & Fluminense Carneiro, A. (2020). A Comprehensive Statistical Analysis of the Six Major Crypto-Currencies from August 2015 through June 2020. Journal of Risk and Financial Management, 13(9), 192.

21. Tu, C., D'Odorico, P., & Suweis, S. (2020). Critical slowing down associated with critical transition and risk of collapse in crypto-currency. Royal Society open science, 7(3), 191450.

22. Fang, F., Ventre, C., Basios, M., Kong, H., Kanthan, L., Li, L.,... & Wu, F. (2020). Cryptocurrency trading: a comprehensive survey. arXiv preprint arXiv:2003.11352.

23. Drożdż, S., Minati, L., Oświęcimka, P., Stanuszek, M., & Wamtorek, M. (2019). Signatures of the crypto-currency market decoupling from the Forex. Future Internet, 11(7), 154.

24. Panagiotidis, T., Stengos, T., & Vravosinos, O. (2019). The effects of markets, uncertainty and search intensity on bitcoin returns. International Review of Financial Analysis, 63, 220-242.

25. Aysan, A. F., Demir, E., Gozgor, G., & Lau, C. K. M. (2019). Effects of the geopolitical risks on Bitcoin returns and volatility. Research in International Business and Finance, 47, 511-518.

26. Panagiotidis, T., Stengos, T., & Vravosinos, O. (2018). On the determinants of bitcoin returns: A LASSO approach. Finance Research Letters, 27, 235-240.

27. Koutmos, D. (2018). Bitcoin returns and transaction activity. Economics Letters, 167, 81-85.

28. Demir, E., Gozgor, G., Lau, C. K. M., & Vigne, S. A. (2018). Does economic policy uncertainty predict the Bitcoin returns? An empirical investigation. Finance Research Letters, 26, 145-149.

29. Balcilar, M., Bouri, E., Gupta, R., & Roubaud, D. (2017). Can volume predict Bitcoin returns and volatility? A quantiles-based approach. Economic Modelling, 64, 74-81.

30. Urquhart, A. (2016). The inefficiency of Bitcoin. Economics Letters, 148, 80-82.

31. Anonymous, investment.com, https://id.investing.com/crypto/bitcoin; access 8 April 2021

32. Anonymous, harga emas, https://harga emas.org/history-harga/2021/April/07/, access 8 April 2021

33. Anonymous, bank Indonesia, https://www.bi.go.id/id/statistic/informasi-kurs/transaksi-bi/Default.aspx, access 8 April 2021

SECTION-5

ACCOUNTING EDUCATION: CHALLENGES AND OPPORTUNITIES

05 The Economic Effect of Bitcoin Halving Events on the U.S. Capital Market

1. INTRODUCTION

Bitcoin emerged as an alternative source of fiat currency that is intended to be fast (i.e., electronic) and peer-to-peer that does not require the need of a third party (i.e., intermediaries like banks or governments). In his 2008 paper that marked the birth of bitcoin, Satoshi Nakamoto describes bitcoin as "a system for electronic transactions without relying on trust" [1]. Bitcoin is a permissionless system that is open to any user. To exchange bitcoin, blockchain technology, a distributed ledger technology (DLT), was developed as a medium of exchanging bitcoin. Blockchain technology, for example, is expected to transform many industrial sectors, reduce the processing costs, increase efficiency, eliminate intermediary costs, and decrease market frictions. Related, bitcoin, the leading cryptocurrency, has become widely traded as a borderless form of payment and is generally perceived as a store of value, such as gold. Unlike the fiat currency, bitcoin has been criticized for not being backed by trusted institutions, having high volatility, and a lack of correlations with other fiat currencies or stock indexes [2]. The present controversy over bitcoin challenges the notion that it is a "store of value".

Bitcoin can be visualized as a reward from solving a puzzle. Participants on the blockchain are usually connected to nodes/computers. To earn bitcoin, participants must solve a cryptographic problem using the "proof-of work" concept to reach consensus among nodes/computers and create a block. Once a block is created, bitcoin is generated as a reward. Every four years, the reward from mining bitcoin is reduced by half, a phenomenon called bitcoin halving. When bitcoin was first mined, the first chunk of mining reward was 50 bitcoin per block. Three halving events have happened since the inception of bitcoin, which were in 2012, 2016 and 2020. In 2012, the halving resulted in rewards from 50 to 25 bitcoin, and from 25 to 12.5 bitcoins after the 2016 halving event. The late halving event occurred on May 11, 2020, where the reward from bitcoin went down from 12.5 to 6.25 bitcoins per block. More interestingly, the trading price of bitcoin, which started around $0.0008 in July 2010, has reached over $40,000 in January 2021, raising the concerns and interests of various market constituencies including current and prospective traders, regulators, and policy makers (Figure 1).

Figure 1. Bitcoin historical prices (2010–2021).

In order to prevent inflation, there are only 21 million bitcoin that can be mined. As of February 2021, the total number of mined bitcoins is 18.5 million. To get to 18.5 million, it took roughly 10 years for miners. With 2.5 million remaining bitcoins to mine, it is uncertain whether the supply of bitcoin will stop at this point. Bitcoin is the first cryptocurrency, but it is not the last. Hundreds of cryptocurrencies are currently circulating in the market. In 2020, the market capitalization of cryptocurrencies went from $200 billion to $1 trillion. Bitcoin holders during COVID-19 witnessed the highest peak in prices since its inception. The rise in bitcoin prices during COVID-19 is claimed to be attributed to the slew of institutional investors who started to view bitcoin as the future of money. For example, MicroStrategy bought 70,000 bitcoins [3]. This unimaginable increase spurred speculation on whether this price surge is a bubble or simply a reaffirmation that it became more popular as a store of value. On December 17, 2017, bitcoin reached nearly $20,000 and a few days later, on December 22, 2017, the price dropped 45% to below $11,000.

The speculative nature of bitcoin has made it a lucrative investment opportunity for risk-takers as well as a threat to the stability of financial markets and innovation due to the high volatility of the ever-changing price. The controversy over the lack of intrinsic value of bitcoin, along with its ability to surpass gold, infused an uncertainty among market participants on whether it is a speculative short-term trading medium or an innovative new currency that is here for the long term. Therefore, regulators had to intervene to provide guidelines on the use, classification, and the trading of bitcoin. This chapter discusses bitcoin as an innovative venture tool of investment. More specifically, this chapter reviews global market regulations of bitcoin, classification, use cases, policies, and economic implications of trading bitcoin in the U.S. market. This chapter helps in understanding the nature of bitcoin, and its potential benefits as well as threats, not only to the U.S. market but also the global economy.

2. MARKET REGULATIONS FOR BITCOIN

2.1 Security Versus Currency

Is bitcoin a currency or investment instrument? The speculative nature of bitcoin, high volatility, low correlation with fiat currencies or gold, and vulnerability to cyber risk made regulators tend to classify it as an investment instrument rather than a currency. To be classified as a currency, bitcoin needs to have three functions: value storage, medium of exchange and account unit [2]. The International Securities Services Association (ISSA) classifies digital assets into four categories [4]: payment (i.e., cryptocurrencies), utility (i.e., provides digital access to an application), asset (i.e., security), and asset-backed (i.e., rights of ownership). Concerns about digital asset's nature, transparency, trading, and valuation have been the prime interests of policy makers and regulators. For example, trading on these assets requires an identification of whether these assets are considered as a "security" under federal jurisdiction. A security can be broadly defined as an investment contract or other instruments such as stocks and bonds. The U.S. Treasury has classified bitcoin as money services but not currency. That is, to subject bitcoin to market rules and regulations such as the Bank Secrecy Act and Anti Money Laundering Laws. For tax purposes, bitcoin is considered as a digital asset and thereby profits on trading bitcoins are taxable.

On April 3, 2019, the SEC released "Framework for 'Investment Contract' Analysis of Digital Assets" to determine whether a digital asset is a security under the Investment Company Act of 1940 and the Investment Advisers Act of 1940. The framework also made it possible to identify whether the security may no longer be a security. In the U.S., an investment contract exists if it meets the Howey test. According to the Howey test, an investment contract exist of there is an investment in an enterprise with attainable expectations of realized profits from the efforts of others [5]. This test extends to the facts and circumstances surrounding sale of digital assets (i.e., sale in the secondary market), if any. Sellers and offers of digital assets that qualify as security (i.e., investment contracts) must abide by the SEC's rules and regulations by either registering their securities or qualifying for an exemption, thereof. During the registration process, sellers would need to provide information about how managers plan to generate profit and exert efforts towards the successful continuation of the enterprise. This type of information provides "full and fair disclosure" to investors who seek investment contract and helps in reducing the asymmetric information among managers and prospective investors.

Elements of the *Howey test* include the following:

1. Investment of money through the sale of digital assets in exchange of value. This condition usually exists because there is always a sale of such assets as the first step of recognizing its existence.

2. Common enterprise must exist.
3. Reasonable expectation of profits derived from efforts of others. The efforts of others could be promoters, sponsors, or active participant. Under the Howey test, price appreciation should not result solely from external market forces. Rather, reasonable expectation of profits comes from the capital appreciation that results from investment in the enterprise. Therefore, to meet the Howey test, the digital asset should give the investor the right to share profits (i.e., dividends) in the enterprise. The federal court examines other characteristics of digital assets such as the economic reality of transaction to identify whether there is reasonable expectation of profit derived from the efforts of others. Among these considerations are: (1) whether digital assets are fully developed, (2) whether holders of such assets can use it immediately, (3) whether the structure of digital assets meets the expectation of holders of such assets, and (4) whether it can be used as to make payments, in case of virtual currency.

A digital asset that meets the criteria of "security" is still a topic of interest by regulators because of the complex issues associated with after selling this security, such as valuation, classification in the balance sheet, and operational risk. For example, the below issues were raised by the SEC in a comment letter [6]:

1. Valuation: cryptocurrencies, for example, are highly volatile and new to the futures market. It is unclear how would managers assess the fair values of such assets.
2. Classification: how would digital assets be classified in financial statements (i.e., short vs. long term)?
3. Operational risk: how would manipulation in the digital asset prices in the financial market affect its trading?

The US federal securities laws and regulations also apply to Decentralized Autonomous Organization (DAO) that uses decentralized or distributed ledger such as blockchain technology. In July 2017, the SEC considered Slock.it UG digital asset as a "security", however, decided against pursuing enforcement action towards it. [7] Slock.it is a DAO, a virtual organization that is executed on a distributed ledger or blockchain. The virtual organization sold 1.15 billion DAO in exchange for 12 million ether (ETH) that was later valued at $150 million at the time of the sale. The SEC concluded that the co-founders of Slock.it promoted their DAO using various platforms, the company was audited by leading security audit companies, and solicited media interest. The DAO tokens that were issued in exchange for Ethereum (ETH), which gave holders certain voting and ownership rights and prospect of earning a return on investment. Therefore, the SEC deemed the DAO token as a security for the following reasons: (1) the SEC securities laws apply to virtual organization making use of distributed ledger technology, (2) investors in the DAO invested money, (3) there was a reasonable expectation of profits, (4) the assumed profits are derived from the managerial efforts of others because the efforts of the co-founders and the DAO's curators were essential to the enterprise.

Cryptocurrencies classification varies across countries. For example, in November 2019, digital assets were recognized as a property/commodity according to the UK Jurisdiction Taskforce [8]. More specifically, digital assets exhibit four characteristics: (1) definable, (2) identifiable by third parties, (3) capable in their nature of assumption by third parties, and (4) having some degree of permanence. The Financial Conduct Authority (FCA), the financial market regulatory authority in the UK, mandated that businesses dealing with digital assets to register with the authority by June 30, 2020, failing to register by the deadline would carry a penalty of case trading [9]. According to the FCA, digital assets can be classified as regulated and unregulated tokens. Regulated tokens are security tokens and e-money tokens, and unregulated tokens are utility and exchange tokens. Rules of classifying tokens include prospectus and transparency requirements, manager's certification regime, and principles of business.

2.2 Bitcoin Use Cases

Because of Bitcoin's features (i.e., irrevocability, anonymity, and low transaction costs) along with the rise of decentralized finance (DeFi), bitcoin has become widely used as a fast payment tool in buying/selling, smart contracts, voting, collateral, donations, and a trading investment. For example, bitcoin can be used as a substitute to cash and as a peer-to-peer electronic cash system as initially envisioned by Satoshi Nakamoto. Bitcoin can be used in smart contracts, which are stored codes that can be automatically excused using bitcoin as the electronic cash. It can also be used as collateral on DeFi networks. Bitcoin is one of the best tools or solutions to cross-border transfer of money without the need of intermediaries and hence considerably reduces the transactions fees. It is widely known as a tool to facilitate internet of value.

2.3 Bitcoin Policies and Regulations

The global capital market regulators realized the need for fostering innovation in the capital market by embracing nascent technologies (i.e., blockchain) and flexible forms of ownership/payment (i.e., digital assets, cryptocurrencies). On the one hand, in line with expectations that global jurisdictions are embracing innovative technologies, regulators around the world (i.e., USA, Singapore, Thailand, Switzerland, and Hong Kong) are issuing guidelines and framework to facilitate exchange of digital assets [4].

On the other hand, the speculative nature of bitcoin and high volatility mandate regulatory government intervention and the subsequent issuance of guidance and rules on the classification and use of bitcoin. The intervention of government regulators is, however, sometimes perceived as a setback to the innovative nature of bitcoin and emergence as peer-to-peer tool that discards intermediaries. Hence, there are unintended consequences with government regulations. Market intervention in cryptocurrency trading, in general, may include communications from regulators and/or issuances of regulatory rules. For example, in September 2017, the Chinese government halted trading on cryptocurrencies and banned initial coin offerings (ICOs). In April 2017, Japan issued the Payment Services Act and the Financial Instruments and Exchange Act that was later revised in 2020 to tighten restrictions on cryptocurrency custodians, but meanwhile allowed the use of crypto as digital assets. Indeed, Japan was the lead country in Asia to allow cryptocurrency to be a safe haven asset. In August 2020, the UK approved its first digital stock exchange, Archax. David Lester, former chief strategy officer of the London Stock Exchange Group mentioned that: "*Blockchain and tokenization are innovations that can empower more frictionless and transparent markets which, combined with an FCA regulated exchange like Archax, can deliver what capital providers, business leaders and founders now really need*" [10].

In 2015, the U.S. classified bitcoin as a commodity. Realizing the need to adapt to flexibility in financial market innovations, the Securities and Exchange Commission (SEC) has been diligently working towards protecting investor's rights as well as fostering innovation in the financial market by allowing it to develop exponentially and at the same time expanding the SEC federal rules and regulations to include digital assets. Additionally, in the US market, the regulatory oversight over digital assets have become more developed and geared towards simplifying the rules and regulations. For example, the SEC modernized the digital asset securities settlement and condensed its steps from four to three to reduce the operational risk for broker-dealer who operate alternative trading system (ATS) [11]. The four steps are: (1) the buyer and seller send orders to ATS, (2) the ATS matches the orders, (3) the ATS notifies the buyer and seller with the matching process, and (4) the transaction is bilaterally settled. The streamlined process involves only three steps: (1) the buyer and seller send orders to ATS and instruct their custodian to settle the transactions when the match is announced on the ATS, (2) the ATS matches the order, and (3) the ATS notified the buyer and seller with the matched and the custodians of the parties execute the instructions. However, digital assets regulations in the US market are not uniform across the states [12]. Some states (i.e., Wyoming, Colorado, Oklahoma) are "crypto-friendly" while others are not (i.e., Iowa). Crypto-friendly states promote bitcoin as a faster and more efficient payment system by reducing regulatory barriers and leveraging investment in the technology and allowing for a wider adoption among the community participants. For example, legislatures in Wyoming supported the initiation of a special purpose depository institutions to handle digital assets. Likewise, lawmakers in Colorado exempted cryptocurrencies from state securities regulations. While the SEC declared Bitcoin and Ethereum not to be securities, it used a double standard with XRP, the Ripple token, when it sued Ripple and two of its executive, claiming that Ripple sold unlicensed securities. Although Ripple has been in circulation since 2012, the SEC only initiated the lawsuit in late 2020, a few days before President Trump administration left SEC leadership, starting speculations about the interference of politics with cryptocurrency regulations. Ripple claims that the SEC suit caused XRP's price to plummet, accumulating in over $15 billion in losses. Notably, President Trump twitted in different occasions about cryptocurrency and bitcoin *"not a fan of highly volatile cryptocurrencies based on thin air that facilitate unlawful behavior,"* causing more volatility in the cryptocurrency market. The disagreement among regulators within the U.S. and outside it makes it more difficult to embrace blockchain technology and the power that digital assets (i.e., cryptocurrency) can bring to the market.

The study made by Park et al. [13] examine the exogenous shocks of local regulations on bitcoin prices and trading activities across six countries. Anecdotal evidence suggests that market regulations have a short-term impact on bitcoin price and a long-term suppressive trading effect. More interestingly, bitcoin prices vary across jurisdictions and although regulations have a short-term influence on bitcoin prices, the market for bitcoin is sought to be globally integrated and local frictions are weak to persist in the face of bitcoin's strong international network.

The size of the global cryptocurrency market is too big to regulate by one government. In fact, anecdotal evidence suggests that regulations on bitcoin create market frictions and long-term decline in trading activities. Bitcoin was invented to cross borders and barriers, facilitate fast payment, reduce market frictions and transactions costs. Global efforts are required to achieve the tangible benefits of bitcoin and lessen the unavoidable negative consequences that usually comes with innovative technologies in times of need such as the unprecedented COVID-19.

3. CHALLENGES FACING BITCOIN

3.1 Bitcoin Substitution

When bitcoin was invented by Satoshi Nakamoto, he developed blockchain as the tool or medium to exchange bitcoin. You may think of bitcoin as the vehicle and blockchain as the road. Hence, one can imagine the power and innovation that comes with the invention of the first vehicle on the road. Yet, the present status of the cryptocurrency industry is that there are thousands of vehicles "cryptocurrencies" invented after bitcoin, each with its own features that may be incremental or decremental to bitcoin in functions. Bitcoin represents roughly 69% of the total market capitalization of cryptocurrencies that reached a peak of over

$1 trillion on January, 6 of 2021. For example, Ethereum (ETH) is an altcoin that is used in a smart contract on the Ethereum network. Another substitute to bitcoin is XPR, which is a Ripple token that is using network of nodes of participating banks and financial institutions. Litecoin is another cryptocurrency that is four times faster than bitcoin and offer four times the amount of bitcoin supply (i.e., the total supply of bitcoin is 21 million while Litecoin's supply is 84 million). While bitcoin will remain the first innovative cryptocurrency, it is difficult to speculate that it is the best one on the road.

3.2 Bitcoin Cross Border Financing

As a peer-to-peer transaction, bitcoin defies the central government sole right to issue currencies and calls for a decentralized flow of currency. The market for bitcoin is concentrated in six major markets (the USA, Japan, China, Europe, UK, and South Korea) that roughly represent 99% of bitcoin trading activities with China taking over 88% of total bitcoin trading as of 2018 [13]. Therefore, it is likely that if there are cross border usage of bitcoin, it will happen mostly among these six countries. The lack of a centralized authority to regulate bitcoin along with its high tendency to be anonymous even though create an opportunity for faster and cheaper cross border transfer of currency, it opens another gate to illegal transfer of money. More specifically, one major risk associated with bitcoin is capital flight. The problem intensifies when bitcoin transaction is anonymized to cover cross-border money laundering. A study [14] examines bitcoin's capital flight from China to USA as the largest two originators of bitcoin transactions. It also examines whether market regulations can be effective in curbing the illegal transfer of bitcoin across countries. They use bitcoin-implied exchange rate discount as a proxy for bitcoin capital flight from China to the USA prior to China's announcement of regulations that banned financial institutions and payment companies from using bitcoin transactions. Further, they document that China's regulatory regime successfully halted this transaction. Therefore, the intervention of financial institutions in regulating bitcoin is becoming more crucial to reduce the likelihood of using it in illicit activities and improve transparency in trading.

3.3 Bitcoin Cyber Risk and Security

Expectedly, bitcoin price variability across exchanges may involve illegal behavior and anomalies related to ask and bid prices [15]. The European Central Bank (ECB) Regulations on bitcoin are meant to curb illegal trading, reduce cyber-attacks, and protect investors. However, it is unclear whether individual bitcoin regulations across different jurisdictions can make a global impact on bitcoin trading activities. Additionally, bitcoin's virtual nature made it subject to lost and disappearance. For example, 20% of the 18.5 million circulated bitcoins are believed to be lost because owners of these bitcoins have lost their password to nearly $140 billion in bitcoins.

In 2014, Mt. Gox trading platform in Tokyo went bankrupt [16] leaving 850,000 bitcoins owners clueless trying to find their passwords. James Howells from the UK mistakenly dumped his computer hard drive that includes 7,500 bitcoins that he mined in 2009. The fact that the identity of bitcoin developer is anonymous also raises speculation on whether bitcoin was originally developed for the dark web. Bitcoin can be used for money laundry and can help perpetrators cover up their identities. Ransomware attacks in the digital age includes demands for bitcoin, which made bitcoin a tool used for cyber-attacks. It is estimated that bitcoin drives ransomware of $1.4 billion in the U.S. Cyber risk and security are one of the key barriers to bitcoin evolution as a mainstream digital currency.

3.4 Bitcoin Other Challenges

Another study [17] raised other concerns not addressed by the SEC in their framework such as whether digital assets traded by "Airdrop" are considered a security and the status of digital assets traded overseas. Lack of regulatory clarity of such important issues hampers the development of digital assets and blockchain technology. Challenges to securities service providers and their clients have been raised by [4] as obstacles towards getting the most out of tokenization. Some of these challenges include lack of common standards and interoperability after the introduction of new concepts by market participants. Issues regarding market stability from digital assets are also of great concerns to investors, regulators, activists, and various stakeholders. Barriers of entry (i.e., fiduciary obligation) of institutional investors into the digital asset world has slowed down the development of digital assets and underlying blockchain technology, at least this was the case before the onset of COVID-19. Among other impediment to the development of digital asset worldwide are various regulations across regulations, fraud, lack of scaling by blockchain technology and balancing scalability and security. Park, Sang, Lee, and Jang (2019) raised two critical issues related to digital assets: privacy and access by third party after death. Related, another study [18] questioned whether people should be able to inherit digital assets and whether to consider social media accounts (i.e., Email accounts, Facebook, Twitter, LinkedIn) as digital assets because they contain monetary value and are real.

4. THE ECONOMIC EFFECT OF BITCOIN HALVING EVENTS ON CAPITAL MARKETS

An interesting question on whether bitcoin came up with net economic benefits to the U.S. financial system is still unanswered. Anecdotal evidence suggests that bitcoin prices are influenced by the quality of financial system (governance and regulations) it exists at. Nevertheless, the major characteristics of bitcoin are its volatility and price unpredictability, two major factors that are more than enough to hinder its international recognition as an innovative payment system that has the potential of replacing fiat currencies. These features are, however, puzzling. Why would bitcoin prices decline by 50% on March 12, 2020 and go up by 36% on November 19, 2013, while the global stock indexes do not synchronize in movement in the same manner? Additionally, anecdotal evidence suggests that bitcoin prices vary across different markets due to differences in market infrastructure, financial frictions, regulatory oversight, and institutional investors [12, 19].

Although the market for bitcoin is dispersed worldwide, it is globally integrated by a diverse group of bitcoin holders. When the total market capitalization reached out a peak of $1 trillion on January 6, 2021, market participants started to contemplate on whether this unimaginable magnitude of the cryptocurrency market that is mainly sparked by bitcoin is frothy. In this section, I empirically test the economic consequences of bitcoin halving events on the U.S. capital market. More specifically, I examine the market reaction to bitcoin's first and second halving events that occurred over the past decade. There are three halving events occurred since 2009. The first halving occurred on November 28, 2012 and ended up with reducing the rewards from mining for bitcoin from 50 to 25 bitcoins per block. The second halving further reduced the reward to 12.5 bitcoins per block when it occurred on July 9, 2016. The last halving at the time of writing this study occurred on May 11, 2020 and reduced the rewards from bitcoin mining to 6.25 bitcoins per block. Due to lack of data on CRSP database post 2019 about stock prices, this study focuses on examining the stock market reactions to the first and second halving events that occurred in 2012 and 2016.

The halving event is intended to reduce bitcoin's inflation rate. It is usually scheduled when miners solve a certain number of blocks and happens every 210,000 blocks. The next halving will happen when miners reach out 840,000 blocks and it is scheduled to happened between February 2024 and June 2024. Litecoin rewards is also halved every four years but it does not sync with bitcoin halving events.

I started my sample by July 18, 2010 and ended on December 31, 2019 as CRSP database does not provide stock returns date for the year 2020 yet. This restriction in the available dataset will not allow the empirical testing of the third halving event as previously stated that occurred on May 11, 2020. To examine the economic effect of bitcoin halving events on the U.S. capital market, I first estimate stock returns using the Capital Asset Pricing Model (CAPM) and then calculate abnormal returns as the difference between actual and estimated returns. Then, I cumulate abnormal returns to calculate Cumulative Abnormal returns (CARs) around difference length of return windows, a short window (2 days) and long window (10 days).

Table 1. Summarizes the Pearson correlations among cryptocurrencies, returns and halving events.

	Pearson correlation coefficients										
	1st_E	2nd_E	Δ BTC	Δ BCH	Δ ADA	Δ LINK	Δ ETH	Δ LTC	Δ XLM	Δ USDT	Δ XRP
CAR	0.001a	0.002a	−0.002a	0.001a	0.004a	0.00a	0.003a	0.00	0.002a	−0.002a	−0.002a
1st_E		−0.00c	−0.00	−0.00	0.00	−0.00	−0.00	−0.00	−0.00	−0.00a	0.00
2nd_E			0.002a	−0.00	0.00	−0.00	−0.00	−0.00	−0.00	0.00a	0.001a
Δ BTC				0.254a	0.264a	0.200a	0.545a	0.45 1a	0.309a	0.068a	0.620a
Δ BCH					0.206a	0.058a	0.450a	0.241a	0.253a	0.113a	0.022a
Δ ADA						0.050a	0.467a	0.211a	0.772a	0.025a	0.042a
Δ LINK							0.097a	0.124a	0.066a	0.018a	−0.016a
Δ ETH								0.564[a]	0.462a	0.082a	0.183a
Δ LTC									0.237a	0.079a	0.236a
Δ XLM										0.068a	0.059a
Δ USDT											−0.026a

I first ran a Pearson correlation among cryptocurrencies, halving events, and stock returns. The results of the correlation analysis are displayed in Table 1 *that shows positive and significant correlations at %1 between the two halving events (1st_E and 2*[nd]*_E) under investigation and contemporaneous stock returns (R). The magnitude of the correlation is very weak. There is a negative significant correlation at 1% between contemporaneous stock returns (R) and change in bitcoin (ΔBTC), suggesting that an increase in BTC corresponds to a decrease in R. However, other altcoins, cryptocurrencies other than bitcoin, such as ADA, LINK, ETH, and XLM seem to be positively correlated with R.*

1st_E is an indicator variable for the first halving event that occurred on November 28, 2012, zero otherwise. 2nd_E is an indicator variable for the second halving event that occurred on July 9, 2016, zero otherwise. Δ BTC is the change in returns on bitcoin as measured by the difference in bitcoin prices in day t and day t-1. Δ BCH is the change in returns on bitcoin cash as measured by the difference in bitcoin cash prices in day t and day t-1. Δ ADA is the change in returns on Cardano coin as measured by the difference in Cardano prices in day t and day t-1. Δ LINK is the change in returns on ChainLink coin as measured by the difference in ChainLink prices in day t and day t-1. Δ ETH is the the change in returns on Ethereum coin as measured by the difference in Ethereum prices in day t and day t-1. Δ LTC is the change in returns on Litecoin as measured by the difference in Litecoin prices in day t and day t-1. Δ XLM is the change in returns on Stellar Lumens as measured by the difference in Stellar Lumens prices in day t and day t-1. Δ USDT is the change in returns on Tether coin as measured by the difference in Tether prices in day t and day t-1. Δ XRP is t the change in returns on Ripple token (XRP) as measured by the difference in XRP prices in day t and day t-1.

[a] *Significance levels at 1%.* [b] *Significance levels at 5%.* [c] *Significance levels at 10%.*

The result of the event study on the effect of bitcoin halving events on the U.S. capital market is summarized in Tables 2 and 3 and Figures 2–5. Table 2 summarizes the results of CARs and lists its correspondence t-test with the level of significance for the test of the first halving event. As shown in Panel A, CARs around 2 days return window of the first bitcoin halving shows that the first bitcoin halving event has a significant negative market reaction on the event date. CARs shows a decline two days before the event date and then an increase starting from day 1+. Panel B shows the results using 10 days return window and the results show large fluctuations around the halving event. The use of a large return window should be interpreted with caution since other market events may confound the results. Figures 2 and 3 confirms the results displayed in Table 2 by showing the negative market reaction on day zero (the event date). Table 3 summarizes the results of CARs and lists its correspondence t-test with the level of significance for the test of the second halving event. Because the second halving event occurred during a holiday, I used July 2016 ,11 as the event date when the market opened to capture the market reaction after the second halving event. Although the results in Panel (A) of Table 3 show significant positive CARs on the event date, the CARs are significantly declining from day 1- to day 0 (the event day, suggesting that the second halving event still causes a downward abnormal stock returns but perhaps not with the same negative magnitude caused by the first halving event.

Table 2. Displays the Cumulative Abnormal Stock Returns (CAR) around two event windows, 2 days as in Panel (A) and 10 days as in Panel (B) for the 1st bitcoin halving event.

CAR_{it} around the 1st Bitcoin Halving Event on Nov. 2012 ,28					
Panel A: CAR_{it} around 2 days return-window					
Days	-2	-1	0	1	2
CAR_{it}	0.0041	0.0014	-0.0015	0.0022	0.0029
t-test	(7.44)***	(3.02)***	(-4.91)***	(5.05)***	(5.59)***
No. Obs.	6654	6655	6656	6653	6652
Panel B: CAR_{it} around 10 days return-window					
Days	-10	-5	0	5	10
CAR_{it}	-0.0034	0.0051	-0.0015	0.0030	0.0029
t-test	(-3.36)***	(7.16)***	(-4.91)***	(4.20)***	(2.63)***
No. Obs.	6644	6652	6656	6640	6631

**Significance levels at 10%*

***Significance levels at 5%*

**** Significance levels at 1%*

Panel (B) of Table 3 displays CARs around 10 days return window and as expected CARs fluctuates around the event and showing the lowest significant statistical decline on the event date. Figure 4 and 5 shows the market reaction around the second halving event and supports the main conclusion reached from Table 3.

Table 3. Displays the Cumulative Abnormal Stock Returns (CAR) around two event windows, 2 days as in Panel (A) and 10 days as in Panel (B) for the 2nd bitcoin halving event.

CAR_{it} around the 2nd Bitcoin Halving Event on July 2016 ,9					
Panel A: CAR_{it} around 2 days return-window					
Days	-2	-1	0	1	2
CAR_{it}	0.0080	0.0063	0.0031	0.0068	0.0046
t-test	(7.44)***	(3.02)***	(9.93)***	(5.05)***	(5.59)***
No. Obs.	7178	7173	7170	7204	7201
Panel B: CAR_{it} around 10 days return-window					
Days	-10	-5	0	5	10
CAR_{it}	0.0043	0.0084	0.0031	0.0050	0.0056
t-test	(-3.36)***	(7.16)***	(9.93)***	(4.20)***	(2.63)***
No. Obs.	7207	7186	7170	7188	7176

**Significance levels at 10%*

***Significance levels at 5%*

**** Significance levels at 1%*

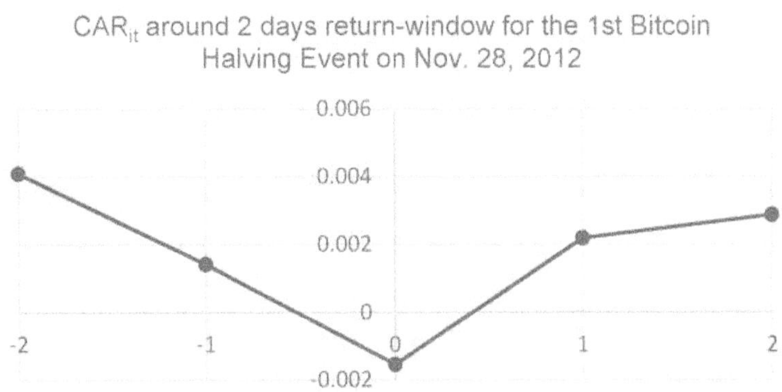

Figure 2. CAR around 2 days return-window of the 1st Bitcoin Halving Event on November 28, 2012.

I also ran an OLS regression by regressing stock returns (R) on the halving events, change in bitcoin, change in altcoin, and industry categorization to get a better understanding on the nature of the economic effect of the halving events on stock returns. The results are displayed in Tables 4 and 5. Table 4 summarizes the OLS regression on the association between contemporaneous stock returns as the dependent variable in all models and 1st bitcoin halving event halving, changes in bitcoin, changes in cryptocurrencies, and industry categorization as the independent variables. The 1st bitcoin halving event (1st_E) is the independent variable of interest. The coefficient on this variable (1st_E) is expected to be negative and significant, consistent with the documented results from the event study.

Figure 3. CAR around 10 days return-window of the 1st Bitcoin Halving Event on November 28, 2012.

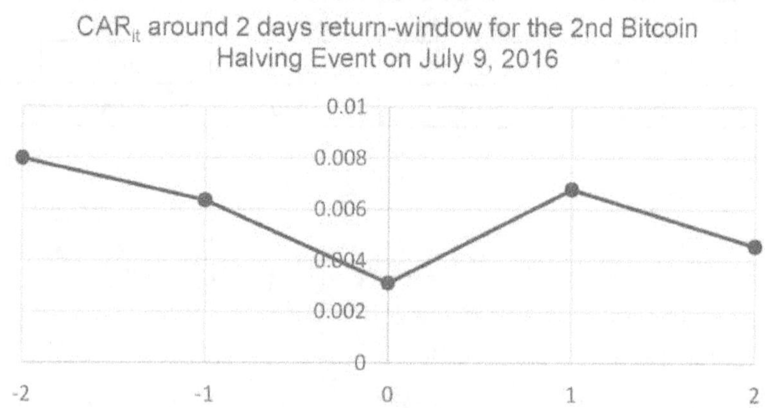

Figure 4. CAR around 2 days return-window of the 2nd Bitcoin Halving Event on July 9, 2016.

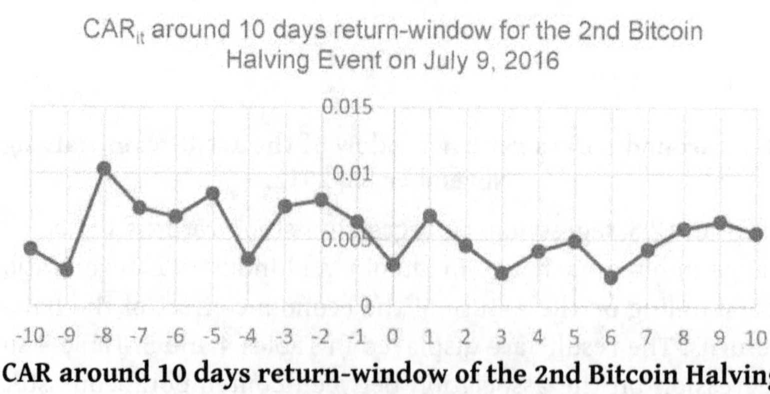

Figure 5. CAR around 10 days return-window of the 2nd Bitcoin Halving Event on July 9, 2016.

Table 4. Summarizes the OLS regression on the association between stock returns and 1st bitcoin event halving and changes in crypto currencies.

	Model (1)	Model (2)	Model (3)	Model (4)		Model (5)	Model (6)	Model (7)
	Dependent variable = R							
Intercept	-0.00002***	-0.00002***	-0.00002***	-0.00001	Intercept	-0.00002**	-0.00002***	-0.00002***
1st_E	-0.00152***	-0.00152***	-0.00153***	-0.00153***	1st_E	-0.00152***	-0.00152***	-0.00152***
Δ BTC		0.00000***	0.00000***	0.00000***	Δ BTC_V	0.00000***	0.00000***	0.00000***
Δ BCH			0.00000	0.00000	Δ BCH_V		0.00000***	0.00000***
Δ ADA			0.01236***	0.01236***	Δ ADA_V		0.00000***	0.00000***
Δ LINK			0.00081***	0.00081***	Δ LINK_V		0.00000***	0.00000***
Δ ETH			0.00001***	0.00001***	Δ ETH_V		0.00000	0.00000***
Δ LTC			0.00000**	0.00000**	Δ LTC_V		0.00000***	0.00000***
Δ XLM			-0.00336***	-0.00336***	Δ XLM_V		0.00000***	0.00000***
Δ USDT			-0.01586***	-0.01587***	Δ USDT_V		0.00000***	0.00000***
Δ XRP			0.00000	0.00000	Δ XRP_V		0.00000***	0.00000***
INDUSTRY	No	No	No	Yes	INDUSTRY	No	No	Yes
F-Ratio	15.69	28	57.89	29.12	F-Ratio	50.14	46.02	23.18
P-Value	<.0001	<.0001	<.0001	<.0001	P-Value	<.0001	<.0001	<.0001
# Obs.	16,621,212	16,621,212	16,621,212	16,621,212	# Obs.	16,621,212	16,621,212	16,621,212

1st_E is an indicator variable for the first halving event that occurred on November 28, 2012, zero otherwise. Δ BTC is the change in returns on bitcoin as measured by the difference in bitcoin prices in day t and day t-1. Δ BCH is the change in returns on bitcoin cash as measured by the difference in bitcoin cash prices in day t and day t-1. Δ ADA is the change in returns on Cardano coin as measured by the difference in Cardano prices in day t and day t-1. Δ LINK is the change in returns on ChainLink coin as measured by the difference in ChainLink prices in day t and day t-1. Δ ETH is the change in returns on Ethereum coin as measured by the difference in Ethereum prices in day t and day t-1. Δ LTC is the change in returns on Litecoin as measured by the difference in Litecoin prices in day t and day t-1. Δ XLM is the change in returns on Stellar Lumens as measured by the difference in Stellar Lumens prices in day t and day t-1. Δ USDT is the change in returns on Tether coin as measured by the difference in Tether prices in day t and day t-1. Δ XRP is t the change in returns on Ripple token (XRP) as measured by the difference in XRP prices in day t and day t-1.

[*] Significance levels at 10%. [**] Significance levels at 5%. [***] Significance levels at 1%.

Table 5. Summarizes the OLS regression on the association between stock returns and 2nd bitcoin event halving and changes in crypto currencies.

	Model (1)	Model (2)	Model (3)	Model (4)		Model (5)	Model (6)	Model (7)
	Dependent variable = R							
Intercept	-0.00002***	-0.00002***	-0.00002***	-0.00001	Intercept	-0.00002**	-0.00002***	-0.00002***
2nd_E	-0.00314***	-0.00315***	-0.00316***	-0.00316***	2nd_E	0.00313***	0.00314***	0.00314***
Δ BTC		0.00000***	0.00000***	0.00000***	Δ BTC_V	0.00000***	0.00000***	0.00000***
Δ BCH			0.00000	0.00000	Δ BCH_V		0.00000v**	0.00000***
Δ ADA			0.01236***	0.01236***	Δ ADA_V		0.00000***	0.00000***
Δ LINK			0.00081***	0.00081***	Δ LINK_V		0.00000**	0.00000***
Δ ETH			0.00001***	0.00001***	Δ ETH_V		0.00000	0.00000
Δ LTC			0.00000**	0.00000**	Δ LTC_V		0.00000***	0.00000***
Δ XLM			-0.00336****	-0.00336***	Δ XLM_V		0.00000***	0.00000***
Δ USDT			-0.01586***	-0.01587***	Δ USDT_V		0.00000***	0.00000***
Δ XRP			0.00000	0.00000	Δ XRP_V		0.00000***	0.00000***
INDUSTRY	No	No	No	Yes	INDUSTRY	No	No	Yes
F-Ratio	72.23	56.39	63.60	31.98	F-Ratio	78.06	51.67	26.00
P-Value	<.0001	<.0001	<.0001	<.0001	P-Value	<.0001	<.0001	<.0001
# Obs.	16,621,212	16,621,212	16,621,212	16,621,212	# Obs.	16,621,212	16,621,212	16,621,212

2nd_E is an indicator variable for the second halving event that occurred on July 9, 2016, zero otherwise. Δ BTC is the change in returns on bitcoin as measured by the difference in bitcoin prices in day t and day t-1. Δ BCH is the change in returns on bitcoin cash as measured by the difference in bitcoin cash prices in day t and day t-1. Δ ADA is the change in returns on Cardano coin as measured by the difference in Cardano prices in day t and day t-1. Δ LINK is the change in returns on ChainLink coin as measured by the difference in ChainLink prices in day t and day t-1. Δ ETH is the the change in returns on Ethereum coin as measured by the difference in Ethereum prices in day t and day t-1. Δ LTC is the change in returns on Litecoin as measured by the difference in Litecoin prices in day t and day t-1. Δ XLM is the change in returns on Stellar Lumens as measured by the difference in Stellar Lumens prices in day t and day t-1. Δ USDT is the change in returns on Tether coin as measured by the difference in Tether prices in day t and day t-1. Δ XRP is t the change in returns on Ripple token (XRP) as measured by the difference in XRP prices in day t and day t-1. ΔBTC_V is the change in trading volume of BTC, ΔBCH_V is the change in trading volume of BCH, ΔADA_V is change in the trading volume of ADA, ΔLINK_V is the change in trading volume of LINK, ΔETH_V is the change in trading volume of ETH, ΔLTC_V is the change in trading volume of LTC, ΔXLM_V is the change in trading volume of XLM, ΔUSDT_V is the change in trading volume of USDT, ΔXPR_V is change in the trading volume of XRP.

* *Significance levels at 10%.* ** *Significance levels at 5%.* *** *Significance levels at 1%.*

As shown in Table 4, there is a significant negative association (coefficient = -0.00152) at 1% significance level between the first bitcoin halving event (1^{st}_E) and stock returns (R). I used different variations of the regression model by regressing the contemporaneous stock returns on bitcoin, returns on other altcoins, industry categorization, and substituting cryptocurrencies returns with trading volumes as displayed in models 1–7 and the results are still the same. Table 5 summarizes the OLS regression on the association between contemporaneous stock returns (R) as the dependent variable and 2nd bitcoin halving event, changes in bitcoin, changes in cryptocurrencies, and industry categorization as the independent variables. The 2nd bitcoin halving event (2nd _E) is the independent variable of interest. The coefficient on this variable (2nd _E) is expected to be negative and significant, consistent with the documented results from the event study.

The results in Table 5 suggests the same conclusion from Table 4 that the second halving event is statistically and significantly associated with negative stock returns. I used different variations of the regression model by regressing the contemporaneous stock returns on bitcoin, returns on other altcoins, industry categorization, and substituting cryptocurrencies returns with trading volumes as displayed in models 1–7 and the results are still the same. The results in this section suggests that bitcoin halving events, which eventually increased the demand on and price of bitcoin, are detrimental to the U.S. capital market because these events are associated with a downward abnormal stock returns around the announcement date.

5. CONCLUSIONS

It is indisputable that regulatory bodies across different countries lack harmony and agreement on bitcoin classification, use cases and policies. Even within the same country such as the case in the U.S., bitcoin regulations diverge widely across different states. And despite regulatory intervention, or lack thereof, across different jurisdictions, bitcoin stood against regulatory constraints in terms of financial performance in the cryptocurrency world. It showed steady increase over the past decade and most notably over the past several months, especially during COVID-19 era that hastened decades of innovation. However, it is unclear whether COVID-19 accelerated the need for financial innovation and hence contributed to a surge in bitcoin price or the market is presently experiencing a bubble. The conclusion from this study is that bitcoin scarce supply as measured by the decline in the reward from bitcoin is detrimental to the U.S. capital market because the halving events are significantly associated with negative abnormal stock returns around the announcement days. The results suggest that the second halving event has less of an impact on the stock market than the first halving event. Future research may study the market reaction to the third halving event and examine whether the results will remain the same.

The theoretical argument and conclusion from this study are of benefits to many market constituencies such as regulators, practitioners, research scholars, and cryptocurrency traders. For example, current and prospective cryptocurrency traders should bear in mind that the price surge in cryptocurrencies that is mainly driven by the past, most recent bitcoin halving event in 2020, and the current pandemic is negatively associated with their investment in the U.S. capital market. Therefore, perhaps having a diverse portfolio to hedge the risk associated with investing solely in one market is a good investment strategy at the present time. Additionally, evidence suggests that the cryptocurrency market is highly volatile, if new traders would like to penetrate this unique market, they should wait until the price drops to a reasonable level they can afford and they should not put all their savings (i.e., pension funds, college savings) into this market. Likewise, it is always a good strategy to exit the cryptocurrency market "temporarily" when traders achieve certain level of profits (i.e., 30%) and then reinvest again when the market experience sudden decline and it will eventually happen because sharp volatility is a primary trait of cryptocurrency market. Regulators should be aware that the gigantic size of bitcoin and other cryptocurrencies is not going to vanish, and it would be beneficial for regulators to work with those in other jurisdictions on a local, national, and international levels to regulate this market. Regulating cryptocurrency market will come up with several tangible advantages. First, it will reduce the risk associated with cryptocurrencies' cyber-attacks. Second, it will stabilize the price of cryptocurrencies so that the market gets the anticipated benefits of using cryptocurrencies in blockchain applications. Scholars who would like to examine the risks and benefits of cryptocurrencies may attempt to investigate the economic consequences of corporate investment in cryptocurrencies on financial performance or financial reporting quality such as accounting conservatism and internal control quality. For example, a firm may use investment in cryptocurrencies to cover up its poor financial performance and signal a better performance. In early 2021, Tesla company invested $1.5 billion in bitcoin where the price was (and still) skyrocketing. Speculators believe that Tesla made between $0.29 to $0.98 billion profit just from investment in bitcoin during a very short period. Notably, Telsa's profit in 2020 per form 10-K was a modest $721 million. This previous example illustrates how some companies can make "everything" from trading in cryptocurrencies. Nevertheless, it does not rule out the possibility that everything can turn into "nothing" if the price of bitcoin tailspins to the opposite direction with the news of reopening the global market and getting vaccinated against the risk of exposure to coronavirus.

It is worthwhile to note that despite the increase in bitcoin in 2020, investors still consider it a venture tool of investment. Proponents of bitcoin argue that it shares characteristics with gold (i.e., scarce, mined, international) and can be used for hedging and diversifying asset. However, gold is "scientifically" not scarce as evidence [20] suggests that gold can be formulated instantaneously within a few tenths of a second in response to earthquakes. With the same token, it is reasonable to assume that bitcoin miners may be able to change its protocol and increase its supply. With too much uncertainty at stake, it is difficult to make a prediction that bitcoin is the future of money. Nevertheless, there is quite agreement that blockchain technology is valuable tool for many applications (i.e., supply chain management) and in order for blockchain to function, an efficient form of cryptocurrency (virtual money) is needed.

The question whether bitcoin will reach $500,000 per coin or dive into $1,000 a decade from today is not the correct answer at the present time. A relevant question would be whether bitcoin can improve our lives, decrease transaction cost, accelerate transfer of money, reduce market frictions, reduce cyber-attacks and fraudulent activities, and eliminate intermediaries' costs. Another interesting question is perhaps whether bitcoin is a safe haven against financial crises? The limited supply of the total amount of bitcoin that can be circulated along with the mining reward that is split into half every four years made it, by definition, a scarce commodity. Using a simple equilibrium scenario, plotting the demand and supply of bitcoin shows that the price is poised to rise in the future, but this is under the assumption that bitcoin is the only cryptocurrency in the market, which is untrue. Related, it is not impossible to change the bitcoin protocol and increase the amount of its supply. Therefore, the economic as well as real benefits of bitcoin to the market still open for discussion and future research is needed to provoke in depth discussion about its assumed risk and benefits to market constituencies.

REFERENCES

1. Nakamoto S. Bitcoin P2P e-cash paper. 2008. Working paper available at: https://bitcoin.org/bitcoin.pdf

2. Yermak D. Is bitcoin a real currency? An economic appraisal. 2013; NBER working paper 19747. DOI 10.3386/w19747

3. Voel Z. Total Cryptocurrency Market Value Hits Record $1 Trillion. 2021. Available at:https://www.coindesk.com/cryptocurrency-market-value-record-1-trillion

4. Harwood-Jones M. Digital and crypto-assets: Tracking global adoption rates and impacts on securities services. Journal of Securities Operations and Custody. 2019; 12: (1) 49–58.

5. SEC. Framework for "Investment Contract" Analysis of Digital Assets. Available at: https://www.sec.gov/files/dlt-framework.pdf

6. SEC. Staff Letter: Engaging on Fund Innovation and Cryptocurrency-related Holdings. 2018. Available at: https://www.sec.gov/divisions/investment/noaction/2018/cryptocurrency-011818.htm

7. SEC. Report of Investigation Pursuant to Section 21(a) of the Securities Exchange Act of 1934: The DAO. 2017. Available at: https://www.sec.gov/litigation/investreport/34-81207.pdf

8. Alderman P. UK High Court recognizes digital assets as property at common law. 2020. Available at: https://www.lexology.com/library/detail.aspx?g=83ae727b-2ff8-445a-aba0-b18a124e5b0a

9. Murray D., and Petrie N. A Mix of Clarity and Confusion: Crypto Asset Law and Regulation in the UK. 2021; The National Law Review XI, 35. Available at: https://www.natlawreview.com/article/mix-clarity-and-confusion-crypto-asset-law-and-regulation-uk

10. Delaney R. Archax authorised as first UK digital securities exchange. 2020. Available at: http://www.assetservicingtimes.com/assetservicesnews/article.php?article_id=10875

11. David E. US SEC issues no-action letter on compressed digital asset settlement process 2020. Available at: https://cointelegraph.com/news/us-sec-issues-no-action-letter-on-compressed-digital-asset-settlement-process/amp

12. Global Legal Insights. Blockchain and cryptocurrency regulation 2021. 2021. Available at: https://www.globallegalinsights.com/practice-areas/blockchain-laws-and-regulations/usa

13. Park C, Tian S., and Zhao B. Global bitcoin markets and local regulations. ADB Economics Working Paper Series No. 605. 2020.

14. Ju L., Lu T, and Tu Z. Capital flight and bitcoin regulation. International Review of Finance. 2015; 16(3): 445–455. https://doi.org/10.1111/irfi.12072

15. Shi F-B, Sun X-Q, Gao J-H, Xu L, Shen H-W, and Cheng X-Q. Anomaly Detection in Bitcoin Market via Price Return Analysis, PLoS ONE, 2019; 14(6): 1–11.

16. Sullivan P. As Bitcoin's Price Surges, Affluent Investors Start to Take a Look. 2021. Available at: https://www.nytimes.com/2021/01/29/your-money/bitcoin-wealth-investors.html

17. Berman K, Hayes M, Kaplan M, Lim B, Murphy G, Do Y, and Steinberg J. SEC framework and no-action letter provide guidance on analyzing whether a digital asset is a security. Journal of Investment Compliance. 2019; 20 (4): 68–71

18. Toygar A, Rohm C, and Zhu J. A New Asset Type: Digital Assets. Journal of International Technology and Information Management. 2013; 22: (4) 113–120.

19. Viglione R. Does Governance Have a Role in Pricing? Cross-Country Evidence from Bitcoin Markets. 2015; http://dx.doi.org/10.2139/ssrn.2666243. Available at SSRN: https://ssrn.com/abstract=2666243

20. Weatherley, D. and Henley R. Flash vaporization during earthquakes evidenced by gold deposits. Nature Geoscience 2013; 6: 294–298. https://doi.org/10.1038/ngeo1759

SECTION-6

RISK MANAGEMENT AND RISK SHARING: FINANCIAL INNOVATIONS

06 What Was Published in Accounting Education Journals About Accounting Teaching?

1. INTRODUCTION

Currently, accounting has spread to all courses in the area of Management and Economics. However, it appears that students are not prepared for this curricular unit that is both interesting and complex. Its specificity leads to learning difficulties where everyone must assume their responsibilities, from the teacher who teaches to the student who learns.

Therefore, teachers must arouse curiosity about this topic in students, helping them learn that what seems difficult is not always the case. The most profoundly traditional teaching methods are not always the most attractive to the student. It is necessary to innovate in accounting, making it more attractive to the target audience.

Considering the above problem and its importance for universities in general and teachers and students in particular, this article aims to identify how the teaching of accounting has been taught in HEIs as it intends, through a systematic literature review based on articles published in journals in this thematic area, understand what the necessary skills that accounting students must have to be successful in learning this curricular unit are.

Students' approaches to the learning context and their perceptions are considered the primary influence on their success [1, 2]. According to Entwistle et al. [1], student learning is more affected by the perception of teaching than by the teaching methods themselves. In this context, teaching includes methods and a strong teacher-student interaction, which is fundamental to a good university learning environment [3, 4].

A fundamental principle of student-centred learning refers to the importance of being consulted about the teaching process of which they are an integral part, leaving the more traditional pedagogical approaches in which teaching was centred on the teacher, thus making the student more passive [5, 6].

Several research types have concluded that student involvement is one of the crucial aspects of their learning, directly influencing retention rates [7, 8, 9]. In this sense, if universities intend to improve retention rates and student satisfaction with the teaching-learning process, they need to pay more attention to students' real needs and expectations [6].

Ramsden and Entwistle [10] refer that the quality of teaching, in whatever area, is directly influenced by teachers' attitude. As a general rule, ineffective teachers promote discouragement of positive attitudes by students.

Students' educational experience and learning background have a substantial influence on their orientation to study [11, 12]. Some authors argue that the student's behavior concerning learning is strongly related to their motivation [13]. However, this also varies according to the learning field [14].

The literature identifies three approaches related to simple, profound and self-fulfilling approaches, being said that a student who takes a more straightforward approach is intrinsically motivated. One who takes a deeper approach is intrinsically motivated [15]. In the context of accounting, it is stated that students must first learn the terminology, basic concepts and procedures and only later can they use their new knowledge acquired according to the context in which they are inserted [16, 17].

In the context of the present research, it appears that the learning of accounting does not escape the rule of what has already been saying about perceptions, attitude, teacher involvement, student involvement and motivation. Accounting teaching is seen as essentially technical [18], which is an area that usually attracts a population with a more advanced academic level. It is recurrent that a graduate student reveals more significant difficulties in learning this subject than a graduate or master student [19]. Some studies reveal that there are some obstacles in the learning of this topic, where the absence of previous school bases, the inexperience resulting from the diversity of the student population, language barriers, socio-economic, cultural and educational contexts are highlighted. Oral and written communication skills are also considered fundamental to the success of accounting learning, and HEIs need to be concerned with finding ways to improve these capacities in order to obtain better future results [20, 21, 22].

These aspects can prove to be obstacles that increase the complexity of the learning environments in HEIs, posing problems related to heterogeneous competencies among students that directly influence learning [23]. In fact, a gap between students 'expectations and what they experience can result in students' resistance to accepting new teaching approaches, leading to less academic performance or even, in extreme cases, abandoning the institution [24, 25].

Universities are faced with the challenge of maintaining a balance between the products (courses) they offer and the actual preferences of their customers (students), trying to optimize this balance in order to remain in the market [26].

Concerning accounting, universities need to keep up-to-date by not shying away from the need to keep up with technological innovation that allows them to take a learning approach that complements traditional teaching [27].

In addition to increasing technological updating in accounting education, it is necessary to make it more practical, encouraging student participation in projects aimed at their learning in the field [28].

The accounting learning approach is influenced by how students view it and can be superficial or profound, leading to different learning outcomes making them capable of solving more or less complex problems as well as making them more or less capable of understanding the social and critical perspectives of accounting [29]. Some studies show that most accounting students learn only superficially this scientific field of knowledge, thus becoming less able to solve problems that prove to be more complex [30, 31, 32, 33].

On the other hand, working in a team is acknowledged as a good accounting learning practice as the exchange of experiences and acquired knowledge allows students to improve their learning skills [34].

The present research intends to fill a gap found in the literature related to the fact that no systematic review of the literature has been found that focuses in detail on the teaching of accounting in HEIs and whose scientific publication has been carried out in one of the most important journals in this field of knowledge: Accounting Education.

2. LITERATURE REVIEW

2.1 Accounting Teaching and Learning in Higher Education

Learning depends on the availability of time one gets assigned and the intellectual resources made available to achieve the expected results. In this sense, one of the main motivations of students is competitiveness with their colleagues [35]. As a result of several types of research, it was possible to identify the main aspects that influence learning, being the structure and relevance given to the contents [36], the conception of learning [37], motivation [38] and the approach to learning [36].

According to various researches, in order to be successful in accounting teaching and learning, several skills are needed, such as an excellent entrepreneurial spirit, good ability to solve practical problems, communication and interpersonal skills, good management and negotiation skills as well as an excellent theoretical background [39, 40]. In this sense, the skills of the professional who teaches and the student who learns must be much more than essentially technical, maturity, interpersonal effectiveness and general psychological well-being are necessary, not forgetting other essential aspects such as oral and written communication skills, sound reasoning and reasoning skills [39, 41].

From the students' point of view, academic success is of paramount importance, as the possibility of failure entails emotional and financial costs [42]. According to these authors, from the point of view of the HEIs, students' failure can promote discredit caused by high retention rates.

Marriott [43] refers that teachers who teach the curricular accounting units assume themselves as extrinsic motivators of their students in the sense of indicating the right path for learning, which, in the vast majority of cases, is essentially superficial. However, students' approaches to learning can be modified through new teaching strategies aimed at improving academic results, that is, teaching methods that are oriented towards a more practical component and more related to the fundamental requirements of the accountant profession [44, 45]. In education in general and of accounting in particular, one of the main concerns is related to the apparent ineffectiveness of the teaching given in the HEIs, and this inefficiency is attributed to the lack of motivation shown by both teachers and students [46]. Bui and Porter [47] refer that in the teaching of accounting, the students lack the desired skills. However, the teachers' lack of time to devote the necessary energy to their teaching is also the problem, making it more stimulating and motivating. In turn, students also report some disappointment as they find that their teachers are not enthusiastic about teaching, which causes demotivation. The latter author mentions in his research that the students see the teacher's enthusiasm as essential to increase their intrinsic motivation in an indirect and extrinsic way directly, assuming itself as a preponderant factor in the evaluation of the quality and effectiveness of teaching. Another aspect mentioned in the literature is related to the gap between the expectations previously established by the students and the reality they encounter in the classroom environment [46].

Patel et al. [48] report in their research that accounting students are influenced by cultural and social factors that interfere with their ability to learn. In this sense, language-related barriers are also important in learning and can constitute obstacles to the interiorization of contents [49].

Students' experience throughout their academic career also influences their orientation towards study, making them more independent as a result of their greater adaptation to the academy in general and to the curricular units in learning in particular [50]. The same author states that the greater the educational experience of students, the less dependent they become on teacher-centred learning as a result of the number of years of presence in the academy. This conclusion is consistent with the research carried out by Lee and Lodewijks [51]. They concluded that students in their final year of university are more likely to change their learning approaches than their peers in the early years. Within this line of thought, several researchers refer that accounting students must experience rigorous and profound learning of topics to apprehend them consistently in the sense that, if they choose this field in the future, they become better professionals [52, 53, 54]. Despite considering the importance of rigor and deepening of learning in accounting, these same authors consider it is challenging to lead students to this intellectual aspiration, saying that it would be essential that this type of learning be experienced as early as the first years of higher education.

Turner and Baskerville [55] also concluded that a general change in accounting students' attitude, focusing on more profound and more rigorous learning in the first weeks of the course, allows you to provide them with a solid basis for their learning be more active and effective.

As research is a constant academic requirement, teachers inevitably have to pay attention to it, sometimes neglecting, even without any intention, the quality of their classes [56]. However, with the impact of accounting research less academically visible and therefore more difficult to value, as in other areas [57], this makes that in many cases, research related to this area does not become an asset that influences students, for research in accounting has been identified as a process that is excessively away from the practical reality that is the one which is more prevalent in the context of the teaching-learning process in HEIs [58].

2.2 Student Learning Skills and Teacher Teaching Strategies -

Crawford et al. [59] refer in their research to the necessary skills that a student should have when entering the job market in the field of accounting and the skills that future employers expect them to have. In fact, knowledge of these skills is a strong help for teachers to adapt their teaching methodologies to fulfill those needs. The study concluded that analytical, oral and writing skills are fundamental, so it should be easily seen that universities have every interest in moving in that direction.

In the context of accounting education, it appears that there is an effort aimed at encouraging students to greater participation through the construction of their knowledge and practices [48]. In this sense, accounting students, to achieve excellence goals, need to integrate and adapt to learning approaches that improve academic performance, progress and seek superior quality learning results [60, 61, 62].

Although students' efforts are crucial to their academic success, the importance of accounting teachers cannot be overlooked, who must, above all, be aware of the needs and difficulties of students in the classroom and outside the classroom [63]. The author mentions in his research that the program's quality, the methodology used, and the resources available prove to be fundamental for the improvement of the accounting learning environment.

Many studies related to teaching and learning focus on certain concrete aspects of teaching, such as strategies, skills and methodologies applied to each context [64]. However, according to these authors, education in general and its strategies, skills and methodologies applied in particular cannot be considered just as an isolated sequence in order to achieve particular objectives. Teaching should be seen as a set of relationships where changing one aspect necessarily requires changes in other aspects [62]. However, in the vast majority of cases, this aim is tough to achieve.

Regarding the methodologies preferred by students, studies show that students prefer expository classes, with step-by-step teaching, resolution of exercises and functional specification of content instead of other methodologies [62]. However, the various teaching methodologies are never completely good or bad, effective or ineffective, appropriate or inappropriate as they depend on several factors that affect the success of the teaching-learning process, such as teacher quality, content difficulty, classroom environment, school background, among others [65].

A single teaching method usually cannot create all the conditions effectively because each topic has its complexity and specificity. It is necessary to adapt to the best method for each situation. Teachers may find it impossible to adopt very sophisticated teaching strategies because the curricular unit is very specific, technical and sometimes also theoretical from a conceptual perspective [66].

In the era of digital technology, it becomes crucial to understand whether the teaching of accounting should initiate innovative changes in its methodology, trying to understand whether this change may or may not bring pedagogical complexities resulting from innovative approaches [67].

Owens and Price [68] found in their researches that the use of technologies is already so every day that, in the classroom, students already consider them as traditional teaching. For this reason, the authors question whether education has already reached a turning point and is on the threshold of being entirely transformed by innovative digital technologies that place it on the next level of qualitative evolution. However, according to Taylor and Newton [69], students are still not convinced that technology can improve their learning experience.

Several researchers say it is a significant challenge to adapt universities to new teaching methodological trends that increase student preferences and teacher motivation [70, 71, 72]. The truth is that many teachers remain accustomed to the usual routine, resisting the necessary change in the teaching paradigm [73, 74, 75], mainly ignoring the necessary change due to apparent lack of knowledge of new technologies [76].

Watty et al. [77], in their research, concluded that some professors are innovative in the application of new technologies. However, there are still many that prove to be inhibitors to their use. These authors discovered four factors that demonstrate resistance to the implementation of new technologies in the teaching of accounting. These factors are (1) resistance of the teaching staff - insofar as it appears that the teaching staff presents resistance to the use of new technologies due to the existence of opposition to the change in teaching methods. This resistance is due to the lack of knowledge/adaptation to the use of new technologies and also to the preference of teachers for more traditional teaching approaches; (2) Individual and solitary innovators - insofar as there are teachers who individually try to implement new technologies, being, in their curricular units, pioneers of innovation. However, they report that when they tried to implement new technologies, they felt strong resistance from their co-workers; (3) Comfort zone and generational attitudes - it appears that the teaching staff is resistant to the use of new technologies due to the existence of opposition to the change in teaching methods. This resistance is due to the lack of knowledge/adaptation to the use of new technologies and also to the preference of teachers for more traditional teaching approaches; (4) Lack of support from teaching staff – the lack of support from the rest of the faculty was found as a form of resistance to the adoption of new technologies. The lack of support is due to the lack of knowledge that some teachers reveal about the use of technology, the need to relearn and the fear of appearing incompetent for not knowing how to use these tools.; (5) Lack of time and overwork by the teaching staff - the teachers revealed that the immense workloads they have do not allow them to spend time learning new technologies that then allow them to have the background to use them properly in the teaching process learning in the classroom.

In line with the previous study, it can be said that while many teachers have been striving to improve the teaching and learning process, others remain stagnant and willing to keep everything as usual [73, 74, 75, 78, 79, 80].

Concerning accounting, the perception of researchers is the same. There are professors interested in being innovative [80] but many others in being inhibitors [73, 78, 81].

The curricular unit of accounting has been somewhat slow in adopting technologies that improve its results [80]. Although there is a growing effort to adopt technology in order to improve the teaching of accounting [82], such an objective remains limited in time and space [81, 83, 84].

In addition to all the aspects already mentioned, it is also interesting to address others explored by the literature that prove to be relevant to the topic highlighted here.

Student feedback is a crucial aspect of the teaching-learning process's success, whether in the area of accounting or any other area. Watty et al. [85] state in their studies that a meaningful way to improve the quality of accounting teachers' classes is related to the need to obtain student feedback regarding the whole process. The authors state that feedback allows students to identify the difference between their performance and their goals. Moreover, on the other hand, it allows students and teachers to adopt new methodologies and strategies of teaching and learning, respectively, in order to achieve the goals of better-quality teaching.

The uniformity of accounting education within a country or between different countries would also be relevant as it would allow an international student to learn this curricular unit in the same way as internal students, this proving to be a helpful teaching tool in order to be able to understand better the educational systems of accounting around the world [86].

The origin of the students who attend the curricular accounting unit is also of relevant analysis to understand the teaching problem of this curricular unit. There are two types of students, those who bring secondary education bases and those whose bases are reduced or practically nil. There are students whose provenance is a professional education and brings many bases because they are directed to a more practical component and students from regular general education who do not have access to any accounting discipline. In that sense, Abhayawansa et al. [87] refer that students exposed to accounting learning before entering university usually achieve better academic results than the rest. This conclusion suggests the need for universities in general and teachers in the classroom to adopt mechanisms and methodologies that allow everyone to have access to learning in an integrated and sustained way, leaving no one behind [88].

The student's cultural background and knowledge of the literature also contribute to the improvement of skills in the area of accounting learning, since the original, creative, imaginative and multicultural thinking added to scientific rigor allows for more excellent reflection and the ability to apply the knowledge acquired in the university context [89]. Students' initial choices when entering higher education also influence their future intention in a particular area, that is, a student who at the beginning of his academic life chooses accounting as one of his areas of choice maintains his dedication to this area typically, becomes a better professional, and his intention to pursue a career related to this topic increases [88].

Cooperative learning through the formation of working groups within the classroom can also condition learning. Suppose the teacher purposefully selects the working groups to promote the exchange of knowledge between the most prepared and the least prepared students. In that case, this increases learning by exchanging ideas and knowledge between students who are in different stages of learning with each other [90]. In the following chapters, the methodology that guided the present research is presented, followed by the same and respective conclusions.

3. METHODOLOGY

According to Barañano [91], the research method adopted was quantitative, confirmatory and descriptive research. This chapter describes the research process adopted, following the research process advised by Tranfield et al. [92]: (1) review planning; (2) systematic review; (3) review disclosure.

It was defined as a base research criterion that only articles published in the Accounting Education magazine and that was indexed in the ISI Web of Science and Scopus databases, whose abstract addressed accounting education in the context of HEIs, would be analyzed. In the initial search, 808 articles were found (130 in WOS and 678 in Scopus) published between 1992 and 2019. Duplicate articles were eliminated, abstracts of all articles were read, and only those that dealt with the topic of teaching accounting in HEIs were considered, leading to the exclusion of 410 articles that, despite dealing with the topic of accounting in general, did not deal with the topic of teaching accounting in HEIs. Figure 1 shows the search criteria used in this study.

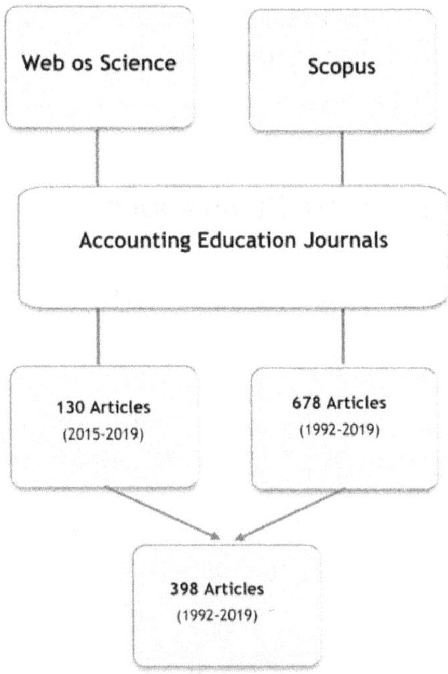

Figure 1. Search criteria.

4. RESULTS

4.1 Final Uutput (N = 398 articles)

4.1.1 Number of Publications by Year

The first and last research work published in Accounting Education on teaching accounting in HEIs was written by Wilson [93] and Coetzee et al. [94].

In the period between 1992 and 2019, which is the period in which the 398 articles included in this study are located, the number of publications varied, with the years 1997 to 1999 having the lowest number of publications (0) and the year 2013, which reached the highest number (39). Analyzing the period in question, we can say that from 2008 onwards, the number of publications was consistently above 20, except in 2019, which at the date of this research had not yet ended (Figure 2).

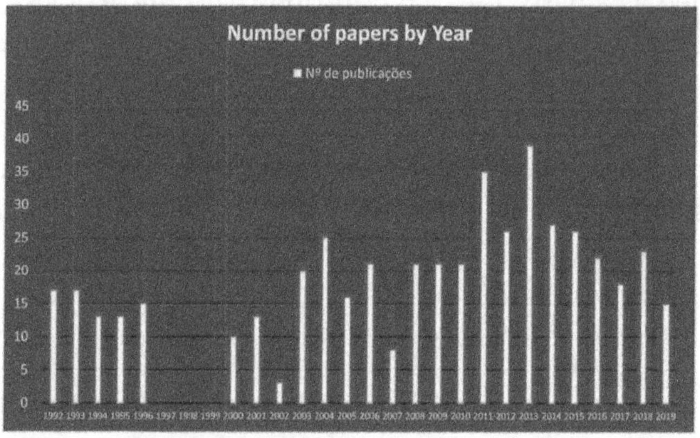

Figure 2. Number of papers evolution (1992–2019).

The years 2011 and 2013 were the most productive, with 35 and 39 articles published respectively.

4.1.2 Authors With Five or More Publications

As the primary author, the number of publications by each author, the analysis of the 485 articles in our database allows us to verify that there are 20 authors with five or more publications on teaching accounting in HEIs, totalling 147 articles from the complete database. The remaining 139 authors have between 1 and 4 articles published on average (Figure 3). The authors with the most significant number of publications are Jackling, Beverley F. (h-index 16); Marriott, Neil (h-index 9) and McHugh, Gerard (h-index 2).

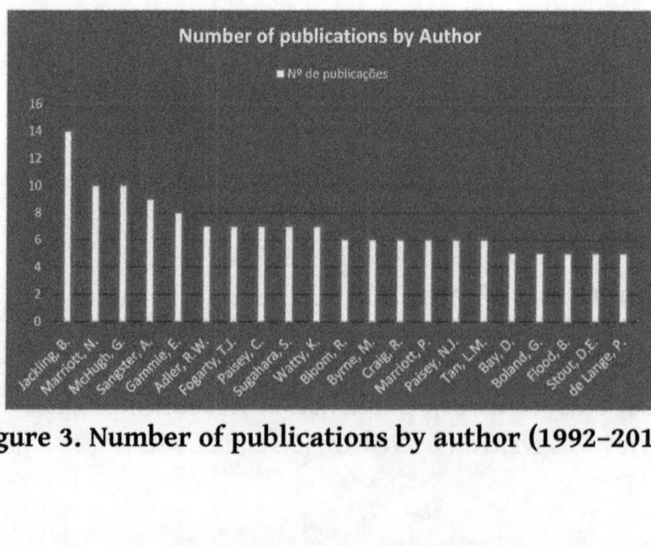

Figure 3. Number of publications by author (1992–2019).

4.1.3 Most Covered Areas of Knowledge

There are several areas of knowledge in which research has focused, with Accounting Educations with 200 articles, Financial Accounting with 62 and International Accounting with 25 as the main areas.

In Figure 4, we can observe the main areas of knowledge on which the research works published in the Accounting Education magazine focused.

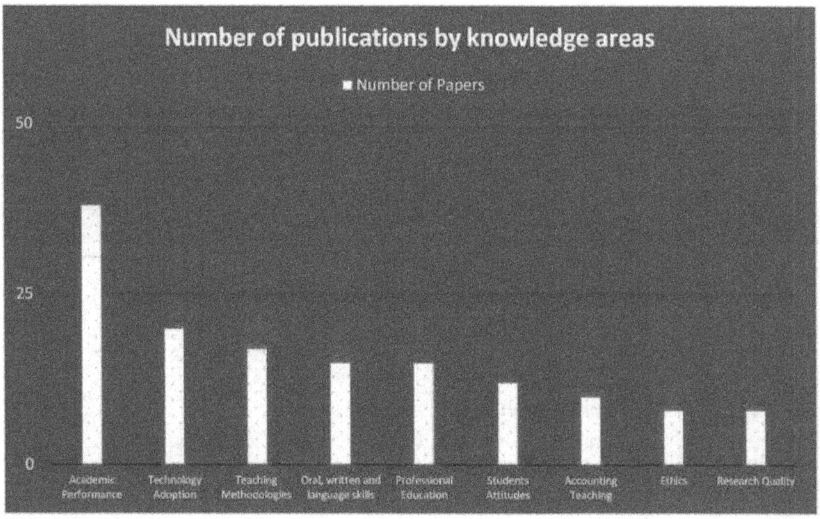

Figure 4. Number of publications by knowledge areas (1992–2019).

4.1.4 Most Covered Topics

Regarding research topics, these are diverse, with the main topics related to academic performance (38 papers), the adoption of technologies in teaching (20 papers) and teaching methodologies (17 papers), among many others being highlighted, as we can see in Figure 5.

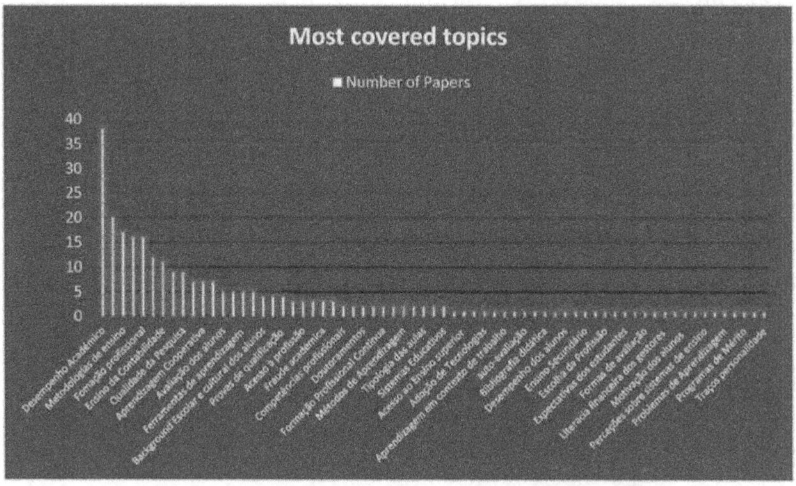

Figure 5. Most covered topics (1992–2019).

4.2 Top 20

4.2.1 Main Authors and Respective Citations

The criteria for presenting results that will be used from now on will be based on the 20 most cited articles. It was necessary to count the citations that occurred in WOS and SCOPUS and thus reach the 20 most cited articles in the totality of the two databases used. Table 1 presents the TOP 20 most cited articles in the sum of both databases.

Table 1. Authors and citations (Top 20).

Position	Authors	Paper Title	Total citations WOS	Total citations SCOPUS	Total citations WOS + SCOPUS
1°	Sangster [95]	You Cannot Judge a Book by Its Cover: The Problems with Journal Rankings	20	26	46
2°	Moya et al. [96]	Performance-based Incentives and the Behavior of Accounting Academics: Responding to Changes	14	17	31
3°	Dull et al. [97]	Achievement Goal Theory: The Relationship of Accounting Students' Goal Orientations with Self-efficacy, Anxiety, and Achievement	12	16	28
4°	Everaert et al. [98]	The relationship between motivation, learning approaches, academic performance and time spent	11	13	24
5°	Daly et al. [99]	Using Group Work to Develop Intercultural Skills in the Accounting Curriculum in Australia	11	13	24
6°	Rackliffe and Ragland [100]	Excel in the accounting curriculum: perceptions from accounting professors	9	12	21
7°	Spraakman et al. [101]	Employers' Perceptions of Information Technology Competency Requirements for Management Accounting Graduates	11	9	20

Position	Authors	Paper Title	Total citations WOS	Total citations SCOPUS	Total citations WOS + SCOPUS
8°	Carenys and Moya [102]	Digital game-based learning in accounting and business education	7	12	19
9°	Levant et al. [103]	Business simulation as an active learning activity for developing soft skills	8	10	18
10°	Aldamen et al. [104]	Does Lecture Capturing Impact Student Performance and Attendance in an Introductory Accounting Course?	8	9	17
11°	Moore [105]	Exploring the Role of Symbolic Legitimation in Voluntary Journal List Adoption	8	9	17
12°	Webb and Chaffer [106]	The expectation performance gap in accounting education: a review of generic skills development in UK accounting degrees	6	11	17
13°	McGuigan [107]	The Impact of Journal Rankings on Australasian Accounting Education Scholarship - A Personal View	7	9	16
14°	Hussain et al. [108]	Journal Rankings, Collaborative Research and Publication Strategies: Evidence from China	7	8	15
15°	Marriott et al. [109]	Experiential Learning - A Case Study of the Use of Computerized Stock Market Trading Simulation in Finance Education	6	9	15
16°	Barac [110]	Helping Disadvantaged Students: Findings from the Thuthuka Programme	7	7	14

Position	Authors	Paper Title	Total citations WOS	Total citations SCOPUS	Total citations WOS + SCOPUS
17°	Wen et al. [111]	Understanding the Intentions of Accounting Students in China to Pursue Certified Public Accountant Designation	7	6	13
18°	Ellington [112]	The impediments to the change to UK university accounting education, a comparison to the USA pathways commission	5	6	11
19°	Lindsay [113]	More than 'continuing professional development: a proposed new learning framework for professional accountants	5	6	11
20°	Cameron and O'Leary [114]	Improving Ethical Attitudes or Simply Teaching Ethical Codes? The Reality of Accounting Ethics Education	9	0	9

4.2.2 Structure and Content of the TOP 20 Articles

Table 2 presents the results extracted from the TOP 20, providing us with relevant information on the main empirical data resulting from the various investigations. Regarding the methodological dimension, the most general studies are quantitative with %55.3 of publications (16), followed by qualitative with 7) %24.1), then mixed methods and literature review have 3) %10.3) each of methodology predominance. Empirical studies with the application of surveys are the most used to research how accounting is taught at HEIs and the necessary skills that the professional in the area of accounting must have to be an effective teacher in higher education. Surveys were used in 15 articles (%51.7), interviews in %20.7) 6), surveys and interviews in %13.8) 4) and the remaining %13.8) 4) were essentially theoretical without application of any inquiry and/or interview.

Table 2. Overview of the main conclusions of published articles on teaching accounting in HEIs - Top 20.

Authors	Sample	Methodology	Review	Main conclusions
Sangster [95]	Not applicable (theoretical)	Qualitative	Accounting Education	The ranking lists of journals in the accounting area have an impact on the quality of accounting research. This means that often the inclusion of the word accounting leads authors to lower the magazines' ranking level.
Moya et al. [96]	Academic articles by Spanish authors on accounting for the period between 1996 and 2005.	Quantitative	Accounting Education	In view of the change in the regulation of publications in Spanish universities, these authors considered a decrease in publications, jeopardizing the relationship between research and professional practice. Additionally, they argued that this is because publication in indexed journals is favored exclusively.
Dull et al. [97]	521 students in the financial accounting course at a US public university.	Quantitative	Accounting Education	They argued that students' goals and their relationship to academic expectations, performance, self-efficacy and test anxiety have a positive relationship. However, the combination of mastery and motivation regarding performance goals can lead to better results in terms of course scores.
Everaert et al. [98]	388 1st year students of a degree in economics and administration from a university in Belgium	Quantitative	Accounting Education	Accounting students can opt for deep or superficial learning. In the study, they concluded that most students opt for deep learning over superficial learning, which is motivated by their motivation to learn, their gender, their skills, and the time they intend to spend studying. This option leads to higher academic performance.

Authors	Sample	Methodology	Review	Main conclusions
Daly et al. [99]	192 international students studying at an Australian university	Quantitative	Accounting Education	Learning based on working alliances between students from different cultural backgrounds allows for a very positive multicultural exchange and higher learning levels compared to control groups. The students participating in these alliances showed higher learning levels of the contents and cultural increases resulting from the exchange of experiences with their colleagues from other nationalities. It is also concluded that accounting students' intercultural learning is fundamental for their future globalized labour market.
Ramachandran et al. [115]	Accounting teachers and of other similar areas	Quantitative	Accounting Education	Most of these teachers use Excel to teach their classes. However, students often do not show skills to work in the classroom with this software. This means that there are still disconnects between teachers and students' skills regarding the use of computer tools in class.
Spraakman et al. [101]	Senior financial advisers and their subordinates in large New Zealand companies.	Qualitative	Accounting Education	They concluded that technology and information tools are crucial for accounting and finance professionals. Their findings explicitly provide information that accounting teachers should integrate the use of these tools in their programs.
Carenys et al. [116]	Not applicable (theoretical)	Literature review	Accounting Education	The results allow us to understand better the effectiveness of using games in these areas.
[103]	Undergraduate and postgraduate students from the university campuses of Paris, Nice and Lille, to apply a business simulator	Quantitative	Accounting Education	They concluded that the skills and abilities of students in the use of the simulator are influenced by the ethnic, cultural and professional experience of the students and that it also requires that there be sharing of practices in a context of global education.

Authors	Sample	Methodology	Review	Main conclusions
Aldamen et al. [104]	254 students in the first year of the introduction to financial accounting course in Qatar.	Quantitative	Accounting Education	There is a weak positive relationship between capture/attention and the performance obtained with the use of lectures, mainly taking into account the variables: average grades, frequency, gender and age. However, students with good performance value these lectures as an efficient pedagogical resource, in contrast to students with lower performance.
Moore [105]	Not applicable (theoretical)	Qualitative	Accounting Education	They concluded, with some caution, that issues of symbolic legitimation in assessing the quality of research can play a crucial role in the processes of listing and classification of journals.
Webb and Chaffer [106]	Application of questionnaires to CIMA interns at UK (valid answers = 1655)	Quantitative	Accounting Education	In order to gain an understanding of how accounting courses are geared towards the professional requirements of the market, they concluded that there is still a need to improve, at the level of students, their oral communication skills, their global view on the organization, their ability to resilience and their ethical conscience.
McGuigan [107]	University and accounting teachers	Quantitative	Accounting Education	The ranking of the journals where scientific articles are published is seen as the main measure of academic performance in the area of accounting. The article concludes that this narrow measurement approach must be abandoned in order to encourage creativity and innovation in business research in order to solve the really important problems that we face in the present and that we will have to face in the future.

Authors	Sample	Methodology	Review	Main conclusions
Hussain et al. [108]	200 participants at an international symposium at Shanghai University of Finance and Economics	Mixed (quantitative and qualitative)	Accounting Education	Most respondents of Chinese origin use the ranking list of the university's own magazines to assess their quality; However, this option generated conflicts for 73% of the interviewees when collaborating with other academics from other universities due to the variation in the classification criteria of the journals being different.
Marriott et al. [109]	97 UK universities with higher education programs in finance.	Mixed (quantitative and qualitative)	Accounting Education	There is effectiveness when presenting educational simulators for the student and the teacher, which leads to a better understanding of the complex concepts inherent in the area of finance.
Barac [110]	12 students from a university in Africa	Qualitative	Accounting Education	The characteristics of a support program, which involves the various interested parties, which aims to help socioeconomically most disadvantaged students to study and simultaneously have a job are fundamental to their success, both academic and professional These support programs are essential so that students can more easily enter the restricted labour market.
Wen et al. [111]	288 accounting students (undergraduate and masters)	Quantitative	Accounting Education	There is a genuine interest in obtaining the title of certified accountant by students, in view of the prospect of becoming independent professionals in the labour market and the influences of professionals of excellence in the area.
Ellington [112]	Theoretical	Qualitative	Accounting Education	By comparing US and UK universities with respect to the changes that business environments demand, they concluded that UK universities should change their programs in accordance with accounting bodies, institutional policies and the identity of professors of universities.

Authors	Sample	Methodology	Review	Main conclusions
Lindsay [113]	Theoretical	Qualitative	Accounting Education	Through the development of a holistic and interactive framework, they have helped accounting bodies and accounting professors to interact and train future accounting professionals
Cameron e O'Leary [114]	Senior year students of accounting	Quantitative	Accounting Education	Regarding the sensitivity that students have about ethical, moral and legal issues and attitudes and their effectiveness in the accounting area, they concluded that training in accounting ethics needs to be reassessed for it to be effective.

4.3 TOP 20 vs. N = 485

4.3.1 Main Research Topics

Regarding the main research topics covered in our research articles, the topic most addressed in the total output is that which is also the most researched in the Top 20. Then there are two topics (Adoption of Technologies and Teaching Methodologies) that are very much addressed in the final output that is not found in our Top 20. The topics located in the 4th and 6th positions of the complete database are also in the same position in our Top 20, together with the topics Cooperative Learning and School and students' cultural background. In Table 3, we can see the complete information of the general overview of the most discussed research topics.

Table 3. Main research topics: TOP 20 vs. N = 485.

Thematic	Final Output (N = 398)	Top 20
Academic Achievement	38	4
Adoption of Technologies	20	X
Teaching methodologies	17	X
Oral, written and linguistic skills	16	3
Professional qualification	16	X
Student Attitudes	12	3
Accounting Teaching	11	X
Ethics	9	X
Research Quality	9	X
Curricular Adjustment	7	X
Cooperative Learning	7	3
International Accounting Standards	7	X
Student evaluation	5	X
Curricular internships	5	2
Learning Tools	5	X
Using Multiple Choices	5	X
School and cultural background of students	4	3
Challenges for teachers	4	X
Qualification tests	4	X
Access to Profession	3	X
Student Choices	3	1
Academic fraud	3	X
Information systems	3	X
Professional skills	2	X

Thematic	Final Output (N = 398)	Top 20
Professional commitment	2	X
Ph.Ds	2	X
Choice of Magazines	2	X
Continuing Professional Training	2	X
International Education Standards (IES)	2	X
Learning Methods	2	X
Plagiarism	2	X
Typology of classes	2	X
Quality of teaching	2	X
Education Systems	2	X
School dropout	1	X
Access to Higher Education	1	X
Accreditation of courses	1	X
Adoption of Technologies	1	X
Professional affiliation	1	X
Work-based learning	1	X
Evaluation activities	1	X
self-evaluation	1	X
Performance evaluation	1	X
Didactic Bibliography	1	X
Curriculum	1	X
Student performance	1	X
Employability skills	1	X
High school	1	X
Student involvement in learning	1	X
Choice of Profession	1	X
Professional Exams	1	X
Student expectations	1	X
Instructional feedback	1	1
Assessment methods	1	X
Accounting research	1	X
Financial literacy of managers	1	X
Mentoring	1	X
Student motivation	1	X
School Organization	1	X

Thematic	Final Output (N = 398)	Top 20
Perceptions about education systems	1	X
First job	1	X
Learning Problems	1	X
Support programs	1	X
Merit Programs	1	X
Problem-solving	1	X
Personality traits	1	X

4.3.2 Research Paradigms (N = 398 vs. TOP 20)

For the classification of articles according to their paradigm, the study of Hopper and Powell [117], shown in Figure 6, which based on a structure defined by Burrell and Morgan [118], synthesized accounting research into a taxonomy based on two axes, where the researcher's variety of ontological and epistemological assumptions is represented on one axis and the assumptions about human nature and its relationship to social change are represented on the other axis.

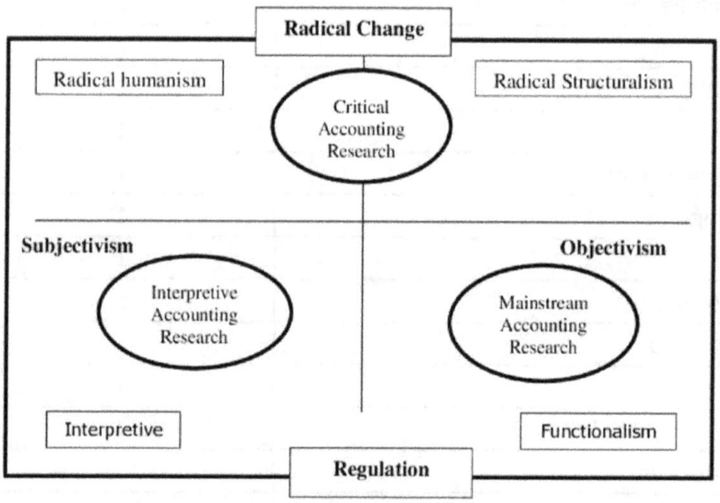

Figure 6. Taxonomy of accounting research. Adapted from: Hopper and Powell [117].

A general analysis made to the final output of the 385 articles allowed us to verify that the main paradigms addressed are the Interpretative with 50% of the occurrences, followed by the positivist with 41%, with 8% we find articles with both approaches simultaneously and with 0.25% the critical paradigm. In the Top 20, we find that the positivist paradigm is the one that is used in most articles with 60% of occurrences, followed by articles with a positivist and interpretive paradigm simultaneously with 30% of occurrences, the interpretive paradigm with 9% and with 1% the critical paradigm.

Tables 4–7 shows the unit of analysis of the articles (Students /Teachers /Students and Teachers/Others), the research paradigms used (Positivist, Interpretative), that is, the theoretical and methodological frameworks for interpreting the phenomena used by the researchers, as well as the essential topics addressed by the authors and the respective authors of the scientific articles that addressed them are also presented.

Table 4. Research paradigms and topics addressed - analysis unit: students.

Analysis Unit	Research Paradigms	Topics covered	Author (s) and Year
Students	Positivist	Student Choices	[111]
		Student attitudes	[104, 97, 98]
		Feedback	[111]
		Academic achievement	[107, 111, 97, 106]
		Curricular internships	[111, 106]
		School and cultural background of students	[104, 114, 98]
		Cooperative learning	[99, 104, 98]
		Oral, written and language skills	[104, 98, 106]
	Positivist e Interpretative	School and cultural background of students	[103]

Table 5. Research paradigms and topics addressed - analysis unit: teachers.

Analysis Unit	Research Paradigms	Topics covered	Author (s) and Year
Teachers	Positivist	Continuing professional training	[113]
		Challenges for teachers	[109, 106, 100]
		Typology of classes	[109, 112]
	Positivist e Interpretative	Technologies Adoption	[101, 103]
		Support programs	[110]

Table 6. Research paradigms and topics addressed - analysis unit: students and teachers.

Analysis Unit	Research Paradigms	Topics covered	Author (s) and Year
Students and Teachers	Interpretative	Learning Tools	[103, 100]

Table 7. Research paradigms and topics addressed - analysis unit: others.

Analysis Unit	Research Paradigms	Topics covered	Author (s) and Year
Others	Positivist	Ethics	[114]
	Interpretative	Quality of research	[105]
	Critic	Choice of quality magazines	[95, 108, 96]

Analyzing the articles that focus on the "Students" analysis unit, we verified the existence of positivist articles (8 articles) and only 1 interpretative positivist article. Concerning the "Teachers" analysis unit, we found that the positivist nature (5 articles) and the positivist/interpretative nature (3 articles) simultaneously in the same article are the observed paradigms. The topic of analysis, "Academic Performance" and the one with the most significant number of articles, is the topic whose research approach differs concerning the paradigms used. It appears that the approaches were different between different authors on the same topic. Three articles each follow the research topics Students' attitudes; School and cultural background of students. Cooperative learning; Oral, written and linguistic skills and Challenges for teachers (Table 4).

By analyzing Table 5, we can see that, concerning the articles that focus on the "Teachers" analysis unit, it is verified that the positivist nature leads with 5 articles, followed by the positivist and interpretative nature with 3 articles, not finding articles of only interpretive nature. The topic with the most significant number of published articles is the topic "Challenges for teachers" with three articles, followed by "Typology of classes" and "Adoption of technologies" with 2 articles each.

By analyzing Table 6, we can see that in relation to the articles that focus on the unit of analysis, "Students and Teachers", there is only interpretative nature (2 articles).

By analyzing Table 7, we can see that concerning the articles that focus on the analysis unit "Other topics", there is a predominance of articles with a critical nature (3 articles), followed by a positivist and interpretive nature with 1 article each.

Analyzing the topics covered in the articles, we can see that the vast majority are centred only on the student. However, there are also topics centred on the teacher and other topics that are not centred on the student or the teacher. The most addressed topics are academic performance (4 articles), followed by the research topics "Students' attitudes";" School and cultural background of students"; "Cooperative learning"; "Oral, written and linguistic skills" and "Challenges for teachers" with 3 articles each.

5. CONCLUSIONS

This systematic review of the literature was directed solely and exclusively to the magazine Accounting Education to identify articles published over 28 years of scientific contribution to knowledge evolution. We identified how many studies related to the Teaching of Accounting in Higher Education Institutions (HEIs) had been published in the Accounting Education magazine since the journal started its scientific activity. We proposed a ranking of articles based on the volume of citations in the WOS and SCOPUS databases. We described the main conclusions and research methodologies used in the TOP 20, described the main research topics and described the research paradigms used in the articles. This issue of the epistemological paradigms used by accounting researchers is relevant and rarely addressed in the literature, being a significant contribution. Based on the results found, we verified that most of the studies carried out used quantitative and qualitative research methodology, which reveals the robustness of the researches carried out, the relevance of the conclusions drawn from each study and the contribution of each research to the increase of knowledge on this thematic area. The systematic review of the literature carried out shows concern in HEIs to promote quality education in general and the curricular accounting unit. It was found that the vast majority of concerns inherent to the research of this topic are encompassed in the students' skills, teaching methodologies and teaching-learning strategies. It was also found that teachers and students' intrinsic and extrinsic motivation are preponderant for increasing commitment and dedication to the accounting area. The way students approach learning, superficial or deep, is also a determining factor for their academic success and professional future in the field.

It was also possible to identify several research areas and topics on which the teaching of accounting in the HEIs is approached, such as the students' school background, oral, written and linguistic skills, cooperative learning, curricular internships, adoption of technologies, among other particular topics of interest, explained throughout this research, for the understanding of the phenomenon under study.

It appears that over the past 28 years, the research on teaching accounting published in this journal is related to good teaching practices, both methodologically. In terms of the skills of those who teach and those who learn, an evolution in the quality of teaching occurring. Researchers' effort has promoted and relaunched the curricular accounting unit to a level of excellence both in research and in the quality of teaching by teachers and learning by students. HEIs and their entire hierarchical organization, with their support and strategic plans, have contributed a lot to make the success and continuous improvement of accounting education in HEIs a reality. The present research is thus able to fill a gap found in the literature by focusing only on one journal, which is a reference in the area of accounting education, summarizing the main published studies on the subject under analysis, enumerating the main topics addressed by the researchers and enunciating the epistemological research paradigms that guided each research. Based on the results found, this article identifies research paths that can be explored to provide greater consistency and substantially increase the theoretical and empirical knowledge related to the teaching of accounting in HEIs.

REFERENCES

1. N. Entwistle, V. McCune, and J. Hounsell, "Approaches to studying and perceptions of university teaching-learning environments: Concepts, measures and preliminary findings," Occas. Rep., vol. 1, 2002.
2. T. Hassall and J. Joyce, "Approaches to learning of management accounting students," Educ. Train., vol. 43, no. 3, pp. 145–153, 2001.
3. C. Asmar, E. Proude, and L. Inge, "'Unwelcome sisters?' An analysis of findings from a study of how Muslim women (and Muslim men) experience university," Aust. J. Educ., vol. 48, no. 1, pp. 47–63, 2004.
4. W. Tan and K. Simpson, "Overseas educational experience of Chinese students: An evaluation of service quality experience in New Zealand," J. Res. Int. Educ., vol. 7, no. 1, pp. 93–112, 2008.
5. J. Biggs, "What the student does: Teaching for enhanced learning," High. Educ. Res. Dev., vol. 18, no. 1, pp. 57–75, 1999.
6. S. J. Lea, D. Stephenson, and J. Troy, "Higher education students' attitudes to student-centred learning: beyond'educational bulimia'?," Stud. High. Educ., vol. 28, no. 3, pp. 321–334, 2003.
7. M. D. Boston and M. S. Smith, "Transforming secondary mathematics teaching: Increasing the cognitive demands of instructional tasks used in teachers' classrooms," J. Res. Math. Educ., pp. 119–156, 2009.
8. S. Martin and J. T. Scott, "The nature of innovation market failure and the design of public support for private innovation," Res. Policy, vol. 29, no. 4–5, pp. 437–447, 2000.
9. G. Scott, Accessing the Student Voice: Using CEQuery to Identify what Retains Students and Promotes Engagement in Productive Learning in Australian Higher Education: Final Report. Department of Education, Science and Training, 2006.
10. P. Ramsden and N. J. Entwistle, "EFFECTS OF ACADEMIC DEPARTMENTS ON STUDENTS'APPROACHES TO STUDYING," Br. J. Educ. Psychol., vol. 51, no. 3, pp. 368–383, 1981.

11. F. Dochy, C. De Rijdt, and W. Dyck, "Cognitive prerequisites and learning how far have we progressed since bloom? Implications for educational practice and teaching," Act. Learn. High. Educ., vol. 3, no. 3, pp. 265–284, 2002.

12. S. Honkimäki, "Tynj{ä}l{ä}, P.-Valkonen, S.(2004): University students' study orientations, learning experiences and study success in innovative courses," Stud. High. Educ., vol. 29, no. 4, pp. 431–449, 2004.

13. H. Christie, L. Tett, V. E. Cree, J. Hounsell, and V. McCune, "'A real rollercoaster of confidence and emotions': Learning to be a university student," Stud. High. Educ., vol. 33, no. 5, pp. 567–581, 2008.

14. A. Heikkilä and K. Lonka, "Studying in higher education: students' approaches to learning, self-regulation, and cognitive strategies," Stud. High. Educ., vol. 31, no. 1, pp. 99–117, 2006.

15. J. H. F. Meyer, "The modelling of 'dissonant' study orchestration in higher education," Eur. J. Psychol. Educ., vol. 15, no. 1, pp. 5–18, 2000.

16. M. Hall*, A. Ramsay, and J. Raven, "Changing the learning environment to promote deep learning approaches in first-year accounting students," Account. Educ., vol. 13, no. 4, pp. 489–505, 2004.

17. D. Watkins and J. Hattie, "Individual and contextual differences in the approaches to learning of Australian secondary school students," Educ. Psychol., vol. 10, no. 4, pp. 333–342, 1990.

18. B. Flood and R. M. S. Wilson, "An exploration of the learning approaches of prospective professional accountants in Ireland," in Accounting Forum, 2008, vol. 32, no. 3, pp. 225–239.

19. V. Beattie IV, B. Collins, and B. Mcinnes, "Deep and surface learning: a simple or simplistic dichotomy?," Account. Educ., vol. 6, no. 1, pp. 1–12, 1997.

20. W. S. Albrecht and R. J. Sack, Accounting education: Charting the course through a perilous future, vol. 16. American Accounting Association Sarasota, FL, 2000.

21. T. Hassall, J. Joyce, M. D. Bramhall, I. M. Robinson, and J. L. Arquero, "The sound of silence? A comparative study of the barriers to communication skills development in accounting and engineering students," Ind. High. Educ., vol. 19, no. 5, pp. 392–398, 2005.

22. M. Loureiro, N. Loureiro, and R. Silva, "Differences of Gender in Oral and Written Communication Apprehension of University Students," Educ. Sci., vol. 10, no. 12, 2020.

23. M. Byrne and B. Flood, "A study of accounting students' motives, expectations and preparedness for higher education," J. Furth. High. Educ., vol. 29, no. 2, pp. 111–124, 2005.

24. S. M. Kift, K. J. Nelson, and J. A. Clarke, "Transition pedagogy: a third generation approach to FYE: a case study of policy and practice for the higher education sector," Int. J. First Year High. Educ., vol. 1, no. 1, pp. 1–20, 2010.

25. V. Sheridan and S. Dunne, "The bigger picture: undergraduate voices reflecting on academic transition in an Irish university," Innov. Educ. Teach. Int., vol. 49, no. 3, pp. 237–247, 2012.

26. A. Cook and J. Leckey, "Do Expectations Meet Reality? A survey of changes in first-year student opinion," J. Furth. High. Educ., vol. 23, no. 2, pp. 157–171, 1999.

27. R. H. Taplin, R. Kerr, and A. M. Brown, "Opportunity costs associated with the provision of student services: A case study of web-based lecture technology," High. Educ., vol. 68, no. 1, pp. 15–28, 2014.

28. C. Farrow, "Pathways for chartered accountants in the 21st century," Emerg. pathways next Gener. accountants, vol. 3, pp. 35–45, 2012.

29. G. Boyce, S. Greer, B. Blair, and C. Davids, "Expanding the horizons of accounting education: Incorporating social and critical perspectives," Account. Educ., vol. 21, no. 1, pp. 47–74, 2012.

30. P. Andon, K. M. Chong, and P. Roebuck, "Personality preferences of accounting and non-accounting graduates seeking to enter the accounting profession," *Crit. Perspect. Account.*, vol. 21, no. 4, pp. 253–265, 2010.

31. P. Booth, P. Luckett, and R. Mladenovic, "The quality of learning in accounting education: the impact of approaches to learning on academic performance," Account. Educ., vol. 8, no. 4, pp. 277–300, 1999.

32. M. Byrne, B. Flood, and P. Willis, "An Inter-Institutional Exploration of the Learning Approaches of Students Studying Accounting.," Int. J. Teach. Learn. High. Educ., vol. 20, no. 2, pp. 155–167, 2009.

33. M. Baeten, E. Kyndt, K. Struyven, and F. Dochy, "Using student-centred learning environments to stimulate deep approaches to learning: Factors encouraging or discouraging their effectiveness," Educ. Res. Rev., vol. 5, no. 3, pp. 243–260, 2010.

34. J. Freeman, R. Dale, and T. Farmer, "Hand in motion reveals mind in motion," Front. Psychol., vol. 2, p. 59, 2011.

35. N. Entwistle, "Motivational factors in students' approaches to learning," in Learning strategies and learning styles, Springer, 1988, pp. 21–51.

36. F. Marton and S. A. Booth, Learning and awareness. Psychology Press, 1997.

37. F. Marton, G. Dall'Alba, and E. Beaty, "Subject:[IFETS-DISCUSSION: 2499] RE: IFETS-DISCUSSION digest 322 From: Jennie Swann (swann_j@ usp. ac. fj) Date: Wed 31 Oct 2001-21: 40: 16 MET," Int. J. Educ. Res., vol. 19, pp. 277–300, 1993.

38. A. Fransson, "On qualitative differences in learning: IV—Effects of intrinsic motivation and extrinsic test anxiety on process and outcome," Br. J. Educ. Psychol., vol. 47, no. 3, pp. 244–257, 1977.

39. G. Boyce, S. Williams, A. Kelly, and H. Yee, "Fostering deep and elaborative learning and generic (soft) skill development: the strategic use of case studies in accounting education," Account. Educ., vol. 10, no. 1, pp. 37–60, 2001.

40. M. Broad, M. Matthews, and A. McDonald, "Accounting education through an online-supported virtual learning environment," Act. Learn. High. Educ., vol. 5, no. 2, pp. 135–151, 2004.

41. T. Davenport, S. Jarvenpaa, and M. Beers, "Improving knowledge work processes," Sloan Manage. Rev., vol. 37, pp. 53–66, 1996.

42. L. Gracia and E. Jenkins, "A quantitative exploration of student performance on an undergraduate accounting programme of study," Account. Educ., vol. 12, no. 1, pp. 15–32, 2003.

43. N. Marriott*, "Using computerized business simulations and spreadsheet models in accounting education: a case study," Account. Educ., vol. 13, no. sup1, pp. 55–70, 2004.

44. J. Cullen*, S. Richardson, and R. O'Brien, "Exploring the teaching potential of empirically-based case studies," Account. Educ., vol. 13, no. 2, pp. 251–266, 2004.

45. A. Manninen, Knowledge in Accounting: An Applied Phenomenological Perspective, vol. 24. University of Jyv{ä}skyl{ä}, 1994.

46. G. Wong, B. J. Cooper, and S. Dellaportas, "Chinese students' perceptions of the teaching in an Australian accounting programme--an exploratory study," Account. Educ., vol. 24, no. 4, pp. 318–340, 2015.

47. B. Bui and B. Porter, "The expectation-performance gap in accounting education: an exploratory study," Account. Educ. an Int. J., vol. 19, no. 1–2, pp. 23–50, 2010.

48. C. Patel, B. Millanta, and D. Tweedie, "Is international accounting education delivering pedagogical value?," Account. Educ., vol. 25, no. 3, 2016.

49. T. A. Ulrich, A. R. Michenzi, and W. E. Blouch, "CPAs assess the development of professional skills of recent accounting graduates," J. Acad. Bus. Educ., vol. 4, no. 3, pp. 126–137, 2003.

50. P. Ramsden, Learning to teach in higher education. Routledge, 2003.

51. K. Lee and H. G. L. C. Lodewijks, "The adaptation of international students' learning styles to different learning contexts.," Coll. Stud. J., 1995.

52.J. A. Ballantine, A. Duff, and P. M. Larres, "Accounting and business students' approaches to learning: A longitudinal study," J. Account. Educ., vol. 26, no. 4, pp. 188–201, 2008.

53.T. Y. Liu and Y. L. Chu, "Using ubiquitous games in an English listening and speaking course: Impact on learning outcomes and motivation," Comput. Educ., vol. 55, no. 2, pp. 630–643, 2010.

54.L. English, P. Luckett, and R. Mladenovic*, "Encouraging a deep approach to learning through curriculum design," Account. Educ., vol. 13, no. 4, pp. 461–488, 2004.

55.M. Turner and R. Baskerville, "The Experience of Deep Learning by Accounting Students," Account. Educ., vol. 22, no. 6, 2013.

56.S. Wright, K. Chalmers, and others, "The future for accounting academics in Australia," 2010.

57. C. Tilt, "The impact of academic accounting research on professional practice," Account. Educ. a Crossroad, vol. 2070, pp. 35–40, 2010.

58. B. Singleton-Green, "The communication gap: why doesn't accounting research make a greater contribution to debates on accounting policy?," Account. Eur., vol. 7, no. 2, pp. 129–145, 2010.

59. L. Crawford, C. Helliar, and E. A. Monk, "Generic skills in audit education," Account. Educ., vol. 20, no. 2, 2011.

60. P. de Lange* and F. Mavondo, "Gender and motivational differences in approaches to learning by a cohort of open learning students," Account. Educ., vol. 13, no. 4, pp. 431–448, 2004.

61. A. Duff, "The role of cognitive learning styles in accounting education: developing learning competencies," J. Account. Educ., vol. 22, no. 1, pp. 29–52, 2004.

62. B. R. Lord and J. Robertson, "Students' experiences of learning in a third-year management accounting class: Evidence from New Zealand," Account. Educ. an Int. J., vol. 15, no. 01, pp. 41–59, 2006.

63. D. Brown and M. Warschauer, "From the university to the elementary classroom: Students' experiences in learning to integrate technology in instruction," J. Technol. Teach. Educ., vol. 14, no. 3, p. 599, 2006.

64. K. L. Hillenburg, R. A. Cederberg, S. A. Gray, C. L. Hurst, G. K. Johnson, and B. J. Potter, "E-learning and the future of dental education: opinions of administrators and information technology specialists," Eur. J. Dent. Educ., vol. 10, no. 3, pp. 169–177, 2006.

65. S. E. Bonner, "Choosing teaching methods based on learning objectives: An integrative framework," Issues Account. Educ., vol. 14, no. 1, pp. 11–15, 1999.

66. L. Leveson, "The things that count: negative perceptions of the teaching environment among university academics," Int. J. Educ. Manag., vol. 18, no. 6, pp. 368–373, 2004.

67. C. J. Bonk, K.-J. Kim, and T. Zeng, "Future directions of blended learning in higher education and workplace learning settings," Handb. blended Learn. Glob. Perspect. local Des., pp. 550–567, 2006.

68. J. D. Owens and L. Price, "Is e-learning replacing the traditional lecture?," Educ. Train., vol. 52, no. 2, pp. 128–139, 2010.

69. J. A. Taylor and D. Newton, "Beyond blended learning: A case study of institutional change at an Australian regional university," Internet High. Educ., vol. 18, pp. 54–60, 2013.

70. G. Kregor, M. Breslin, and W. Fountain, "Experience and beliefs of technology users at an Australian university: Keys to maximising e-learning potential," Australas. J. Educ. Technol., vol. 28, no. 8, 2012.

71. F. C. Saunders and A. W. Gale, "Digital or didactic: Using learning technology to confront the challenge of large cohort teaching," Br. J. Educ. Technol., vol. 43, no. 6, pp. 847–858, 2012.

72. S. D. Smith and J. B. Caruso, The ECAR study of undergraduate students and information technology, 2010. Educause Colorado, 2010.

73. F. Blin and M. Munro, "Why hasn't technology disrupted academics' teaching practices? Understanding resistance to change through the lens of activity theory," Comput. Educ., vol. 50, no. 2, pp. 475–490, 2008.

74. G. Conole, "E-learning: The hype and the reality," J. Interact. Media Educ., vol. 2004, no. 2, 2004.

75. N. Selwyn, "The use of computer technology in university teaching and learning: a critical perspective," J. Comput. Assist. Learn., vol. 23, no. 2, pp. 83–94, 2007.

76. C. C. Lewis, C. E. Fretwell, J. Ryan, and J. B. Parham, "Faculty Use of Established and Emerging Technologies in Higher Education: A Unified Theory of Acceptance and Use of Technology Perspective.," Int. J. High. Educ., vol. 2, no. 2, pp. 22–34, 2013.

77. K. Watty, J. McKay, and L. Ngo, "Innovators or inhibitors? Accounting faculty resistance to new educational technologies in higher education," J. Account. Educ., vol. 36, pp. 1–15, 2016.

78. G. Kirkup and A. Kirkwood, "Information and communications technologies (ICT) in higher education teaching—a tale of gradualism rather than revolution," Learn. Media Technol., vol. 30, no. 2, pp. 185–199, 2005.

79. J. Paver, D. A. Walker, and W.-C. Hung, "Factors that predict the integration of technology for instruction by community college adjunct faculty," Community Coll. J. Res. Pract., vol. 38, no. 1, pp. 68–85, 2014.

80. E. Zarei, E. F. Kargar, and S. Bazyar, "The level at which accounting professors use information technology at universities," J. *Account. Res.*, vol. 4, no. 2, pp. 159–174, 2014.

81. R. Senik and M. Broad, "Information technology skills development for accounting graduates: Intervening conditions.," Int. Educ. Stud., vol. 4, no. 2, pp. 105–110, 2011.

82. P. McCourt Larres, J. Ballantine, and M. Whittington, "Evaluating the validity of self-assessment: measuring computer literacy among entry-level undergraduates within accounting degree programmes at two UK universities," Account. Educ., vol. 12, no. 2, pp. 97–112, 2003.

83. G. Jones and A. Abraham, "Education implications of the changing role of accountants: perceptions of practitioners, academics and students," 2007.

84. Z. J. Lin, X. Xiong, and M. Liu, "Knowledge base and skill development in accounting education: Evidence from China," J. Account. Educ., vol. 23, no. 3, pp. 149–169, 2005.

85. K. Watty, P. de Lange, R. Carr, B. O'Connell, B. Howieson, and B. Jacobsen, "Accounting Students' Feedback on Feedback in Australian Universities: They're Less Than Impressed," Account. Educ., vol. 22, no. 5, 2013.

86. K. Watty, S. Sugahara, N. Abayadeera, and L. Perera, "Developing a Global Model of Accounting Education and Examining IES Compliance in Australia, Japan, and Sri Lanka," Account. Educ., vol. 22, no. 5, 2013.

87. S. Abhayawansa, I. Tempone, and S. Pillay, "Impact of Entry Mode on Students' Approaches to Learning: A Study of Accounting Students," Account. Educ., vol. 21, no. 4, 2012.

88. L. M. Tan and F. Laswad, "Understanding students' choice of academic majors: A longitudinal analysis," Account. Educ., vol. 18, no. 3, 2009.

89. R. J. Lister, "A Role for the compulsory study of literature in accounting education," Account. Educ., vol. 19, no. 4, 2010.

90. J. van der Laan Smith and R. M. Spindle, "The impact of group formation in a cooperative learning environment," J. Account. Educ., vol. 25, no. 4, 2007.

91. A. M. Barañano, Métodos e técnicas de investigação em gestão: manual de apoio à realização de trabalhos de investigação. 2004.

92. D. Tranfield, D. Denyer, and P. Smart, "Towards a methodology for developing evidence-informed management knowledge by means of systematic review *," Br. J. Manag., vol. 14, pp. 207–222, 2003.

93. R. M. S. Wilson, "Editorial," Account. Educ., vol. 1, no. 1, pp. 1–2, 1992.

94. S. A. Coetzee, K. Leith, and A. Schmulian, "Accounting students access to social media related resources and the risk of tacit social exclusion," Account. Educ., vol. 28, no. 5, pp. 465–483, 2019.

95. A. Sangster, "You Cannot Judge a Book by Its Cover: The Problems with Journal Rankings," Account. Educ., vol. 24, no. 3, SI, pp. 175–186, 2015.

96. S. Moya, D. Prior, and G. Rodríguez-Pérez, "Performance-based Incentives and the Behavior of Accounting Academics: Responding to Changes," Account. Educ., vol. 24, no. 3, pp. 208–232, 2015.

97. R. B. Dull, L. L. F. Schleifer, and J. J. McMillan, "Achievement Goal Theory: The Relationship of Accounting Students' Goal Orientations with Self-efficacy, Anxiety, and Achievement," Account. Educ., vol. 24, no. 2, pp. 152–174, 2015.

98. P. Everaert, E. Opdecam, and S. Maussen, "The relationship between motivation, learning approaches, academic performance and time spent," Account. Educ., vol. 26, no. 1, pp. 78–107, 2017.

99. A. Daly, S. Hoy, M. Hughes, J. Islam, and A. S. Mak, "Using group work to develop intercultural skills in the accounting curriculum in Australia," Account. Educ., vol. 24, no. 1, pp. 27–40, 2015.

100. U. R. Rackliffe and L. Ragland, "Excel in the accounting curriculum: perceptions from accounting professors," Account. Educ., vol. 25, no. 2, pp. 139–166, 2016.

101. G. Spraakman, W. O'Grady, D. Askarany, and C. Akroyd, "Employers' Perceptions of Information Technology Competency Requirements for Management Accounting Graduates," Account. Educ., vol. 24, no. 5, pp. 403–422, 2015.

102. J. Carenys and S. Moya, "Digital game-based learning in accounting and business education," Account. Educ., vol. 25, no. 6, pp. 598–651, 2016.

103. Y. Levant, M. Coulmont, and R. Sandu, "Business simulation as an active learning activity for developing soft skills," Account. Educ., vol. 25, no. 4, SI, pp. 368–395, 2016.

104. H. Aldamen, R. Al-Esmail, and J. Hollindale, "Does Lecture Capturing Impact Student Performance and Attendance in an Introductory Accounting Course?," Account. Educ., vol. 24, no. 4, pp. 291–317, 2015.

105. L. Moore, "Exploring the Role of Symbolic Legitimation in Voluntary Journal List Adoption," Account. Educ., vol. 24, no. 3, SI, pp. 256–273, 2015.

106. J. Webb and C. Chaffer, "The expectation performance gap in accounting education: a review of generic skills development in UK accounting degrees," Account. Educ., vol. 25, no. 4, SI, pp. 349–367, 2016.

107. N. McGuigan, "The Impact of Journal Rankings on Australasian Accounting Education Scholarship – A Personal View," Account. Educ., vol. 24, no. 3, 2015.

108. S. Hussain, L. Liu, Y. Wang, and L. Zuo, "Journal Rankings, Collaborative Research and Publication Strategies: Evidence from China," Account. Educ., vol. 24, no. 3, pp. 233–255, 2015.

109. P. Marriott, S. M. Tan, and N. Marriott, "Experiential Learning – A Case Study of the Use of Computerised Stock Market Trading Simulation in Finance Education," Account. Educ., vol. 24, no. 6, pp. 480–497, 2015.

110. K. Barac, "Helping Disadvantaged Students: Findings from the Thuthuka Programme," Account. Educ., vol. 24, no. 2, 2015.

111. L. Wen, Q. Hao, and D. Bu, "Understanding the Intentions of Accounting Students in China to Pursue Certified Public Accountant Designation," Account. Educ., vol. 24, no. 4, pp. 341–359, 2015.

112. P. Ellington, "The impediments to the change to UK university accounting education, a comparison to the USA pathways commission," Account. Educ., vol. 26, no. 5–6, pp. 576–598, 2017.

113. H. Lindsay, "More than 'continuing professional development': a proposed new learning framework for professional accountants," Account. Educ., vol. 25, no. 1, pp. 1–13, 2016.

114. R. A. Cameron and C. O'Leary, "Improving Ethical Attitudes or Simply Teaching Ethical Codes? The Reality of Accounting Ethics Education," Account. Educ., vol. 24, no. 4, pp. 275–290, Jul. 2015.

115. U. Ramachandran Rackliffe and L. Ragland, "Excel in the accounting curriculum: perceptions from accounting professors," Account. Educ., vol. 25, no. 2, pp. 139–166, 2016.

116. J. Carenys, S. Moya, and J. Perramon, "Is it worth it to consider videogames in accounting education? A comparison of a simulation and a videogame in attributes, motivation and learning outcomes," Rev. Contab., 2016.

117. T. Hopper and A. Powell, "Making sense of research into the organizational and social aspects of management accounting: A review of its underlying assumptions [1]," *J. Manag. Stud.,* vol. 22, no. 5, pp. 429–465, 1985.

118. G. Burrell and G. Morgan, "Social paradigms and organizational analysis," Aldershop, Gower, 1979.

SECTION-7

ENTREPRENEURSHIP AND WORKING CAPITAL MANAGEMENT

07 Knowledge and Skills Required in Accounting Education: A Comparative Study

1. INTRODUCTION

We are witnessing an unprecedented acceleration of the evolution of the business environment, particularly in terms of globalization, market liberalization and the diffusion of new technologies [1]. This results in a constant pressure on higher education institutions, so that they take into account these new constraints and adapt constantly. Accounting education is no exception to the rule, and it has now become necessary to make it evolve by introducing new goals, new tools and new courses.

This development is all the more urgent since some researchers [2, 3, 4] have highlighted two disturbing phenomena in the United States: increasingly fewer students opt for educations in accounting, and it is the least brilliant of them who are now choosing this discipline. We can question the extrapolation of these trends in our case, Tunisia. Developments related to globalization, liberalization of markets and the diffusion of new technologies require expanding both the knowledge and the skills from professional accountants in order to meet the needs of the profession in a changing environment. Several previous studies have examined the question of what should be the knowledge and skills components in accounting education programs [5, 6, 7].

This research fits into this context. Through a questionnaire-based survey administered to Tunisian professional accountants, we will seek, first, to highlight the knowledge, skills, and teaching methods seen as important for professional accountants and, secondly, we will conduct a comparative study regarding the knowledge and skills perceived as necessary by professional accountants practicing in the United States, China, and Tunisia. Thus, to adapt to the environmental changes mentioned above, accounting education must evolve in order to prepare future professionals for these new requirements. Hence the interest of our research questions: What kind of knowledge, skills and teaching methods are seen as important for professional accountants? And secondly, do the needs of Tunisian accountants professionals match to those of Americans and Chinese's professionals?

The remainder of the paper is organized as follows. The Section 2 presents the study background and reviews the relevant literature. The third section describes the research methodology. Perceptions of the Tunisian professional accountants are described and discussed in Section 4. Finally, we conclude in Section 5 with implications for further research and practice.

2. STUDY BACKGROUND AND LITERATURE REVIEW

In recent decades, considerable changes have occurred in the business environment, as well as in the nature and the role of the accounting profession. These changes have led accounting education to fundamentally call itself into question [1, 2, 8, 9, 10, 11]. Indeed, in western countries, several academic studies and professional reports have identified issues related to the accounting curriculum [5, 6, 7]. These latter are considered traditional because they are focused on the training of students to prepare for professional qualifying exams, to the detriment of teaching a broader base of knowledge and professional skills [12, 13, 14, 15, 16, 17]. These significant criticisms from the accounting profession, as well as the rapid evolution of technologies [1], economic globalization, and increasing competition in the business world have led teachers in the accounting field to undertake a reform of accounting education, both in the United States and in other countries [18, 19, 20, 21, 22]. Thus, in the American context, since 1986 and in order to cope with these changes, the major accounting firms (the "Big Four") created a dedicated commission to study the correlation between accounting education programs and the requirements of the accounting profession resulting from new economic conditions. Due to perceived deficiencies in accounting education, a great number of studies have been conducted, seeking to improve it. Several studies were conducted in the United States, including the report prepared by the Bedford Committee [12] promoting the reform of accounting education in the United States. Later, one report focused on the prospects of international accounting firms and education [23] and, in 1990, the Accounting Education Change Commission (AECC) published a report entitled: *Objectives of Education for Accountants*, stating that the main objective of accounting education is to prepare students to become professional accountants, instead of being professional accountants when they enter the profession [24]. In 1992 the AECC finally recognized the existence of a mismatch between the desired profile of the professional accountant and the qualities offered by accounting education programs. Furthermore, in its report on the future of the profession, the American Institute of Certified Public Accountants (AICPA) called for a change in the accounting curriculum in order to meet the requirements of the accounting profession [25]. For example, these different studies have demonstrated the need to extend the accounting curriculum towards a general accounting education, rather than focusing on traditional training that is overly focused on preparing students for professional qualification exams [9, 13]. Indeed, in higher education institutions in many countries, most accounting programs have been built too narrowly, with limited knowledge and a lack of skills needed to perform the accounting profession [2, 12, 24, 26, 27].

In their report entitled *Accounting Education: Charting the Course through a Perilous Future*, the same view is shared by Albrecht and Sack [2]. These authors have reached the conclusion that accounting education should change if it is to be relevant and add value to the students and the community. Some educators have heard these warnings and have made significant changes to their programs and curricula. However, in general, the changes undertaken in accounting education have not been expansive enough or were too superficial. A change is all the more urgent since Albrecht and Sack [2] found a decrease in the number of students enrolled in accounting. They also noted that both accounting practitioners and teachers have made alarming statements about students enrolled in accounting, saying that students completing their studies in accounting would not be real specialists in accounting. These are serious problems and we believe that the criticisms are well-founded. Not to mention the threats resulting from market changes and the fact that some factors are not controlled. In addition, Albrecht and Sack argue that the current accounting education should focus on teaching professional skills and greatly expanding the knowledge base. In their report, Albrecht and Sack list a set of knowledge, professional skills, technological skills, and teaching methods, and study the perceived importance of American practitioners and teachers regarding the components of this list. They found that there is a gap in the perception of the importance as well as at the level of the ranking of the knowledge, skills and methods. Teachers are following in the path of the practitioners in recognizing the importance of teaching a number of skills and extra-accounting knowledge [2]. The authors essentially recommend reconsidering the content of programs, focusing on the development of skills at the expense of the excessive accumulation of knowledge, and changing the pedagogy.

Later, in 2002, Francisco and Kelly proposed a continuation of Albrecht and Sack's work, particularly in the area of skills development. To do this, students were asked to assess different professional skills in order to identify those that were the most important for their future career. They identified differences in the perceived importance of these skills between students enrolled in accounting education and those registered in other disciplines. Although there are some variations in the perceptions of students with practitioners and teachers, all stakeholders nevertheless agreed on the need for an immediate and thorough reform in accounting education [2, 28, 29]. Since the report by Albrecht and Sack [2], concerns about the curriculum, seemingly unchanged in the post-Enron era, have been renewed. Attempts to fill in the gaps have not achieved a significant change, and accounting education continues to be "limited, focusing strictly on technical accounting" [30]. Several authors have criticized the limited reaction of academics following the accounting scandals, and advocated broadening the base of accounting education by addressing the economic, social, cultural, and political roles of accounting [31, 32, 33, 34, 35]. More specifically, Ravenscroft and Williams [31] argue that "there are currently serious omissions in the accounting curriculum which must be rectified, and that accounting students are poorly trained in some critical areas. Almost, a decade later, the Pathways Commission [5] identified a need for a new model of education that is better aligned with the contemporary environment and evolving demands on accounting professionals. It is the integrated competency-based framework developed as part of a research project of Lawson et al., [6], the first report of the Task Force established in 2010 by the Institute of Management ccountants (IMA) and the Management Accounting Section (MAS) of the American Accounting Association, to address certain issues of accounting education and make curriculum recommendations for all accounting majors.

Although resistance to changes in accounting education seems to be considerable [2, 17, 36], the above studies and reports produced a positive impact on the development of the accounting education in the Chinese context. Indeed, several studies have focused on the context of an emerging country as China [37, 38, 39]. In recent years, due to the rapid evolution of economic reforms and the internationalization of Chinese accounting, accounting education underwent considerable changes to adopt western systems [40, 41, 42]. However, after more than two decades of reforms, the Chinese system of accounting education is now quite similar to the U.S. model, deemed traditional [43]. It is in this context that Lin et al., [37] estimate that the Chinese accounting profession should now expect a higher level from the students enrolled in accounting who will be the future professionals. For this, the authors have sought the views of students, teachers and accounting practitioners about their perception of the importance of the require knowledge, skills, and pedagogy, and their assessment of whether or not the specified knowledge and skills component have effectively been delivered by the existing accounting curriculum and pedagogy in China. Although there is some variance in the survey responses, they generally agreed on a set of knowledge and skills and methods deemed important for the training of students. The results also reveal a gap between the most important knowledge and skills for the profession and those taught. Thus, it appears that the reform of accounting education in China is not only necessary, but indispensable.

At the international level, the problem of professional accounting education has become increasingly important, which led the International Federation of accountants (IFAC) to conclude that it is imperative to develop a general framework and standards governing accounting education. To do this, the IFAC Education Committee, International Accounting Education Standards Board (IAESB) has developed International Education Standard (IES) aimed at professional accountants. In addition, the International Educational Guideline (IEG) No. 9 of IFAC asserts that "the objective of theoretical education in accounting is to prepare future competent professional accountants (...) it is necessary to offer an education that provides them with knowledge, skills and rules that allow them to continue to enrich their background and adapt to change throughout their active life" [44]. The IAESB sets standards to increase the "competence of the global accountancy profession and contribute to strengthened public interest" [45]. Indeed, the IAESB declares that adopting IES practice will enhance education in the public interest by "contributing to the ability of the accountancy profession to meet the needs of decision makers" [46]. However, the challenge to the IAESB to motivate education practice in its organizational field goes beyond influencing professional bodies and international regulators with an interest in globalized accounting practice. Audiences involved in professional accountancy education also include, for example professional bodies operating in countries at different stages of development, national governments, private training providers, universities, and employers [47].

In conclusion, the experience of the reforms in accounting education in the United States, in China, as well as in other countries is a relevant reference from which we can draw the inspiration to change the accounting education in other contexts. Given the rapid integration of the Tunisian economy in the global markets through its production of high technology products and the globalization of its trade activities, accounting education in Tunisia is similar to that of the western world. It is, as such, also confronted with this new requirement which has the objective of training students in order to meet the challenges arising from the changing business environment. It seems to us that it is time to suggest changes in the accounting education in order both to broaden the base of knowledge and to develop skills, and change teaching methods. The timing is particularly appropriate since the Tunisian government, after implementing LMD reform (License-Master-Doctorate) [48], is currently putting implementing a new reform of higher education [49].

3. METHODOLOGICAL APPROACH

In light of our research questions and our purposes, we conducted a survey using a questionnaire prepared based on the literature focused on the theme of the accounting profession needs and accounting education, on the IES and, lastly, on the various existing questionnaires on this theme. The first draft was submitted to three phases of pre-testing. Once finalized, the questionnaire was administered to the 615 Certified Public Accountants (CPA) enrolled in the Association of CPA of Tunisia, as well as to the 444 Certified Public Accountant trainees (CPAt) who passed the national CPA examination and were, at the time, doing their internship.

The survey instrument includes a list of knowledge (19 items), professional, and technological skills (respectively, 22 items and 18 items), as well as teaching methods (12 items). We asked respondents to express their views about their perception of the importance of the required knowledge, skills, and pedagogy on a scale of 1–4 (1 represents not at all important; 4 is very important).

CPA education seems appropriate to our object of research for three reasons. Firstly, in the Tunisian context, CPA education is training that deals with a very broad program, encompassing different subject matter already studied in the master of accounting (level: high school diploma +4 years). Secondly, the Tunisian CPA education leads to a prestigious national examination. Thirdly, success in this exam allows students to become a CPA after the completion of three years of internship.

An initial release of our survey instrument was conducted by e-mail in September 2010. We then presented the questionnaire by hand to the 350 CPA and CPAt who had not yet responded to our email. After four reminders, we received 131 questionnaires from the CPA and 175 questionnaires from the CPAt. Altogether, 306 usable questionnaires were collected and were entered into SPSS. The overall response rate was 37%, including 26% for the CPA and 48% for the CPAt. Statistical tests carried out in this study are descriptive statistics and comparison of means tests.

4. PROFESSIONAL ACCOUNTANTS' PERCEPTIONS

In this part of the study we will present the perceptions of professional accountants. First, we will put forward the differences in perception between the Tunisian CPA and CPAt about the importance of the needs (4.1.). These needs are seen in terms of knowledge, professional and technological skills, and finally, in terms of teaching methods. Then, we will propose a comparison of perceptions in terms of needs from professional accountants who are in developed, emerging, or developing countries. These countries are the United States, China and Tunisia (4.2.).

4.1 Perceptions About the Needs

Tables 1-4 present the descriptive statistics of our survey results. Mean scores and standard deviations for each item of the knowledge, skills and teaching methods are listed in Panel 3 ,2 ,1, and 4 respectively. The ranking order of the perceived importance of those items (based on their mean scores) is indicated as well. A significance test of means was also carried out based on the one-way ANOVA.

Table 1. Importance ranking of knowledge.

Panel 1: Knowledge	Total population N = 306			Certified Public Accountants N = 131			Certified Public Accountants trainees N = 175			F (P)
	Mean	Standard deviation	Rank	Mean	Standard deviation	Rank	Mean	Standard deviation	Rank	
Taxes	3.777	.508	1	3.748	.501	1	3.800	.514	1	.780(.378)
Auditing/Assurance services	3.620	.616	2	3.717	.468	2	3.548	.700	3	5.711(.017)*
Financial accounting	3.604	.558	3	3.580	.540	4	3.622	.572	2	.437(.509)
Business law	3.588	.617	4	3.679	.530	3	3.520	.668	4	5.066(.025)*
Managerial accounting	3.477	.633	5	3.549	.584	5	3.422	.663	6	3.021(.083)
Information systems	3.447	.732	6	3.542	.623	6	3.377	.799	8	3.829(.051)
Finance	3.402	.604	7	3.343	.565	8	3.445	.630	5	2.148(.144)
Technology topics	3.385	.880	8	3.351	.822	7	3.411	.923	7	.350(.554)
Business strategy	3.153	.741	9	3.274	.784	9	3.062	.696	9	6.223(.013)*
Electronic commerce	3.009	.932	10	3.190	.912	10	2.874	.926	12	8.864(.003)**
Statistics/Quantitative methods	2.990	.986	11	3.076	.873	13	2.925	1.061	10	1.750(.187)
Organizationalbehavior/ Human resource management	2.928	.948	12	3.152	.808	11	2.760	1.011	13	13.359(.000)**
Accounting research methods	2.892	.848	13	2.877	.784	14	2.902	.894	11	.065(.799)
Ethics and social responsibility	2.849	.990	14	3.099	.918	12	2.662	1.003	16	15.227(.000)**

Operations/Supply-chain management	2.771	.968	15	2.824	.854	15	2.731	1.046	14	.690(.407)
Global/International business	2.722	.907	16	2.793	.865	16	2.668	.937	15	1.430(.233)
Economics	2.408	.856	17	2.740	.837	17	2.160	.786	18	38.620(.000)**
Marketing	2.343	.870	18	2.557	.833	18	2.182	.864	17	14.480(.000)**
Retail and sales	2.192	.904	19	2.404	.857	19	2.034	.909	19	13.047(.000)**

*Significant at the 5% level.

**Very significant at the 1% level.

Table 2. Importance ranking of professional skills.

Panel 2: Professional skills	Total population N = 306			Certified Public Accountants N = 131			Certified Public Accountants trainees N = 175			F (P)
	Mean	Standard deviation	Rank	Mean	Standard deviation	Rank	Mean	Standard deviation	Rank	
Analytical/Critical thinking	*3.692*	*.558*	*1*	*3.694*	*.509*	*5*	*3.691*	*.593*	*1*	*.002(.960)*
Oral communication	*3.673*	*.582*	*2*	*3.786*	*.429*	*1*	*3.588*	*.662*	*4*	*8.866(.003)***
Foreign language	*3.653*	*.576*	*3*	*3.732*	*.493*	*3*	*3.594*	*.626*	*3*	*4.378(.037)**
Written communication	*3.627*	*.620*	*4*	*3.709*	*.488*	*4*	*3.565*	*.698*	*7*	*4.084(.044)**
Professional demeanor	*3.617*	*.622*	*5*	*3.626*	*.501*	*6*	*3.611*	*.701*	*2*	*.041(.840)*
Measurement	*3.601*	*.651*	*6*	*3.626*	*.572*	*7*	*3.582*	*.705*	*6*	*.327(.568)*
Risk analysis	*3.578*	*.674*	*7*	*3.618*	*.561*	*8*	*3.548*	*.747*	*8*	*.801(.371)*
Teamwork	*3.545*	*.637*	*8*	*3.488*	*.636*	*15*	*3.588*	*.635*	*5*	*1.851(.175)*
Continuous learning	*3.509*	*.692*	*9*	*3.534*	*.611*	*13*	*3.491*	*.749*	*9*	*.287(.593)*

Panel 2: Professional skills	Total population N = 306			Certified Public Accountants N = 131			Certified Public Accountants trainees N = 175			F (P)
	Mean	Standard deviation	Rank	Mean	Standard deviation	Rank	Mean	Standard deviation	Rank	
Computing technology	*3.500*	*.678*	*10*	*3.557*	*.570*	*12*	*3.457*	*.748*	*10*	*1.633(.202)*
Interpersonal	*3.483*	*.697*	*11*	*3.564*	*.569*	*11*	*3.422*	*.775*	*12*	*3.127(.078)*
Entrepreneurship	*3.470*	*.729*	*12*	*3.526*	*.586*	*14*	*3.428*	*.819*	*11*	*1.358(.245)*
Decision-making	*3.408*	*.728*	*13*	*3.458*	*.659*	*16*	*3.371*	*.776*	*13*	*1.058(.304)*
Research	*3.388*	*.739*	*14*	*3.580*	*.594*	*9*	*3.245*	*.803*	*14*	*16.088(.000)***
Leadership	*3.356*	*.760*	*15*	*3.564*	*.608*	*10*	*3.200*	*.823*	*15*	*18.245(.000)***
Negotiation	*3.294*	*2.419*	*16*	*3.755*	*3.515*	*2*	*2.948*	*.866*	*20*	*8.544(.004)***
Project-management	*3.232*	*.729*	*17*	*3.351*	*.619*	*17*	*3.142*	*.793*	*16*	*6.204(.013)**
Customer orientation	*3.169*	*.779*	*18*	*3.213*	*.723*	*20*	*3.137*	*.818*	*17*	*.723(.396)*
Resource-management	*3.150*	*.748*	*19*	*3.305*	*.689*	*19*	*3.034*	*.772*	*18*	*10.106(.002)***
Change-management	*3.039*	*.800*	*20*	*3.129*	*.778*	*21*	*2.971*	*.812*	*19*	*2.949(.087)*
Salesmanship	*3.003*	*.892*	*21*	*3.335*	*.760*	*18*	*2.754*	*.904*	*21*	*35.394(.000)***
Business Decision Modeling	*2.846*	*.833*	*22*	*3.084*	*.702*	*22*	*2.668*	*.880*	*22*	*19.763(.000)***

** Significant at the 5% level.*

*** Very significant at the 1% level.*

Table 3. Importance ranking of technological skills.

Panel 3: Technological skills	Total population N = 306			Certified public accountants N = 131			Certified Public Accountants trainees N = 175			F (P)
	Mean	Standard deviation	Rank	Mean	Standard deviation	Rank	Mean	Standard deviation	Rank	
Spreadsheet software (e.g. Excel)	3.735	.559	1	3.763	.477	1	3.714	.614	1	.575(.449)
Word processing software (e.g. Word)	3.585	.612	2	3.542	.598	2	3.617	.622	2	1.130(.289)
World-Wide Web searching	3.503	.673	3	3.442	.622	5	3.548	.708	3	1.853(.174)
Systems analysis	3.441	2.878	4	3.519	2.707	4	3.382	3.007	6	.167(.683)
Windows	3.437	.736	5	3.442	.703	6	3.434	.761	4	.010(.921)
Presentation software (e.g. Power Point)	3.392	.726	6	3.412	.642	8	3.377	.784	7	.174(.677)
Database software (e.g. Access)	3.388	.743	7	3.519	.648	3	3.291	.795	8	7.161(.008)**
File & directory management	3.379	.742	8	3.351	.678	10	3.400	.787	5	.324(.570)
Project management	3.303	.827	9	3.412	.711	7	3.222	.897	9	3.963(.047)*

Panel 3: Technological skills	Total population N = 306			Certified public accountants N = 131			Certified Public Accountants trainees N = 175			F (P)
	Mean	Standard deviation	Rank	Mean	Standard deviation	Rank	Mean	Standard deviation	Rank	
Communication software (e.g. Outlook)	3.261	.766	10	3.381	.717	9	3.171	.790	11	5.728(.017)*
Intra/Extranets	3.225	.859	11	3.282	.777	11	3.182	.916	10	1.005(.317)
Electronic commerce	3.114	.917	12	3.061	.892	14	3.154	.937	12	.772(.380)
Information systems planning & auditing	3.062	.805	13	3.175	.673	13	2.925	.982	15	4.602(.033)*
Technology management & budgeting	3.062	.833	14	3.213	.822	12	2.948	.825	14	7.753(.006)**
Graphics software (e.g. Adobe)	2.957	.924	15	3.000	.841	15	2.925	.982	15	.483(.487)
Other operating systems	2.526	.955	16	2.916	.868	16	2.234	.914	17	43.477(.000)**
HTML programming	2.392	.993	17	2.595	.942	17	2.240	1.005	16	0.871(.002)**
Programming languages	2.303	.913	18	2.427	.804	18	2.211	.980	18	4.231(.041)*

* *Significant at the 5% level.*

** *Very significant at the 1% level.*

Table 4. Importance ranking of teaching methods.

Panel 4: Teaching methods	Total population N = 306			Certified Public Accountants N = 131			Certified Public Accountants trainees N = 175			F (P)
	Mean	Standard deviation	Rank	Mean	Standard deviation	Rank	Mean	Standard deviation	Rank	
Assignments with real companies	3.594	.681	1	3.687	.497	1	3.525	.786	1	4.239(.040)*
Team teaching	3.500	.678	2	3.542	.558	2	3.468	.756	2	.876(.350)
Case analysis	3.460	.632	3	3.519	.573	3	3.417	.671	3	1.952(.163)
Team (group) work	3.392	.735	4	3.458	.659	5	3.342	.785	4	1.842(.176)
Role playing	3.392	.799	5	3.503	.672	4	3.308	.875	6	4.520(.034)*
Technology assignments	3.352	.845	6	3.396	.751	7	3.320	.909	5	.620(.432)
Oral presentations	3.150	.787	7	3.442	.609	6	2.931	.834	9	35.130(.000) **
Lecture	3.127	.764	8	3.328	.625	8	2.977	.823	8	16.633(.000) **
Feedback exercises (e.g. Quizzes)	3.101	.759	9	3.221	.682	11	3.011	.802	7	5.818(.016)*
Reading textbooks	3.039	.808	10	3.259	.697	10	2.874	.848	10	17.941(.000)**
Writing assignments	2.993	.805	11	3.267	.677	9	2.788	.834	11	28.851(.000) **
Videos	2.555	.871	12	2.740	.780	12	2.417	.911	12	10.641(.001)**

** Significant at the 5% level.*

*** Very significant at the 1% level.*

In addition, Table 1 presents the means and the standard deviations for the CPA and CPA trainees. For the knowledge components, it is important to note that both CPAs and CPA trainees recognized tax as the most important knowledge. However, some variations exist in the scores of perceived importance and the ranking among the two groups of respondents. Regarding the top five most important knowledge items, CPA have ranked auditing/assurance services as the second most important knowledge item, although auditing was ranked as the third most important knowledge item by the CPA trainees. Financial accounting is recognized by CPA as the fourth most important knowledge item, but it was ranked the second most important knowledge item by the CPA trainees. In addition, CPA ranked Ethics and social responsibility as the twelfth most important knowledge, but ethics was seen as only the sixteenth most important knowledge item by the CPA trainees. We also note rather significant differences in ranking regarding several knowledge items, such as, for example, Information systems, Finance and Electronic commerce. Mean scores of the two groups of respondents concerning the less important knowledge items varied considerably. However, retail and sales were ranked last in accordance with perceptions of the two groups.

With regard to the three most requested professional skills, CPA and CPA trainees are consistent in the identification of the third most important skill, namely a foreign language. While analytical/critical thinking was ranked by the CPA trainees as being the most important professional skill, it was ranked the fifth professional skill by the CPA. Regarding oral communication, although it is considered to be the most important professional skill by CPA, it is only recognized by CPA trainees as the fourth most important skill. It should be noted that CPAs perceive decision-making as a relatively unimportant professional skill (ranked 16th), lower than it was perceived by CPA trainees (ranked 13th). It is also interesting to note that CPA trainees ranked written communication seventh, a skill which practitioners gave a much higher ranking to (fourth most important skill). Other findings seem quite striking, in fact, while some skills are relatively important for CPA trainees, CPAs considered them much less important, for example, teamwork, learning, and entrepreneurship. Conversely, some skills appear to be important for CPAs but not at all for CPA trainees. The most striking example is the one relating to negotiation. Indeed, the group of CPAs perceives negotiation as the second most important professional skill while CPA trainees relegated it to twentieth (Table 2).

Turning now to technological skills, responses displayed in Table 3 show a convergence of opinion between CPA and CPA trainees in the ranking concerning the two most important technological skills. The two groups of respondents find that mastering spreadsheet software and word processing software are the two most important technological skills respectively. However, differences in rankings between the two groups are numerous. For example, while mastering databases is considered the third most important technological skill by the CPA, CPA trainees ranked it eighth. Similarly, world-wide web searching was ranked the third most important technological skill by CPA trainees, but was considered only the fifth most important by CPA. Other differences in ranking between the two groups may be observed, for example, concerning the use of file & directory management and communications software. However, both CPA and CPA trainees agreed that programming languages is the least important technological skill.

With regard to the most important teaching methods, surprisingly, both CPA and CPA trainees identified assignments with real companies, team teaching, and case analysis as the three most important methods. Similarly, the two groups of respondents agreed on the least important teaching method, namely the use of videos. However, Table 4 highlights some differences in ranking, particularly with regard to role playing, technology assignments, and oral presentations. Finally, it is important to emphasize the importance given to writing assignments by CPA (ranked 9th), while CPA trainees ranked them eleventh.

4.1.2 Findings Discussion

Our survey results reveal that respondents recognize the importance of a series of knowledge, skills and teaching methods for the training of future professional accountants in the changing business environment in Tunisia. In particular, respondents have a consistent perception of the top five most important knowledge items. As shown in Table 1, the knowledge items perceived as being important are mainly traditional accounting subjects such as auditing, financial accounting, and managerial accounting, while most of the broader types of knowledge received relatively lower scores, for example, ethics and social responsibility, global business, and economics. This result may suggest that the importance of receiving broader knowledge in the accounting education is not fully recognized by the respondents. We can conclude that at present time, accounting education of CPA in Tunisia has a relatively narrow focus manifested in particular by the concentration on traditional or content-mastery knowledge, while multidisciplinary roles such as management and other areas in social sciences and humanities are not sufficiently addressed.

Regarding professional skills, and particularly those ranked highest, it is interesting to note that CPA' averages are higher than those of CPA trainees. The two groups of respondents rank oral communication among the four most important skills. This seems to contradict the stereotypical impression of isolated professional accountants recording accounting documents throughout the day. It appears that the respondents understand the interpersonal nature of the accounting environment. It is not surprising that CPA trainees consider written communication as the seventh most important professional skill while the professionals consider it to be more important. In fact, CPA are more accustomed to writing business reports and audit opinions, and are therefore more likely to consider the importance of such a skill.

At the aggregate level, analytical/critical thinking is one of the three most important professional skills. However, in our context, only the CPA trainees placed it at the forefront. This can be explained by the fact that most CPA trainees of our sample were exposed to situations that require them to think critically.

Mastering foreign languages were unanimously ranked as the third most important professional skill, both for CPA and CPA trainees. This result is not surprising given the current emphasis on globalization. Apparently, the two groups felt that English was the language of business and, therefore, they should master it.

Moreover, CPA trainees gave much more importance to professional demeanor (ranked 2nd) than CPA (ranked 6th). We can explain this result by the fact that, at the beginning of their careers, CPA trainees are more sensitive to ethics and eventually give tremendous respect to their accreditation body. The ranking of negotiating skill was very high in the CPA sample. Indeed, they regard it as the second most important professional skill because, after many years of practice, they are able to recognize that negotiation plays a major role in their everyday life. Conversely, CPA trainees are still at the level of their internship and haven't faced such situations yet. In the course of their internship, they are assigned tasks that do not require the use of negotiation, for example, bookkeeping and auditing.

The ranking of respondents regarding the five least important skills show less striking diversity than at the level of the five most important skills. Actually, both groups of respondents ranked the following items: customer orientation, resource-management, change-management, salesmanship, and business decision modeling, close together and were unanimous regarding their importance. The results also show that customer orientation is not considered as a very important skill for both CPA trainees and CPA. This seems surprising on the part of the CPA who work in firms that depend on their customers. Therefore, they should take more account of the present and future needs of their customers and should meet their requirements and strive to meet their expectations. Change management was considered more important by trainees than by practitioners. This result is surprising since practitioners have had experience in the real world and should therefore be aware that change is part of life. Despite their young age, CPA trainees are aware that all companies must evolve in order to survive in today's dynamic environment.

The rankings of technological skills highlight the agreement of CPA and CPA trainees regarding the importance given to spreadsheet software and word processing software. Thus, this result shows the importance of the use of spreadsheet software and word processing software in the daily tasks that Tunisian professional accountants are required to carry out, including bookkeeping and the preparation of audit reports. However, it appears that the two groups of respondents do not share the same opinion when it comes to world-wide web searching. CPA trainees give more importance to web searching. This finding could be explained by a shift between two generations. The new generation of Tunisian professional accountants gives more importance to web searching. They therefore understood the relevance of search engines when it comes to seeking information. While it seems that CPA prefer using more conventional means when it comes to looking for information. HTML programming and programming languages do not appear to be important for the two groups of respondents. We can explain this result by the existence of programming experts who are more likely than professional accountants to carry out programming.

Finally, concerning the teaching methods in accounting education, both groups of respondents have similar views on the importance of the various methods. One notable difference is that practitioners have given greater weight to writing assignments compared to feedback exercises (e.g. Quizzes), while CPA trainees have an opposite point of view. This may be interpreted by the fact that Tunisian CPA trainees should be aware of the importance of the written communication skills that CPA need (ranked 4th).

4.2 Comparative Study

After having studied the perceptions of the Tunisian respondents about their needs, we will now offer a comparison of the perceptions of the importance of knowledge, professional skills, technological skills, and teaching methods for professional accountants coming from different economic and cultural environments. Table 5 shows the ranking of the different components of the knowledge, skills, and teaching methods items. The ranking order is determined by the average score of the perceived importance of each item or component. The Tunisian sample data were collected from our survey. U.S. and Chinese data results from studies conducted by Albrecht and Sack [2] and by Lin et al., [37] respectively (data for accounting practitioners). Some differences in the perceptions of the importance of knowledge, professional and technological skills and teaching methods among Tunisian, Chinese and Americans respondents must be noticed.

Table 5. Importance ranking of Tunisian, Chinese and American accounting practitioners.

Professional Accountants			
	Tunisia: Khemiri, 2012	**China: Lin & al, 2005**	**USA: Albrecht & Sack, 2000**
Panel 1: Knowledge			
Taxes	1	2	3

Professional Accountants			
Auditing/Assurance services	2	7	6
Financial accounting	3	1	1
Business law	4	6	10
Managerial accounting	5	4	7
Information systems	6	8	2
Finance	7	3	3
Technology topics	8	10	8
Business strategy	9	14	5
Electronic commerce	10	13	9
Statistics/Quantitative methods	11	17	14
Organizational behavior/Human resource management	12	16	17
Accounting research methods	13	—	15
Ethics and social responsibility	14	5	12
Operations/Supply-chain management	15	18	16
Global/International business	16	12	11
Economics	17	9/111	13
Marketing	18	15	18
Retail and sales	19	19	—
Panel 2: Professional skills			
Analytical/Critical thinking	1	4	2
Oral communication	2	8	3
Foreign language	3	9	22
Written communication	4	3	1
Professional demeanor	5	1	10
Measurement	6	—	20
Risk analysis	7	—	13
Teamwork	8	6	5
Continuous learning	9	—	9
Computing technology	10	2	4
Interpersonal	11	7	7
Entrepreneurship	12	14	19
Decision-making	13	5	6
Research	14	1	18
Leadership	15	10	8
Negotiation	16	15	15

Professional Accountants			
Project-management	17	11	10
Customer orientation	18	16	16
Resource-management	19	12	17
Change-management	20	17	14
Salesmanship	21	18	21
Business Decision Modeling	22	13	12
Panel 3: Technological skills			
Spreadsheet software (e.g. Excel)	1	—	1
Word processing software (e.g. Word)	2	—	3
World-Wide Web searching	3	—	4
Systems analysis	4	—	15
Windows	5	—	2
Presentation software (e.g. Power Point)	6	—	6
Database software (e.g. Access)	7	—	8
File & directory management	8	—	6
Project management	9	—	11
Communication software (e.g. Outlook)	10	—	10
Intra/Extranets	11	—	16
Electronic commerce	12	—	12
Information systems planning & auditing	13	—	12
Technology management & budgeting	14	—	14
Graphics software (e.g. Adobe)	15	—	19
Other operating systems	16	—	20
HTML programming	17	—	21
Programming languages	18	—	22
Panel 4: Teaching methods			
Assignments with real companies	1	3	2
Team teaching	2	—	8
Case analysis	3	2	5
Team (group) work	4	—	3
Role playing	5	7	7

Professional Accountants			
Technology assignments	6	4	1
Oral presentations	7	—	6
Lecture	8	—	12
Feedback exercises (e.g. Quizzes)	9	—	10
Reading textbooks	10	—	11
Writing assignments	11	5	4
Videos	12	—	9

[1] *According to the study of Lin et al. [37], item economy was split in microeconomics (ranked 9th) and macroeconomics (11th).*

According to Table 5, the ranking of the first three knowledge items is relatively uniform for both American and Chinese samples, namely financial accounting, taxes, and finance. Gaps exist for other knowledge items. For example, there are considerable differences in the ranking of information systems, business law, ethics, and social responsibility. Indeed, information systems was ranked as the second most important knowledge item by U.S. practitioners [2], but ranked eighth by Chinese respondents [37], and placed sixth by professional accountants in Tunisia. This difference is probably due to the fact that information systems are much less developed in China and Tunisia than in the United States. Thus, the Tunisian respondents could not give the same high ranking for this item as their counterparts in the United States. In addition, business law which was classified by Chinese practitioners as the sixth most important knowledge item and by their American counterparts as the tenth most important one has been ranked by Tunisian practitioners as the fourth most important knowledge item. The reason for this may be due to the importance given by the Tunisian accounting profession to the issues of rights. Thus, business law is, at present, considered a very important component of the accounting education in Tunisia.

Another difference to note concerns ethics and social responsibility, which were ranked as the fifth most important knowledge item by Chinese practitioners, the twelfth most important by U.S. practitioners [2] and the fourteenth most important knowledge item by Tunisian practitioners. Such a difference can be explained by the fact that the accounting profession at the worldwide level has established a major emphasis on ethics and social responsibility in recent years. This happened as a response to public concerns following the Enron and Arthur Andersen case at the beginning of 2001. So, it seems that Chinese have recognized the ethics and social responsibility as a very important knowledge item for accounting education. Obviously, Tunisian practitioners are still not aware of the importance of such knowledge in accounting education.

In addition, as shown in panel 2 of Table 5, there are considerable differences in the perceived importance of the professional skills necessary for professional accountants in the Tunisian, Chinese and American contexts. The major items which received scores of varied importance by Tunisian, Chinese and Americans respondents are especially analytical/critical thinking, professional demeanor, foreign language, computing technology, communications (written and oral), decision-making, change-management and research. Thus, while Chinese respondents gave information technology a higher rank than American respondents did, Tunisian respondents, for their part, assigned it a rank lower than that of the Americans and Chinese (ranked 10th). This ranking by the Tunisian professionals seems surprising because computerization is now gaining ground in Tunisia. Indeed, the level of computer culture is high in Tunisia and such skills may have been taken for granted by Tunisian professional accountants. Similarly, professional demeanor is ranked by Tunisian respondents as the fifth most important skill, while Chinese practitioners put it in first place and American practitioners only in tenth place [2]. The difference may be due to the different business environments of the three countries. Further, as the accounting profession is less mature in Tunisia, Tunisian respondents may feel that it is important to develop professional demeanor to improve the social status and reputation of the Tunisian accounting professionals.

Foreign languages are ranked ninth by the Chinese, while it was perceived as the least important professional skill by American practitioners. However, the Tunisian practitioners put it in the third place. Since the gradual integration of the Tunisian economy in the world market, especially after the entry of Tunisia in the World Trade Organization (WTO) in 1995, mastering foreign languages has become a very important professional skill and one that is useful for Tunisian professional accountants, allowing them to work for foreign clients or Tunisian companies which possess subsidiaries abroad or working in cooperation with foreign companies. Regarding the American CPAs' ranking of foreign languages, it is possible that respondents consider the English language to be the universal language of business and that communications around the world are generally made in English. Therefore, they minimize the value of foreign languages by considering them to be useless.

Critical thinking, oral, as well as written communications are considered in the Albrecht and Sack [2] study to be the three most important professional skills in the eyes of American professionals. This view is shared by Tunisian professionals. Chinese respondents, however, give these skills relatively low ranking. This finding may reflect the fact that accounting practices and transactions are quite complicated, so Tunisian professionals employ the analytical and critical thinking and professional judgment in their practice. In addition, the high rankings given to oral and written communication by Tunisian respondents seem surprising. Indeed, this result contradicts the influence of the eastern culture in which individuals are supposed to be humble and must strictly obey the orders or instructions of their superiors. In such a cultural context, bidirectional communication is generally not encouraged and the value of communications skills could be underestimated. These skills are crucial for accountants in a changing and dynamic business world and they should take a greater role in accounting education in Tunisia.

Regarding technological skills, only the U.S. and Tunisian professionals have expressed themselves about their perception of the level of importance of such skills. Moreover, it is interesting to note the convergence of the two groups of respondents particularly at the level of the ranking of the most important technological skills and the least important. On the one hand, U.S. and Tunisian practitioners agree on the importance of spreadsheet software, word processing software and world-wide web searching for the accounting profession. It seems that these three technological skills are widely used in the daily tasks of the practitioners. In addition, this consistency in the perceptions of importance of the two groups of respondents may reflect the level of computerization among the Tunisian accounting professionals who seem seduced by its multiple benefits: speed, reliability, traceability, inventory management, paper saving and teleconsultation of documents. On the other hand, the two groups of respondents pointed the same technological skills which appear to them to be least important for accounting practice. This is the case, for example, for HTML programming and programming languages. It seems that these skills are considered overly technical specialties for professional accountants and that it is more appropriate to employ a specialist when necessary.

Lastly, the perceived level of importance of teaching methods by U.S., Chinese and Tunisian professionals reveals some differences. While Tunisian respondents rank team teaching second, American respondents rank it eighth. In addition, technology assignments are considered by American practitioners as the most important teaching method. Chinese practitioners rank it fourth, while Tunisian practitioners rank it only sixth. This result shows that the use of technology is part of the American educational landscape. It helps to explain the importance given by American professionals, on the one hand, to technology as being one of the ten most important knowledge items and, on the other hand, to computing technology as being the fourth most important professional skill. We can also notice that Tunisian professionals have not been made sensitive to the completion of technological skills; this could be due to the fact that technological tools have not yet made their appearance in the accounting education of CPA. Similarly, respondents do not agree on the importance of writing assignments. While American professionals believe that writing assignments are the fourth most important pedagogical method, Chinese and Tunisian respondents ranked them seventh and eleventh respectively.

Such a result confirms the importance given to written communications by American practitioners (ranked the most important skill), which is not the case for other respondents. So, it seems that writing assignments help to initiate the future professionals in the writing of numerous reports that they will be required to carry out, for example, audit reports.

However, the three groups of respondents have similar views in terms of the perceived importance of assignments with real companies, team (group) work, and role playing. These different methods enable developing certain skills required for the accounting practice. For example, assignments with real companies can develop the critical and analytical mind of students. Team teaching could teach students leadership and importance of collaboration. And role-playing introduces students to negotiation. The use of textbooks doesn't seem to be an important teaching method for both American and Tunisian professional accountants. Indeed, the use of textbooks seems to be abandoned in favor of other methods that extend the scope of knowledge and also have the possibility of updating.

5. CONCLUSION

Major changes in the environment of affairs throughout these last decades have greatly impacted the accounting profession. The development of globalization and technology has resulted in new requirements for professional accountants. For example, these needs are reflected in the emergence of new missions with high added value, whose demand is ever increasing, such as consulting and opinion services. To carry out these new missions, professional accountants must get an academic education that enables them to develop new competencies (knowledge and skills). The identification of these competencies has been the subject of both academic [6, 11, 28, 37, 38] and professional studies [5, 12, 25, 50].

All the studies converge and identified a set of knowledge and skills as well as technical, personal [51], and in the field of Information and Communication Technology (ICT). Technology forces today are significantly changing many professions, including the accounting profession. Hood [52] reports the result of interviews with thought leaders throughout the accounting profession, noting their three "biggest nightmares:" (1) technology-induced changes that devalue longstanding core services of the profession, (2) finding new employees with the right mix of skills and retraining current employees who need new skills, and (3) keeping up with the pace of technology change [52]. Further evidence of the impact of technology forces on the accounting profession may be seen in significant offshoring of tasks (to lower costs) and increasing automation of accounting/ finance jobs. The result is an increasing skills gap in accounting/finance [1]. However, if the Anglo-Saxon countries, including the United States, were the first to respond to this new economic situation in adopting educational systems capable of providing the future professional knowledge and skills mentioned above, Tunisia, for its part, has set up a higher education system on the License-Master-Doctorate model, without so far, providing a specific accounting educational path for CPA. Can we say that the current system of CPA education in Tunisia is adapted to the needs of the accounting profession?

We conducted a survey on Tunisian CPA and CPA trainees. The results revealed a range of knowledge, skills and teaching methods considered to be the most important. The results also highlight similarities in the perception of knowledge and skills required by professional accountants, whether they are Tunisians, Chinese or Americans. Differences of perception are probably due to the differences in terms of economic and technological development, as well as social and cultural influences that differ from one country to another. Thus, this research has helped to form two convictions. The first one is that we must continue to think about the pedagogy to adopt in the context of accounting education, as well as the manner in which the knowledge is transmitted [11, 51]. The second is that academic accounting education curriculum plays a crucial role to meet the needs of the profession and influences the development of the profession.

In conclusion, this work cannot claim to have responded to all issues related to the problems and challenges facing accounting education, even less to have found the solutions. One of the main objectives of this study was to try to put the problem in its context and to propose a model for analyzing the situation. Academics in the field of accounting face the challenge of repositioning their discipline in a position of excellence. Indeed, the accounting discipline should be organized in order to benefit from the experience gained particularly over the last decades, to evolve and adapt to new challenges and new expectations of the accounting profession. This can be accomplished only if the academic world agrees to abandon its conformity and its commitment to traditional teaching methods. It is obvious that in the current state, higher education institutions have no choice than to change their methods. The costs associated with the implementation of these changes are much lower than the costs that would be generated by a possible lack of action.

REFERENCES

1. Pincus K V, Stout D E, Sorensen J E, Stocks K D, Lawson R A. Forces for change in higher education and implications for the accounting academy. Journal of Accounting Education. 2017; 40: 1-18. DOI: 10.1016/j.jaccedu.2017.06.001

2. Albrecht W S, and Sack R J. Accounting education: charting the course through a perilous future. Accounting Education, American Accounting Association; 2000; Sarasota, FL. Series 16.

3. Sanders B, and Romeo L B. The supply of accounting graduates and the demand for pubic accounting recruits. 2000, New York: American Institute of Certified Public Accountants.

4. Sanders B, Goldfarb S and Romeo LB. The Supply of Accounting Graduates and the Demand for Public Accounting Recruits--200J. For Academic Year 1999-2000; 2001; New York: American Institute of Certified Public Accountants.

5. Pathways Commission. Charting a National Strategy for the Next Generation of Accountants. [Internet]. 2012. Available at: http://commons.aaahq.org/files/0b14318188/Pathways_Commission_Final_Report_Complete.pdf

6. Lawson R A, Blocher E J, Brewer P C, Cokins G, Sorensen J E, Stout D E, Sundem G L, Wolcott S, and Wouters M J F. Focusing accounting curricula on students' long-run careers: Recommendations for an integrated competency-based framework for accounting education. Issues in Accounting Education. 2014; 29 (2): 295-317. DOI: 10.2139/ssrn.2342306.

7. Lawson R A, Blocher E J, Brewer P C, Morris J T, Stocks K D, Sorensen J E, Stout D., and Wouters M J F. Thoughts on competency integration in accounting education. Issues in Accounting Education. 2015; 30 (3): 149-171. DOI: 10.2308/iace-51021

8. Sundem G L, and Williams D Z. Changes in accounting education: preparing for the twenty-first century. Accounting Education: An International Journal. 1992;1(1), 55-61. DOI.org/10.1080/09639289200000006

9. Williams D Z. Reforming accounting education. Journal of Accountancy. 1993, 176(2): 76-82.

10. Nelson IT, Bailey J A, and Nelson A T. Changing accounting education with purpose: market-based strategic planning for departments of accounting. Issues in Accounting Education. 1998; 13(2): 301-326.

11. Khemiri R. L'enseignement supérieur en comptabilité : enjeux et perspectives pour la profession comptable, cas de la Tunisie [thesis]. Université de Toulouse I Capitole, France; 2012.

12. American Accounting Association. Future accounting education: preparing for the expanding profession. Issues in Accounting Education. 1986; 1(1): 168-195.

13. Sundem G L. Changes in accounting education in the United States: the impact of the accounting education change commission. International Handbook of Accounting Education and Certification. ed. A. ANYANENTOW. NY: Pergamon Press; 1992.

14. Kimmel P. A framework for incorporating critical thinking into accounting education. Journal of Accounting Education. 1995; 13: 299-318. DOI: 10.1016/0748-5751(95)00012-B

15. Cummings B, Bennett R E and Normand C J. Meeting the challenge: the university accounting program corporate American needs. Management Accounting Quarterly. 2001; (Winter): 4-13.

16. Barsky N P, Catanach A H, and Kozlowski B M. Creating strategic responses to critical risks facing accounting education. Issues in Accounting Education. 2003; 18(4): 445-459. DOI: 10.2308/iace.2003.18.4.445

17. Gibbin A L. The crisis in accounting education. Journal of Accountancy. 2002; 193(4), 81-86.

18. Montano J A, Anes J A D, Hassall T and Joyce J. Vocational skills in the accounting professional profile: The chartered institute of management accountants (CIMA) employer's opinion. Accounting Education: An International Journal. 2001; 10(3): 299-313. DOI: 10.1080/09639280210122339

19. Burnett S. The future of accounting education: a regional perspective. Journal of Education for Business. 2003; 78(3): 129-136. DOI: 10.1080/08832320309599709

20. Forristal T. CAP Forum: The future of accounting education: the response of charted accountants. Canadian Accounting Perspectives. 2002; 1(1): 80-88.

21. Howieson B. Accounting practice in the new millennium: is accounting education ready to meet the challenge. The British Accounting Review. 2003; 35(2): 69-78. Doi:10.1016/S0890-8389(03)00004-0

22. Taylor V A and Rudnick M. Accounting education: designing a curriculum for the 21st century. Journal of American Academy of Business. 2005; 6(2): 321-323.

23. Arthur Andersen and Co. Perspectives on education: capabilities for success in the accounting profession. New York; 1989: Arthur Anderson and Co. et al.

24. Accounting Education Change Commission. Objectives of education for accountants: position statement number one. Issues in Accounting Education. 1990; 5(2): 307-312.

25. American Institute of Certified Public Accountant. The CPA vision project, 2011 and beyond. 1998; AICPA web site.

26. Nelson A T. The future for accounting education: A view from rocking chair. Journal of Accounting Education. 1996; 14(2): 245-254. DOI: 10.1016/0748-5751(96)00014-0

27. Aly I M and Islam M. Audit of accounting program on oral communication apprehension: a comparative study among accounting students. Managerial Auditing Journal. 2003; 18(9): 751-760. DOI: 10.1108/02686900310500514

28. Francisco B, and Kelly A. Beyond Albrecht and Sack: a comparison of accounting professionals and college students [Internet]. 2003. Retrieved June 27, Available from http://www.aicpa.org/download/career/edu/Beyond_Albrecht_Sack.pdf, 2002.
29. Russell K and Smith C. Accounting education's role in corporate malfeasance: its time for a new curriculum. Strategic Finance. 2003; 85(6): 46-52.
30. Boyce G. Critical accounting education: teaching and learning outside the circle. Critical Perspectives on Accounting. 2004; 15(4-5): 565-586. DOI: 10.1016/S1045-2354(03)00047-9
31. Ravenscroft S P and Williams P. Accounting education in the U.S. post-Enron. Accounting Education: An International Journal. 2004; 13(1): 7-23. DOI: 10.1080/0963928042000310760
32. Cooper D J, Everett J and Neu D. Financial scandals, accounting change and the role of accounting academics: a perspective from North America. European Accounting Review. 2005; 14(2): 373-382. DOI: 10.1080/09638180500124905
33. Diamond M. Accounting education, research and practice: after Enron, where do we go? European Accounting Review. 2005; 14(2): 353-362. DOI: 10.1080/09638180500124855
34. Ferguson J, Collison D, Power D, and Stevenson L. What are recommended accounting textbooks teaching students about corporate stakeholders? The British Accounting Review. 2005; 37(1): 23-46. DOI: 10.1016/j.bar.2004.08.002
35. Ferguson J, Collison D, Power D, and Stevenson L. Accounting textbooks: exploring the production of a cultural and political artifact. Accounting Education: An International Journal. 2006; 15(3): 243-260. DOI: 10.1080/09639280600850679
36. Fedoryshyn M W, and Tyson T N. The impact of practitioner presentations on student attitudes about accounting. Journal of Education for Business. 2003; 78(5): 273-284. DOI: 10.1080/08832320309598614
37. Lin Z J, Xiong X, and Liu M. Knowledge base and skill development in accounting education: Evidence from China. Journal of Accounting Education. 2005; 23(3): 149-169. DOI: 10.1016/j.jaccedu.2005.06.003
38. Lin Z J. A factor analysis on knowledge and skill components of accounting education: Chinese case. Advances in Accounting. 2008; 24(1): 110-118. DOI: 10.1016/j.adiac.2008.05.009
39. Chen TTY. A comparative study of what accounting employers in the United States and Hong Kong expect: Implications for curriculum and pedagogical design. Global Perspectives on Accounting Education. 2013; 10: 121-132.

40. Tang Y. The recent accounting development and internationalization of accounting education in China. Issues in Accounting Education. 1997; 12(2): 219-228. ISBN: 1558-7983

41. Chan L. Accounting education and economic reform in the people's Republic of China. International Studies of Management and Organization. 1999; 29: 37-55. DOI: 10.1080/00208825.1999.11656770

42. Rahaman A S. Accounting and socio-economic development paradigms. Journal of American Academy of Business. 2005; 6(2): 217-222.

43. Wu T, and Tong Y. Issues and challenges of accounting education in China: practitioners and academic perspectives. Journal of American Academy of Business. 2004; 4(1/2): 208-219.

44. International Federation of Accountants. International education Guideline N° 9: Prequalification education, assessment of professional competence and experience requirements of professional accountants. Education Committee; 1991.

45. International Accounting Education Standards Board. IAESB factsheet [Internet]. 2013. Available from: https://www.ifac.org/sites/default/files/uploads/IAESB/IAESB.pdf.Accessed April 2013.

46. International Accounting Education Standards Board. Handbook of international education pronouncements. ed.2010. New York: IFAC ; 2010a.

47. Crawford L, Helliarc C, Monka E, Veneziani M. International Accounting Education Standards Board:Organisational legitimacy within the field of professionalaccountancy education. Accounting Forum. 2014; 38: 67-89. DOI: 10.1016/j.accfor.2013.09.001

48. Khemiri R, Ben Chahida M. Introduction of Information and Communication Technologies Teaching in Accounting Education Following the LMD Reform in Tunisia: Toward a Market Orientation. The Journal of African Research in Business & Technology. 2010; V2010: 1-14. DOI: 10.5171/2010.206493

49. Commission Nationale de la Réforme de l'Enseignement Supérieur: CNR. Plan stratégique de la réforme de l'enseignement supérieur et de la recherche scientifique 2015 – 2025. MESRS; 2015.

50. American Institute of Certified Public Accountant. AICPA Core Competency Framework & Educational Competency Assessment Website [Internet]. 2015. Available from: <http://www.aicpa.org/interestareas/accountingeducation/resources/pages/corecompetency.aspx> Accessed 02.15.

51. Chabrak H, and Craig R. Student imaginings, cognitive dissonance and critical thinking. Critical Perspectives on Accounting. 2013 ; 24(2): 91-104. DOI: 10.1016/j.cpa.2011.07.008

52.Hood D. Losing sleep: Leaders of the profession on its biggest nightmares. Accounting Today. 2015; 29(10).

SECTION-8

CORPORATE GOVERNANCE AND PERFORMANCE MEASURES

08 Funded Pension Schemes in Aging Societies: A Pure Economic Argument?

1. INTRODUCTION

The western world deals with continuous aging, low fertility, and debt crisis that push governments toward funded-capitalized pension schemes [1, 2, 3]. A common trend indicates a decline in public pension benefits [4]. Moreover, systemic reforms have changed the nature of pension provisions, shifting more risks onto pension earners. The privatization of pension plans worldwide and the global process toward the appearance of more funded plans raise important thoughts regarding the adequacy and sustainability of pension schemes, their benefits, and falls [5, 6].

According to Milev, "The sharp downturn in the value of financial assets between 2007 and 2009 and the current financial crisis due to the COVID-19 pandemic serve as sharp examples of how risky assets quickly lose a significant part of their value" ([7], p. 2). The financial crises and continuing concerns about retirement security have generated a new interest regarding the role of the country to provide adequate old-age benefits to its citizens. We are witnessing a great wave of pension withdrawals from funded-capitalized schemes, moving toward more governmental intervention. Indeed, according to Altiparmakov, "most of the countries experiencing similar crises were the first to implement new liberal pension schemes during the 1990s" ([8], p. 4).

Late research has demonstrated the importance of balancing funded schemes with unfunded components to increase adequacy and sustainability [6, 9, 10]. These studies strengthen the expanding policy and efforts of worldwide governments to start the economies after the pandemic shocks and in parallel insure old participants from the turmoil markets [11, 12].

In conjunction with the current fiscal expenditures lies the classic economic argument that countries should shift to funded pension schemes due to low fertility [13]. "The shrinking tax base and negative influence of governments on markets are the flags of the Washington Consensus, the World Bank during the 1990s, and other economic institutes" ([14], p. 2).

This composition argues that, from a wide perspective, the rush of governments toward funded pension schemes due to low fertility and fiscal constraints may not be optimal. The current complex environment influenced by the pandemic strengthens this argument. We base this on simple equilibriums in the pension markets based on different macro-economic assumptions. The novelty of this research is demonstrated in the wide array of interests taken into consideration. We avoid treating participants as a single-player and allow intergeneration and intra-generational risk sharing. The adjacent generations allow us to examine the cyclical tax burden, the influence of fertility on future generations, and the statistical returns in the long term. The split to earning cohorts demonstrates different interests of hedging capabilities and different optimal contribution rates, considering tax burden and insurance components in old-age benefits [15].

We suggest balancing funded pension schemes with "unfunded boxes," which may increase the sustainability of the pension system, improving the utility of all players. It is found that in some cases, which are common in Western economies, the optimal pension scheme is surprisingly the pay-as-you-go (PAYG) pension system, even in aging societies.

The next section details the interests of the different players in the pension field as well as the assumptions to the economic model. In Section 3, we set the stochastic model of the pension system, which maximizes the participants' utility, and analyzes how it is best to finance the guaranWtee. Section 4 provides the main results of the simulations and sensitivity analysis. In Section 5, we discuss the results and their implications, and the last section provides the conclusion.

2. THE GOVERNMENT AND THE PARTICIPANTS' INTERESTS

It is common to determine that the government wishes to decrease its fiscal risks and obligations and hence push for a shift toward an unfunded pension scheme. The fiscal exposure of the government is obviously levied on its citizens [1]. Consequently, it should be the interest of the citizens to shift from the comfort PAYG DB pension scheme to a funded pension scheme. Indeed, some scholars, mainly during the 1990s, supported the transition to a funded scheme, trying to convince people that the alternative is a heavy tax burden [2, 3].

Disassembling the answer to this question to society and different players seems much more complex and far from unambiguous. Since information is not a free asset but a risk in pension systems, framing the argument in the second-best terms starts from the multiple objectives of pension systems. "Policy has to seek the best balance between consumption smoothing, poverty relief, and insurance, and this balance will depend in each society on the weights given to those and other objectives and to the different constraints that societies face" [5].

This composition focuses on the central planner, which has the responsibility to balance the interests of all players—recognizing a variety of earning cohorts and adjacent generations. That variety of actors throughout its length and breadth may represent the entire government perspective. With that, we continue with Altiparmakov [8] and Wolf and Ocerin [9], who suggest that stable pension systems must seek an equilibrium between earning cohorts. Otherwise, the chances are high for pension reforms and reversals [16].

We expand previous overlapping generations (OLG) models [17] by including debt. The consideration of cycle government debt obligates the central planner to make sure that future generations will not be used as a heavy tax source. In the current research, we take future generations' utility as part of the total preferences of the society by simply discounting them. One may claim that the weight for future generations in preferences equations does not necessary derives from the participant's discount factor and may suggest greater weight. We agree with that argument and claim that the equilibrium in that case should still be calculated specifically for every market separately.

The second dimension is the differentiation between high- and low-earning cohorts. Wolf and Del Rio [10, 11, 18] have shown that by shifting to the funded pension scheme, a socio-economic anomaly exists because of the high exposure of low-earning cohorts to market and credit risk without the ability to hedge themselves. They also claim that the optimal contribution rates are generally close to high-earning preferences (see also [9]). In that case, the funded pension market should be included as "externalities," where high earners compensate low earners by risk-sharing. That may include, for example, minimum pension guarantee, intergenerational/intra-generational risk sharing of social security benefits. These processes clearly justify differentiating the considerations and interests of earning cohorts.

3. MODEL SETUP

We employ a simple OLG model to characterize optimal pension pillars' sizes. In each period, a new generation of unit mass is borne. We employ this model for four generations. For simplicity, each generation includes three equal life periods cycle frameworks as in Knell [19]: "Individuals work during the first two parts of their life, while they are retired in the third part. The first pillar is unfunded social security, and the second is in the form of individual accounts" ([19], p. 6).

3.1 Consumers

The consumer works over two periods of 23 years each and retires at the age of 67 ($s=T_R$). They live for another 23 years, represented by the third period, and are assumed to die at the age of 90 ($s=T_D$).

During the first 46 years, consumers work and earn a real labor income of W_{t1}. We allow for differentiation in wage levels across earning deciles. From this wage, the individual contributes to social security tax and funded pension fund. The participant consumes the residual after contributions.

During the retirement period (TR≤s<TD), the individual's consumption, C_t, T_R, is given by the benefits both from public and funded pension pillars. These benefits are collectively denoted by P_t. The consumption of the generation t in time s can be described as follows:[1]

$$c_{t,s} = \left\{ \begin{array}{c} W_{t,s}(1-\tau), during\ work\ period \\ p^U_{T_R} + p^F_{T_R}, during\ retirement \end{array} \right\} \quad (1)$$

Individuals have a constant relative risk aversion (CRRA) utility function defined over a single nondurable consumption good. Let us define δ as the discount factor; α measures the curvature of the utility function or risk aversion level, so the individual's preferences are then defined by

$$U_t = \sum_{s=1}^{s=2} \delta^{s-1} \frac{1}{1-a} (c_{t,t+s-1})^{1-a} + \delta^2 \frac{1}{1-a} \left(c_{t,T_R} - mpg_{t,T_R} \right)^{1-a} \quad (2)$$

Here, $C_{t,s}$ is the consumption level of generation t in periods, and $mpg_{t,s}$ is the level of government guarantee for generation t in period s.

Consumption is a function of the participant's wage and deductions due to pension contributions (funded and unfunded) and taxes financing government debt. Government's debt can be made due to financing pension guarantees or financing intergenerational gaps in PAYG DB due to aging. These payments are detailed in Table 1. In fact, the aging effect realizes in twofold positions. First, by increasing the real debt cost of the government, as fewer people participate in a specified burden. Second, by reducing PAYG benefits per specified contribution rate.

Table 1. Consumption in each pension scheme.

Consumption	Defined benefit	Mix pension scheme	Mix pension scheme with pension guarantee
During working phase	Wage-pension contributions—tax-financing aging effect (the cost of shrinking tax base)	Wage-pension contributions	Wage-pension contributions—tax-financing guarantee cost of earlier generations
During Retirement	Unfunded pillar with no aging effect	Funded + unfunded pillar	Funded + unfunded pillar + minimum pension guarantee up to the poverty line

Consistently with the life cycle model of Ando and Modigliani [20], the participant is aware of future interest rate risks and adapts his consumption during the working phase accordingly. If the government supposes to collect extra tax payments to finance the interests of its debts, the individual adapts his/her consumption accordingly.

3.2 Mix Pension Scheme with Dominant Funded Pillar

Rates of returns are uncertain (*ex ante* expected utility). The GDP per capita growth rate approximates the aggregate wage income, following the same method of Masten and Thorgesen [21], and Wolf and Ocerin [9]. We also assume that the real PAYG rate of return, g_{s+1}, is equal to the growth rate of wages or the change in the GDP per capita.

The parameter g_t describes the evolution of wage,W, which follows a Brownian motion of the following form:

$$\frac{dW(t)}{W(t)} = dg_t = \mu_g dt + \sigma_g dB^W(t), \tag{3}$$

where μ_g stands for the constant expectation of the instantaneous variation rate in the wage, σg denotes its constant standard deviation, and B^Wrepresents a standard Brownian motion. The first phrase is a constant drift, and the second phrase is the volatility drift. The term g_{t+1} is the growth of labor income or the return on human capital.

The individual pays a fixed contribution rate τ. From that contribution, a share of γ is invested in a private-funded pillar and a share of (-1γ)-1 finances in the unfunded pillar or the public social security. The pension benefit for generation t in the retirement period is denoted by

$$p_{T_R} = p^F_{T_R} + p^U_{T_R}. \tag{4}$$

Here, p^F_{t+2} and p^U_{t+2}represents the funded fund and social security (PAYG), respectively.

We allow a correlation between the GDP per capita and the fund asset return rate, thus

$$dB^W(t)dB^A(t) = \rho_{w,A}dt, \tag{5}$$

with the condition 1≥ρw,A≥-1.

We assumed a constant social security benefit based on time of contributions. In each period, the working population's contributions are equal to the total benefit payments to retirees. Consequently, the public unfunded pension benefit is determined using the balanced budget condition of

$$\varphi\tau^U\{\overline{W}_{t+1,T_R}N_{t+1} * A + \overline{W}_{t+2,T_R}N_{t+2} * A^2\} = \sum_{n=1}^{N_{T_R}} p_t^U \tag{6}$$

Here, τ^U is the contribution rate to social security, N_t is the size of the generation born in period t, and p_t^U is the unfunded pension benefits paid to generation t in the period T_R. The term φ is the constant social security's old-age benefits/ contribution ratio. The residual share (-1φ)-1 of contributions finance other social expenses pertaining to Medicare, means-tested, minimum pension guarantee, disability benefits, unemployment benefits, and other social expenses. The tax base in each generation is shrinking due to the aging of societies. Consequently, A represents the aging factor of each contributor generation to social security.

Under the assumption of constant population growth, nitni, the contribution $\tau^U w_{t,s}$ is paid by generation *t* in time s; thus, there is a return of $g_{s+1}=(W_{t,s+1}/W_{t,s})-1$. In addition, we assume the economic principle of Aaron [22] that the notional interest rate or the population growth rate is set equal to the growth rate of wages: $ni_t=g_t$. Hence, the unfunded benefit at retirement can be described in the following reduced form:

$$P_{t,T_R}^U = \varphi(1-\gamma)\tau \sum_{t=1}^{T} \partial_d \overline{W}_{t+1,T_R} * \left(A + A^2\right), \tag{7}$$

where ∂_d is a constant parameter per earning decile that adjusts the benefit to contribution level. This mechanism is similar to the Notional Defined Contribution (NDC) pension scheme and ensures higher benefits for high earners in relation to their contributions.

The funded-capitalized pillar is a private collective defined-contribution (DC) system with a fixed contribution rate. Individuals start with zero initial asset holdings. Subsequently, the individual adds the fraction of γw_t to his accumulations during the working phase, which is invested in a constant portfolio mix of financial assets (equities, bonds, etc.). This accumulation earns an average annual rate of return of r_t. This rate of return also follows a Brownian motion of the following form

$$dr_s = \mu_r dt + \sigma_r B^A dt \tag{8}$$

Here, r_t denotes the continuous rate expectation of the asset instantaneous return rate, σ_r stands for its constant standard deviation, and B^A indicates the standard Brownian motion. The first phrase from the left is a constant drift, and the second phrase is the volatility drift.

The funded pillar is equal to the accumulated capital from the contributions to the private collective defined-contribution fund during every working period until retirement (T_R). The real capital is given by

$$p_t^F = \left(1 - T^f\right)\left(1 - I^f\right)\tau^F \sum_{s=t}^{T_R} W_{t,s} {r_t}^{T_R - t} \tag{9}$$

Here, T^f is the effective tax rate on old-age funded fund's benefits. I^f is the fraction from the contributions that represent insurance contributed from the pension fund, such as disability. Funded fund's liabilities are based on the current and future retiree's benefit payments. The funded benefit can be described more specifically as

$$p_t^F = \gamma \tau W_t r_{s+1} r_{s+2} + \gamma \tau W_{t+1} r_{s+2} \qquad (10)$$

Due to the assumption that there is only one period of retirement, it is not necessary to specify how the pension capital of the funded pillar is annuitized or amortized, that is, transformed into annual pension installments.

3.3 Pension Guarantee

The government considers implementing a minimum pension guarantee when imposing the funded pension scheme. The periodical guarantee is at the poverty level, meaning 0.6 of the median earnings decile. We calculate the cost of the guarantee as

$$Guarante\ cost\ at\ time\ t = p.\,l\ at\ time\ t - \left(p_t^F + p_t^U\right) \qquad (11)$$

The poverty line itself is growing every period by the GDP per capita growth rate. However, the guarantee cost depends on the income inequality in the market and stays constant as a percentage from the GDP. The guarantee cost is financed by the government in the form of tax levied on future generations.

3.4 PAYG DB Pension Scheme

Pension benefits are calculated using the same method of the unfunded pillar described above. The difference is that total contributions are for the unfunded pillar (γ=0)=0. In addition, retirees benefit from the constant contribution level. The government, through debt, finances the exposure of aging, which reduces the intra-generational financing base.

$$P_{t,T_R}^{DB} = \varphi \tau \sum_{t=1}^{T} \partial_d \overline{W}_{t+1} * 2 \qquad (12)$$

As the government keeps benefit retirees at the same original level before transition, the shrinking tax base is translated to a fiscal expenditure. That expenditure is financed by future generations as tax payments in the amount of

$$P_{t,T_R}^{DB}\ government\ share = \varphi \tau \sum_{t=1}^{T} \partial_d \overline{W}_{t+1} * \left(2 - \left(A + A^2\right)\right) \qquad (13)$$

3.5 Government Debt

Government finances two different obligations through debt and future tax. The first is the guarantee cost in mix funded pension scheme. The second is the aging influence of the intra-generational tax base from generation to generation.

For each of these expenses, we assume a debt cycle of four periods. In the first period, the fiscal expense is realized. Over the next two periods, the working population pays the interest rate component as tax, while during the fourth period, return also the principle in addition to the periodical interest payment. In total, in each period, the working generation pays three interest rate components of past debts and a single principle of past debt.

3.6 Different Earning Cohorts

We allow different preferences among earning cohorts. In fact, this diversity is one of the most important novelties of this research. We assume that high-earning cohorts benefit from a higher share of GDP growth than low earners, in increasing order. In parallel, high earners levy a higher share of tax payments, progressively. For example, the tax burden on decile 4 is only 5% from payment, while it is 30% on the highest-earning decile. Figure 1 summarizes the differentiation across different earning deciles.

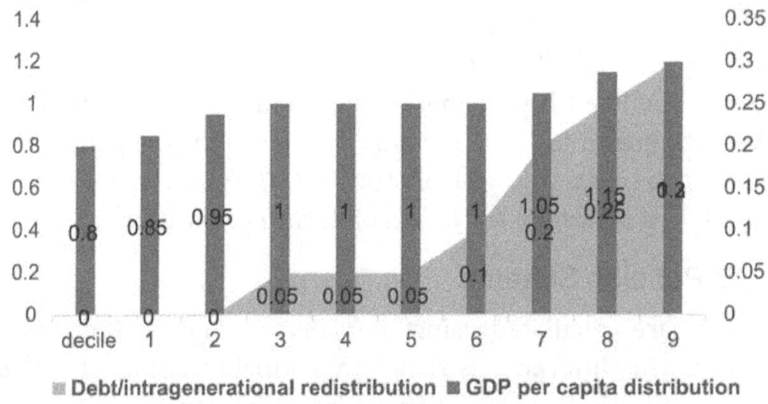

Figure 1. Earning deciles.

We value the preferences of earning cohorts to the different pension schemes by the change of average utility computed according to each of the three pension schemes analyzed. For simplicity, we group these preferences by deciles 1–4 for low-earning cohorts and 7–10 for high-earning cohorts.

4. SIMULATION AND CALIBRATION

The GDP per capita stochastic yields turn to be stochastic the variables of periodic wage, poverty line, defined benefit pension scheme, and social security. The market yield affects the funded pension pillar stochastically. We use Monte Carlo simulations to simulate the level of the guarantee cost in each generation and the level of governmental debt due to imposing defined benefits in each generation. Another set of Monte Carlo simulations is conducted to compute the preferences of each earning cohort for each generation among funded pension schemes, funded schemes with guarantees, and defined benefit pension schemes.

For each generation, the preference of pension scheme depends on the utility of each earning cohort in each generation. For comparability, we compute the relative preference of the mix pension scheme over the DB and respectively the preference of the mix pension scheme with a guarantee over the DB. Monte Carlo simulations simulate these pairs of ratios.

Analyzing the results, we make a differentiation between low- and high-earning cohorts. For each set of results, we discount the preferences of the four generations to a single number.

We calibrate the model as of the average western OECD country, using its updating database [4]. In the base scenario, the government capital cost is 0.5%, the GDP per capita is 1.6% per year, and the average net pension market yield is 3.74%. The contribution rates to pension pillars are derived from countries such as Denmark and Israel that run dominant funded pension schemes [4]. We take into consideration the aging trend in Western countries. We assume the high aging influence as conservative in analyzing the rush toward the funded scheme. In that case, similar to Germany and Spain, the dependency ratio increases by 0.4% every year. The sensitive analysis is conducted to map the trends of preferences as a function of risk aversion and interest rate gap. We summarize the calibrations variables in Table 2.

Table 2. Calibration.

Wage and pension systems	
Contribution rate	0.3
Funded rate from contributions	0.75
Annual Expected S.D. of funded pillar	18%
Gross return [4]	4.3%
Admin. Cost	0.5%
The funded Benefit tax rate	20%
Annual Expected GDP per capita – g	1.6%
Annual GDP S.D	2%
Social Security Benefit / Contribution coeff.	60%
Insurances in funded pension funds from contribution	25.00%
Macro-economic parameters	
Risk Aversion Coeff. (Base Scenario)	3
Annual Interest rate (Base Scenario)	0.10%
Total population annual growth	0.30%
Dependency ratio annual change	0.4%
Annual discount factor	G + 1.3%

5. RESULTS AND INSIGHTS

While there is no debt financing the funded pension scheme, there is small debt financing the DB pension scheme (the aging effect) with a constant percent from GDP. We map higher debt level financing the guarantee, reducing in time, if >r_f>.

In the Western market, the government interest rate is generally lower than the GDP per capita rate, while the market yield (r) is higher than both. In times when the difference between the market yield and the GDP per capita increases, markets will prefer to shift to a funded pension scheme and vice versa. Here, we point out the government capital price as also an important factor as it affects the preferences of future generations. A coherent pension system, which considers multiplayers' preferences, cannot avoid the tax/PAYG burden levied on the working population or future generation in the form of cycle tax payments.

5.1 PAYG DB Scheme vs. Funded Pension Scheme

For each generation, we check the preferences between PAYG DB and the funded pension scheme via 2100 Monte Carlo simulations. Each simulation calculates the OLG model with the aforementioned assumptions. Figure 2 describes these preferences by earning cohorts and as a function of the rate of returns gaps (GDP per capita minus the government interest rate). The more positive the preference value, the more the preference tends toward the funded scheme. By the same logic, the more negative the value, the more they prefer the DB pension scheme.

Panel A: Low Earning Deciles

Interest rate gap / Generation Preference		A	B	C	D	Preference to end of genertion A
g-r	1.50%	-2.21%	-1.31%	-0.73%	-0.39%	-3.7%
	1.30%	-2.03%	-1.14%	-0.64%	-0.36%	-3.2%
	1.10%	-1.77%	-1.05%	-0.59%	-0.31%	-2.8%
	0.90%	-1.54%	-0.94%	-0.51%	-0.27%	-2.4%
	0.70%	-1.38%	-0.80%	-0.43%	-0.22%	-2.1%
	0.50%	-1.26%	-0.69%	-0.37%	-0.17%	-1.8%
	0.30%	-1.06%	-0.58%	-0.28%	-0.12%	-1.5%
	0.00%	-0.74%	-0.37%	-0.15%	-0.03%	-1.0%

Panel B: High Earning Deciles

Interest rate gap / Generation Preference		A	B	C	D	Preference to end of genertion A
g-r	1.50%	-3.34%	-2.74%	-3.82%	-2.91%	-8.5%
	1.30%	-0.32%	0.35%	-0.01%	1.59%	0.4%
	1.10%	3.23%	2.67%	1.93%	4.43%	7.1%
	0.90%	5.00%	5.74%	8.03%	8.84%	14.0%
	0.70%	8.88%	9.22%	10.96%	12.91%	21.5%
	0.50%	12.59%	13.76%	15.70%	17.89%	29.3%
	0.30%	16.14%	18.00%	19.92%	22.19%	35.8%
	0.00%	22.37%	24.91%	26.66%	29.82%	46.7%

Figure 2. Generations' preferences of PAYG DB vs. funded scheme in the base scenario (a=3=3).

As expected, high earners prefer the funded pension scheme, while low earners tend to prefer the DB scheme. For high earners, the reasons for this are the potential for higher benefits and the avoidance of financing pension gaps of unfunded transfers due to aging and the shrinking labor force.

Low-earning cohorts prefer the DB pension system as it enables insurance although the benefits in the funded scheme are higher on average. As time goes by, in both earning cohorts, the attractiveness of the funded scheme increases as the average returns of the funded scheme is higher than the GDP per capita, and naturally, the insurance for the long term is less considered in the utility measure.

When increasing the risk aversion coefficient from 3 to 5, low earners become almost indifferent between funded and unfunded pension schemes. This is because, in high-risk aversion measures, participants put considerable weight on their current consumption more than their old-age benefits. Since consumption does not change, the total utility change is almost constant.

According to Figure 3, for high earners, the preferences concerning unfunded pension schemes are dramatic. That tendency is moderated with generations and when government debt cost increases. In other words, even when the tax burden due to aging is levied on high earners' consumption and their old-age benefits are lower than in the funded pension scheme, they will rather strongly prefer unfunded pension schemes along most of the returns gap array. Additionally, when risk aversion increases, high earners' preferences for the PAYG DB pension system increases as opposed to mix pension with pension guarantee. We explain that as of high insurance embedded in the first option and lower tax burden. That conclusion is highly important mainly in times of turmoil markets.

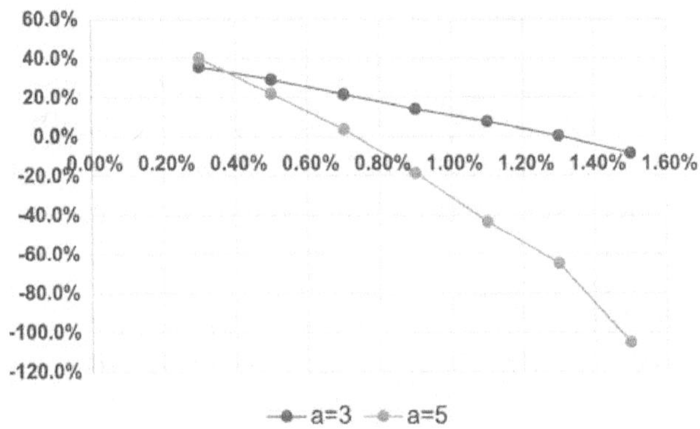

Figure 3. High earners' preference when risk aversion increases.

5.2 PAYG DB Scheme vs. Mix Pension Scheme with Pension Guarantee

Figure 4 compares along with the base scenario the preferences for PAYG DB scheme and mix pension scheme with pension guarantee. According to the results, there is not much difference between the two possibilities (the blue line) according to low earners. The benefit level is quite similar; in both cases, there is an insurance component, and in both cases, the tax burden does not fall on this earning cohort's shoulders. As the gap between the GDP per capita and the government's interest rate decreases, the discounting factor diminishes and the attractiveness of the PAYG DB decreases. It is most interesting to understand the results for high earners, who finance the insurance components in both of these pension systems. It is significant to determine that high earners would prefer the PAYG DB pension scheme over the alternative. The reason for this is mostly the high financing cost of the guarantee. Figure 4 depicts that when government's interest rate increases (small gap), the preference for PAYG DB increases accordingly, avoiding a higher tax burden.

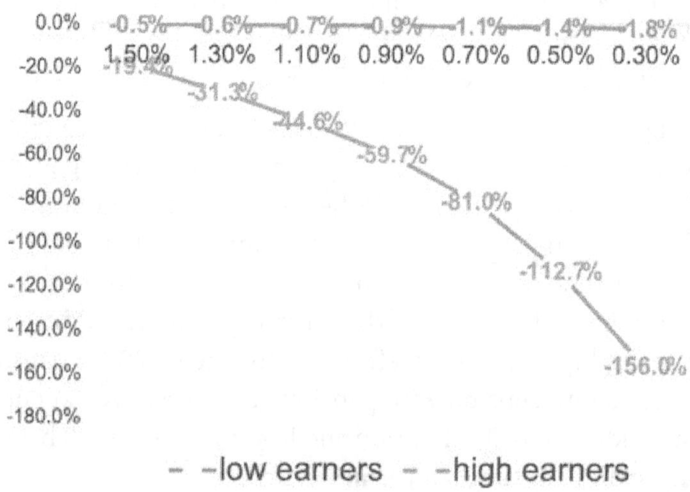

Figure 4. The preference between PAYG DB and mix pension system.

As we allow differentiation in deciles' wealth growth, the income inequality increases with time. The poverty line is indexed to the GDP per capita while high-earning deciles' wealth growth faster. That makes the guaranteed price to be relatively lower along with generations, which comes to realize by decreasing percent from total GDP.

In general, if the GDP per capita is higher than the government interest rate, clearly, the central planner would prefer to accumulate debt and roll it over the years, as the principal and interest rate payment decrease as percent from the GDP. Along with generations, the preferences toward the DB pension scheme tend to decrease as the average return effect increases. However, for high earners, the attractiveness between the two pension schemes is not ambiguous. High earners prefer the DB pension scheme because of the lower tax burden during the working phase. In other words, they prefer to pay lower old-age benefits than to pay the relatively high tax burden due to the guarantee.

5.3 Finding an Equilibrium Point

Equilibrium in pension systems is not only dealing with a question of the economy but also involves social targets [23]. Even when poverty alleviation is highly weighted among the central planner's considerations, it is not straightforward to implement mix pension system with a minimum guarantee. Although low earners only slightly prefer the unfunded scheme over the mix with the guarantee, high earners significantly prefer the unfunded scheme and avoid financing the high costs of the guarantee. Consequently, among these two options, from a wider perspective of all players, the system should be set at the PAYG DB pension system.

That conclusion is certainly relevant in an aging society having clear economic characteristics of Western countries. In other words, the potential old-age benefits for high benefits in the funded pension scheme are offset with the tax burden to fund social targets.

In this research, we show that the PAYG DB is a common equilibrium even when releasing the assumption of social targets. One can see that in Figure 2, wherein the gap between the GDP per capita and the government debt cost is large (1.5–1.3%), the players would prefer the PAYG DB. That simple equilibrium is also relevant when risk aversion increases or the yield's standard deviation increase. Naturally, in these situations, participants prefer safer benefits even in the cost of lower consumption during the working phase. That conclusion is most relevant when markets are not stable, for example, during the COVID-19 pandemic crisis.

More complex scenarios can be found when the gap between the GDP per capita and government debt price is narrowed. For example, in Figure 2, when the gap is at 1.1%, low earners prefer the unfunded pension scheme (measure of -2.8%). Similarly, high earners prefer the funded scheme (measure of 7.1%) while resisting the mix scheme (measure of -44.6% in Figure 4). The lack of preference of neither of the players toward the mix pension system suggests it's from the realistic equilibrium variety.

Between the unfunded and the funded pension scheme, we seek a point satisfying the players' interests, which in turn increases the chances to system sustainability. With a given macroeconomic parameters, we seek a new mix pension system, which includes an "unfunded box," shifted from high earners to low earners, at retirement. That shift compensates low earners to excess market risk and their low abilities to hedge it. From another economic angle, high earners finance this compensation due to the characteristics of contribution rates being close to being optimal for high earners and sub-optimal for low earners [10, 11, 18]. In fact, this shift creates equilibrium as part of the "externalities" theory and alleviates the inherent socio-economic anomaly in funded pension schemes, which is in favor of high earners.

Panel A GDP per capita - government interst rate = 1.1%						
Earning cohort	Box size (%GDP)	A	B	C	D	Preference to end of genertion A
The Base Scenario						
low	3.30%	-1.77%	-1.05%	-0.59%	-0.31%	-2.8%
high	3.30%	2.80%	3.00%	3.63%	4.34%	7.6%
Finding Equilibirium Point						
high	3%	-7.63%	-8.82%	-8.45%	-9.00%	-19.7%
high	2%	-4.35%	-4.66%	-3.84%	-4.24%	-10.3%
high	1%	-1.24%	-1.39%	0.27%	0.66%	-1.9%

Panel B GDP per capita - government interst rate = 0.9%						
Earning cohort	Box size (%GDP)	A	B	C	D	Preference to end of genertion A
The Base Scenario						
low	3.60%	-1.77%	-1.05%	-0.59%	-0.31%	-2.7%
high	3.60%	2.80%	3.00%	3.63%	4.34%	7.2%
Finding Equilibirium Point						
high	2%	-1.71%	-1.59%	-1.02%	-0.71%	-3.3%
high	1%	3.08%	2.48%	3.61%	4.81%	7.3%

Panel C GDP per capita - government interst rate = 0.7%						
Earning cohort	Box size (%GDP)	A	B	C	D	Preference to end of genertion A
The Base Scenario						
low		-1.38%	-0.80%	-0.43%	-0.22%	-2.1%
high		8.88%	9.22%	10.96%	12.91%	21.5%
Finding Equilibirium Point						
high	3%	-0.37%	-1.06%	-0.23%	-0.65%	-1.2%
high	2%	3.02%	2.84%	3.10%	3.96%	6.8%
high	1%	6.89%	5.93%	7.27%	8.93%	15.2%

Figure 5. Finding an equilibrium point in the funded pension scheme.

Finding the unfunded "box" size, we analyze the preferences while low earners benefit from it and high earners finance it. Figure 5 plots the convergence process to equilibriums based on the funded scheme along with the unfunded box. We learn that even is a small amount of shifting (low box size), high earners would prefer to stay in the DB PAYG scheme. That is valid even for debt levels that are far lower than the PAYG DB base scenario. For example, in panel A, when the returns gap is %1.1, high earners would prefer the PAYG DB even with a minimum level of the box (%1 of GDP). In panel B, when the gap is shorter, the equilibrium will be set at the funded scheme with an unfunded box of %2 of the GDP. In these two cases, one can determine that the equilibrium is extremely fragile, meaning it is actually the PAYG DB scheme. In panel C, when the returns gap is at %0.7, the suggested equilibrium is the funded scheme with an unfunded box of %3 of the GDP. From that gap level and lower, the model suggests equilibrium involving the funded pension scheme.

6. DISCUSSION

The influence of aging is perceived as an intergenerational burden [24], which increases over the years. That was used in the base arguments of the World Bank in convincing economies to shift to funded pension systems during the 1990s [25]. The motivation to converge to equilibrium is first of the government's itself, avoiding fiscal expenses on reverting and ensuring political support from all players [26].

The fiscal concerns due to the aging process are indeed intuitive; however, it might push governments to endorse funded pension schemes too fast. According to the findings, the insurance effect of the unfunded pension scheme is beneficial even at the cost of a shrinking tax base. A low-interest rate environment and a sufficient gap between the GDP per capita and the government's interest rate mostly suggest keeping unfunded pension schemes. In markets with a narrowed gap, equilibriums can be established with a funded pension scheme with some unfunded box strengthening low earners pensions at retirement. One has to mention that the equilibrium with the funded scheme is mostly fragile, where a slight change in the macroeconomic variables, will cause even high earners to prefer the unfunded pension scheme. In addition, the preferences toward unfunded schemes are strengthened in times of unstable markets.

In addition to the results, supporting a mix pension design with a risk-sharing mechanism, we count another fiscal motive of the government to avoid extensive funded scheme, surprising, as it may be sound. Altiparmakov [8] shows that CEE countries revert to unfunded pension schemes to control all sorts of contributions and taxes of their citizens. In other words, in times of financial crisis, governments wish to raise chip money, and unfunded contribution is a fast way to do that.

7. CONCLUSION

The key feature of this research is the consideration of multiplayers in the field, as the pension system effects across generations and earning cohorts. By treating society as one single entity managing financial risks, we may lose the opportunities to disclose other interests and avoid potential equilibriums in the markets. Seeking stable pension markets is one of the top priorities of central planners, especially during the period of uncertainty in other markets due to the pandemic and global debt crisis.

While the preferences for low earners are clear toward the unfunded pension scheme, for high earners, it is most interesting to examine their preferences. Here, we consider the assumptions of mutual risk-sharing among earning cohorts, solving the inherent socio-economic anomaly in the funded scheme, which favors high earners at the expense of low earners [10, 11, 18].

The findings point that central planners must not rush for funded pension funds although societies are aging. The rush after funded pension schemes in aging markets must not be turned to way out of governments to consider multiplayers game and avoid other macro-economic parameters, such as debt level, debt price, and GDP per capita factors. Here, we mention the global trend of shifting to funded schemes even in non-aging markets, such as in Israel [27]. We find in this composition that the unfunded pension scheme should be considered as most efficient to all actors in a wide variety of macroeconomic conditions, especially when the interest rates are very low, as it is in this period.

In times of the pandemic, central planners have to minimize the possibilities of unstable pension markets and reversals. The period for itself increases the motive to find a sustainable equilibrium in the market. In addition, governments have to reconsider the frightened in the markets in these times. In our model, that comes to realize by the higher standard deviation of the market yield and higher risk aversion. Both realizations imply higher chances for equilibrium in the unfunded pension scheme. These results come despite the aging of societies.

REFERENCES

1. Clements B, Dybczak K, Gaspar V, Gupta S, Soto M. The fiscal consequences of shrinking and ageing populations. Ageing International. 2018;43:391-414. DOI: 10.1007/s12126-017-9306-6

2. Feldstein M. Structural reform of social security. Journal of Economic Perspectives. 2005;19(2):33-55. DOI: 10.1257/0895330054048731

3. Holzmann R, Hinz R. Old-Age Income Support in the 21st Century: An International Perspective on Pension Systems and Reform. Washington, DC: The World Bank; 2005. DOI: 10.1596/0-8213-6040-X

4. OECD. Pension at Glance 2020: OECD and G20 Indicators. Brussels: OECD Publishing; 2019. DOI: 10.1787/b6d3dcfc-en

5. Barr N, Diamond P. Reforming pensions: Principles, analytical errors and policy directions. International Social Security Review. 2009;62(2):5-29. DOI: 10.1111/j.1468-246X.2009.01327.x

6. Ebbinghaus B. Multi-pillarisation remodelled: The role of interest organizations in British and German pension reforms. Journal of European Public Policy. 2019;26(4):521-539. DOI: 10.1080/13501763.2019.1574875

7. Milev J. The pandemic crisis and the resulted risks for the fully funded pension funds in Central and Eastern Europe. Research Papers of UNWE. 2021;2(1):203-216

8. Altiparmakov N. Another look at causes and consequences of pension privatization reform reversals in Eastern Europe. Journal of European Social Policy. 2018;28(3):224-241. DOI: 10.1177/0958928717735053

9. Wolf I, Ocerin JMC. The transition to a multi-pillar pension system: The inherent socio-economic anomaly. *Journal of Financial Economic* Policy. 2021. DOI: 10.1108/JFEP-07-2020-0162

10. Wolf I, Del Rio LCL. Funded-capitalized pension designs and the demand for minimum pension guarantee. Public and Municipal Finance. 2021;10(1):12-24. DOI: 10.21511/pmf.10(1).2021.02

11. Wolf I, Del Rio LCL. Benefit adequacy in funded pension systems: Micro-simulation of the Israeli pension scheme. International Journal of Economics & Business Administration. 2021;9(2):143-164. DOI: 10.10.35808/ijeba/694

12. Feher C, Bidegain I. IMF Report. July 2020

13. Gruber J, Wise DA. Social Security and Retirement Around the World. Chicago: University of Chicago Press; 2008. DOI: 10.7208/9780226309996

14. Heneghan M, Orenstein MA. Organizing for impact: International organizations and global pension policy. Global Social Policy. 2019;19(1-2):65-86. DOI: 10.1177/1468018119834730

15. Wolf I. Political stress and the sustainability of funded pension schemes: Introduction of a financial theory. Journal of Risk and Financial Management. 2021;14(11):1-12. DOI: 10.3390/jrfm14110525

16. Ortiz I, Durán-Valverde F, Urban S, Wodsak V. Reversing Pension Privatizations: Rebuilding Public Pension Systems in Eastern Europe and Latin America. Geneva: International Labour Organization; 2018. DOI: 10.2139/ssrn.3275228

17. Cipriani G, Fioroni T. Social security and endogenous demographic change: Child support and retirement policies*. Journal of Pension Economics and Finance. 2021:1-19. DOI: 10.1017/S1474747220000402

18. Wolf I, Del Rio LCL. Pension reforms and risk sharing cycle: A theory and global experience. International Journal of Economics & Business Administration (IJEBA). 2021;9(1):225-242

19. Knell M. The optimal mix between funded and unfunded pension systems when people care about relative consumption. Economica. 2010;77(308):710-733. DOI: 10.1111/j.1468-0335.2009.00797.x

20. Ando A, Modigliani F. The "life cycle" hypothesis of saving: Aggregate implications and tests. The American Economic Review. 1963; 53(1): 55-84. Available from http://www.jstor.org/stable/1817129 [Retrieved: February 23, 2021]

21. Masten E, Thorgesen O. Designing social security—A portfolio choice approach. European Economic Review. 2004;48(4):883-904. DOI: 10.1016/j.euroecorev.2003.09.006

22. Aaron H. The social insurance paradox. Canadian Journal of Economics and Political Science. 1966;32(3):371-374. DOI: 10.2307/139995

23. Barrientos A. Social protection in Latin America: One region two systems. In: Cruz-Martínez G, editor. Welfare and Social Protection in Contemporary Latin America. London: Routledge; 2019

24. Bohn H. Should public retirement plans be fully funded? Journal of Pension Economics and Finance. 2011;10(2):195-219. DOI: 10.1017/S1474747211000096

25. Noy S. Healthy targets? World Bank projects and targeted health programmes and policies in Costa Rica, Argentina, and Peru, 1980–2005. Oxford Development Studies. 2018;46(2):164-183. DOI: 10.1080/13600818.2017.1346068

26. Guardiancich I, Guidi M. The political economy of pension reforms in Europe under financial stress. Socio-Economic Review. 2020:mwaa012. DOI: 10.1093/ser/mwaa012

27. Lurie L. Pension privatization in Israel. In: Paz-Fuchs A, Mandelkern R, Galnoor I, editors. The Privatization of Israel. New York: Palgrave Macmillan; 2018. DOI: 10.1057/978-1-137-58261-4_5

SECTION-9

INTERNATIONALIZATION AND ACCOUNTING QUALITY

09 Investigating the Viability of Applying a Lower Bound Risk Metric for Altman's z-Score

1. INTRODUCTION

This study investigates a perspective of using a lower bound risk metric on Altman's z-score variables to determine the lower limits for Altman's z-score.

The lower bound risk metric is intended to help in assessing a default risk during an economic distress or in situations of extreme volatility and calamity of business. Altman's model uses values for its variables from a past year's financial statements. Based on these values, a result of Altman's formula shows whether a company is in a distressed zone and whether a bankruptcy is expected in the next two years. In situations where financial results of a company are very volatile, Altman's formula may show a good result, but the result and a health of the company may degrade very rapidly because of a volatility inherent to the company. The volatility may be a result of several factors, including a bad management or a cyclicity of a business. In such instances, Altman's z-score alone is not the best option for depicting the riskiness of the business. Therefore, it needs another metric which considers the volatility in the variables and which can estimate the risk of having a potentially sharp drop in Altman's z-score value. The lack of a proper risk estimation in Altman's z-score model prompted this study to examine methods to construct the lower bound risk metric.

The risk metric is extensively based on the Value at Risk (VAR) methodology. The VaR is used to estimate a maximum loss of value over a certain period of time with a determined probability level. The VaR methodology was developed by J. P. Morgan during the 1980s and the 1990s to measure the riskiness of their assets required by the Basel I set of international banking regulations [1]. Since then, it has become the central theory in a risk management in banking, insurance and asset management. The stress testing is a complement to the VaR and it looks at the riskiest but yet plausible events. The use of a model to predict Altman's z-score variables in distress situations were not identified in the literature. Previous studies mainly suggest new models or other improvements to Altman's formula. Altman's z-score is giving a default risk figure based on the historical information. It does not try to predict extreme situations in which a firm's position may deteriorate much faster than the equation is able to predict based on the historical information.

The aim of this study is to use the VaR methodology for variables in Altman's z-score to analyse whether it is a helpful risk metric to describe the depth of variance and to add a factor of predictability. To do that, Altman's z-score results for the FTSE 250 companies during the crisis of 2008 are compared with the results produced by the new risk metric using the pre-crisis data for Altman's formula. The assumption is that Altman's variables in a modelled distress situation help to better understand the depth of insolvency risk a company possesses. The study uses London Stock Exchange index FTSE 250 companies to carry out the empirical research. The panel data from Capital IQ is used for the Monte Carlo simulation to model the base distribution for Altman's variables. The simulated values for the variables are used to form the new risk metric. It gives the lower bound values for Altman's z-scores, which inform the underlying volatility and the worst-case scenarios with defined confidence levels. To confirm its validity, the results from the risk metric and stress tests should be back- and forward tested. The analysis reveals the limitations in the study, but it also points out options for further improvement.

2. LITERATURE REVIEW AND RESEARCH HYPOTHESES

2.1 Bankruptcy Prediction Models

Bankruptcy prediction models can be classified into three general groups [2]: the statistical models [3, 4, 5, 6, 7, 8, 9], the Artificial Neural Network (ANN) models [10, 11, 12, 13] and the kernel based learning models [14, 15, 16].

The statistical methods have the longest application history and are the most common still today. There are many methods, models and their variations. Some of the prevalent methods are simple ratio analysis [5], univariate analysis [4], multivariate analysis [3], logit method [7, 9]. Soon after Beaver's research, Altman [3] used a multivariate discriminant analysis (MDA) and was able to get more accurate results and predict the failure over a longer time horizon. His model received wide acceptance and since then, the multivariate approach has been broadly used to develop bankruptcy models for different sectors, indexes, countries and so on. Even when the artificial intelligence and the computer learning methods achieve better results, the statistical models are fairly simple to understand and have continued to prove to be highly reliable.

2.2 Altman's Z-Score Bankruptcy Model

The aim of this research is not to be using the best model possible for the lower bound risk metric calculations, but rather to use the most common and widely used bankruptcy model for which it is appropriate to adapt. Taking it into account, the most commonly used model is Altman's z-score bankruptcy model [17].

He introduced five financial ratios with highest default prediction power: *working capital to total assets*(x_1), *retained earnings to total assets*(x_2), *earnings before interests and taxes* (EBIT) *to total assets*(x_3), *market value of equity to book value of total liabilities*(x_4), *sales to total assets*(x_5):

$$\text{Z Score} = 1.2x_1 + 1.4x_2 + 3.3x_3 + 0.6x_4 + 1.2x_5 \quad (1)$$

Altman [3] divided the formula's results into three categories. The firms which achieve a score above 2.99 are considered to be in a safe area and far from default; results in the range of 1.81–2.99 are considered to be in a grey zone and need attention; results below 1,81 are in a distress zone and firms have a risk to become insolvent.

Altman found his model to be accurate over 70% of times, predicting bankruptcy two years before a default, and 95% accurate one year before a default [3]. In 6% of times the model predicted a default for a survived company. The accuracy rate diminished increasingly after two years. Heine [18] investigated the accuracy of Altman's model over a period of 31 years from 1968 to 1999 and found that the model was still working fairly well. His findings showed over 80% accuracy in defaults one year before the actual event. Regardless of the results, Hillegeist et al. [19] argue that book value based models are by design limited in predicting defaults, as annual reports are prepared on a going-concern basis. There have been other numerous comparisons which find contradictory as well as supportive evidence for using book and financial ratios, for instance, the works of Balcaen and Ooghe [20], Appiah et al. [21], Mousavi et al. [22], Charalambakis [23], Agarwal and Taffler [24].

Commonly, the insolvency models use annual data, but the accuracy of book value models could be increased by using a quarterly data according to [25]. They did not find significant difference between the quality of quarterly and annual reports. The multivariate discriminant analysis conducted in their research provided more accurate and timely results using unaudited quarterly reports instead of just using annual reports.

2.3 Value at Risk

VaR has three main methods of calculation: historical, variance-covariance and Monte Carlo (MC) method [26]. Each of the methods has its own advantages and drawbacks. The historical method is easy to apply for a collected data and it does not need a distributional assumption. The historical simulation assumes that the future events can be described by past events and that recent past trend represents the near future fairly accurately [1]. Such assumption is better than no assumption, but the historical data may consist of events that are not relevant for the future and thus should be treated with care. The variance–covariance method is easy to compute and use to manage portfolio risk. On the other hand, the biggest deficiency for the variance–covariance method is the failure to capture fat tails in the distribution [27]. A normal distribution creates a bias to underestimate the true VaR. Monte Carlo (MC) method overcomes most of the mentioned deficiencies, but has some of its own. MC method is flexible and can be used for shorter and longer time periods, whereas it is considered to be the most accurate method of the three for longer time periods ([1], p. 270). Another advantage of MC is that it can be applied to non-normal distribution, which more accurately describes many of the practical applications [28]. The two main setbacks are the model risk and the time to compute MC simulations ([1], p. 270).

Breuer [29] stresses the setbacks that arise due to the assumptions used in calculating VaR. The first issue he raises is the assumption that the market conditions are static throughout the future. Such assumptions are correct if the future market characteristics are repeating itself and are similar to the present or historical values. It should also be noted that every risk prediction measure has to cope with this dilemma in some scale, it is not specific to VaR. The second major problem that Breuer mentions is the assumption of data following a normal multivariate distribution in many VaR models. This holds true only in some cases and in majority of situations produces an imprecise outcome. He demonstrates such a case with a very illustrative example about 1987 market crash. The crash had a fall in stock prices between 10 to 20 standard deviations. Considering that seven standard deviations fall in a normal multivariate distribution would happen on average one day in three billion years, the assumption of normality in this particular case seems exceptionally poor. Nonetheless, VaR is flexible enough to allow to use more distributions than just a normal distribution, although the prevalence is to use a normal distribution for its simplicity and ease of use. Apart from the previously mentioned setbacks, Krause [30] discusses the limitations in choosing a confidence level and a horizon. The longer the horizon the bigger the variance and the less reliable is the outcome. A selected confidence level also sets the quantile value, beyond which VaR does not describe the losses. To understand the most extreme scale of losses, there are supplementary methods such as the expected shortfall (ES), maximum loss or other stress tests to assist with this information [1]. However, the applicability of stress tests depends on the characteristics of the data, which may limit their suitability in certain analysis.

2.4 Stress Testing

Nearly all models try to predict the bankruptcy based on the trend in the business operations, finances and other accessible information. Not so much has been done to investigate hypothetical stress or worst-case scenarios that happen to every business during its lifecycle.

Stress testing is basically a complementary measure for VaR to capture the extreme losses in the tails. There is no one to tell the probability and depth of such extreme scenarios. An important constituent is the plausibility of such scenario. Although such scenarios are rare, they do happen, but the case should neither be too shallow nor almost impossible in terms of severity. The main difference between VaR and historical stress testing methods is the time period. VaR uses relatively short time periods, usually from a day up till one year, and some VaR models weigh recent time more heavily. Historical stress testing, to the contrary, uses periods of distant past and includes market crashes and periods of extreme volatility. Breuer [29] examines four types of common stress testing methods: historical, expected shortfall, maximum loss and Monte Carlo method. He finds that the choice of the methods depends on the aim and data, but acknowledges that the Monte Carlo method performed relatively better than other methods in many observed cases.

2.5 Predictive Power and Model Verification

A model risk always remains, but it can be minimized using back- and forward testing for a model validation. Back-testing compares the actual outcomes with the predicted estimate of VaR before the sample period [26]. Forward testing compares actual outcomes with an estimate after the sample period. If the losses exceed VaR estimate more than the set confidence level, the model is not accurate and needs modification [31]. Halilbegovic and Vehabovic [26] highlight that the values which exceed VaR should be equally distributed along the horizon and be independent. The first and the most referenced test for back-testing is Kupiec [32] "proportion of failures" coverage test. Banking industry is also using the "traffic lights" test published by the Basel Committee [33].

2.6 Research Hypotheses

The lower bound risk metric is expected to provide a lower limit for Altman's z-score within the selected confidence level. It provides a precautionary gauge and includes the measure for downside volatility. The supplementary information from risk metric gives a more informative decision-making tool and indicates the weaknesses of the subject firms on a more extensive scale. To test the hypotheses, Altman's z-score values of FTSE 250 firms during the selected 2008 recession period are compared with the calculated pre-crisis risk metric values. If the risk metric is reliable, there should not be more outlier firms than the confidence limit allows. It is determined whether the simulated pre-crises risk metric values are providing relevant and sufficient information besides the standard Altman's z-score values to be a practical risk measure. The research hypotheses are as follows:

H_0- The lower bound risk metric does not provide the lower limit for Altman's z-score within the selected confidence level.

H_1- The lower bound risk metric provides the lower limit for Altman's z-score within the selected confidence level.

3. METHODOLOGY

This study investigated a perspective of using the lower bound risk metric on Altman's z-score variables to determine the lower limit for the score. The core methodology used in this research is based on Value at Risk (VaR) and Altman's z-score bankruptcy model. VaR methodology has been widely adopted in measuring financial and market data figures and to report a business or market risk. Using the verified and tested solution on the same type of data and in a similar way, although in a different setting, assured the validity of the approach. The different setting represented the use of VaR approach on Altman's formula to calculate the lower bound risk metric.

The research was carried out on a sample of firms from FTSE 250 index. The index is consisting of similar midsize companies, whose values and operations tend to follow well the fluctuations in the economy. Therefore, the firms were good subjects to estimate the performance of a lower bound risk metric.

The data was retrieved from S&P Capital IQ [34] database; primarily from financial statements. Annual financial statements did not give many data points for correct volatility evaluation. To compensate the lack of data points, quarterly financial reports were used instead of the annual reports. Consequently, it also provided the basis for a risk horizon to be one quarter ([28], p. 216; [1], p. 311). The risk horizon gave the results to which the risk metric was compared. Quarterly reports provided more data to analyse and this became important considering the limited information available.

The study by Nallareddy et al. [35] mentioned that the Financial Conduct Authority (FCA) in the UK did not require quarterly reporting before 2007. They pointed out that it was mandatory between 2007 and 2014, after which it was overruled by the EU Transparency Directive in 2013. It ruled FCA to stop requiring mandatory quarterly reporting from 2014. Relatively few FTSE 250 companies reported quarterly results voluntarily and on a consistent basis before millennia. However, it became more common thereafter, regardless of legal requirements. From year 2001 onwards, there was enough data for the study, and therefore it was a suitable starting point for the data collection. The data collection period had to be relatively long to provide a sufficient amount of data for the time series analysis. It was also preferable to have the risk horizon during a period of high volatility to examine whether the risk metric model actually worked, or it needed to be modified before further testing. The tipping point of financial crisis was in 2008, which made it a suitable period for the risk horizon. Hence, the period for collecting data to calculate the risk metric was from [2001–2007] and the risk horizon was the first quarter of 2008. The firms listed during that time period are not the same as the firms listed in FTSE 250 in July 2017, which were the firms used in this study. There have been changes in the index, when comparing the companies listed during the seven-year period to July 2017. There are firms, which left the stock market, went bankrupt or were simply excluded from the FTSE 250 list. Nonetheless, in order to allow future data analysis of the same firms in later periods than 2008, the data was collected from firms that were listed in FTSE 250 from 1st of January 2001 until 1st of July 2017. This decision drew some limitations as it excluded firms that could have potentially offered a valuable information. On the other hand, the selected time period and firms provided an opportunity for forward testing and some limited scale back-testing for further studies.

Seven years of quarterly data provided 28 data points per firm. Altman's z-score was not used for finance firms as this sector is known to be particularly leveraged, regulated and consists of many disguised risks. Therefore, all finance firms were excluded from the list of FTSE 250 for a data analysis purposes, which left 176 firms. The z-score was calculated for all 28 quarters for the 176 firms. Many did not report quarterly results or did it only for short periods and inconsistently, which was not enough for calculating acceptable standard deviation from the variables. Also, many of the observed firms were not listed during the examined period and thus, did not have the data. Therefore, only firms that had enough data to calculate Altman's z-score for minimum 20 quarters, were included and the rest were excluded. Twenty quarters was an arbitrary figure that provided just enough data points to make meaningful analysis. The limitation of minimum 20 quarters of data left 78 firms with enough quarterly data to conduct the research. Outliers were identified and revealed in a box plots diagram at the end phase of the data analysis. It illustrated well the serious deviations in the data, which could be further investigated to find the root causes of such irregularities.

The examined variables of Altman's z-score were total assets, total liabilities, working capital and retained earnings from the statement of financial position; sales and EBIT from the income statement; market value of equity was received from market data. To calculate the bankruptcy z-score, the quarterly data, which was derived from income statement, had to be annualized. To do that, the results from previous three quarters for sales and EBIT were combined. Calculations of the average value and standard deviation of each of Altman's variables for each firm gave the basic data to derive the risk metric using Monte Carlo simulation.

The first assumption about Monte Carlo simulation was that the base distribution is a suitable proxy for the nature of the data [36]. Monte Carlo simulation was the most flexible of previously reviewed methods and it could assume any distribution as its base distribution [27]. A typical simplifying assumption is that the variable is independent and identically distributed (i.i.d.) and that it follows a normal distribution. Such assumptions are often valid, especially in the case of big sample sizes [36]. However, testing a data for normality is a prerequisite for a more accurate model. Samples of all seven variables were plotted on graphs using histograms and Anderson-Darling normality test. Illustrations of both graphs depicting the distribution of standardized total assets can be found in Appendix A. Although graphical interpretation is subjective, it allows to draw fast and simple conclusions. A sample of histograms and Anderson-Darling tests suggested that the variables did not fulfil the requirements for normality and did not follow a normal distribution. A normality requirement was fixed simply by Monte Carlo simulation, where the generated iterations created a big enough sample size to fulfil the normality requirement. Histograms suggested that the distributions were not normal, but more likely followed a fat-tailed leptokurtic t-distributions. Using a multivariate Student t-distribution for the model, all the marginal distributions had to follow the same degrees of freedom parameter. For the analysis in this research both distributions were used. Firstly, it was described the process of getting risk metrics using normal distribution and secondly, using the Student t-distribution as there were only slight differences in implementing a t-distribution compared to a normal distribution.

It was assumed that the variables follow a stochastic process referred to as Geometric Brownian Motion ([1], p. 309). It was stochastic in a sense that changes in the variance were random and did not depend on a past information [37]. The equation for Monte Carlo simulation with Geometric Brownian Motion is

$$x = \mu + \sigma z \tag{2}$$

Where x is the value of the variable, μ is the expected value of the variable, σ is the standard deviation, and z is the standard score expressed as

$$z = \frac{x - \mu}{\sigma} \tag{3}$$

To make the variance change randomly, Monte Carlo simulation method with a designed random number generator was used. Random numbers were generated repeatedly a large number of times for each of the seven variables. This created a typical Monte Carlo simulation, where there were a number of variables that could be easily tested in a simulation, but which may have lacked the data or resources to test experimentally. Simulations are simple to create using random numbers.

There are two random number generating techniques. The non-deterministic, in which case each time the random number is generated, it exhibits a different output number. The deterministic technique, which creates pseudo random numbers that keep their output numbers fixed. It is fixed by using a seed number. The latter makes analysis easier by enabling to run the simulations repeatedly and allows to modify and recreate iterations.

For the simulation, a Lehmer random number generator (RNG) with different seed for each variable was used to generate the random integers. Lehmer RNG belongs to a group of linear congruential generators. It generated a uniformly distributed random numbers k between 0 and 1. The equation for Lehmer RNG is

$$k_i = (ak_i) \bmod m \tag{4}$$

a≥0 is the constant multiplier.

m is the modulo m.

k_i is the random integer.

Lehmer RNG generated pseudo random numbers in the range of [0,a−1]0−1, where aa was the Mersenne prime. Dividing that range with Mersenne prime gave a uniformly distributed probability values ε_i in the range of [01.[0,1.

$$\varepsilon_i = \frac{k_i}{a} \tag{5}$$

ε_i is the pseudo random number in the range of [01.[0,1.

k_i is the generated pseudo random integer in the range of [0,a1−0.[1−.

a is the Mersenne prime

The generated probability values were fed into the inverse base-distribution selected for Monte Carlo simulation [27]. The inverse function generated the statistical standard score values. Hence, the formula (III.1) could also be written in a form

$$x = \mu + \sigma\Phi^{-1}(\alpha) \tag{6}$$

Monte Carlo simulation was used to create 15,000 iterations of described standard score values for each of the seven Altman's z-score variables. The independent iterations of standard scores had to be adjusted for the correlation between Altman's variables. The complexity of calculations in multivariate analysis for correlation adjustments required the use of matrices [37]. Several matrix calculations were performed for each Altman's variable and this was done for each firm under observation. The matrices performed were correlation matrix, variance matrix, variance-correlation matrix, covariance matrix, Cholesky decomposition matrix and the result matrix [37]. The result matrix provided the product of correlated standard scores and the standard deviation of each variable. The results showed how much the expected mean of each variable can deviate. Therefore, when the expected mean was added to each of the calculated results, it provided variable values that followed the chosen base distribution for Monte Carlo simulation. Finally, the produced values were inserted to Altman's formula to produce 15,000 Altman's z-scores for each of the observed firm. The selected confidence level determined the lower quantile value, which became the lower bound risk metric for Altman's z-score

$$Z < Z_h = Z_{h\alpha} \tag{7}$$

where ZZ is the simulated iterations, ZhZh is Altman's z score for risk horizon h. The lower bound risk metric for Altman's z-score is noted as ZhαZhα. It marks the α quantile of the simulated iterations for risk horizon h.

4. DATA AND ANALYSIS

This study examines how the methods and formulas brought out in Methodology are applied to retrieved data. Because a simulation generates a large amount of data, it is not presentable in such a scale. Instead, specific examples are presented to provide comprehension on the subject matter.

4.1 Random Number Generator

The Lehmer random number generator is used to generate pseudo random numbers k_i with chosen seed numbers

$$k_i = (ak_0) \bmod m \tag{8}$$

For instance, the Lehmer RNG with parameters $a=2^{31}-1$, $m=7^5$, $k_0=231$ and 15,000 iterations generate randomly distributed numbers plotted on Figure

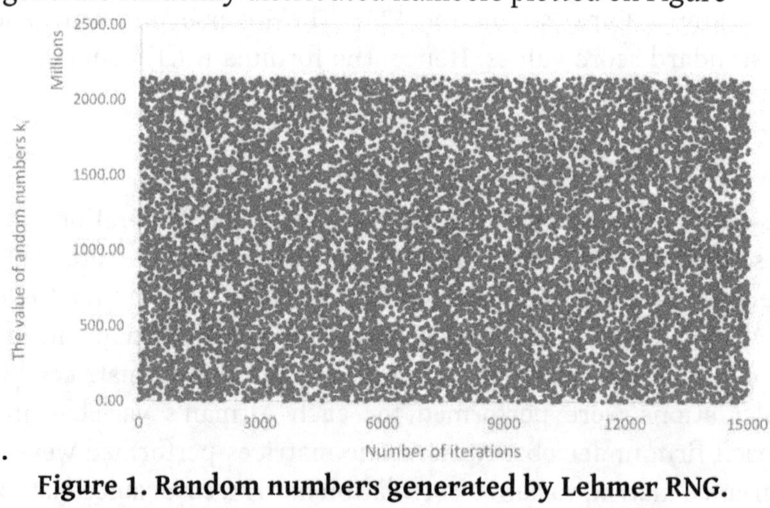

Figure 1. Random numbers generated by Lehmer RNG.

Park and Miller, in 1988, suggested specific parameters for $a=2^{31}-1$ (Mersenne prime) and $m=7^5$. The random integer requires an initial value k_0. It is typically called a seed value. The seed value is used to run the initial random number. To randomize variance, each of the seven Altman's variables need a seed number to run its own 15,000 iterations. Thus, each variable is assigned a seed number. The seed number does not have to be random, but for Lehmer RNG, the seed needs to be a coprime to the modulus m. A coprime is such a number that the only number which divides the coprime and the modulus is 1. The seven variables are assigned the coprime seeds as follows: total assets 231, total liabilities 331, working capital 431, retained earnings 531, sales 631, EBIT 731 and market value of equity is assigned a seed value of 831. When all the parameters are applied to the above mentioned random number generator, it generates pseudo random numbers in the range of [0, a-1]-1, where a is the Mersenne prime.

4.2 Probability distributions

In order to derive a probability function, the generated random numbers within the range of [0,a−1]0−1 need to be divided by the Mersenne prime. The division gives pseudo random numbers ε_i in the range of [01.[0,1.

$$\varepsilon_i = \frac{k_i}{a} \tag{9}$$

The formula creates numbers, which follow a uniform distribution. For instance, the uniform distribution for total assets with a seed 231 is depicted in Figure 2.

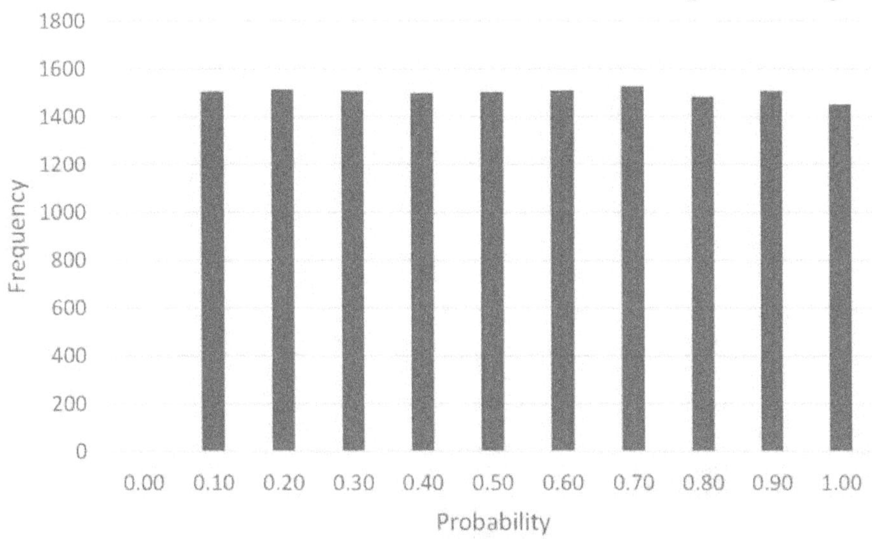

Figure 2. Uniform probability distribution.

The generated pseudo random numbers are uniformly distributed and can be fed into the inverse standard normal cumulative distribution $\Phi^{-1}(\alpha)$ to provide standard score statistic z. Each outcome of the cumulative distribution gives a standard score, which is the corresponding quantile to any given value of α. $\Phi^{-1}(\alpha)$ Φ^{-1}, which produces the standard score, shows how common are samples that are less than or equal to this value. As a reminder, the standard score statistic and Altman's z-score are not the same and should not be confused. Figures 3 and 4 depict the cumulative standard normal distribution function and the standard normal probability density function respectively.

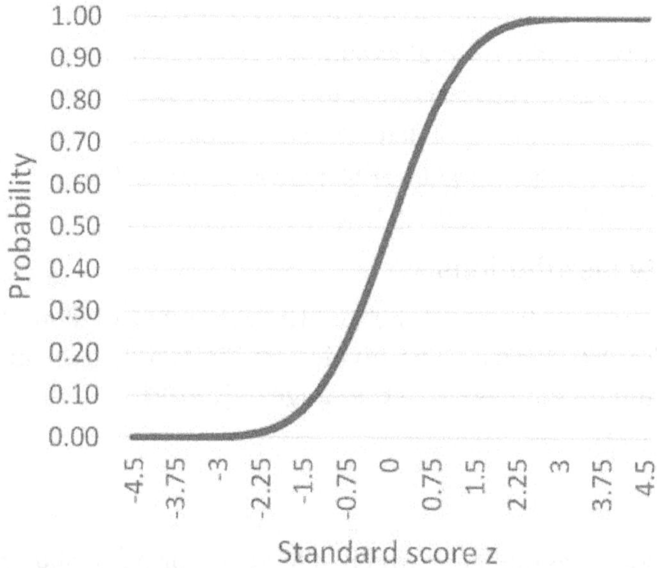

Figure 3. Cumulative standard normal distribution function (CDF).

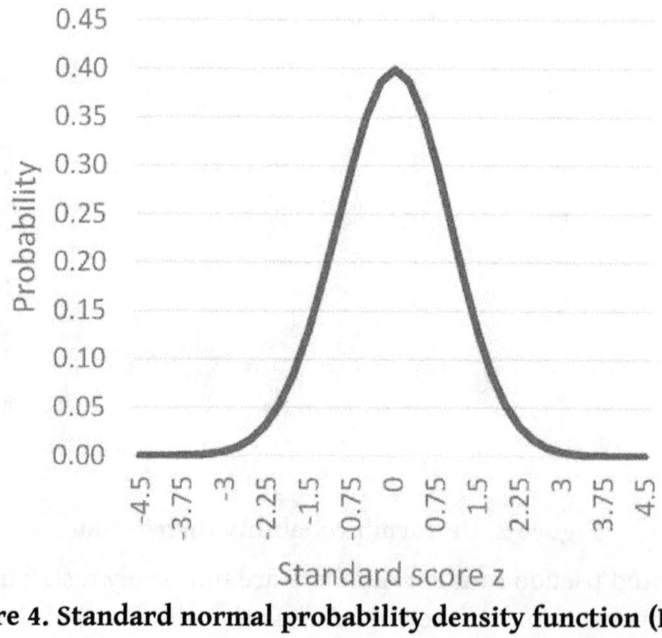

Figure 4. Standard normal probability density function (PDF).

Setting z=Φ−1(α), then

$$x = \mu + \sigma\Phi^{-1}(\alpha) \quad (10)$$

When α is replicated 15,000 times, x takes values along a normal distribution. Depending on the chosen significance level α, the α quantile is the value of x below which the x is not expected to go with a confidence level of -1α For instance, Workspace Group PLC value of assets x can be described by a function x=619+229* $\Phi^{-1}(\alpha)$. Replicating α randomly by 15,000 times and taking a lower %5 quantile of the distribution gives an asset value 259 M. Therefore, in theory, it means that with %95 confidence, the value of assets is not expected to go below 259 M.

The function can be written in another way

$$x = \sigma\Phi^{-1}(\alpha) - \mu \quad (11)$$

in which case, the x now represents a risk metric similar to Value at Risk and is already presented in absolute terms.

It is possible to plug the generated probability values directly to derive the values for each variable. But doing so, a correlation between variables is totally ignored. The correlation has an impact on the deviation, and it characterizes how each deviation is correlated to the deviations in other variables. Correlation is simple to calculate when using only two variables. In this situation, it is seven variables, which requires a matrix based methodology. The process of producing a correlation between the variables can be divided into six separate calculation steps, which make it easier to understand.

5. CORRELATION MATRICES FOR SIMULATED VARIABLES

The first step is to create a correlation matrix. Each individual correlation between variables is entered into the matrix table. The diagonal is always 1, because the correlation of the variable with itself is 1. Normally the upper area from the diagonal is left empty, but in this case, it is filled for computational reasons. The covariance between each variable and the correlation coefficient are calculated. An example of resulting matrix for Workplace Group PLC is illustrated in Table 1.

Table 1. Correlation matrix.

Correlation matrix	Total assets	Total liabilities	Working capital	Retained earnings	Total revenue	EBIT	Market capital
Assets	1.00	0.95	-0.56	0.91	0.97	0.95	0.91
Liabilities	0.95	1.00	-0.32	0.81	0.94	0.96	0.94
Working	-0.56	-0.32	1.00	-0.72	-0.48	-0.37	-0.33
Retained	0.91	0.81	-0.72	1.00	0.82	0.78	0.82
Total	0.97	0.94	-0.48	0.82	1.00	0.99	0.92

Correlation matrix	Total assets	Total liabilities	Working capital	Retained earnings	Total revenue	EBIT	Market capital
EBIT	0.95	0.96	-0.37	0.78	0.99	1.00	0.94
Market	0.91	0.94	-0.33	0.82	0.92	0.94	1.00

$$\sigma_{x,y} = \frac{\sum_{i=1}^{N}(x_i - \bar{x})(y_i - \bar{y})}{(n-1)} \quad (12)$$

$$\rho_{x,y} = \frac{\sigma_{x,y}}{\sigma_x \sigma_y} \quad (13)$$

The second step is to create a variance matrix as shown in Table 2. It is achieved by simply adding the standard deviations of each variable diagonally.

Table 2. Variance matrix.

Variance matrix	Total assets	Total liabilities	Working capital	Retained earnings	Total revenue	EBIT	Market capital
Assets	228.54	0.00	0.00	0.00	0.00	0.00	0.00
Liabilities	0.00	136.98	0.00	0.00	0.00	0.00	0.00
Working	0.00	0.00	11.96	0.00	0.00	0.00	0.00
Retained	0.00	0.00	0.00	164.03	0.00	0.00	0.00
Total	0.00	0.00	0.00	0.00	10.20	0.00	0.00
EBIT	0.00	0.00	0.00	0.00	0.00	6.11	0.00
Market	0.00	0.00	0.00	0.00	0.00	0.00	213.07

The third step is to produce a variance-correlation matrix. It is the product of the correlation and variance matrices and it can be calculated only when the matrix is positive definite. The equation to multiply the above matrices is illustrated and the calculated matrix is presented in Table 3.

Table 3. Variance-correlation matrix.

Variance - correlation matrix	Total assets	Total liabilities	Working capital	Retained earnings	Total revenue	EBIT	Market capital
Assets	228.54	217.58	-128.92	207.96	221.92	216.53	207.35
Liabilities	130.41	136.98	-44.11	110.85	128.61	131.13	128.68
Working	-6.74	-3.85	11.96	-8.67	-5.69	-4.47	-3.90
Retained	149.26	132.74	-118.88	164.03	134.78	127.42	134.29
Total	9.90	9.57	-4.86	8.38	10.20	10.06	9.34
EBIT	5.79	5.85	-2.29	4.75	6.03	6.11	5.74
Market	193.32	200.16	-69.42	174.44	195.22	200.05	213.07

$$\sum = \begin{pmatrix} \rho_{1,1} & \rho_{1,2} & \cdots & \rho_{1,d} \\ \rho_{2,1} & \rho_{2,2} & \cdots & \rho_{2,d} \\ \vdots & \vdots & \ddots & \vdots \\ \rho_{d,1} & \rho_{d,2} & \cdots & \rho_{d,d} \end{pmatrix} \begin{pmatrix} \sigma_{1,1} & & & \\ & \sigma_{2,2} & & \\ & & \ddots & \\ & & & \sigma_{d,d} \end{pmatrix} \tag{14}$$

The fourth step is to produce variance–covariance matrix. It is the product of the variance-correlation matrix and the variance matrix and the results are presented in Table 4.

Table 4. Variance–covariance matrix.

Variance - covariance matrix	Total assets	Total liabilities	Working capital	Retained earnings	Total revenue	EBIT	Market capital
Assets	52229.12	29804.56	-1541.41	34110.54	2263.11	1323.70	44180.06
Liabilities	29804.56	18764.59	-527.43	18182.95	1311.60	801.65	27418.56
Working	-1541.41	-527.43	142.96	-1421.38	-58.06	-27.33	-829.99
Retained	34110.54	18182.95	-1421.38	26904.86	1374.51	778.99	28613.43
Total	2263.11	1311.60	-58.06	1374.51	104.00	61.53	1990.79
EBIT	1323.70	801.65	-27.33	778.99	61.53	37.37	1222.98
Market	44180.06	27418.56	-829.99	28613.43	1990.79	1222.98	45398.90

The fifth step is to produce a Cholesky decomposition [38]. It is produced by taking a square root of variance–covariance matrix as illustrated in Table 5 [39].

Table 5. Cholesky decomposition matrix.

Cholesky decomposition matrix	Total assets	Total liabilities	Working capital	Retained earnings	Total revenue	EBIT	Market capital
Assets	228.54	0.00	0.00	0.00	0.00	0.00	0.00
Liabilities	130.41	41.91	0.00	0.00	0.00	0.00	0.00
Working	-6.74	8.40	5.18	0.00	0.00	0.00	0.00
Retained	149.26	-30.59	-30.41	52.60	0.00	0.00	0.00
Total	9.90	0.48	0.91	-1.16	1.88	0.00	0.00
EBIT	5.79	1.10	0.47	-0.71	1.27	0.52	0.00
Market	193.32	52.66	6.05	29.56	42.64	17.61	47.07

The methodology of step one to step five is similar to producing a correlated bivariate distribution from two samples of uncorrelated normal variables [40]. It is more straightforward and makes the calculations of above matrices easily understandable. For instance, the first sample of uncorrelated variable is produced as described above by feeding a uniformly distributed random number into an inverse standard normal cumulative distribution Φ−1(α) to arrive at standard score statistic z_i. When applying the standard score into an equation for the first variable, it produces as follows

$$x_1 = \mu_1 + \sigma_1 z_1 \tag{15}$$

To make the second sample of uncorrelated variable to correlate with the first one, the variables need to be combined. The combining factor is the correlation between both z-scores, Z_1 and Z_2 [40]. The resulting for the second variable is presented below

$$x_2 = \mu_2 + \sigma_2\left(z_1\rho + z_2\sqrt{1-\rho^2}\right) \tag{16}$$

Instead of two variables, the five step calculations ending with Cholesky decomposition produces a correlation between seven variables.

Finally, the sixth step produces the results for each variable by summing the product of Cholesky matrix and the matrix of standard score iterations to the mean of each variable. The results for Workspace Group PLC are displayed in Table 6.

Table 6. Result matrix.

Iterations	Total assets	Total liabilities	Working capital	Retained earnings	Total revenue	EBIT	Market capital	Altman z-score
1	-241.36	-307.70	-45.49	-379.30	4.32	-2.34	-970.90	-4.37
2	563.74	301.84	-19.78	137.20	35.47	19.17	97.82	0.67
3	642.62	295.42	-32.76	145.85	51.18	28.71	393.65	1.28
4	978.49	567.92	-26.31	344.62	64.14	37.60	656.50	1.35
5	301.96	134.73	-16.47	-2.07	31.73	17.81	107.79	0.70
...	...	...	...	...	...	...	...	...
15,000	537.72	250.66	-37.58	223.63	42.57	24.29	303.46	1.45

Altman's z-score value in the table is calculated simply by using Altman's bankruptcy formula and the calculated variables in the row. Given the 15,000 iterations, the 5% and 1% quantile are the smallest 749th and 149th values respectively. In the example about Workplace Group PLC, Altman's z-score 5% and 1% quantile values are -0.23 and -6.86 respectively.

As stated earlier, the variables are following a fat-tailed distribution that is similar to a leptokurtic t-distribution. Figure 5 is illustrating the comparison of a leptokurtic and a standard normal distribution that are created by using the Lehmer random number generator and seed 231. The entire process for a t-distribution is very similar to that of a normal distribution which was described above. The only difference is that the standard z-score is replaced with t, which is the statistic for t-distribution. To arrive at standardized Student t values, the independent standard Student t simulations are multiplied by $\sqrt{\nu^{-1}(\nu-2)}$, where ν where v is the degree of freedom ([28], p. 228).

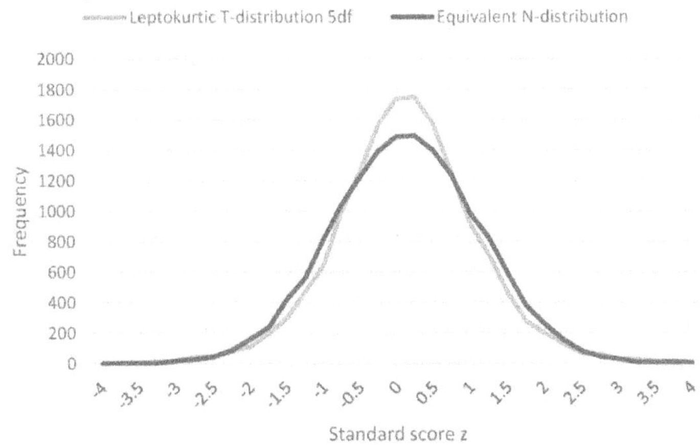

Figure 5. Comparison of leptokurtic and standard normal distribution.

There are several ways to estimate degrees of freedom. Suggested methods for multivariate Student t-test are the *maximum likelihood estimation* and *method of moments* [41]. Both methods are estimating the parameters of the statistical model. For this analysis, the degrees of freedom are estimated approximately. Considering that the unknown parameters are the seven observations and the two known parameters are the mean and variance, the difference of it is the five unknown parameters, which are also the five degrees of freedom.

6. RESULTS

Before presenting the calculated risk metric values, it is good to understand how many of the 78 firms were already in distressed zone in terms of Altman's z-score limits. The distressed zone for manufacturing firms was defined by Altman as a score lower than 1.81. This study was based on the standard formula of Altman's z-score and it was used for all the companies despite their primary industry classification. The industry classifications for the 78 firms are displayed in Table 7.

Table 7. Industry classifications.

Industry Classifications	Frequency
Consumer Discretionary (Primary)	18
Consumer Staples (Primary)	6
Energy (Primary)	4
Healthcare (Primary)	3
Industrials (Primary)	25
Information Technology (Primary)	5

Industry Classifications	Frequency
Materials (Primary)	4
Real Estate (Primary)	11
Utilities (Primary)	2
Total	78

All energy, industrials and materials companies were considered to be manufacturing companies and the rest in the list were non-manufacturing. A similar approach has been applied by many researchers and organizations, including the research by Miller [17] and the reports by market intelligence provider S&P Capital IQ. Table 8 provides an overview of distressed firms in each four-quarter period.

Table 8. Distressed firms.

	Manufacturing	Non-manufacturing	Total
0 quarters	20	24	44
4 quarters	6	2	8
8 quarters	2	0	2
12 quarters	2	3	5
16 quarters	1	3	4
20 quarters	1	4	5
24 quarters	1	3	4
28 quarters	0	6	6
Total	33	45	78

Around 33% of the 78 companies experienced the distressed period for longer than one year according to Altman bankruptcy model. It is also known that the type two error, which classifies firm as bankrupt when it does not go bankrupt, is around 15–20%. In that respect, the 33% figure is too high. The reason could be that the standard Altman's z-score is not that accurate for non-manufacturing firms, which had 42% of firms in distressed zone. Whereas the number of distressed firms for manufacturing industry was 19%. Anyhow, this could be investigated further.

Returning to calculated Altman's z-score limits. In Table 9, both, the 95% and 99% confidence level limits from the normal and t-distribution are used to compare them with the actual first quarter results of 2008. In addition, the two calculated Monte Carlo (MC) limit values are compared with 95% and 99% confidence level limits, which were calculated from the actual quarterly Altman's z-scores from [2001–2007]. Table 9 provides a good comparison of the effectiveness of the calculated MC limit values. From 78 firms, only 64 of them reported first quarter results in 2008. The outliers section on the left hand of Table 9 shows how many of the 64 firms crossed the applied confidence level limits. The failure rate section on the right hand of Table 9 presents the confidence level limit differences between the MC limit values and the limit values from the seven years of quarterly results. Therefore, the right-hand section considers all of the 78 firms not only 64.

Table 9. Outliers and failure rate.

Confidence level	outliers		Pass 95% N-dist	Fail 95% N-dist	Failure rate
95% N-dist.	3	95% N-dist. MC	50	28	0.36
95% N-dist. MC	3	95% t-dist. MC	49	29	0.37
95% t-dist. MC	3				
99% N-dist.	1		Pass 99% N-dist	Fail 99% N-dist	Failure rate
99% N-dist. MC	0	99% N-dist. MC	56	22	0.28
99% t-dist. MC	0	99% t-dist. MC	61	17	0.22

Three companies are determined as outliers, which remains in 95% confidence level as 3 out of 64 is less than 5%. Therefore, the results show, that both distributions are giving valid results for the first quarter of 2008. Moreover, the calculated MC limits perform at least as well as the 95% level limit figures from actual quarterly results. Nevertheless, it does not mean that the model is valid. To test validity, the model needs to be back- and forward tested. Testing the validity is discussed afterwards.

Analyzing the number of firms ending up in the distressed zone using the confidence limits and above-mentioned distributions, gives a good estimate of how badly firms may do in terms of Altman's z-score.

Table 10 shows the firms during the period [2007–2001] that have Altman's z-score less than 1.81. For calculated %95 and %99 confidence limit, the firms having score less than 1.81 range from 17 to 28 firms. There is a great difference between the %95 and %99 limit for manufacturing firms. Almost %60 more firms fall into distressed zone compared to %95 confidence level. For non-manufacturing firms, such difference is smaller. Again, the discrepancy is likely to come from the standard Altman's formula used for non-manufacturing firms. The comparison also unveils that the results for the normal and t-distribution are almost the same for each confidence level. It is known from the properties of the two distributions that the difference between them is not big for the %95 confidence level, but when the confidence level is getting bigger, the difference is expected to widen considerably. For the period and firms investigated, the results do not confirm it, which may imply that the variables were nevertheless following a distribution fairly similar to a normal distribution. However, definite conclusions can only be drawn when the model has been back- and forward tested.

Table 10. Confidence limits.

	Manufacturing out of 33	Non-manufacturing out of 45	Total out of 78
95% N-dist. MC	17	13	30
95% Student t-dist. MC	17	13	30
99% N-dist. MC	26	16	42
99% Student t-dist. MC	28	18	46

All the results that the previous tables are based on can be found in Appendix B. To make these results easily accessible in one set, the outcomes are represented on a box plot diagram as seen in Figure 6. The *x* on the diagram represents the mean and the line within the box represents the median value, which is also the second quartile or 50th percentile. The lower end of the box is the first quadrant and the higher end of the box is the third quadrant.

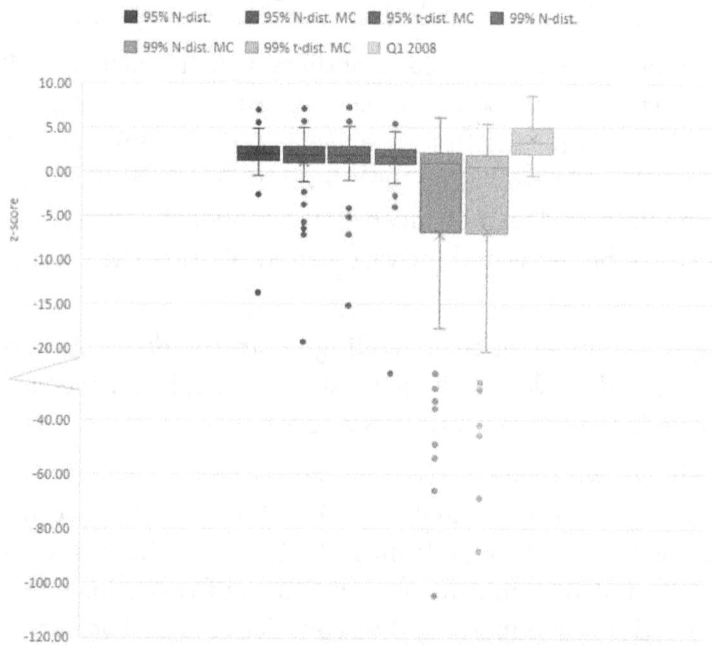

Figure 6. Box plots of Altman's z-score results.

The box plots reveal how the statistical 95% and 99% confidence limit results are greatly more constrained than the calculated MC results. Especially it can be said for 99% confidence limit, when compared to MC 99% normal or 99% t-distribution box plots. The box plots also illustrate that the results of the 95% limit are closer to each other compared to the 99% limit, where the differences in the results are wider. The two 99% Monte Carlo box plots of the normal and t-distribution display that the t-distribution confidence limits have a somewhat wider and deeper negative range. Box plots also reveal that the means are close to the first quartile boundary, except the first quarter results of 2008, which has a mean higher than the median. It is explainable by the fact that the top quartile has more variation than the lower quartile, resulting in further higher values than lower values relative to the median value.

The T-shaped projections are the whisker lines that represent the highest *local maximum* and the lowest *local minimum*. All values outside the local maximum or minimum are outliers and marked by dots. The outliers are calculated by using John W. Tukey convention. It determines outliers as data points, which are further than 1.5 times the interquartile range from either end of the box [42]. The interquartile range is the length of the box, from quartile 1 to quartile 3. Tukey determined the length of the whiskers so that it would not be either too exclusive nor too inclusive and established that 1.5 times the interquartile range is a good compromise [42].

The diagram unveils also risks posed by the first four box plots compared to the Q1 2008 box plot. If the following quarters were extremely bad, the results of recent quarters may not have had enough impact for the trailing seven years of data to estimate the confidence limits correctly. Therefore, it is risky to rely on any other confidence limit than the 99% limit of Monte Carlo normal or t-distribution. The range of the two latter confidence limits is more appropriate considering the vulnerability of Altman's z-score values to potential sharp falls. On the other hand, there are trade-offs because the values of some z-scores tend to go extremely negative and may not appropriately express the economic limits of actual situations. Nevertheless, the deep negative values should be a good indication of how bad the situation can go with a specific firm.

The diagram displays how the lower bound risk metric provides a metric to look beyond Altman's z-score values and determine the real risk metric of bankruptcy the firm may possess. The range of values is much wider and the values have fluctuated considerably more when comparing the 99% confidence level results to the original first quarter results for 2008. An example of an individual firm brings more clarity as it is difficult to interpret the group result on a diagram to individual firms. The data for the following example was taken from the results in Appendix B. For instance, the IMI plc had the first quarter Altman's z-score result of 2008 as 3.21 and the 95% and 99% t-distribution confidence limit scores as 2.33 and 2.05 respectively. HomeServe plc had a little higher bankruptcy score for 2008, it was 3.95, but the 95% and 99% t-distribution confidence limit scores were far worse, 0.76 and −1.24 respectively. Although, it may seem that HomeServe plc had better bankruptcy score for 2008 and was better protected from insolvency, the lower bound risk metric indicated the opposite. It shows how the lower bound risk metric adds another necessary risk measure to Altman's z-score to interpret and consider the inherent risk in the results.

The diagram shows inconsistencies in the data of at least with some of the outlier firms. Whether there were mistakes in quarterly reports or the mistakes lay somewhere else, either way the data in these few cases do not appear to be trustworthy. In other instances, there appeared to be no apparent reason in the big deviations, when inspecting the variables and data used. In such situations, it is important to look at the financial statements and other fundamental values of the interested outlier firms to determine the source of inconsistencies.

7. DISCUSSION

This study did not identify any previous research that would have specifically tried to expand Altman's study by using confidence limits for Altman's z-score values. Considering that the limits are providing a very valuable information for a risk evaluation and prevention, this study deemed it necessary to fulfil this research gap. The study produced a lower bound risk metric for Altman's z-score and identified it to be a good gauge for the lower limit measure using a 99% confidence level. It provided satisfactory results for the tested period and for the sample used, but the model needs a more rigorous testing to modify and verify its performance.

7.1 Evaluation

In a bankruptcy literature, a research has tried to establish the best model for a bankruptcy prediction by using ever more complicated methods such as the highly computerized Artificial Neural Networking or kernel based learning models. Instead, this research examined the most popular bankruptcy model, Altman's z-score, in relation to the worst-case scenario. It examined the variability and correlation between variables with an aim to produce a simulation that repetitively calculates Altman's z-scores from which it is possible to find the worst-case scenario with a selected confidence level. Not only is this approach applicable for Altman's z-score model, but this methodology can be used similarly for almost any other bankruptcy model. The Value at Risk methodology, used throughout this study, is very flexible and applicable in a variety of situations.

The biggest drawbacks were not related to the methodological approach, but rather to the availability of data and resources to conduct the study in the most appropriate way possible. Some of the limitations faced during this study were purely related to the lack of resources. Having had necessary resources would have helped to improve and modify the system, resulting in less limitations and better outcomes. It would have given more credibility for the study. Some limitations, such as the lack of data, was practically impossible to overcome. Although simulations help in situations of limited data, the simulations are as good as the quality of data. One option to overcome some of the data related issues, would be to choose a model that uses a data, which has a long historical record and which future outcomes are more predictable. Even then, the model depends on the selected sample size. The size and industry of companies, the culture and regulations of different countries. Has an impact on variables that would be difficult to measure with one standard model. Hence, the model developed in this study is most appropriate to use on FTSE250 index firms or on firms that have similar characteristics. As it was pointed out in the analysis of data, the model is best to use on manufacturing firms as the results may not describe as accurately the riskiness of service firms. For service firms, it could have been more accurate to use the modified z-score model specifically developed for non-manufacturing firms. Its distressed region is also defined as having z-score results of less than 1.1. This would have changed the obtained results, although not considerably.

The positive side of this model is that it is observing a range and it gives the lower quantile figure based on a confidence level. It is much more difficult to overestimate this figure compared to the standard Altman's z-score. The lower bound risk metric depends on the volatility of variables. Therefore, the firms, whose results from the risk metric are above the distressed zone limit of 1.81 can be considered as relatively safe option in terms of insolvency during times of economic distress. The results from the example introduced in finding display that HomeServe plc was more exposed to the negative economic and adverse business situations. It had a higher risk of insolvency if such situations would have had become true and had continued for an extended period. As can be seen from that example, Altman's z-score does not give a full and accurate overview. Therefore, the lower bound risk metric developed in this research, provides a valuable supplementary information for a well-informed decision making.

The outcomes in Table 9 showed that there were no material differences between the results from a normal and a t-distribution used in Monte Carlo simulation. It indicates that the distribution does not have the expected fat tails, but it is somewhat closer to a normal distribution. For instance, it could also be a t-distribution with a different degrees of freedom parameter. Nevertheless, this could only be determined with back- and forward testing and with more refinements to the model.

The 99% MC confidence limits have lower and wider z-score range compared to the statistically calculated 99% normal confidence limits. The right-hand section of Table 9 showed that more than %70 of firms had lower z-score when MC limits were used compared to the %99 normal confidence limits. Even when the rest of the values, over %20, were higher, the model did not perform worse. The left-hand section of Table 9 showed that the number of outliers was the same, which indicates that the Monte Carlo method was following the distribution of variables more closely than the statistical limit method. It gives more confidence in using

MC method. Even when the limits with MC method come very negative, there is reason behind it. It indicates a considerable risk and that the financials and the volatility of variables in observed firms need more investigation.

Whilst the outliers remained within the confidence limits as indicated in Table 9, the potential downside effect may not be included when using the 95% MC limits as can be deduced from Table 10 and from the box plots presented by Figure 6. The 99% MC limits provide the confidence even in more adverse situations such as a financial crisis. Same requirement has been also applied by Basel Accords ([28], p.385).

Considering that the number of outliers in Table 9 stayed within the specified confidence limits, we can reject the null hypothesis and accept the alternative hypothesis. The VaR methodological approach to create a lower bound risk metric and determine the lower limits for Altman's z-score has been demonstrated to be working within the specified boundaries.

8. CONCLUSION

The research analysed FTSE 250 companies with the aim of providing a lower bound risk metric for Altman's z-score. The time period examined was from 2001 to 2007 and Altman's z-score limits were estimated for the first quarter of 2008. Data was collected from quarterly reports. After all limitations and exclusions, 78 firms were analysed. Essentially, the methods applied in this research were based on the Value at Risk methodology. The VaR methodology was used to generate a new risk metric that set a lower bound confidence limit for Altman's z-score bankruptcy model. The model used Monte Carlo simulation and correlation matrices to produce the new risk metric.

The results obtained were compared to statistical confidence limits and to Altman's z-scores from the first quarter of 2008. The number of outliers stayed within the selected confidence limits, which showed that the model does work in the specified limits. The first limitation was set by the chosen sample. The aim of the research was to focus on UK based firms and therefore the FTSE 250 index appeared to be the most appropriate in size, data availability and of interest to study. To actually verify the model, it must be back- and forward tested, neither of which was carried out in this research. It was suggested to use a 99% confidence limit for the model in order to include the potential adverse situations. The contribution of this paper is the new risk metric provides a measure of risk to Altman's z-score that was not considered before. It produces essential information on the quality of the z-score and helps to make more profound decisions.

Appendix

A. Examples of test for normality

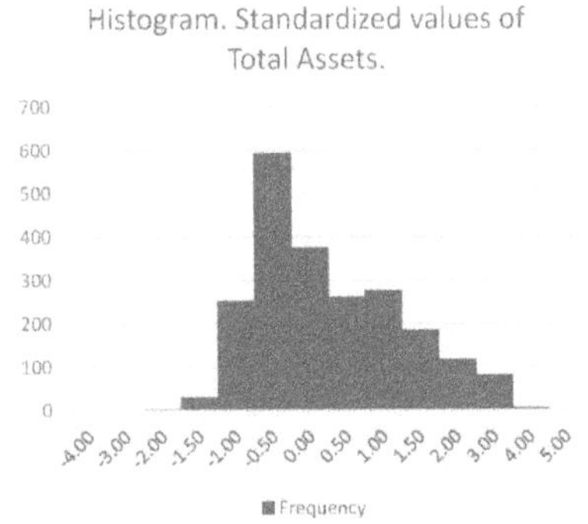

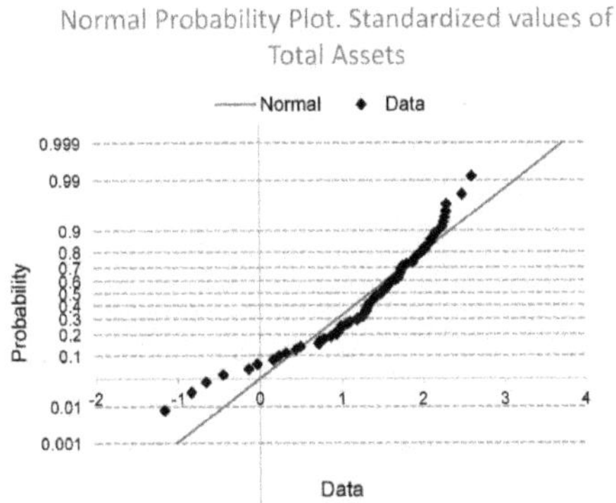

1.8584	AD test statistic
<0.0005	P-value

The chosen risk horizon throughout this analysis has been one quarter, because this is the minimum period of a financial statement and provides most data points to carry out this analysis. There are possibilities to change the risk horizon. The obvious way is to replace a quarterly result with a half a year result or longer term and carry out the whole calculation process again. Another way is to convert the short-term risk horizon to a long-term, which is called scaling. Assuming that the variables are normally distributed, the values can be approximately scaled by the following equation

$$x = \mu r + \sqrt{r}\sigma z \qquad (17)$$

where r is the multiplier to obtain required risk horizon ([28], p.22). Therefore, in the current analysis, all variable values x need to be recalculated. It also means the recalculation of all the subsequent values of Altman's z-scores and the confidence limit for each firm.

1.8584	AD test statistic
<0.0005	P-value

B. Table of Results

Company Name	Industry Classifications	95% N-dist.	95% N-dist. MC	95% t-dist. MC	99% N-dist. MC	99% t-dist. MC	99% N-dist.	Q1 2008
A.G. BARR p.l.c. (LSE:BAG)	Consumer Staples (Primary)	4.29	4.20	4.21	3.47	3.08	3.94	5.31
Aggreko plc (LSE:AGK)	Industrials (Primary)	2.60	2.21	2.27	1.02	0.12	2.20	3.50
Amec Foster Wheeler plc (LSE:AMFW)	Energy (Primary)	1.12	1.38	1.37	1.15	1.07	0.67	3.74
AVEVA Group plc (LSE:AVV)	Information Technology (Primary)	4.09	-19.18	-15.07	-104.54	-88.12	2.82	7.51
Balfour Beatty plc (LSE:BBY)	Industrials (Primary)	1.52	1.56	1.56	1.41	1.36	1.34	2.00
BBA Aviation plc (LSE:BBA)	Industrials (Primary)	1.48	1.50	1.50	1.35	1.33	1.36	1.95
Bellway p.l.c. (LSE:BWY)	Consumer Discretionary (Primary)	2.97	2.56	2.62	1.06	0.31	2.65	4.33
Bodycote plc (LSE:BOY)	Industrials (Primary)	1.19	1.18	1.19	0.91	0.86	0.94	1.66
Bovis Homes Group PLC (LSE:BVS)	Consumer Discretionary (Primary)	2.94	2.92	2.95	2.31	2.07	2.37	4.65
BTG plc (LSE:BTG)	Healthcare (Primary)	-13.66	-6.39	-7.03	-22.86	-45.32	-22.50	2.81
Cairn Energy plc (LSE:CNE)	Energy (Primary)	1.54	-3.72	-3.90	-65.73	-68.63	-0.79	5.19
Carillion plc (LSE:CLLN)	Industrials (Primary)	1.61	1.55	1.53	-7.36	-5.72	1.28	1.43
Clarkson PLC (LSE:CKN)	Industrials (Primary)	1.80	-5.62	-4.15	-32.77	-28.93	1.26	2.54
Cranswick plc (LSE:CWK)	Consumer Staples (Primary)	2.92	2.04	2.16	-14.92	-9.86	2.43	3.86

Company Name	Industry Classifications	95% N-dist.	95% N-dist. MC	95% t-dist. MC	99% N-dist. MC	99% t-dist. MC	99% N-dist.	Q1 2008
Dairy Crest Group plc (LSE:DCG)	Consumer Staples (Primary)	2.33	2.35	2.35	2.16	2.12	2.11	2.38
Dechra Pharmaceuticals plc (LSE:DPH)	Healthcare (Primary)	3.32	3.13	3.16	2.41	2.01	2.96	5.10
Diploma PLC (LSE:DPLM)	Industrials (Primary)	4.93	4.71	4.71	3.63	3.16	4.43	5.14
Domino's Pizza Group plc (LSE:DOM)	Consumer Discretionary (Primary)	2.16	0.19	0.44	-6.59	-9.48	0.41	8.44
Euromoney Institutional Investor PLC (LSE:ERM)	Consumer Discretionary (Primary)	0.96	-7.03	-4.80	-48.77	-41.36	0.64	1.25
Firstgroup plc (LSE:FGP)	Industrials (Primary)	1.79	1.64	1.66	1.27	1.12	1.61	2.44
Galliford Try plc (LSE:GFRD)	Industrials (Primary)	2.40	-2.19	-0.97	-28.46	-20.32	2.11	2.22
Grafton Group plc (LSE:GFTU)	Industrials (Primary)	2.36	1.91	1.97	-4.22	-3.84	2.16	3.43
Greencore Group plc (LSE:GNC)	Consumer Staples (Primary)	1.10	1.12	1.12	0.97	0.95	0.90	2.39
Greene King plc (LSE:GNK)	Consumer Discretionary (Primary)	0.99	0.99	0.99	-3.71	-2.65	0.83	1.20
Greggs plc (LSE:GRG)	Consumer Discretionary (Primary)	5.76	5.74	5.74	5.50	5.41	5.43	6.86
Halma plc (LSE:HLMA)	Information Technology (Primary)	4.34	4.78	4.77	4.35	4.26	3.57	5.92
Hays plc (LSE:HAS)	Industrials (Primary)	1.58	1.97	1.84	-53.82	-41.64	-0.81	5.95

Company Name	Industry Classifications	95% N-dist.	95% N-dist. MC	95% t-dist. MC	99% N-dist. MC	99% t-dist. MC	99% N-dist.	Q1 2008
Hill & Smith Holdings PLC (LSE:HILS)	Materials (Primary)	1.47	1.40	1.40	1.06	0.62	1.21	1.77
HomeServe plc (LSE:HSV)	Industrials (Primary)	1.82	0.84	0.76	−0.80	−1.24	0.90	3.95
Hunting plc (LSE:HTG)	Energy (Primary)	2.36	2.10	2.11	1.40	1.04	2.08	2.02
IMI plc (LSE:IMI)	Industrials (Primary)	2.29	2.31	2.33	2.09	2.05	2.00	3.21
Inchcape plc (LSE:INCH)	Consumer Discretionary (Primary)	3.11	3.08	3.08	2.66	2.45	2.74	3.41
J D Wetherspoon plc (LSE:-JDW)	Consumer Discretionary (Primary)	1.60	1.68	1.69	1.55	1.51	1.39	2.18
Kier Group plc (LSE:KIE)	Industrials (Primary)	2.59	2.59	2.59	2.48	2.43	2.49	3.01
Ladbrokes Coral Group plc (LSE:LCL)	Consumer Discretionary (Primary)	-2.53	-5.17	-3.80	-35.48	-25.93	-3.90	-0.44
Marston's PLC (LSE:MARS)	Consumer Discretionary (Primary)	0.96	0.96	0.95	0.83	0.69	0.87	1.01
Meggitt PLC (LSE:MGGT)	Industrials (Primary)	1.23	−1.06	−0.48	−15.72	−10.10	0.87	1.35
Mitie Group plc (LSE:MTO)	Industrials (Primary)	4.04	4.20	4.18	3.38	−2.60	3.63	4.05
N Brown Group plc (LSE:B-WNG)	Consumer Discretionary (Primary)	2.82	3.17	3.17	2.90	2.82	2.27	3.69
Northgate plc (LSE:NTG)	Industrials (Primary)	1.11	1.07	1.07	−2.80	−3.06	0.91	1.46
PageGroup plc (LSE:PAGE)	Industrials (Primary)	7.07	4.66	4.61	−17.65	−17.25	5.92	8.36
PZ Cussons Plc (LSE:PZC)	Consumer Staples (Primary)	1.48	2.56	2.63	0.86	0.69	−1.18	4.67

Company Name	Industry Classifications	95% N-dist.	95% N-dist. MC	95% t-dist. MC	99% N-dist. MC	99% t-dist. MC	99% N-dist.	Q1 2008
Redrow plc (LSE:RDW)	Consumer Discretionary (Primary)	3.35	3.22	3.20	2.84	2.71	3.13	3.82
Renishaw plc (LSE:RSW)	Information Technology (Primary)	7.18	7.58	7.53	6.19	2.06	5.77	13.20
RPC Group Plc (LSE:RPC)	Materials (Primary)	1.89	1.77	1.79	1.35	1.18	1.74	2.67
Savills plc (LSE:SVS)	Real Estate (Primary)	2.29	1.33	1.36	-6.70	-7.53	1.80	4.04
Senior plc (LSE:SNR)	Industrials (Primary)	1.90	1.86	1.87	1.57	1.50	1.70	2.63
Serco Group plc (LSE:SRP)	Industrials (Primary)	1.29	1.41	1.37	-6.89	-4.82	0.66	3.07
Spectris plc (LSE:SXS)	Information Technology (Primary)	1.55	1.73	1.74	1.27	1.11	0.97	3.58
Spirax-Sarco Engineering plc (LSE:SPX)	Industrials (Primary)	2.86	3.08	3.11	2.37	2.21	1.98	5.47
St. Modwen Properties PLC (LSE:SMP)	Real Estate (Primary)	1.26	1.08	1.04	-7.39	-6.16	1.06	1.39
Stagecoach Group plc (LSE:SGC)	Industrials (Primary)	0.90	1.06	1.06	0.84	0.74	0.60	1.73
Tate & Lyle plc (LSE:TATE)	Consumer Staples (Primary)	2.21	2.22	2.22	2.12	2.07	2.01	2.98
Ted Baker PLC (LSE:TED)	Consumer Discretionary (Primary)	5.61	5.10	5.24	2.47	0.38	4.63	8.40
The Berkeley Group Holdings plc (LSE:BKG)	Consumer Discretionary (Primary)	1.65	2.72	2.68	1.86	1.17	0.37	5.78
The Go-Ahead Group plc (LSE:GOG)	Industrials (Primary)	2.35	2.33	2.33	1.21	0.31	2.00	3.01

Company Name	Industry Classifications	95% N-dist.	95% N-dist. MC	95% t-dist. MC	99% N-dist. MC	99% t-dist. MC	99% N-dist.	Q1 2008
Travis Perkins plc (LSE:T-PK)	Industrials (Primary)	1.93	2.04	2.04	-12.96	-7.23	1.35	2.54
Tullow Oil plc (LSE:TLW)	Energy (Primary)	0.92	-6.35	-5.12	-34.31	-25.13	0.49	2.02
UBM plc (LSE:UBM)	Consumer Discretionary (Primary)	0.00	-0.32	-0.26	-0.89	-1.14	-0.44	1.51
UDG Healthcare plc (LSE:UDG)	Healthcare (Primary)	3.76	3.75	3.74	3.34	3.24	3.55	4.05
Ultra Electronics Holdings plc (LSE:ULE)	Industrials (Primary)	2.93	2.69	2.71	2.02	1.72	2.61	3.52
Victrex plc (LSE:VCT)	Materials (Primary)	7.06	7.25	7.28	-2.44	-8.15	5.75	8.60
WH Smith PLC (LSE:SM-WH)	Consumer Discretionary (Primary)	2.66	2.59	2.58	1.86	1.34	2.06	5.42
William Hill plc (LSE:W-MH)	Consumer Discretionary (Primary)	-0.43	0.86	0.81	-0.36	-0.99	-2.71	2.06

REFERENCES

1. Jorion P. *Value at risk: the new benchmark for managing financial risk.* New York: McGraw-Hill; 2001

2. Xu X, Chen Y, Zheng H. The comparison of enterprise bankruptcy forecasting method. Journal Of Applied Statistics. 2011;38(2):301-308. DOI: 10.1080/02664760903406470

3. Altman EI. Financial Ratios, Discriminant Analysis and the Prediction of Corporate Bankruptcy. Journal of Finance. 1968:189-209. DOI: 10.1111/j.1540-6261.1968.tb00843.x

4. Beaver WH. Financial ratios predictors of failure. Journal of Accounting Research. 1966;4:71-111

5. Fisher RA. The Use of Multiple Measurements in Taxonomic Problems. Annals of Eugenics. 1936;7:179. DOI: 10.1111/j.1469-1809.1936.tb02137.x

6. Merton R. On the Pricing of Corporate Debt: The Risk Structure of Interest Rates. The Journal of Finance. 1974;29(2):449-470. DOI: 10.2307/2978814

7. Ohlson J. Financial Ratios and the Probabilistic Prediction of Bankruptcy. Journal of Accounting Research. 1980;18(1):109-131. DOI: 10.2307/2490395

8. Springate GLV. Predicting the possibility of failure in a Canadian firm (Unpublished master's thesis). Canada: Simon Fraser University; 1978

9. Zmijewski ME. Methodological issues related to the estimation of financial distress prediction models. Journal of Accounting Research. 1984;22:59-86

10. Chou C, Hsieh S, Qiu C. Hybrid genetic algorithm and fuzzy clustering for bankruptcy prediction. Applied Soft Computing. 2017. DOI: 10.1016/j.asoc.2017.03.014

11. Coats PK, Fant LF. Recognizing Financial Distress Patterns Using a Neural Network Tool. The Journal Of The Financial Management Association. 1993;22(3):142-155

12. Perez M. Artificial neural networks and bankruptcy forecasting: a state of the art. Neural Computing & Applications. 2006;15(2):154-163. DOI: 10.1007/s00521-005-0022-x

13. Tam KY, Kiang MY. Managerial applications of neural networks: the case of bank failure predictions. *Management science.* 1992;38(7):926-947

14. Barboza F, Kimura H, Altman E. Machine Learning Models and Bankruptcy Prediction. Expert Systems With Applications. 2017. DOI: 10.1016/j.eswa.2017.04.006

15. Van Gestel T, Baesens B, Martens D. From linear to non-linear kernel based classifiers for bankruptcy prediction. Neurocomputing. 2010;73. DOI: 10.1016/j.neucom.2010.07.002

16. Zhao D, Yu F, Huang C, Wei Y, Wang M, Chen H. An Effective Computational Model for Bankruptcy Prediction Using Kernel Extreme Learning Machine Approach. Computational Economics. 2017;49(2):325-341. DOI: 10.1007/s10614-016-9562-7

17. Miller W. Comparing Models of Corporate Bankruptcy Prediction: Distance to Default vs. In: Z-Score. 2009 Retrieved 25 June 2017, from https://corporate.morningstar.com/us/documents/MethodologyDocuments/MethodologyPapers/CompareModelsCorpBankruptcyPrediction.pdf

18. Heine ML. Predicting Financial Distress Of Companies: Revisiting The Z-Score and Zeta models. (Unpublished paper. New York: Stern School of Business; 2000

19. Hillegeist S, Keating E, Cram D, Lundstedt K. Assessing the Probability of Bankruptcy. Review Of Accounting Studies. 2004;9(1):5-34. DOI: 10.1023/B:RAST.0000013627.90884.b7

20. Balcaen S, Ooghe H. 35 years of studies on business failure: an overview of the classic statistical methodologies and their related problems. The British Accounting Review. 2006;93. DOI: 10.1016/j.bar.2005.09.001

21. Appiah KO, Chizema A, Arthur J. Predicting corporate failure: a systematic literature review of methodological issues. International Journal Of Law & Management. 2015;57(5):461. DOI: 10.1108/IJLMA-04-2014-0032

22. Mousavi MM, Ouenniche J, Xu B. Performance evaluation of bankruptcy prediction models: An orientation-free super-efficiency DEA-based framework. International Review Of Financial Analysis. 2015;75. DOI: 10.1016/j.irfa.2015.01.006

23. Charalambakis EC. On the Prediction of Corporate Financial Distress in the Light of the Financial Crisis: Empirical Evidence from Greek Listed Firms. International Journal Of The Economics Of Business. 2015;22(3):407-428

24. Agarwal V, Taffler RJ. Comparing the performance of market-based and accounting-based bankruptcy prediction models. Journal Of Banking And Finance. 2008. DOI: 10.1016/j.jbankfin.2007.07.014

25. Baldwin J, Glezen GW. Bankruptcy Prediction Using Quarterly Financial Statement Data. Journal Of Accounting, Auditing & Finance. 1992;7(3):269-285

26. Halilbegovic S, Vehabovic M. Backtesting Value at Risk Forecast: the Case of Kupiec Pof-Test. European Journal Of Economic Studies. 2016;17(3):393-404. DOI: 10.13187/es.2016.17.393

27. Cheung YH, Powell RJ. Anybody can do Value at Risk: A Teaching Study using Parametric Computation and Monte Carlo Simulation. Australasian Accounting, Business and Finance Journal. 2012;6(5):101-118

28. Alexander C. Value-at-risk models. 1st ed. Chichester, England: Wiley; 2010

29. Breuer T. Providing against the worst: Risk capital for worst case scenarios. Managerial Finance. 2006;32(9):716-730. DOI: 10.1108/03074350610681934

30. Krause A. Exploring the Limitations of Value at Risk: How Good Is It in Practice? The Journal Of Risk Finance. 2003;(2):19

31. Lambadiaris G, Papadopoulou L, Skiadopoulos G, Zoulis Y. VAR: history or simulation? Risk. 2003;16(9):122-127

32. Kupiec P. Techniques for Verifying the Accuracy of Risk Management Models. Journal of Derivatives. 1995;3:73-84

33. Nieto MR, Ruiz E. Review: Frontiers in VaR forecasting and backtesting. International Journal Of Forecasting. 2016;501. DOI: 10.1016/j.ijforecast.2015.08.003

34. S&P Capital IQ. (2017). FTSE 250 Index Financial Data. Retrieved 1 July 2017, from S&P Capital IQ database.

35. Nallareddy, S., Pozen, R., and Rajgopal, S. (2017). Consequences of Mandatory Quarterly Reporting: The U.K. Experience. *Columbia Business School Research,* 17(33).

36. Marathe R, Ryan SM. On The Validity of The Geometric Brownian Motion Assumption. The Engineering Economist. 2005;50(2):159-192. DOI: 10.1080/00137910590949904

37. McCrary, S. (2015). Implementing a Monte Carlo simulation: Correlation, skew, and kurtosis. Retrieved 29 June 2017, from http://www.thinkbrg.com/media/publication/687_McCrary_MonteCarlo_Whitepaper_20150923_WEB.pdf

38. Moore T. Generating Multivariate Normal Pseudo Random Data. Teaching Statistics. 2001;23(1):8-10

39. Hunt N. Generating Multivariate Normal Data in Excel. Teaching Statistics. 2001;23(2):58-59

40. Parramore K. On Simulating Realizations of Correlated Random Variables. Teaching Statistics. 2000;22(2):61-63

41. Villa, C., & Rubio, F. J. (2017). Objective priors for the number of degrees of freedom of a multivariate t distribution and the t-copula. Retrieved 20 July 2017, from https://arxiv.org/abs/1701.05638

42. Krzywinski M, Altman N. Points of Significance: Visualizing samples with box plots. Nature Methods. 2014;11(2):119-120. DOI: 10.1038/nmeth.2813

10 Informality and Entrepreneurship in Developing Economy: Case for Entrepreneurial Financing

1. INTRODUCTION

Seeking and taking advantages of emerging entrepreneurial opportunities in a socio-economic environment that is saddled with volatility, shock, turbulence, munificence and disruption could be an arduous task for entrepreneurship to evolve, thrive, and grow the economy at a space and speed that are desirable for fast economic growth and development. The fact that entrepreneurship is both formal and informal makes such opportunity-seeking and advantage-taking to be diverse, complex and highly competitive.

Unarguably in the extant literature, entrepreneurship is considered an engine and a key driver of growth [1, 2]. However, this notion of entrepreneurship-driven growth is often downplayed in most of the developing economies [3], because the substantial part of their economies is largely informal [4]. This informality engenders entrepreneurship to be significantly influenced by the economic policies and institutional forces to the extent that emerging and localised innovative ideas and financing of such opportunities have become a critical interplay of the economic activities [5].

This paper aims at discussing gaps that were observed in the extant literature and empirical evidence relating to the entrepreneurial financing of the informal sector, and explores how the domain of accounting knowledge, specifically the management accounting field, could play a key role in advancing the frontier of informal entrepreneurship financing in the twenty-first century.

In this chapter, the key issues surrounding informal sector entrepreneurship are problematized while the emerging financial technology (FINTECH) and new outlets for funding existing and new business ventures, innovative products and technology are discussed alongside the potential impacts on informal entrepreneurship.

To navigate how the theoretical gaps could be closed, theoretical framework that demonstrates the linkages among different variables of the entrepreneurial phenomenon and charts the pathways to which the suggested contributions mitigate the financing bottlenecks of the informal entrepreneurship is conceptualised.

In conclusion, this paper has implications on accounting research both theoretically and in practice. First, it highlights core areas of management accounting that are relevant to the knowledge exposure of the entrepreneurial financing where fragmentation of theory and pragmatism have tended to limit the impacts of academic research on practitioners and impedes clarity of communication between theory and practice [6].

Second, where accounting profession can be more appreciated and be seen as co-pilots that drive standardisation and innovativeness of information management and tools that are relevant to entrepreneurial ventures in the informal sector, particularly in the developing or emerging economies.

2. INFORMAL ENTREPRENEURSHIP AND DEVELOPING ECONOMY

2.1 Introduction

The informal sector of an economy depicts a channel through which unregulated but organised business endeavours take place among different stakeholders, particularly the people at the bottom of the pyramid in an environment that is characterised by poverty and inequality. The business activities within the sector are mostly transacted outside the boundary of government regulations but firmly reside within the confines of informal structures that are encapsulated in culture, norms, convention and rules [7].

The understanding of informal entrepreneurship is ambiguous and has diverse conceptualisation in the literature. This is because the insight into informality as an economic unit, varies across scholars [8]. While some scholars see informality in the sense of legality, which denotes those informal businesses are compulsorily brought into being as a result of rigid and strict regulations, others see it under the lens of structuralists, as a "safe-haven" for those who could not find jobs in a formal structure of the economy.

Informality is also perceived under the purview of voluntarists as a "necessity-driven" avenue for seeking entrepreneurial opportunities when there is no hope in the formal sector. By whatever way we perceive the informality phenomenon, there is evidence that the informal entrepreneurship sector contributes positively to the growth and wealth of the economy, although in some cases, it also dilutes economic growth [4, 9].

2.2 Informal Sector Entrepreneurship and its Economic Impacts

Scholars continue to debate the extent to which numerous firms and individual actors in the informal economic environment impact growth of the economy, despite having a larger population of the economy engaged in trading, street vendors, public markets, subsistence farming and self-employment among other informal economic activities [9]. In this paper, informal entrepreneurship is viewed under the lens of opportunity discovery and innovativeness dimensions of entrepreneurial orientation. An entrepreneurial opportunity was succinctly put as "situations *in which new goods, services, raw materials, markets and organisational methods can be introduced through the formation of new means, ends, or means-ends relationship*" [10]. The author argues further that although opportunities are discovered, the locus of changes in product, services, etc., sources of the opportunities regarding information asymmetry, demand and supply sides, the dichotomy of rent-seeking and productivity-enhancing, as well as the quality and influence of the change initiator, are of utmost importance.

The dimension of innovativeness, on the other hand, is characterised by a new product, new technology, new channel and new market that are unique and create differentiation advantage over the existing products, channels or markets [11].

Considering that there is a linkage between formal and informal entrepreneurship, it is apparent that such interconnectedness is an avenue for informal entrepreneurs to discover entrepreneurial opportunities to create new products, services or technologies. Moreover, the limitation of opportunities in the formal sector arising from over-regulation or excessive legal constraints can also become a source for entrepreneurial opportunities for the informal sector to explore and exploit [11].

Similarly, when a section of formal sector products or services is transitioned or outsourced to informal markets, this could inspire an entrepreneurial opportunity for informal entrepreneurs to exploit. However, it is argued that, rather than gaining from collaborative and mutual benefits of the formal-informal sector linkage, the informal sector is cannibalised by the formal sector which preys on the innovativeness of informality through free-riding and risk-shifting. Hence, the frugality of innovation tending towards a reconfiguration of informal sector opportunities and innovativeness to further the growth of the formal sector [12].

Notwithstanding the above, the question as to whether informality helps entrepreneurs to achieve firm growth still lingers, and if it does, how does the firm growth translate to economic growth? The main issue is that the informal sector has been seen in the shadow of the formal sector because of its lower productivity, less technology-driven, poor access to qualified or competent human capital, poor access to financial credit and out of formal institutional coverage [4, 13]. With these characteristics, the informal sector in the developing countries has not been growing in tandem with the growth of the overall economy. It rather shrinks and gives ways to further development of the formal sector.

This position is supported by IMF Regional Economic Outlook (REO, 2017) which suggests that the productivity levels of informal firms are strictly lower than that of formal firms based on the real output per worker (*25% of small formal firms & 19% of medium-sized formal firms*).

In contrast to the widely held notion of the lower economic performance of informal sectors, some scholars have argued that informality did contribute positively to economic growth and has become a destination for the development of a country rather than continues as a journey. For instance, there was a finding that a strong positive correlation exists between informality and firm growth, and the probability of informal entrepreneurs achieving their set objectives is higher than the formal entrepreneurs achieving theirs [14].

The other positive areas of informality to economic growth in developing nations can be traced to trade and self-employment. Trade liberalisation has the consequence of spillovers of workers from the formal sector to the informal sector as a result of the drop in demand and supply of goods and services. This unabsorbed labour may then take a new opportunity or be self-employed [15, 16]. This situation plays crucial roles in the reallocation of resources to the informal sector, thus reducing apparent unemployment in the economy. Given the above, it can be concluded that informality has some positive correlations to the growth of the economy, particularly in sub-Saharan Africa which has the largest settlement of informal economic activities in the world.

To illustrate this with data, IMF Regional Economic Outlook shows that the informal economy in sub-Saharan Africa contributed between 25% and 65% to the Gross Domestic Product (GDP) of the region. The regional informality also accounts for 30–90% of the total employment in the non-agricultural sector, while the unweighted average share of the informal sector as a percentage of GDP between 2010 and 2014 was 38%, despite that informality is shrinking both in the region and globally [17].

2.3 Institutional Forces, Economic Policies and Informal Entrepreneurship

The regulatory environment, economic policies and informal institutional forces of norms, conventions, etc., have significant influences on the choice, prevalence and performance of both informal and formal entrepreneurship. An empirical finding reveals that a unit (standard-deviation) increase in the quality of political and economic institutional roles could halve the rates of informal entrepreneurship, but double the rates of formal entrepreneurship [18].

This means that the degree to which the informal sector is impacted by the vagaries of government regulations and policies is much more than that of the formal sector. It is these economic and political-institutional forces that confer advantages of legitimacy to firms in the formal sector which in turns skew the allocation of entrepreneurial efforts and resources towards formality. This is understandable since informal firms and individual actors within the sector operate outside the confines of formal business laws, rules and property rights protection. The caveat is that some of these formal legitimacies carry the implications of disincentives to capital accumulation and investment in the informal sector.

However, informal firms leverage on the social legitimacy confers on them by their stakeholders including government authority. Social legitimacy is governed by norms, values, conventions and beliefs that are prevalent in the environment and make informal firms and individual actors within the environment to be legitimate in dealings with their customers, suppliers and other stakeholders [7, 14].

In most developing nations, the drives and quests for revenue mobilisation have made some relevant government authorities extend the hand of regulation to the informal sector in some spheres of informal trade activities. For instance, in Nigeria, state and local government have mandates of local taxes, operational licences, environmental pollution controls for organised informal markets, which are enforced through umbrella associations and leaders of the market communities.

Regardless of the issue of legitimacy and regulation, what matters most in the institutional framework of the informal sector is the interconnectedness of formal and informal entrepreneurship, and how well or otherwise does the regulatory and policy environment support or impede the progress of informality in terms of opportunity discovery and innovativeness. First, the quality and efficiency of government regulations and policy, determine the choice, size and prevalence of formal or informal entrepreneurship.

Most important are the tax regimes, credit policies and property rights protection. Many undifferentiated government policies and actions between the two sectors in form of taxes, revenue mobilisation, environmental pollution, financial credits, property rights and labour laws are hostile to informal entrepreneurial firms and are gradually used to exiting them from the economy, although informal firms also define structural and political clout of the economy.

Second, the perception of 'all-inclusive' or 'frugal' innovation in the linkage between formal and informal economies, particularly in developing countries has been argued by some scholars that rather than promoting and rewarding informal entrepreneurs for their innovative and collaborative endeavours, the relationship of formal and informal firms tends to suppress and cannibalise the informal sector for the profit motives and institutional gains of the formal sector. Meaning that firms in the formal sector simply take the existing routine innovation in the informal markets and scale it up, thus formalising what is already informal through free riding, by-passing and risk-shifting [12].

Third, the institutional linkage that binds informal and formal entrepreneurship also implies information asymmetry and networking. Informal firms leverage occupational and social networking when seeking an opportunity for innovative ideas, new products, technology advancement, and when regulating the behaviours of the individual actors within the sector [19]. On the other hand, formal firms substantially rely on changes in laws, regulations, policies and a few open-channel information to guide their legitimate economic activities. The resulting information asymmetry and superior social networking on the part of informal firms often create unfair competition for the firms operating in the same market.

Lastly, contentious issues of product counterfeiting and passing-off on the part of informal entrepreneurs tend to further the illegitimacy concerns of the informal sector. However, in some cases, counterfeit products are socially acceptable in the informal market as a result of exorbitant prices on similar products, or simply to fill the gaps in the market [7]. Nonetheless, in the institutional relationship between the two sectors, criminal and illegitimate activities of some of the informal firms should be viewed separately within the linkage and do not make informality illegal in the entire economy.

3. FINANCING OF INFORMAL ENTREPRENEURSHIP SECTOR

3.1 Traditional Financing of Business Venture and Impacts on Informal Entrepreneurship

The traditional roles of financial intermediary in nurturing and promoting new business creation and innovation are fast changing in the modern entrepreneurial economy. Consequent to this changing dynamic is that venture capitalist, angel investor, commercial and investment banking are confronted with globalisation and technological disruption. Similar to this situation is the increasing trend of local venture capitalist and entrepreneurship philanthropist as a modern-day angel investor who is financially promoting local business ideas through their foundation platforms. Hence, the need for greater focus on the evolving roles of financial intermediaries and their linkage to the financial and ownership structure of the entrepreneurs, as major determinants for innovation and firm growth [20].

It is, therefore, no gainsaying that emerging entrepreneurs from either formal or informal sector are becoming viable sources for new business and job creation, new product and technology that will lead to productivity growth. However, the major constraint in fostering these economic growth-enhancing activities is the difficulty in accessing appropriate financial resources for innovative endeavours.

The focal area in this paper centres on the sourcing and process of financing informal sector entrepreneurial opportunity and innovation, since the actors in this sector are largely unregulated within the ambit of formal sector financial institutions. Their ownership and financial structure are also non-conforming with the formal contractual obligations and property rights framework. These then pose some questions regarding; (i) the ideal financial outlets to raise funds for innovative products, services and technology, (ii) effectiveness of financial intermediation to support informal firms within the financial industry to raise funds critical to financing a new business, products, and (iii) the conditionalities for accessing funds in terms of financial and ownership structure.

These questions and more, deserve scholastic attention to expand the frontier of informal sector financing [21]. Nevertheless, there has been some coverage of this issue in the literature, albeit not specific to informal entrepreneurship [22, 23].

The process of raising funds by informal entrepreneurs to finance novel ideas, create new business, new product, innovate or renovate technology and process, has not only been complex but also difficult. Stemming from inadequate or lack of internal cash flows and prominently, lack of adequate collaterals, asymmetric information, agency problems, most of the entrepreneurial projects in the informal entrepreneurship sector usually die on arrival.

Notwithstanding, informal entrepreneurs have the privilege of accessing financial resources from traditional channels either internally or externally. Internal traditional sources such as accumulated savings, retained reserves, business assistance or inheritance from families, and loans from friends. On the external traditional sources, bank loans, microfinancing, and cooperative loans are options. In most cases, internalised funding options are unarguably inadequate for funding serious innovation, hence there are needs for alternative sources [24, 25].

3.2 Emerging Trend of Financial Technology (FINTECH) and Alternative Fund Providers

In recent times, new channels and platforms of entrepreneurial financing have emerged. These new avenues are necessitated by the inadequacy of supply side market for funding entrepreneurship, and are expected to mitigate funding barriers and fill the gaps of the dwindling financial intermediation [21].

The shortcomings of informal borrowing and bank lending to the entrepreneurial opportunity and innovation, have culminated in investors turning to angel investor network and venture capital for equity capital contributions. However, due to some limitations leading to adverse selection and credit rationing, new channels of entrepreneurial financing such as crowdfunding, accelerator and incubators, specialised seed funding and government venture funding have emerged in the financial industry [21, 25, 26, 27].

Angel investors are rich individuals who take interest to fund innovation projects with their personal wealth and expertise. They usually focus on the start-up and early-stage innovation and remain passive in the entrepreneurship structure. This source of fund is seen as a second call, when bank loans and other traditional financing fail. On the other hand, venture capital is an intermediated source of capital that is raised from set of limited investors for an early-stage or seed phase innovation projects of young entrepreneurs. It is equity finance capital with the objective of earning returns on the investment for the investors. Venture capitalists are active in the in the entrepreneurial innovation to add value, but with temporary ownership structure.

As a result of funding gaps that continue to exist regardless of robust angel investor and venture capital financing, crowdfunding platform has emerged as a big disruptor in the venture financing market. Crowdfunding allows for direct on-line mobilisation of funds for entrepreneurial and innovation projects, particularly the ones at the early-stage, from clusters of small investors (equity crowdfunding) or from group of potential consumers of the project (reward-based crowdfunding). This channel is a disintermediated finance source of small investors with no standard financial intermediaries. What makes crowdfunding successful are strong network of personal investors, underlying quality of the entrepreneurial projects and geography of the entrepreneurship [28].

There are also accelerators and incubators funding channels which focus on gathering network and mentors for the entrepreneurship innovation. These channels are cohort-based funding supports that also provide financing in exchange for equity [25]. Although, the aforementioned financing options are induced by supply-push factors, however, with some shortcomings in the financial industry, government intervention in funding entrepreneurship innovation has become a response to a demand-pull factor of technology transfer [27]. Some countries are coming out to support new business creation, innovation and corporate venturing by direct intervention of venture funding through relevant agencies, while others are supporting the financial industry with tax and other public investment policies to mitigate prevalent bottlenecks between the investors and the entrepreneurs.

Conversely, the challenge is how the informal sector could explore these new alternative sources of funds to support its emerging inventions, innovations, and other entrepreneurial opportunity discovery in the sector. The issue of legitimacy, informal ownership and financial structure do not position informal entrepreneurship appropriately to benefit from venture capitalist. However, crowdfunding and angel investor network can be of immense benefits to the potential entrepreneurs in the informal sector.

4. REVIEW OF LITERATURE

In the extant literature of entrepreneurial financing, no significant work has yet been done on the peculiarity of informal sector entrepreneurship funding. This apparent gap could be attributed to the afore-mentioned agency problems of information asymmetry and moral hazard, lack of formal financial contract agreement, ambiguous ownership and financial structure, and the issue of legitimacy. It follows that the informal sector entrepreneurship has long been stigmatised with these problems. However, the terrain of financing entrepreneurial opportunity and innovation is not so different for formal and informal entrepreneurs, particularly for new business creation, opaque firms, and young entrepreneurship. Therefore, the streams of funds emanating from the traditional bank loans and trade credits, informal loan from friends and families, coupled with the emergence of alternative sources such as angel investor network, venture capital, crowdfunding, accelerator financing and specialised venture capital, can no longer be overemphasised in the emerging financial markets and technologies [21, 26].

In this regard, scholars are expected to position the phenomenon of entrepreneurial financing in the literature as an important link between entrepreneurial opportunity and economic growth of which the informal sector is paramount. Unfortunately, the literature of finance, strategic management and accounting are yet to fully extend the informality perspective into the theory of finance. Hence, the necessity to integrate into the theory of financing, those gaps associated with the informal entrepreneurship sector in order to bridge the theoretical laxity.

First and foremost, the issue of information asymmetry as a principal-agent problem between two related parties has largely been stressed in some literature [29, 30, 31, 32]. However, little has been done to extend this notion of agency theory to the relationship between entrepreneurial firms and potential investors [21], particularly in the area of informal entrepreneurship-investor nexus. This issue which is profound in the informal market suggests that the entrepreneurs are likely to hold or hide vital information from the knowledge of potential investors when seeking for external funds [33]. This attitude is usually as a result of fear that competitors or rivals might take undue advantages of the innovative ideas or products, hence the reluctance of the entrepreneurs to divulge the core information of such innovation to the potential investors [34].

Aside the withholding or divulging of vital information by the entrepreneurs, the other dark side of informational asymmetry that create gaps in the financing of informal entrepreneurial opportunities is the failure to provide good track of business records and the commitment to business acumen and demonstration of credit worthiness. In this situation, the cost of screening or ascertaining credible information on the history of business endeavours in the informal sector which is considered opaque by investors, is usually prohibitive [24]. Moreover, the opacity of the informal firms dictates the financing strategy and tactics that may be employed by the potential investors [25]. This is because some of the new and young firms, particularly the informal ones have no track records, either with suppliers, customers, lending institutions and other stakeholders.

The second agency related issue that contributes to the financing gap of informal entrepreneurship is the moral hazard conflict. In this instance, informal entrepreneurs might misallocate funds raised from investors and utilise same for their benefits rather than for mutual benefits which was the original purpose of financing [23]. In the extant literature, moral hazard is simply referred to as 'shirking' of responsibility by an agent in a principal-agent relationship [32], meaning that the agent has not effectively render his efforts as agreed in the relationship. It has also been argued that moral hazard conflict stems from the fact that investors often lack the ability to fully incentivise the information asymmetries of the entrepreneurs [35]. For instance, dispersed investors like crowdfunding providers or angel investor network might not have the capacity to monitor or coordinate the activities of the investors to identify manifestations of moral hazard. Thus, goal-congruence is lacking between the potential investor and informal entrepreneurs where the entrepreneurs may disregard the interests of the potential investors [21].

Although, assumptions of self-interest, bounded rationality, risk aversion and information asymmetry play key roles as precursors to agency problems in the relationship between the agent and his principal, the fact that the two parties have different and divergent interests often leads to goal incongruency and once this issue manifests, necessary governance mechanisms and incentives need to be put in place to mitigate the problems [36].

The other fundamental issues facing the informal entrepreneurship sector in raising adequate funding is the lack of formalised financial contract agreement and the high probability of enforcement failure. Contractual relationship between the informal entrepreneurs and potential investors are substantially informal and relational, meaning that the variability by the third party such as court or arbitration, is absent, often lacks rigours, ambiguous, and such contract agreement suffers from incompleteness or holding-up which could result in 'arm-twisting' between the entrepreneurs and the investors [20, 37, 38].

Although, many informal firms and individual actors are organised to some extent, as some of them belong to umbrella associations or recognised professions, nonetheless, the financial contract existing in this environment is largely relational and as such, does not guarantee establishing an appropriate financial contract and agreement within the sector. Moreover, the transactional costs and enforcement are prominent issues surrounding informal contracts. It is costly to establish and enforce informal contract agreements because of the failure to provide adequate and convincing evidences of the breach of contract before the courts or arbitration [37].

In most of the literature on entrepreneurial financing and particularly, the financial contracting between investors and entrepreneurs, the issues that stand out are, the finding of equilibrium in the shared risks among the contracting parties, incentives to mitigate incongruency at the early stage of entrepreneurial opportunity and innovation, and enforcement of financial contractual agreement. Therefore, the quest for investors' robustness on financing decisions, either in the anticipation or against the potential information asymmetry, inexperience or moral hazard conflict of the entrepreneurs has become very important element in the financial contract agreement and transactional costs for informal entrepreneurial opportunities [39].

Most importantly is the enforcement of the contractual agreement. The dichotomy between weak and strong enforcement is significant in determining the default rate of entrepreneurial finance made available by investors. Thus, the supply of funds by investors and the ability to repay by the entrepreneurs are determinants to the enforcement resources available to the investors [40].

Similarly, the nature of ownership structure of most informal firms is either family-oriented or sole actors which do not necessarily have formal organisational structure, standardised financial bookkeeping and financial disclosure, robust financial planning and controls. The absence of these structures can lead to 'cognitive bias' in making financing decisions from both the entrepreneurs and the investors [26]. To illustrate, informal entrepreneurs depend much more on cognitive bias to appeal to investors to fund their entrepreneurial opportunities, regardless of their structure, the amount and accuracy of information they disclose.

In fact, the cognitive bias carries different levels of persuasion and risk mitigation towards entrepreneurial financing. In the literature, cognitive bias is conceptualised in the context of 'perception and reasoning' errors that could influence judgement and decision-making to deviate from the normative rationality [41]. Unlike in the formal sector, informal entrepreneurial intents, opportunity discovery and innovation are shrouded in cognitive bias than in organisational structure and standardised financial disclosure.

Equally, it is very important to note that 'mental accounting' bias also play prominent roles on how informal entrepreneurs keep and present their financial records for the purpose of seeking funds from investor or for any other requirements [42]. This follows that the entrepreneurs organise, process, keep, and report their accounting records based on variety of criteria that are mostly subjective. Finally, the policy and regulatory environment that informal entrepreneurship sector resides and share with the formal sector is also one of the determining factors that constrain easy funding accessibility to informal entrepreneurs and often pose some disincentives for the entrepreneurial firms and the investors to take calculative risks. Although, it is argued that non-conformity with the institutionalised policies and regulations of taxes, financial credit facility, compliance, etc., deprive informal entrepreneurship sector of some of the privileges of legitimacy accorded to the formal sector, however the same environment has helped informal entrepreneurs with the emergence of various financing outlets and technology that are specific to informal debt financing [43].

In the developing economies, microfinancing, cooperative societies, 'esusu' group contributions and lending and on-line loan facility are the new financing opportunities that are reshaping the informal sector entrepreneurship. This attests to the fact that the traditions, rules and conventions that govern the financing of informal entrepreneurship opportunity could be moderated by the formal institutional policy and regulation [44]. Nevertheless, regulative and policy incentives are also part of the environmental variables that can influence the opportunity and innovation of informal entrepreneurship, create a favourable climate for enhancing productive relationship between investors and the entrepreneurs and also create avenues to ease information asymmetry and incongruency of interests in the informal sector [45].

5. CONCEPTUAL MODEL AND PROPOSITIONS

Having discussed and problematised the phenomena of informality and entrepreneurial financing in the developing economy, this paper further attempts to expand the domains of entrepreneurship and accounting by developing a theoretical model that conceptualises the interconnectedness among informal entrepreneurship, institutional environment that constrain the legitimacy of informal entrepreneurship, entrepreneurial financing together with bottlenecks arising from informality and the potential contributions to the conceptual and theoretical framework of financing (Figure 1).

This model has implications for the theoretical underpinning of strategic management, finance and accounting disciplines and exposes agency theory, resource-based theory, transaction cost theory, financial contracting theory and new institutional theory as relevant underlying theories. However, the context of this paper delimits elucidation and amplification of these theories.

The potential theoretical contributions to the literature are limited to the discipline of accounting, and specifically to the management accounting research which is perceived as an applied and quantitative study of strategic management, and belongs to 'method theory' rather than 'domain theory' [27]. In essence, management accounting research is regarded as an interventionist research area that could be explored to demonstrate the practicability of some theoretical postulations of entrepreneurial financing in the informal sector of an economy.

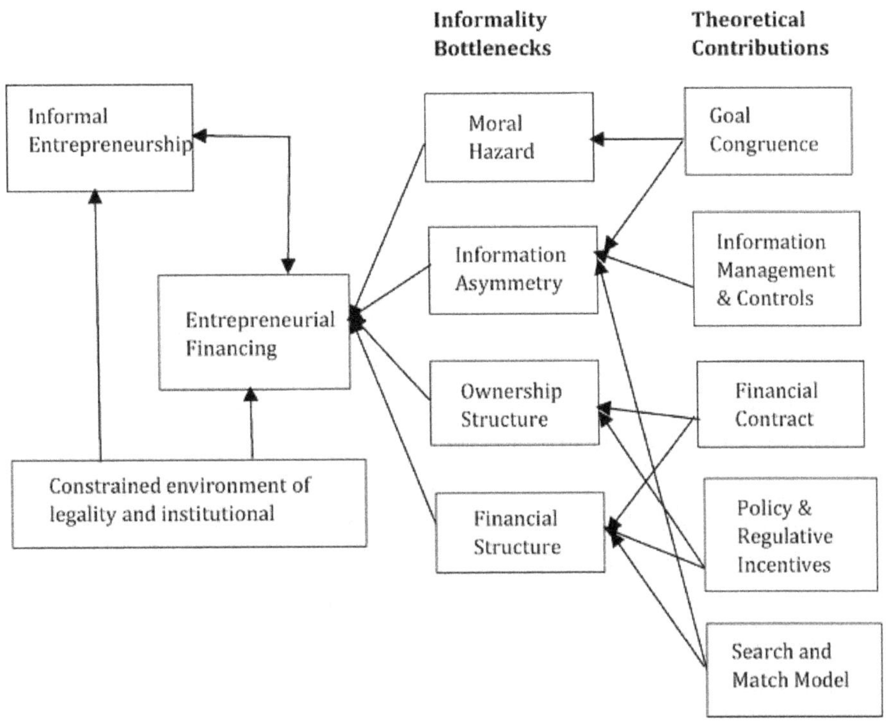

Figure 1. Conceptual model of informal entrepreneurship financing. Source: Author's adaptation, 2021.

This thought process has two consequences. First, the bridging of entrepreneurship and finance domains in the context of informal entrepreneurial financing. Consequently, the underlying but diverse theories would also be unified into a single and augmented scholastic platform. Second, accounting practitioners, knowledgeable entrepreneurs, and policy makers can leverage on the knowledge enhancement in form of management accounting information and tools to further the practice that will develop the accounting profession and also inform appropriate policies for enhancing informal entrepreneurship in the developing economies.

5.1 Conceptualisation of the Model

Informal entrepreneurship is conceptualised into two-fold; the entrepreneurial opportunity and innovativeness emerging from informal sector of the economy. Entrepreneurial opportunity is expressed in terms of recognition and motivation of intents and can be geared towards search or alertness, meaning that potential informal entrepreneur can desire (i.e., to create) or notice (i.e., to discover) opportunity to innovate product, process or service in the informal market. In this context, opportunity can be operationalised in terms of (i) percentage of the unemployed population that recognises start-up of new business, and (ii) percentage informal business activity initiated because of opportunity start-up motive.

Innovativeness refers to innovative ideas and projects that culminate in the newness of product, process, technology amidst competitive brands and varieties in both the formal and informal markets. Innovation can be radical (i.e., completely new) or can be incremental (i.e., renovated). Operationalisation of innovativeness can take the form of (i) number of new products in the market, (ii) number of renovated products in the market, (iii) new technology in the market and (iii) new informal market in the economy.

Both the opportunity discovery and innovativeness exist in the informal environment which is influenced or moderated by institutional policies, regulations and informal rules, conventions and shared values. Although, informality as an environment may be difficult and ambiguous to measure because it is largely seen as a shadow economic unit with the prevalence of numerous informal activities such as small firms trading including street-trading, subsistence farming and agricultural occupation, self-employment, it nevertheless comprises of organised sectors of artisans, technicians, professionals, transporters of goods and persons that are grouped into household businesses and non-wage workers.

It follows that the informal environment has a relationship with the entrepreneurial opportunity and innovativeness respectively. This linkage could therefore establish whether informal firms drive the discovery of entrepreneurial opportunities and innovativeness in the informal markets amidst the disruption in the entire economy.

The interlinkage between the environment and the informal entrepreneurship leads to the emergence on how the new products, technology and process are being financed and brought into the market. Entrepreneurial financing in the context of the informal sector is conceptualised as the process of seeking for and raising appropriate financing for business start-up, renovating new products or technological process and the expansion of capacity that is driven by product and technological innovation. This process runs through informal lending outlets such as borrowing from family, friends, savings, or through financial intermediary such as banks, cooperative societies, microfinance institutions or through the emerging new investment platforms such as crowdfunding, corporate venture, angel investor, accelerators and government specialist financing.

The next phase of the model shows that the paths to seek for fund providers and source appropriate finance for informal entrepreneurial opportunity and innovation are clogged with bottlenecks. Unlike formal entrepreneurial firms, in formal entrepreneurs are faced with informality-specific bottlenecks which are; information asymmetry, moral hazard conflict, ambiguous and unformalized financial contract agreement that is laden with enforcement problems, informal ownership structure and unstandardised financial structure, and mental accounting bias.

In the last phase of the conceptual model, redress propositions in form of contributions to the theory, are made to address the financing bottlenecks in the informal entrepreneurship sector. These contributions are contingent on the frontiers of management accounting research, considering similar theoretical propositions from other disciplines such as finance, economics, strategic management. The contributions to the theory and practice are linked to the relevant bottlenecks that should be addressed in the flow accordingly. For instance, the theoretical expansion envisaged on goal congruence is focused on the agency problems of moral hazard conflict and information asymmetry. Similarly, information management and controls, search and match model are also expected to hinge on the issue of information asymmetry.

The problems of ownership structure would be addressed by the enhancement of management accounting literature in the areas of financial contract agreement and policy and regulative incentives, while the issue of the informal financial structure would be addressed via the expanded theory of the financial contract agreement, search and match model and policy and regulative incentives.

6. IMPLICATIONS FOR MANAGEMENT ACCOUNTING RESEARCH

6.1 Contributions to Theory and Quest for Further Study

Management accounting is considered a purely applied discipline of strategic management. Hence, it is believed that its relevance and intervention in the issues of entrepreneurial orientation and entrepreneurial financing in the informal sector of the economy is prominent.

In the views of some scholars, management accounting research carries a dichotomy of roles in theory While some scholars are of the view that management accounting being a pure applied field, can only adapt or import theories from other disciplines to use in its research, others believe that the field is distinct, and has its own sets of theories [46]. In my view, these two roles are indistinguishable.

Further, management accounting has often been challenged for not doing enough in providing practical solutions to some theoretical or conceptual issues which are fundamental in expanding the knowledge of the field [6, 28]. Thus, it is important to know how accounting research situates in the realms of knowledge and examine how it intervenes in the research theories of other domains.

In the context of management accounting research, this paper contributes in multiple fold to the literature and theories that underly the phenomenon of entrepreneurial financing by identifying how the bottlenecks of information asymmetry, moral hazard conflict, ownership and financial structure hampering informal entrepreneurship could be bridged.

First, the issue of moral hazard conflict is an agency problem, and could be further theorised using the concept of Goal Congruence. This means that the extant theory of agency should be extended to 'goals model' which emphasises the congruency of goals between two or more contrasting parties. In other word, the theory of agency should be expanded to harness the nexus of informal entrepreneurship and financing. Normally, incentives management are employed in resolving goal congruency issues between agent and his principal, but in the context of entrepreneur and investor relationship, resolution should start with modelling of the interests and goals of informal entrepreneurs and investors, after which the two goals are harnessed to anticipate reduction in monitoring cost, reduce bad investment decisions and mitigate impacts of individual opportunism.

The goal congruency modelling should be able to differentiate ostensible and actual goal congruence, whilst proffering different views of congruency that can harmonise common goals and mutual benefits regarding the funding of entrepreneurial opportunities and innovativeness in the informal sector of the economy. In designing the goal model, cooperative behaviours, consensus and control mechanism should all be embedded in order to derive economic benefits of the goal congruency [47].

Second, the problem of information asymmetry could be theoretically salvaged through accounting information management and control, search and match model, and goal congruence. In the nexus of entrepreneurship and financing, information asymmetry occurs when the relevant oversight by investors who normally finance informal entrepreneurial opportunities and innovation is mostly lacking [48]. For instance, angel investors, crowdfunding investors, traditional fund providers like banks, etc. are mostly passive in the management of the entrepreneurship projects, coupled with lack of standardised information systems in the informal sector.

Likewise, the possibility of informal firms concealing vital information to his advantage which is hidden to the potential investor, or the same behaviour posed by investor [23]. These two issues are common in the informal entrepreneurship and financing nexus and contribute to information asymmetry in the financial industry.

Management accounting research will add value to the theory of organisation when it focuses on the design of 'combined control mechanism' that encompasses both behavioural and information systems management and control [49], and to the theory of contingency, when the contingent nature of accounting and management information in the constantly changing environment of financing is explored and included as an additive package to the combined information system mechanism [50]. Management accounting research needs to adapt the model of contingency to the disruptive environment of financial industry, focusing on the prevalence of funding outlets, platforms and providers which are dynamic, to help informal entrepreneurs and investors share and match relevant information which enable both parties to derive economic benefits of standardised accounting and management information.

Similarly, feedback control should also be embedded in the overall management information mechanism to give prominence to 'cognitive dissonance' in the relationship between informal entrepreneurship and entrepreneurial financing. The feedback control should be designed to guard against either of the party hiding information for selfish tendency and to achieve goal congruence, since there is inherent control weakness in the human interaction system between the informal entrepreneurs who are likely to be dominant in information retention and the potential investors who exploit such information are also passive in the relationship.

Cognitive dissonance implies that a party in the relationship agree with and accommodate information, data and reports that is favourable to his position while discerning the ones at variance with his position. In the process, factual information that is vital to make decisions that could be of mutual benefits to the contractual parties are withheld or grossly be absent. Thus, the antecedents and consequence of cognitive biases in an informal setting of entrepreneurial financing in the twenty-first century, should provide both the informal entrepreneurs and investors with adequate and open information that reflects the symmetry of information that is persuasive of good decision making.

On the other hand, accounting scholars can also theoretically bridge the gap of information asymmetry in the relationship between informal entrepreneur-investor relationship, by leveraging on the extant theoretical work on the search cost model and extend it to the '*search and match*' model in the relationship between informal entrepreneurs and potential investors and with the view of enhancing information symmetry and financial contracting between the two parties. Therefore, management accounting models and tools can effectively be deployed in similarity with the model of search and matching [51].

With the advent of Fintech and a variety of new financing instruments, the cost of searching and accessing investors for promising entrepreneurial opportunity and innovation in the informal sector of the economy are fast becoming a concern for informal firms and individual actors within the sector. It follows that search and match model is a valuation tool used in calibrating and matching of demand and supply forces of labour market [52]. Normatively, search and match tool is designed to exploit wealth of information between two contrasting parties (i.e., employer and employee groups) in response to a change in environmental variable and market friction (i.e., job opening requirements or policy changes). Further, it is an estimating tool designed to provide behavioural responses to the employment issues confronting the labour market [53].

In the context of search and matching model, management accounting research needs to extend the model to bridge the gaps of information asymmetry and financial structure in the relationship of informal entrepreneurship and financing. Quantitative calibration, using empirical data appropriate to the relationship such as background data of informal entrepreneurs and investors, parameters for choice of funds, geographical consideration in terms of financing outlets and providers, cost of search, intermediation cost, cost of fund, forecast data on innovation projects, etc., should be factored in the model calibration.

The third implication centres on the inadequacy of financial contracting in the informal entrepreneurship sector, and its consequential effects on the financial and ownership structures. The underlying theory is the transaction cost and contract. Unlike the formal sectors where contractual agreement, financial and ownership structure are formalised and registered in line with some institutionalised directions, informal firms and individual actors within the informal sector are naturally outside such coverage of legality and formal institutional environment. However, the illegitimacy arising from this externality to informal entrepreneurship could be addressed with two accounting tools.

First, the melding of financial models that aim to put informality around the boundary of formality. In this instance, the financial modelling should encompass financial lending, a structure-oriented funding sources and investor-compliance ownership structure. Second, informal incentive contract model should be explored in quantitative terms to evaluate and analyse the standardised setting of the entrepreneur-investor relationship in the context of informal sector. In this instance, the incentive model should be designed to induce the entrepreneurial opportunity and innovation towards acceptability by potential investors based on predetermined criteria that include unhindered flow of information, remediation, and arbitration process amidst other consideration.

Overall financing contract model should reflect a valid intermediation role and also have the capability to serve as a robust check on the internal logic of decision making and controls for the informal sector entrepreneurship which consequently should assist in standardising bookkeeping, accounting records, budgetary controls and management information system.

6.2 Contributions to Accounting Practice

One of the implications of this paper is the dematerialisation of the impacts that some regulatory policy has on the informality of entrepreneurship and financing. Management accounting research should expand its frontier to accommodate studies on economic incentives of regulatory policy that is peculiar to informal markets. In this respect, management accounting research should explore the designs and qualitative analysis for tailor-made economic incentive model that brings informal markets closer to the border of formalities and regulatory framework and which can also avail informal entrepreneurs with some of the benefits that formal firms do enjoy, particularly in the areas of taxes, registration and compliance. Such an incentive model should provide governance authority with constructive directions for taking policy decisions, enhance entrepreneurship blueprint and good advocacy for standardised information system for informal entrepreneurship rather than an accounting model.

7. DELIMITATION

In this paper, the focus is mainly on the domains of observation and their relationships. That means, the domains of entrepreneurship, finance and accounting. The underlying theories of agency, new institutions, financial contract, transaction costs are not explored, but are justified as the basis for theoretical expansion.

In the same way, the proposed focus for expanding the frontiers of entrepreneurial financing is hinged on the management accounting research instead of multiple disciplines such as finance, economics and strategic management. This intentional focus is to explore the interventionist research agenda of management accounting, being the perceived applied strategic management study. It is also to re-awaken accounting practitioners of their vital roles in the knowledge building of entrepreneurship studies, using accounting information controls and tools.

8. CONCLUSION

Informality in the setting of the entrepreneurial economy in developing countries connotes that, informal firms and individual actors within the informal sector do not add significant values to the economy as much as formal firms add, irrespective of the fact that the informal sector employs large numbers of workers and also harness much bigger resources in the value chain of the economy.

Notwithstanding, entrepreneurship opportunity and innovativeness dimensions of entrepreneurial orientation have relevance in the informal sector entrepreneurship, but with the constraints of sourcing and accessing adequate financial resources to fund innovative products, services and new localised technology in the informal markets.

The apparent emergence of financial technology platforms (FINTECH) and new sources of funding, such as crowdfunding, accelerators and incubators are alternative complements to the traditional and informal financing outlets of bank loans, family and friends, as well as angel investor network, venture capital and government venture fund. The new alternative sources are also filling the gaps for considering small firms and start-ups financing, albeit with no visible informal projects in the envelopes. Nevertheless, the on-line provision of capital funds for entrepreneurship has been enormous.

In the informal sector, an opportunity to take advantage of such new sources to close funding gaps are usually marred by the lack of collaterals, poor accounting records, illegitimacy concerns of no formal registration, tax avoidance, no formal contracting and non-coverage of institutionalised policies. These concerns also extend to the issues of information asymmetry, moral hazard, financial and ownership structure.

In an attempt to reposition the understanding of informality in the context of entrepreneurship and financing, and to expand the frontiers of strategic management and accounting literature, this paper suggests that management accounting research could play vital roles in further exploring the problematised issues of entrepreneurial informality and financing by bridging the domains of accounting, finance and entrepreneurship. In this arena, five areas for theoretical contributions were highlighted as, goal congruence, accounting and management information controls, financing contract modelling, regulative policy incentives and search and matching model.

Theoretical model that conceptualises interrelationship among different variables with their underlying theories was proposed. The model demonstrates that informal entrepreneurship has opportunity discovery and innovativeness as antecedents of entrepreneurial orientation. The informal entrepreneurs operate in an institutionalised environment where regulation, policies, culture, traditions and shared values play prominent roles. In this institutionalised environment, it is contingent for the informal entrepreneurs to seek for funds to finance their innovative products, process or technology. There are diverse sources and platforms in the financial industry for the choice either direct or through financial intermediation. However, there many bottlenecks confronting informal entrepreneurship innovation in accessing appropriate and adequate funding.

In this paper, management accounting research is focused to explore various management information systems, models and tools to bridge the theoretical gaps, while also focuses on economic incentives for regulative policy to address gap in policy making concerning informal entrepreneurship sector. The justification for the choice of management accounting research is to position the literature to contribute and expand the frontiers of agency theory, contingency theory, organisational theory, transaction cost theory, financial contracting theory and the model of search and match, all of which underly the highlighted bottlenecks of the informal sector financing.

The other cogent reason is that, management accounting is positioned in between the paradigms of positivism and interpretivism, however, the focus is more on the ontology, epistemology and methodology of interpretivist paradigm, simply because of the social science nature of the discipline rather than considering it as a pure natural science which confers positivist paradigm [54]. While positivism is a scientific paradigm and focus on a realistic natural phenomenon that is independent of the researcher, the interpretivist paradigm is subjective, it focuses on relativism where meanings to objects are discovered and constructed through interaction between researcher conscience and the real world [55].

The knowledge realm of management accounting research is also informed by inductive reasoning for analysing and evaluating qualitative data that will produce reliability and validity of findings [56]. It therefore follows that the perspectives of management accounting research are dynamic and has metamorphosed from just number analysis to qualitative and quantitative decision making and human interaction facilitator [57]. There are instances where management accounting has influenced entrepreneurship studies adopting inductive and qualitative approach such as case studies, interviews, focus groups, etc. Moreover, management accounting has also been found as an important resource and capability for international entrepreneurship and assumes effectuation and causality logic [58]. In these instances, this paper suggests that the theoretical contributions highlighted can be taken through qualitative or quantitative methodology as each case may warrant.

REFERENCES

1. Chowdhury F, Terjesen S, Audretsch D: Varieties of entrepreneurship: institutional drivers across entrepreneurial activity and country. 2014; DOI: 10.1007/s10657-011-9464-x

2. Van Vuuren J, Alemayehu B. Z: The role of entrepreneurship in transforming efficiency economies to innovation-based economies. 2018; 10(1) :1-12. DOI: 10.4102/sajebm. v10i1.40

3. Edoho F. M: Entrepreneurship and socioeconomic development: Catalyzing African transformation in the 21st century. 147-127: (2)6 ;2015. https//doi. org/10.1108/AJEMS0030-2013-03-.

4. La Porta R, Shleifer: Informality and Development. The Journal of Economic Perspectives. 2014 ;28(3) :109-126.

5. Zoogah D. B, Peng M. W, Woldu H: Institutions, Resources and Organizational Effectiveness in Africa. 2015;29(1):7-31. http//dx.doi.org/10.5465/amp.2012.0033

6. Jansen E. P: Bridging the gap between theory and practice in management accounting: Reviewing the literature to shape interventions. 2018; 31(5) :1486-1509. DOI: 10.1108/AAAJ-10-2015-2261.

7. Webb J. W, Ireland R. D, Ketchen D. J: Toward a Greater Understanding of Entrepreneurship and strategy in the Informal Economy. 2014 ;8 :1-15. DOI: 10.1002/sej.1176.

8. Chen M. A: The Informal Economy: Definitions, Theories and Policies. 2012.

9. Meagher K: The Scramble for Africans: demography, globalization and Africa's informal labour market. 2016 ;52(4) :483-497. DOI: 10.1080/00220388.2015.1126253.

10. Eckhardt J. T, Shane S. A: Opportunities and entrepreneurship. 2003;29(3):333-349. DOI: 10.1177/014920630302900304.

11. Lechner C, Gudmundsson S. V: Entrepreneurial orientation, firm strategy and small firm performance. 2014 ;32(1) :36-60. DOI: 10.1177/0266242612455034.

12. Meagher K: Cannibalizing the Informal Economy: Frugal Innovation and Economic Inclusion in Africa. 2018; 30 :17-33. https//doi.org/10.1057/s41287-017-0113-4

13. Sparks D. L, Barnett S. T: The Informal Sector in Sub-Saharan Africa: Out of the Shadows to Foster Sustainable Employment and Equity? 2010 ;9(5):1-11.

14. Krasniqi B. A, Williams C. C: Does informality help entrepreneurs achieve firm growth? Evidence from a post-conflict economy. 2020 ;33(1) :1581-1599. DOI: 10.1080/1331677x.2020.1756369.

15. Anyigba H, Bugbilla D, Omotosho S, Asiedu M, Gomado D: Economic Globalisation, Informality and Informal Employment: The African Perspective. 2020 https//ssrn.com/abstract=3638708.

16. Pham T. H. H: Impacts of globalisation on the informal sector: Empirical evidence from developing countries. 2017; http://dx.doi.org/10.1016/j.econmod.2017.01.001

17. IMF: Regional economic Outlook: Sub-Saharan Africa, Restarting the growth engine. 2017.

18. Autio E, Fu K: Economic and political institutions and entry into formal and informal entrepreneurship. 2015 ;32: 67-94. DOI: 10.1007/s10490-014-9381-0.

19. Ketchen D.J, Ireland R. D, Webb J. W: Toward a Research Agenda for the Informal Economy: A Survey of the Strategic Entrepreneurship Journal's Editorial Board. 2014 ;8 :95-100. DOI: 10.1002/sej.1175.

20. Chemmanur T. J, Fulghieri P: Entrepreneurial Finance and Innovation: An Introduction and Agenda for Future Research. 2013; DOI: 10.1093/rfs/hht063.

21. Bellavitis. C, Filatotchev I, Karimuwo D. S, Vanacker T: Entrepreneurial Finance: new frontiers of research and practice. 2017 ;19(1-2):1-16. DOI: 10.1080/13691066.2016.1259733

22. Block J. H, Colombo M. G, Cumming D. J, Vismara S: New players in entrepreneurial finance and why they are there. 2018 ;50 :239-250. DOI: 10.1007/s11187-016-9826-6.

23. Cumming D, Groh A. P: Entrepreneurial finance: Unifying themes and future directions. 2018 ;50 :538-555. https://doi.org/10.1016/j.jcorpfin2018.01.011.

24. Fraser S, Bhaumik S. K, Wright M: What do we know about entrepreneurial finance and its relationship with growth. 2015 ;33(1) :70-88. DOI: 10.1177/0266242614547827.

25. Mitter C, Kraus G: Entrepreneurial finance- issues and evidence revisited. 2011 ;14(2/3) :133-150.

26. Drover W, Busenitz L, Matsuki S, Townsend D, Anglin A, Dushnitsky G: A Review and Roadmap of Equity Financing Research: Venture Capital, Corporate Venture Capital, Angel Investor, Crowdfunding and Accelerators. 2017; 20(10): 1-34. DOI: 10.1177/0149206317690584.

27. Colombo M. G, Cumming D. J, Vismara S: Governmental venture capital for innovative young firms. 2014; DOI: 10.1007/s10961-014-9380-9.

28. Mollick E: The Dynamics of Crowdfunding: An Exploratory Study. 2014; 29: 1-16. DOI: 10.1016/jbusvent2013.06.005.

29. Alvi F. H, Carsrud A. L: Strategic Entrepreneurial Agency in Emerging Market. 2017; 26(1): 77-101. DOI: 10.1177/0971355716677394.

30. Jerzemowska M: The Main Agency Problems and Their Consequences. 2006; 14(3): 9-17.

31. Bitler M. P, Moskowitz T. J, Vissing-Jorgen A: Testing agency Theory with Entrepreneur Effort and Wealth. 2005; 60(2): 539-576.

32. Eisenhardt K. M: Agency Theory: An assessment and Review. 1989; 14(1): 57-74.

33. Cosh A, Cumming D, Hughes A: Outside Entrepreneurial Capital. 2009; 119: 1494-1533. DOI: 10.1111/j.1468-0297.2009.0227. x.

34. Giordani P. E: Entrepreneurial Finance and Economic Growth. 2015; 115: 153-174. DOI: 10.1017/s00712-014-0411-7

35. Momtaz P. P: Entrepreneurial Finance and Moral Hazard: Evidence from Token offerings. 2020; DOI: 10.1016/j.jbusvent.2020.106001.

36. Bendickson J, Muldoon J, Liguori E, Davis P. E: Agency Theory: the times, they are changin'. 2009; 54(1): 174-193. DOI: 10.1108/MD-02-2015-0058.

37. Gil R, Zanarone G: Formal and Informal Contracting: Theory and Evidence. 2017; 13: 141-159. DOI: 10.1146/annurev/lawsocsci-110316-113413.

38. Gil R, Zanarone G: On the determinants and consequence of informal contracting. 2018; 1-16. DOI: 10.1111/jems.12246.

39. Ling A, Miao J, Wang N: Robust financial Contracting and Investment. 2021; Working paper 28367. http://www.nber.org/papers/w28367.

40. Drodz L. A, Serrano-Padial R: Financial contracting with enforcement externality. 2018; 178: 153-189. DOI: 10.1016/j.jet.2018.09.002

41. Adomza G. K, Astebro T, Yong K: Decision biases and entrepreneurial finance. 2016; DOI: 10.1007/s11187-016-9739-4.

42. Virigineni M, Rao M. B: Contemporary Developments in Behavioral Finance in. 2017; 7(1): 448-459. http://www.econjournals.com

43. Wu J, Si S, Wu X : Entrepreneurial Finance and Innovation : Informal Debt As an Empirical Case. 2016 ; 10 : 257-273. DOI: 10.1102/sej

44. Lee C, Hung S: Institutional Entrepreneurship in the Informal Economy: China's Shan-Zhai Mobile Phones. 2014; DOI: 10.1002/sej.1174

45. Greenwood M. J, Baylis R. M, Tao L: Regulatory incentives and financial reporting quality in public health care organisations. 2017; DOI: 10.1080/00014788.2017.1343116

46. Lukka K, Vinnari E: Domain theory and method theory in management accounting research. 2014 ;27(8):1308-1338. https//doi.org/10.1108/AAAJ-03-2013-1265.

47. Buillon M. L, Ferrier G.D, Stuebs M. T, West T. D: The economic benefit of goal congruence and implications for management control systems. 2006; 25: 265-298. DOI: 10.1016/j.jaccpubol.2006.03.003

48. de Bettignies J-E: Financing the Entrepreneurial Venture. 2008 ;54(1):151-166. http://dx.doi.org/10.1287/mnsc.1070.0759.

49. Malmi T, Brown D. A: Management control systems as a package- Opportunities, challenges and research directions. 2008; 19:287-300. DOI: 10.1016/j.mar.200809.003

50. Otley D: The contingency of management accounting and control:1980-2014. 2016; 31:45-62. DOI: 10.1016/j.mar.2016.02.001

51. Di Porto E, Elia L, Tealdi C: Informal work in a flexible labour market. 2017 ;69(1) :143-164. DOI: 10.1093/oep/gpw010.

52. Lise J, Seitz S, Smith J: Evaluating search and matching models using experimental data. 2015; 4(16):2-35. DOI: 10.1186/s40172-015-0031-7

53. Lubik T. A: Estimating a Search and Matching Model of the Aggregate Labour market. 2009 ;95(2):101-120.

54. Lukka K: Exploring the possibilities for causal explanation in interpretive research. 2014 ;39 :559-566. http://dx.doi.org/10.1016/j.aos.2014.06.002.

55. Scotland J: Exploring the Philosophical Underpinnings of Research: Relating Ontology and Epistemology to the Methodology and Methods of the Scientific, Interpretive, and Critical Research Paradigms. 2012; 5(9):9-150 DOI: 10.5539/elt.v5n9p9.

56. Thomas D. R: A General inductive approach for Analyzing Qualitative Evaluation Data. 2006 ;27(2) :237-246. DOI: 10.1177/1098214005283748.

57. Shields M. D: A Perspective on Management accounting Research. 2018; 30(3): 1-11. DOI: 10.2308/j.mar-10618

58. Mitter C, Hiebl M. R. W: The role of management accounting on international entrepreneurship. 2017; 13(3) :381-409. https//doi.org/10.1108/JAOC-02-2016-0006.

11 Impact of Working Capital Management on Profitability: A Case Study of Trading Companies

1. INTRODUCTION

An attempt has been made in this empirical study to know the impact of working capital management on profitability, both the factors are important concerns of management. If working capital is not managed perfectly it will reduce the liquidity of the company and ultimately effects profitability.

The working capital should be maintained at a desired level depending upon the size of the firm, excessive working capital leads to the unnecessary accumulation of inventories causing losses and wastages. The large debtors indicate the defective credit policy which might lead to bad debts. On the other hand, with the inadequate working capital, the firm will not be in a position to pay short-term liabilities. The firm may not be able to pay its day-to-day expenses which creates inefficiencies and reduces profits.

The success of any business depends on its profitability, liquidity, and solvency. Liquidity plays an important role in the successful running of a business. The crucial functions of financial managers to ensure the liquidity of a firm, that it must be in a position to meet its short-term obligation without which it cannot survive. The working capital which consists of current assets and current liabilities which measure the liquidity has been chosen as the main independent variable to study its relationship with the profitability. The collection period, payment period, inventory days and cash conversion cycle has been used as a measure of working capital.

Many prior studies have been conducted to measure the relationship between working capital and profitability as examined by Azhar [1]. The impact of liquidity and management efficiency on the profitability of select power sectors using different ratios as independent variables, where debtor turnover ratio, collection efficiency, and interest coverage showed a significant impact. Rathiranee and Sangeetha [2] examine the impact of working capital on financial performance in select trading firms where the regression analysis results showed that the high investment in inventories and receivables is associated with lower financial performance i.e., Return on Assets (ROA). They found a negative relationship between Return on Assets and Inventory turnover and Cash conversion cycle for the trading firms listed in Colombo Stock Exchange. Mansoori and Muhammad [3] have studied the same picture with the evidence from Singapore found that Management performance would be improved by managing working capital efficiently. Their results demonstrate that firm's profitability is increased by decreasing in receivable conversion period and inventory conversion period. Saradhadevi found in her study that there exists a highly significant negative relationship between the profitability and cash conversion cycle and a highly significant positive relationship between the time it takes the firm to pay its (Average payment period) which implies the longer a firm takes to pay its creditors the more profitable it is.

Keeping in view the above scenario the present study is designed to know the direct impact of working capital on profitability by choosing the days of collection, days of payment, days inventory converts to sales and finally the cash conversion cycle. Many studies have been conducted for manufacturing companies, cement and textile companies, oil and gas companies only a few have been focused on trading companies. Hence the present study has its focus on working capital management and its impact on profitability in relation to trading sector.

2. REVIEW OF LITERATURE

Working capital management and profitability [4]: This study aims to find out the impact of working capital management on profitability. Return on assets, Current ratio, debt to equity ratio, operating profit to debt ratio, and inventory turnover ratios of the firms are the variables that are used in this study carried out for electrical equipment firms listed on Karachi stock exchange for a period of six years i.e. 2007–2012. Regression analysis was applied to the data. Normality and linearity test was also applied. Results showed significant positive results. T-test is applied to see for individual variable significance, it tells that each variable is significant. It is concluded that working capital management has positive significant impact on profitability of the firms.

The relationship between working capital management and profitability [5]: A sample of 67 companies is used for a period of ten years (2007–2016). Quantitative method using multiple linear regression and pooled data set is used for analysis. The study investigates the relationship between working capital management and profitability in non-financial companies listed in the Saudi Stock Exchange. The results indicate a positive relationship between working capital management and profitability. The results indicate a weak linear relationship between WCM and profitability, indicating that no single constant practice or strategy would suit every company, managers should identify the optimal level of working capital that suits their company's situation. The results showed a statistically positive relationship between WCM, measured by CR, RCP, APP, INP, and profitability; however, there was a weak linear relationship.

Working capital management and firms' profitability: Dynamic panel data analysis of manufactured firms [6]: This paper examines the impact of working capital management on firm's profitability performance of manufacturing firms by using not only static models such as ordinary least square (OLS), fixed and random effects but also dynamic models difference generalized method of moments (GMM) and system generalized method of moments (SGMM) over the period from 2007 to 2018. The results show that inventory conversion period (ICP) and payable deferral period (PDP) have a positive relationship with return on asset while the cash conversion cycle (CCC) has a negative effect on return on assets.

Working capital management and profitability: Empirical evidence [7]: Empirical findings suggest that granting longer extensions to customers does not affect profitability. The results of the other variables showed a negative relationship with the profitability of the companies, suggesting that the investment in inventories and the obtaining of extensions from suppliers determine additional costs that negatively impact profitability. This paper examines the working capital management policies in 105 manufacturing companies in the Czech Republic for five years, from 2014 to 2018.

The relationship between working capital management and profitability: A case study of cement industry in Pakistan [8]: Ikram ul Haqq, Muhammad Sohail, Khalid Zaman and Zaheer Alam examines the effect of working capital on profitability for the period of six years from 2004 to 2009 by using the data of fourteen companies in the cement industry. The ratios relating to capital management have been selected and computed for the study. The main objective of the study was to find whether financial ratios affect the performance of the firm in the special context of cement industry in Pakistan. They found that the ROI is negatively correlated with the current assets to sales ratios and cash turnover ratio while ROI is positively correlated with the current ratio, liquid ratio current assets to total assets ratio, debtors turnover ratio, inventory turnover ratio, and credit turnover ratio.

Relationship between inventory management and profitability: An empirical analysis of Indian cement companies [9]: Dr. Ashok Kumar Panigrahi has discussed the importance of inventory management practices of Indian Cement Companies and their impact on working capital efficiency over a period of ten years from 2001 to 2010. The study uses Regression analysis. The findings indicate that there exists a significant negative linear relationship between inventory conversion period and profitability. It was also found that when profitability increases with the decrease in the financial debt ratio. Further, it showed a positive relationship between profitability and firm size, as the profitability increases with an increase in firm size. Lastly, the relationship between the current ratio and profitability was negative.

Effects of working capital management on profitability: The case for selected companies in Istanbul stock exchange (2005–2008) [10]: The study was carried out by Hasan Ajan Karaduman, Halil Emre Akbas, Arzu Ozsozgun, and Salih Durer with the aim to provide some empirical evidence on the effects of working capital management on profitability for a sample of 140 selected companies listed in the Istanbul Stock Exchange (ISE) for the period of 2005–2008. The return on assets of the sample companies increases with a decrease in the number of days accounts receivable, accounts payable, and a number of days of inventory. Also, the reduction in the cash conversion cycle results in higher returns on assets. Furthermore, the results of control variables like the size have a positive effect on profitability while the debt ratio negatively affects the profitability.

Working capital management in indian oil and gas industry—A case study of Reliance Industries Ltd. [11]: Sankar Thappa has used liquidity ratios to assess the significance of working capital for a period of ten years 2004–2013.The analysis of liquidity ratios, liquidity position, item-wise analysis of components of gross working capital and liquidity ranking have been done. The results showed that the coefficient of correlation between the profitability ratio compared to the current ratio, working capital turnover ratio, and inventory turnover ratio indicates the low degree of positive correlation whereas the coefficient of correlation between profitability ratio compared to the quick ratio (liquid ratio) and absolute liquid ratio indicates that there is a low degree of negative correlation. The overall working capital position is not very much satisfactory.

Relationship between working capital management and firm profitability manufacturing sector of Pakistan [12]: Muhammad Safdar Sial and Aqsa Chaudry measure the relationship between working capital management and firm profitability in the manufacturing sector with a sample of 100 firms covering a period of ten years from 1999 to 2008. The coefficient of size was positive which means that the bigger the size have more profitability as compared to firms of smaller size. The debt ratio has been used for leverage which showed a significant negative relationship with Return on Asset which means increase in leverage adversely affect on return on assets. The results show that there is a strong negative relationship between variables of working capital management and profitability of the firm which means as the cash conversion cycle increases it will lead to a decrease in profitability of the firm.

Effect of working capital management on profitability by Asif Iqbala and Zhuquan Wang [13]: They found a diverging effect of working capital management on the profitability of manufacturing firms of Pakistan. They suggest that "paying full attention to the cash conversion cycle" has enormous effect on working capital. Minimizing the inventory level frees the capital for other use.

Relationship between working capital management and profitability by Puteri Shahirah Binti Ghazal [14]: This paper is an evidence from the UAE market focusing on real estates and construction companies from the Abu Dhabi market. The finding of this study presented that there is a negative relationship between cash conversion cycle and profitability; longer the CCC, the profitability decreases. Another finding showed that the amount of payable days is negatively related to profitability.

The effect of working capital management on profitability [15]: A sample of three (3) manufacturing companies listed on the Dar es Salaam Stock Exchange (DSE) is used for a period of ten years (2002–2012). They found negative relationship between liquidity and profitability showing that as liquidity decreases, the profitability increases, average collection period and profitability indicating that a decrease in the number of days a firm receives payment from sales affects the profitability of the firm positively.

To analyze relationship between working capital management and profitability [16]: This paper basically analysis the relationship between working capital and profitability of the Indian IT Company (TCS). This Study shows negative relationship of inventory turnover ratio with ROA excluding and including Revaluation which shows that with the inventory turnover the firm should increase its return on assets. And also study shows negative relationship of debtor turnover ratio with Return on Capital Employed.

3. RESEARCH QUESTION

The main objective of any business is to earn profit and manage the funds efficiently and effectively which has direct impact on profits. So, working capital is the major constituent to measure liquidity. This study examines the association between the profitability and working capital using the data of 15 US trading companies for the period of 2015 to 2019.

4. HYPOTHESES DEVELOPMENT

Working capital is an important issue during financial decision making. The crucial part in managing working capital is required to maintain its liquidity in day-to-day operation for the smooth running of business and meeting its obligations in time. Thus, working capital is selected as one of the independent variables to know that how it effects profitability.

H1: There is a significant relationship between Working Capital Management and profitability.

H2: Working capital management has strong impact on profitability.

Keeping in view the above studies the following objectives have been outlined for the present study.

5. OBJECTIVES OF THE STUDY

1. To study the relationship between profitability and working capital management.
2. To examine the impact of average collection period, average payment period, inventory turnover days and cash conversion cycle on profitability.

6. METHODS

The choice of the variables for the present study is influenced by the previous studies on working capital management. They include dependent, independent and some control variables. The profitability in terms of Return on assets, Gross profit ratio, Operating profit and Net income are taken as dependent variable in previous studies.

The dependent variable is the one which is affected during the experiment, for the present study profitability is taken as dependent variable i.e., in terms of Net Income. The independent variable is the one which effects the dependent variable. Average collection period, cash conversion cycle, average payment period, inventory turnover ratio, current ratio, liquid ratio, etc. were taken as independent variables in previous studies. For this study the independent variables are the average collection period, average payment period, inventory turnover days and cash conversion cycle. The study aims at to find out the association between the variables through different statistical analysis (Table 1).

Table 1. Showing the key research variables.

Variables	Type	Measured	Abbreviations used
Net income	Dependent variable	Net Income/Net sales*100	NI
Average collection period	Independent variable	Account receivable/net sales*365	ACP
Average payment period	Independent variable	Account payable/Cost of goods sold*365	APP
Inventory turnover days	Independent variable	Inventory/Cost of goods sold* 365	ITD
Cash conversion cycle	Independent variable	ACP+ITD-APP	CCC

The following equation is used to estimate the impact of working capital on profitability.

$$NI(it) = \hat{a}0 + \hat{a}1(ACP\,it) + \hat{a}2(APP\,it) + \hat{a}3(ITD\,it) + \hat{a}4(CCC\,it)$$

NI (it) = profitability of the firms at time 5 years, i = 15 firms.

β0 = the intercept of an equation.

β = coefficients of independent variables.

T = time 5 years 2015–2019.

Average collection period ACP.

Average payment period APP.

Inventory turnover days ITD.

Cash conversion cycle CCC.

In the above general equation, the Profitability is the dependent variable, and it is influenced by the independent variables i.e., ACP, APP, ITD and CCC.

7. SAMPLE AND DATA COLLECTION

The main source of data is the S&P Capital IQ website. Many studies have been conducted to examine the relationship between the financial performance and working capital management. These studies have been done relating to the cement companies, trading companies, manufacturing companies, pharmaceutical companies and only a few have been carried out about trading companies. So for the present study sample is taken from trading companies.

The present study aims at to provide some empirical evidence of impact of working capital management on profitability for a sample of 15 trading companies for the period of five years from 2015 to 2019. These companies are randomly selected from all listed companies in the New York Stock Exchange (NYSE). The sample companies includes: 1) Applied Industrial Technologies Inc. (AIT), 2) DXP Enterprises Inc., 3) Eco Shift Power Corp. (ECOP), 4) EVI Industries Corp., 5) General Finance Corp. (GFN), 6) Gypsum Management and Supply Corp. (GMS), 7) W.W. Grainger (GWW), 8) H&E Equipment Inc. (HEES), 9) HD Supply Inc. (HDS) 10) Houston Wire and Cable Company (HWCC), 11) Huttig Building Products Inc. (HBP) 12) Kaman Corporation (KAMN), 13) MRC Global Inc., 14) MSC Industrial Direct Co. Inc. (MSM), 15) ProShares Ultra Health Care (RXL).

The Net Profitability is taken as the dependent variable and the average collection period (ACP), average payment period (APP), inventory days converted to sales (ITD) ad cash conversion cycle (CCC) are considered as independent variables.

8. RESULTS

The analysis of data is done using descriptive statistics, correlation matrix and regression analysis.

1. The following observations are made from the above Table 2 compiled with five years data for 15 trading companies:
2. The Net profitability for these companies ranges from -7.308 to 31.895 with a mean of 3.637 and standard deviation 5.85 which shows high variance.
3. ACP ranges between 18.57 and 133.28 days with an average of 51 days and standard deviation of 16.88 signifying very high variability across the companies.
4. The APP ranges between 9.6 and 79.69 with an average of 36.76 and standard deviation of 14.62. The minimum time taken to make the payment is 9 days which is unusual.
5. The ITD ranges between 30.62 and 139.53 with an average of 71.24 and standard deviation of 26.05. The maximum time taken to convert inventory into sales is 139 days which is a very large time period to convert inventory into sales.
6. The CCC ranges between 18.02 and 193.18 with an average of 85.85 and standard deviation of 36.63. The maximum time taken for cash conversion cycle is 193 days which is a large time taken to convert cash.

Table 2. Descriptive statistics of 15 companies for the years from 2014 to 2019.

Variable	Mean	Standard deviation	Minimum	Maximum
Net profitability	3.637	5.859	-7.308	31.895
ACP	51.38	16.886	18.576	133.28
APP	36.766	14.617	9.61	79.698
ITD	71.24	26.05	30.62	139.53
CCC	85.85	36.63	18.024	193.18

9. CORRELATION ANALYSIS

Correlation analysis is used to measure the degree of association between different variables under consideration. Correlation matrix of all variables included in the analysis is presented in Table 3 which is calculated based on data of 15 trading companies for a period of five years 2015 and 2019.

An attempt has been made to find the relationship between profitability and WC, for this purpose Pearson's coefficient of correlation analysis is done. As indicated in the above studies there exist a negative correlation between the profitability and the collection period, the lower the average collection period higher will be the profitability. The correlation between average payment period and profitability is 0.127 which shows a positive relationship if there is an increase in payment period it leads to an increase in profitability. There exist a negative correlation between profitability and the cash conversion cycle is -0.271 which indicates an increase in collection period leads to increase in CCC and vice versa and ultimately effects profitability The correlation between inventory conversion days and profitability is positive which is beyond expectation. There exists a negative correlation between cash conversion cycle and average payment period.

Table 3. Correlation matrix of 15 companies for the year 2015 and 2019.

	NP	ACP	APP	ITD	CCC
NP	1				
ACP	-0.353391495	1			
APP	0.127879206	0.25544055	1		
ITD	0.225071917	0.20822956	-0.140703	1	
CCC	-0.271955653	0.50715839	-0.381359	0.8633495	1

It is recommended that the companies should avoid an increasing cash conversion cycle because it means that the business is becoming more operating inefficient, locking more and more cash into its processes. They should maintain a lowest cash conversion cycle compared to their peers, or at least a decreasing one. A decreasing CCC represents a more efficient company that converts its inventories faster as well as gets paid faster and probably is paying its suppliers later thus, holding cash for more time (Table 4).

Table 4. Regression results of 15 companies for the year 2015 to 2019.

Regression statistics	
Multiple R	**0.782**
R square	0.584
Adjusted R square	0.425
Standard error	0.515
Observations	75

10. REGRESSION ANALYSIS

The regression analysis showed the value for the R-squared in the model is 0.584, i.e., 58.4% of the variation in the dependent variable (NI) is explained by the independent variables working capital of the model, which is represented by CCC, APP, ACP, and ITD and 42% is affected by other factors.

11. SUMMARY AND CONCLUSIONS

The study is carried out for a sample of 15 trading companies for the period of five years from 2015 to 2019. These companies are randomly selected from all listed companies in the New York Stock Exchange (NYSE).

This study examined the relationship between Net Profitability and several variables of working capital management such as average collection period, average inventory turnover in days, average payment period and cash conversion cycle. The results showed that there exist a negative relationship between the profitability and the average collection period, the lower the average collection period higher will be the profitability. The correlation between average payment period and profitability is 0.127 which shows a positive relationship if there is an increase in payment period it leads to an increase in profitability. It is found that the cash conversion cycle decreases it will lead to an increase in profitability of the firm, and managers can create a positive value for the shareholders which indicates that it has been maintained.

The results of this study show that there is a strong relationship between the working capital and profitability of the firms. It means if the financial managers keep an eye on the liquidity it will lead to profitability. So, it is recommended that Companies should always maintain a sound collection policy and it is further suggested that managers can create value for their shareholders by reducing the number of days accounts receivable, increasing the number of days accounts payable and inventories to a reasonable minimum.

The hypotheses is accepted for working capital management that it has strong impact on profitability. There is a significance relationship between Working Capital Management and profitability. The study has examined the impact in terms of average collection period, average payment period, inventory turnover days and cash conversion cycle on profitability.

Furthermore, On the basis of the above analysis the results can be further strengthened if the firms manage their working capital in more efficient ways. Management of Working capital means the management of current assets and current liabilities. If these firms efficiently manage their cash, accounts receivables, accounts payables, and inventories, this will ultimately increase profitability of these companies.

12. LIMITATIONS OF THE STUDY

1. The study is carried out for a period of five years only i.e., 2015 to 2019.
2. The study is based on secondary data collected from the website of S&P Capital IQ.
3. The study is carried out about 15 Trading companies.

REFERENCES

1. Azhar, Syed. Impact of liquidity and management efficiency on profitability: An empirical study of selected power distribution utilities in India. Journal of Entrepreneurship, Business and Economics 2015. https://iranept.rcv.org.uk/empirical_analysis_of_entrepreneurship_and_economic_growth_international_studies_in_entrepreneurship.pdf

2. Yogendrarajah, Rathiranee. Working capital management and its impact on firms' financial performance: An analysis of trading firms. Research Gate 2011. https://www.researchgate.net/publication/256088750_Working_Capital_Management_and_its_Impact_on_Firms'_Financial_Performance_An_Analysis_of_Trading_Firms

3. Mansoori, Ebrahim. The effect of working capital management on firm's profitability: Evidence from Singapore. Interdisciplinary Journal of Contemporary Research in Business 2012. https://papers.ssrn.com/sol3/papers.cfm?abstract_id=2185840

4. Rimsha Khalid, Tehreem Saif, Abdul Rehman Gondal, and Hamza Sarfraz. Working capital management and profitability. Mediterranean Journal of Basic and Applied Sciences (MJBAS) 2018;2(2):117-125.

5. Nasser A. Alsulayhim. The relationship between working capital management and profitability. International Business Research 2019;12(8). DOI: 10.5539/ibr.v12n8p142

6. Kafeel, Ali, J., Ud Din, M., Waris, A., Tahir, M., and Khan, S. Working capital management and firms' profitability: dynamic panel data analysis of manufactured firms. Journal of Financial Risk Management 2020;9:494-517. DOI: 10.4236/jfrm.2020.94027

7. Arnaldo Arnaldi, Barbara Novak, Remo Roscigno Wu Zhan. Working capital management and profitability: Empirical evidence. International Journal of Business Management and Economic Research (IJBMER) 2021;12(2).

8. Ul Haq, Ikram, Muhammad Sohail, Khalid Zaman, and Zaheer Alam. The relationship between working capital management and profitability: A case study of cement industry in Pakistan. Research Gate 2011. https://www.researchgate.net/publication/288946070

9. Panigrahi, CMA (Dr.) Ashok. Relationship between inventory management and profitability: An empirical analysis of Indian cement companies. SSRN 2013. https://papers.ssrn.com/sol3/papers.cfm?abstract_id=2342455.

10. Karaduman, Hasan Agan, Halil Emre Akbas, Arzu Ozsozgun, and Salih Durer. Effects of working capital management on profitability: The case for selected companies in the Istanbul stock exchange (2005-2008). Research Gate 2010. https://www.researchgate.net/publication/290164649_Effects_Of_Working_Capital_Management_On_Profitability_The_Case_For_Selected_Companies_In_The_Istanbul_Stock_Exchange_2005-2008

11. Thappa, Sankar. Working capital management in Indian oil and gas industry – A case study of Reliance Industries LTD. Academica Science Journal 2014. https://www.researchgate.net/publication/334442075_Working_Capital_Management_In_Indian_Oil_Gas_Industry_-_A_Cas_Study_of_Reliance_Industries_LTD

12. Safdar Sial, Muhammad, and Aqsa Chaudhry. Relationship between working capital management and firm profitability: Manufacturing sector of Pakistan. Research Gate 2012. https://www.researchgate.net/publication/255855851_Relationship_between_Working_Capital_Management_and_Firm_Profitability_Manufacturing_Sector_of_Pakistan

13. Asif Iqbala and Zhuquan Wang. Effect of working capital management on profitability. 2018 5th International Conference on Key Engineering Materials and Computer Science (KEMCS 2018).

14. Puteri Shahirah Binti Ghazali. Relationship between working capital management and profitability. https://www.researchgate.net/publication/336720653_Relationship_Between_Working_Capital_Management_and_Profitability

15. Ntui Ponsian, Kiemi Chrispina, Gwatako Tago, Halim Mkiibi. The effect of working capital management on profitability. International Journal of Economics, Finance and Management Sciences 2014;2(6):347-355. DOI: 10.11648/j.ijefm.20140206.17

16. Rajwinder Kaur. To analyze relationship between working capital management and profitability. International Journal of Management, Technology and Engineering.https://www.researchgate.net/publication/343162003_To_Analyze_Relationship_between_Working_Capital_Management_and_Profitability

12 The Effect of Internal Corporate Governance of the Firm's Performance and Firm Value in Five GCC Countries

1. INTRODUCTION

There is agreement among scholars with regard to the limitation of CG research or studies in emerging markets. According to Nenova [1], CG in the developing countries is suffering from the effects of a number of issues including transferring the value from minority to controlling shareholders, a poor legal system, the problem of auditing practice and non-transparency disclosure. A critical glance at the literature review of GCC countries, firm performance and firm value shows that the literature does not adequately consider the uniqueness of an institutional setting such as the presence of royal family members and government officials' members on the board. Additionally, noticeable features are not accounted for in the previous literature, such as a large involvement of relatives and the presence of a female on the board of directors. It is important to understand whether these variables matter or not in this region as this then influences the firm's performance and firm value. In addition, this question considers some features of an audit committee and their effect on a firm's performance and firm value. An audit committee is an important committee within the board committee. An audit committee is not just for supporting management by giving advice for major business decisions but also for monitoring and overseeing the management to protect shareholders' interests and to provide an independent view of corporate executives and their affairs [2]. It has been argued that an audit committee is more beneficial due to its skills and resources, which in turn affects their ability to enhance EQ, firm performance and firm value [3]. With respect to females and relatives, it is interesting to note that the region is considered a collectivistic under Hofstadte's cultural dimensions. Due to the culture and social norms, there is a fear of involving females on the board [4]. However, lately, females further engagement in the economy has grown [5]. In addition, as family ownership prevails in the region, there is a substantial involvement of relatives, which cannot be ignored [4]. Finally, the rationale of using both firm performance and firm value in the paper is that firm performance measurements (ROA and ROE) reflect performance based on historical information. This reflects previous firms' operation, and the efficiency of the firm using equity funds to generate profits [6, 7] where the firm value measurements (Tobin's Q) show performance based on firm value by market evolution of the assets [8], which in turn reflects current action [9]. In other words, firm value measurements indicate the perception of the market with respect to the firm's performance [10]. It also refers to growth and investment opportunities [11]. Firm value measurement also accounts for risk and is less likely to be manipulated as accounting measures [12]. Thus, it helps investors to estimate the growth and risk potential and shows the size of the firm. Management and investors have different interests and ways to evaluate CG; therefore, management attempt to use firm performance measurement (ROA and ROE) as the measurement to show how the wealth affects CG mechanisms. On the other hand, investors seem to prefer to value the firm structure of CG based on firm value measurement (Tobin's Q) [13].

2. GCC COUNTRIES BACKGROUND

A brief background of GCC countries is needed to have some understanding of the institutional setting. The Gulf Cooperation Council (GCC) countries, was founded in 1981 and consists of six Arab states namely Bahrain, Kuwait, Oman, Qatar, Saudi Arabia (SA), and the United Arab Emirates (UAE), all of which are Gulf Monarchies. GCC countries are located in the Middle East. Specifically, Arabian Peninsula and their total population are 50.1 million people [14]. They also share similar Arabian culture and traditions, the faith of Islam, social structures, wealth, political development (Monarchy), and demography [15]. The primary purpose of the establishment of GCC was to enhance the cooperation and integration as well as to strengthen their economy and development through their participation in different fields such as the economy, financial affairs, education, cultural activities, social, medical, agricultural development, research development and joint projects. Between them, they can issue similar policies and regulation to achieve unity [16]. It is also worth mentioning that each country has an independent government and their own independent currencies.

GCC countries are developing countries in Asia but enjoy prosperity due to natural resources and the rapid development of their capital market [17]. Some features make GCC countries interesting when examining the effect of CG on EQ, firm performance and firm value. Recently, the GCC countries share in the world's GDP has doubled to 2.2 percent, which refer to the development of a dynamic economy [18]. This also increases the significance and importance of GCC countries in the global economy [19]. Additionally, they have followed some global norms and standards to work with international organisations. This engagement with the world raises the status of the region, which brings more benefit and increases regarding trade and investment. This marks the region as "one of the most prosperous in the world" [19].

3. THEORETICAL FRAMEWORK

3.1 Agency Theory

Agency theory focuses on the relationship between the principals (owners) and the agents (managers). Agency theory's justification for its existence is to establish appropriate and adequate incentives in order to eliminate opportunistic behaviours by the company's management and to ensure that they pursue and maximise not only the company's wealth and interests but, also, work on behalf of the company's shareholders [20]. From agency theory's perspective, a reduced agency problem leads to maximising the company's value and the returns on investments to its shareholders. Furthermore, agency theory suggests ways of reducing agency costs in order to increase the company's EQ. These are: namely, monitoring costs; bonding costs; and residual losses which stem from the company's internal CG structure [21, 22]. Monitoring costs are borne by the principals and are the basis of the company's monitoring mechanisms, such as internal CG mechanisms, which are used to monitor management behaviour. Bonding costs relate to the financial or non-financial mechanisms which are used to ensure the agents make an effort to maximise the principals' wealth. Residual losses happen despite the involvement of monitoring cost and bonding cost because either these can fail or be insufficiently effective to align the principals' (owners) interests with those of the agents (management). Consequently, the owners can reduce the incentives to look after themselves by using some tools such as monitoring managers' behaviours and by introducing a contract which provides an incentive to align their interests with those of the company's management [21, 23].

4. LITERATURE REVIEW

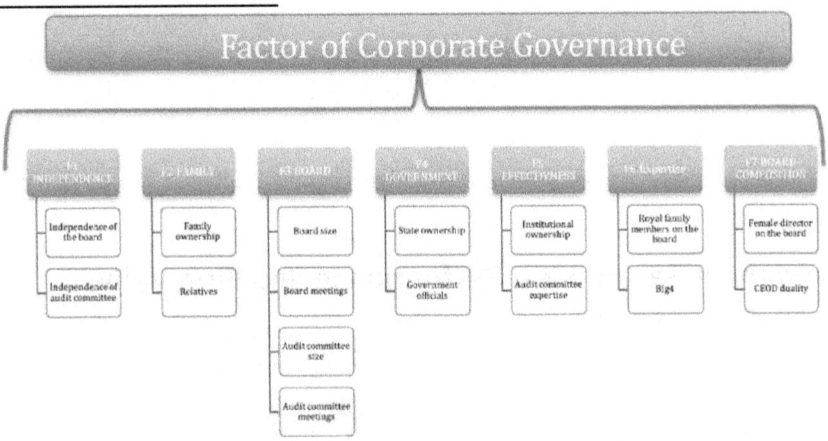

4.1 Independence Factor, Firm Performance, and Firm Value

The independent factor includes independent directors on the board of directors and audit committee. Arguably, a high percentage of independent directors on the board of directors and audit committee influence firm performance positively due to their effective monitoring [24]. However, others argue that independent directors in emerging countries are not applicable as it is "symbolic" but they are more likely to follow the management [15, 25, 26]. Nevertheless, the study follows the notion of CG code in the international practice and GCC countries and the majority of findings [27, 28] and hypothesises that:

$H_{01:}$ There is a positive association between independence factor, firm performance and firm value.

4.2 Family Factor, Firm Performance and Firm Value

Family factor encompasses family ownership and relatives on the board. Based on a prior discussion on relatives and family ownership, the research argues that these two variables are prevalent in the emerging markets [29] to protect family wealth and power [30], which in turn, lead to better performance [31, 32, 33]. Thus, they would play an effective role in the company, which results in better financial performance. Accordingly, the research hypothesises that:

$H_{02:}$ There is a positive association between family factor, firm performance and firm value.

4.3 Board Factor, Firm Performance and Firm Value

Board factor contains board size, board meetings, audit committee size and audit committee meetings. Referring back to discussed literature of board size, meetings, audit committee size and meetings; even though there are few negative findings in the literature, the majority of prior studies argue that a large board and audit committee and the high frequency of board and audit committee meetings leads to better firm performance and firm value. Accordingly, despite different findings, the study follows the majority of prior studies' findings, the recommendation of CG code and claims that the board factor leads to high firm performance and hypothesises that:

$H_{03:}$ There is a positive association between board factor, firm performance and firm value.

4.4 Government Factor, Firm Performance and Firm Value

Government factor encompasses government ownership and government officials on the board. Based on the prior discussion on these two variables, the research argues that the involvement of these two groups is common in the emerging markets [29] to retain their power on the firms. Thus, they may not play an effective role in the company, which results in poor performance. Accordingly, the study follows the majority of the studies [34, 35, 36, 37] and hypothesises that:

$H_{04:}$ There is a negative association between government factor, firm performance and firm value.

4.5 Effectiveness Factor, Firm Performance and Firm Value

The researcher had difficulty giving a name to this factor initially. However, other researchers such as Larcker et al., [38] mention the difficulties in assigning a name to some factors. This factor captures institutional ownership and audit committee expertise and the study calls them effectiveness because both are expected to have effective monitoring. Based on a literature review of institutional ownership and an audit committee, despite some negative findings, the majority of the studies' findings concludes that institutional ownership [39] and audit committee expertise [40, 41] lead to better firm performance and firm value. Therefore, the research follows these studies and hypothesises that:

$H_{05:}$ There is a positive association between effectiveness factor, firm performance and firm value.

4.6 Expertise Factor, Firm Performance and Firm Value

Expertise factor includes royal family members on the board and Big4 audit firms. Based on the discussion of royal family members and Big4 firms literature, the study argues that by giving the royal family members legitimacy, privileges and status, their involvement has benefits for the firms and their shareholders which result in better firm financial performance [42, 43, 44, 45, 46, 47]. Additionally, despite the mixed results in the literature of Big4 firms, the majority of the studies [48, 49, 50, 51, 52] conclude that Big4 firms increase firm performance and firm value. Accordingly, the research hypothesises that:

$H_{06:}$ There is a positive association between legitimacy factor, firm performance and firm value.

4.7 Board Composition Factor, Firm Performance and Firm Value

Board composition factor captures females on the board and CEO duality. Halawi & Davidson [4] document a low female involvement on boards, around 1.5% in the GCC. Accordingly, the research argues that since there are few female directors on the board and because of the culture in emerging markets, it is likely they have a lack of qualifications, skills and business expertise needed for directorship, which might negatively influence firm performance and firm value [5, 53, 54, 55, 56]. With regard to CEO duality, the code of GCC countries and best practice requires separation between the two roles. In addition, this study follows the majority of literature, which finds a negative association between CEO duality and firm performance [28, 57, 58]. Therefore, the study hypothesises that:

$H_{07:}$ There is a negative association between board composition factor, firm performance and firm value.

5. METHODOLOGY

5.1 Measurement of Firm's Performance and Firm Value

Regarding the evolution of firm performance and firm value, there is no consensus within the literature [57]. Nevertheless, the majority of prior studies have relied on return on assets (ROA) and return on equity (ROE) which are an accounting-based measure and a measure of profitability [59, 60] and Tobin's Q which is market-based measure [13, 61, 62, 63, 64]. ROA shows performance based on historical information, which reflects previous firms' operation, where ROE reflects the efficiency of the firm using equity funds to generate profits [6, 7]. Moreover, Tobin's Q shows performance based on firm value by the market evolution of the assets [8], which in turn reflects current action [9]. It also refers to growth and investment opportunities [11]. Tobin's Q accounts for risk and is less likely for manipulation of accounting measures [12]. Management and investors have different interests and ways to evaluate CG; therefore, management attempt to use ROA and ROE as the measurement to show how the wealth affects CG mechanisms. On the other hand, investors seem to prefer to value the firm structure of CG based on Tobin's Q and measurement [13]. Therefore, a higher ratio represents a higher return in each of these measurements.

Some studies of CG have used ROA and ROE as a measurement method (as the proxy of financial performance) [57, 65, 66, 67]. Tobin's Q is the measure used to reflect how management effectively manages assets to generate value for its shareholders and reflects the perception of a firm's financial performance by market [57]. Chung & Pruitt [68] asserts that Tobin's Q has great theoretical and practical relevance. It has been widely used in CG literature as the proxy for firm performance [61, 62, 65]. Following previous paper the author control a couple of variables as influence the analysis. These variables growth Copeland & Dolgoff [69], leverage Haniffa & Hudaib [57], Jang & Park [70], firm size performance [71, 72] and big 4 Al-Hussaini & Al-Sultan, [73] and Wang & Huang [74]. The investigation of the effect of CG on firm performance and firm value based on the principal component analysis (PCA).

5.2 Principal Component Analysis (PCA)

It uses the three sets of internal CG mechanisms namely: ownership structure, the board of directors and audit committee. Due to a large number of variables and the nature of CG mechanisms (variables) especially the board of directors' composition, these variables correlated with each other. Not all 16 variables of CG can be included in one regression without facing the econometric problem, which leads to difficult interpretation and involvement of measurement error. The study does not use the CG index as suggested by Larcker et al., [38]. Larcker et al., [38] argues that using CG index leads to many econometric problems. Therefore, to alleviate the measurement error and avoid multicollinearity, the principal component analysis (PCA) has been used which is a data reduction method to extract the relevant factor which is used in regression methodology to analyse the data. This method reduces the data set to a better size while continuing to hold on to the original information. PCA is identifying a parsimonious set of CG variables that affect firm performance and firm value.

6. REGRESSION

Firm performance and firm value are a dependent variable to the explanatory variables, which include individual internal CG factors and control variables. Table 1 summarises the CG factor and control variables investigated in this question, which include the definition of each variable and shows how they were measured.

Table 1. Variables definition of model: CG, firm performance and firm value.

Symbol	Name of variable	Predicted sign	
Dependent variable			
Firm performance	LN_ROA	The natural logarithm of Return on assets	
	LN_ROE	The natural logarithm of Return on equity	
Firm value	LN_TOBIN'S Q	The natural logarithm of Tobin's Q	
Independent variable			
F1 (INDEPENDENCE)	IND	Independent directors on the board	+
	AUDITIND	Independence of audit committee member	
F2 (FAMILY)	FAMC	Family ownership	+
	RELATIVE	Relatives on the board	
F3 (BOARD)	BSIZE	Board size	+
	BMEET	Board meetings	
	AUDITSIZE	Audit committee size	
	AUDITMEET	Audit committee meetings	
F4 (GOVERNMENT)	STATC	State ownership	—
	GOV	Government officials on the board	
F5 (EFFECTIVENESS)	INSTITIC	Institutional ownership	+
	AUDITEX	Audit committee expertise	

Symbol	Name of variable	Predicted sign	
F6 (EXPERTISE)	ROYAL	Royal family member on the board	+
	BIG 4	Big 4 audit firms	
F7(BOARD COMPOSITION)	FEMALE	Female directors on the board	+
	CEOD	CEO duality	
Control variables			
LN_GROWTH	The natural logarithm of Firm growth		
LN_LEVERAGE	The natural logarithm of Leverage		—
LN_SIZE	The natural logarithm of the Firm size		
BIG 4	Big 4 audit firms		
COUNTRY	Country dummy		?
INDUSTRY	Industry dummy		?
YEAR	Year dummy		?

$$Y = \alpha + \beta_1\, F1\, (INDEPENDENC_{it}) + \beta_2\, F2\, (FAMILY_{it}) + \beta_3\, F3\, (BOARD_{it}) + \beta_4\, F4\, (GOVERNMENT_{it}) + \beta_5\, F5\, (\text{EFFECTIVENESS}_{it}) + \beta_6\, F6\, (EXPERTISE_{it}) + \beta_7\, F7\, (BOARD\ COMPOSITION_{it}) + \beta_8\, LN\_GROWTH_{it} + \beta_9\, LN\_LEVERAGE_{it+} + \beta_{10}\, LN\_SIZE_{it} + \varepsilon_{it.}$$

Coefficients predict that β1 will have positive value where β2 will have negative value. Expected to is that β3 has a positive influence on firm performance where β4 has a negative association with firm performance. Predictions are that β5 and β6 will have a positive value where β7 will take a negative value. Regarding control variables, predictions are that β8 will also have a positive influence on firm performance while β9 will have negative value. Finally, β10 will have a positive value.

7. RESULTS AND ANALYSIS

7.1 Descriptive Statistics and Correlation Matrix

Table 2 presents descriptive statistics for the main model variables. These preliminary findings show the relationship between firm performance, firm value, ownership structure and CG. The ownership structure shows that 14 percent of shares are family owned (FOC), whereas governments own 13.8 percent of shares (STATC). Approximately 21.4 percent of shares are retained by institutional investors (INSTITC), and this indicates a high percentage of institutional ownership in the region. On average, the board of directors is composed of eight members (BSIZE). In addition, there is a small representation of females (FEMALE) on the board of approximately 0.2 percent. Not surprisingly, (RELATIVES) relatives represent 11.6 percent of the boards in the region. Among these members, 59 percent are independent directors (IND). The table also reveals that CEO duality (CEOD) is approximately 7.4 percent of sampled firms. The average number of board meetings (BMEET) in the financial year is six. There are very few royal family members (Royal) and government officials (Gov) represented on these boards. This is an average 3 percent and 1.3 percent respectively.

Table 2. Descriptive statistics-CG and firm performance and firm value-GCC countries.

Variable	Mean	Median	Std. Dev.	Min	Max
TOBIN'SQ	1.542	1.274	0.951	0.283	4.657
ROA	0.063	0.054	0.073	-0.090	0.264
ROE	0.108	0.099	0.120	-0.197	0.376
FAMC	0.141	0.065	0.190	0	0.991
STATC	0.138	0	0.213	0	0.893
INSTITC	0.214	0.115	0.256	0	1
BSIZE	7.882	8	1.693	4	18
FEMALE	0.002	0	0.023	0	0.571
RELATIVE	0.116	0	0.188	0	1
IND	0.595	0.571	0.270	0	1
CEOD	0.074	0	0.263	0	1
BMEET	5.634	5	2.025	1	19
ROYAL	0.027	0	0.053	0	0.2
GOV	0.013	0	0.041	0	0.285
AUDITSIZE	3.300	3	0.804	0	6
AUDITIND	0.628	0.666	0.342	0	1
AUDITMEET	4.659	4	2.213	0	21
AUDITEX	0.280	0.333	0.098	0	0.5
BIG4	0.610	1	0.487	0	1
LEVERAGE	0.380	0.350	0.222	0.068	0.820
LN_SIZE	12.691	12.609	1.662	10.100	16.078
GROWTH	0.029	0.018	0.145	-0.441	0.458

N = 1,096.

Notes: TOBIN'S Q is market value measure. ROA, is return on assets and ROE is return on equity. FAMC is the percentage of family ownership. STATC is the percentage of state ownership. INSTITC is the percentage of institutional ownership. BSIZE is board size. FEMALE is the ratio of female to the total board directors. RELATIVE is the ratio of relative to the total board of directors. IND is the ratio of independent director to the total board of directors. CEOD a dummy variable that takes the value of one if the CEO also serve as Chairman of the board and Zero otherwise. BMEET is the number board of meetings per year. ROYAL is the ratio of royal family member to the total board of directors. GOV is the ratio of government official to the total directors. AUDITSIZE is the number of directors on the audit committee. AUDITIND is the ratio of independent director in audit committee. AUDITMEET is the number of audit committee meeting per year. AUDITEX is the ratio of member with financial or accounting expertise to the total director. BIG4 is a dummy variable that takes the value of one if the company is audited by one of the BIG4 and zero otherwise. LEVEVERGE is total liabilities divided by total assets. LN_SIZE is the natural logarithm of the total assets. GROWTH is change in net sales divided by total assets.

With regard to audit committee characteristics, the average size of the committee is three members (AUDITSIZE); of which 62.8 percent are independent (AUDITIND). This committee meets approximately five times per annum (AUDITMEET). On average, 28 percent of the audit committees have at least one member who possesses financial or accounting expertise (AUDITEX). More than half of the companies hire one of the Big4 external auditors (BIG4).

Regarding control variables, on average, the firm size (SIZE) is $12.69 million. The mean of Leverage (LEVERAGE) is about 38 percent. The mean of the growth (GRWOTH) is 2.9 percent.

The cross-correlation matrix for the variables is reported in Table 3. The results show that institutional ownership is indirectly related to firm value. Family ownership shows a positive association with firm performance. Board size is positively correlated to firm performance. Contrary to the expectation, there is a negative correlation between independence of board of directors, independence of audit committee members and firm performance and firm value, which is also significant. The CEO duality has indirect association with firm performance. The presence of royal family members and government officials has a direct correlation with firm performance. Interestingly, the number of board meetings is significantly negative with firm performance. All other correlations are relatively low indicating no problem of multicollinearity. In addition, all VIF (Variance Inflation Factor) are below a reading of 10. This may indicate that there is no problem of multicollinearity among the variables. Therefore, this also indicates the validity of data [75, 76, 77].

Table 3. Correlation Martrix-CG and firm performance and firm value-GCC countries.

	TOBIN'S Q ROA	ROE	FAMC	STATC	INSTITC	BSIZE	FEMALE	RELATIVE	IND	
TOBIN'S Q	1									
ROA	0.371*	1								
ROE	0.274*	0.798*	1							
FAMC	0.056	0.096*	0.137*	1						
STATC	0.022	0.038	0.030	-0.287*	1					
INSTITC	-0.112*	-0.043	0.022	-0.213*	-0.249*	1				
BSIZE	-0.048	0.087*	0.075*	-0.183*	0.067*	-0.127*	1			
FEMALE	-0.042	0.020	0.000	0.022	0.068*	-0.044	0.010	1		
RELATIVE	0.052	0.011	0.016	0.378*	-0.229*	-0.104*	-0.096*	-0.016	1	
IND	-0.059*	-0.135*	-0.067*	-0.024	-0.087*	0.168*	-0.198*	-0.060*	-0.078*	1
CEOD	-0.004	-0.072*	-0.100*	0.051	-0.063*	-0.087*	0.034	0.068*	0.076*	-0.068*
BMEET	-0.042	-0.139*	-0.068*	-0.067*	0.211*	-0.057	0.002	-0.040	-0.007	0.083*
ROYAL	-0.045	0.080*	0.066*	0.033	-0.003	-0.055	0.076*	-0.020	0.111*	-0.108*
GOV	-0.019	0.063*	0.120*	-0.139*	0.267*	-0.008	0.006	0.024	-0.126*	0.019
AUDITSIZE	-0.052	-0.048	-0.016	-0.006	0.081*	0.029	0.158*	0.076*	-0.044	0.130*
AUDITIND	-0.069*	-0.154*	-0.092*	0.073*	-0.123*	0.190*	-0.134*	-0.064*	0.007	0.681*
AUDITMEET	-0.015	-0.053	0.000	-0.047	0.174*	-0.078*	0.090*	-0.075*	-0.021	0.096*
AUDITEX	0.085*	-0.003	0.024	-0.022	-0.131*	-0.053	-0.056	-0.112*	-0.021	0.059*
BIG4	-0.022	0.084*	0.136*	-0.093*	0.132*	0.033	0.103*	-0.000	-0.071*	-0.046
LEVERAGE	-0.115*	-0.139*	0.105*	0.095*	-0.020	0.176*	-0.050	-0.038	0.013	0.096*

	TOBIN'S Q	ROA	ROE	FAMC	STATC	INSTITC	BSIZE	FEMALE	RELATIVE	IND		
LN_SIZE	-0.013		-0.007	-0.054	-0.076*	0.160*	-0.426*	0.279*	0.030	0.065*	-0.314*	
GROWTH	-0.076*		0.175*	0.166*	0.050	-0.060*	0.018	0.005	-0.008	0.022	-0.031	
	CEOD	BMEET	ROYAL	GOV	AUDITS~E	AUDITIND	AUDITMEET	AUDITEX	BIG4	LEVERAGE	SIZE	GROWTH
TOBIN'S Q												
ROA												
ROE												
FAMC												
STATC												
INSTITC												
BSIZE												
FEMALE												
RELATIVE												
IND												
CEOD	1											
BMEET	-0.006	1										
ROYAL	0.066*	-0.033	1									
GOV	-0.081*	0.088*	-0.004	1								
AUDITSIZE	-0.019	0.157*	-0.063*	0.054	1							
AUDITIND	-0.059*	0.062*	-0.035	-0.002	0.102*	1						
AUDITMEET	-0.020	0.311*	-0.077*	0.047	0.253*	0.083*	1					
AUDITEX	-0.025	-0.083*	-0.046	0.118*	-0.163*	0.146*	0.187*	1				

	TOBIN'S Q	ROA	ROE	FAMC	STATC	INSTITC	BSIZE	FEMALE	RELATIVE	IND		
BIG4	-0.035	-0.007	0.103*	0.092*	0.019	-0.043	0.009	0.107*	1			
LEVERAGE	-0.101*	0.113*	-0.084*	0.042 *	0.111*	0.090*	0.154*	-0.007	0.137*	1		
LN_SIZE	0.079*	0.053	0.158*	0.065*	0.003	-0.281*	0.078*	0.03	0.068*	-0.0304	1	
GROWTH	-0.038	-0.028	-0.040	-0.006	0.075*	-0.055	0.036	-0.005	0.090*	0.117*	-0.035	1

*Notes: *,** and *** denote significant at10%, 5% and 1% levels respectively.*

TOBIN'S Q is market value measure. ROA is return on assets and ROE is return on equity. FAMC is the percentage of family ownership. STATC is the percentage of state ownership. INSTITC is the percentage of institutional ownership. BSIZE is the board size. FEMALE is the ratio of female to the total board directors. RELATIVE is the ratio of relative to the total board of directors. IND is the ratio of independent director to the total board of directors. CEOD a dummy variable that takes the value of one if the CEO also serve as Chairman of the board and Zero otherwise. BMEET is the number board of meetings per year. ROYAL is the ratio of royal family member to the total board of directors. GOV is the ratio of government official to the total directors. AUDITSIZE is the number of directors on the audit committee. AUDITIND is the ratio of independent director in audit committee. AUDITMEET is the number of audit committee meeting per year. AUDITEX is the ratio of member with financial or accounting expertise to the total director. BIG4 is a dummy variable that takes the value of one if the company is audited by one of the BIG4 and zero otherwise. LEVEVERGE is calculated as total liabilities divided by total assets. LN_SIZE is the natural logarithm of the total assets. GROWTH is change in net sales divided by total assets.

7.2 Regression Analysis

The regression analysis for the variables is reported in Table 4. A positive significant relationship is seen between expertise factors and firm performance (LN_ROA; LN_ROE: coefficient = 0.006; 0.007 p-value <5% and 10%, respectively). The expertise factor encompasses royal family members on the board as well as hiring one of the Big 4-auditing firms. This result is in line with a theoretical claim (agency theory), the research question expectation and empirical evidence. According to Algamdi [78], the presence of ruling family members on a board increases firm performance as they may expand the company's competitive environment and therefore, benefit the companies through networking and their privileges, leading to better performance. This supports the majority of politically connected firms literature [42, 43, 44, 45, 46, 47].

Table 4. GMM regression-CG, firm performance and firm value- model 1-GCC countries.

	Expected sign	LN_TOBIN'SQ	LN_ROA	LN_ROE
_CONS		-0.126	0.002	0.073
		-3.42	-0.22	-0.35
INDEPENDENCE FACTOR	+	-0.032	-0.001	0
		-0.07	0	0
FAMILY FACTOR	+	-0.04	-0.001	0.007
		-0.13	-0.01	-0.01
BOARD FACTOR	+	-0.059	0.001	0.001
		-0.04	0	0
GOVERNMENT FACTOR	—	0.029	0	-0.005
		-0.09	0	-0.01
EFFECTIVENESS FACTOR	+	-0.041	0.001	0.004
		-0.06	0	0
EXPERTISE FACTOR	+	-0.022	0.006**	0.007*
		-0.08	0	0
BOARD COMPOSITION FACTOR	—	-0.049	-0.002	-0.001
		-0.04	0	0
LN_GROWTH	+	-0.052	0.013	0.002
		-0.27	-0.02	-0.04
LN_LEVERAGE	—	-0.098	-0.057	0.035
		-0.76	-0.05	-0.07
LN_SIZE	+	0.029	0.013	0.014
		-0.26	-0.02	-0.03

	Expected sign	LN_TOBIN'SQ	LN_ROA	LN_ROE
L.LN_TOBINQ		-0.028		
		-0.03		
L.LN_ROA			-0.164**	
			-0.08	
L.LN_ROE				-0.046
				-0.1
YEAR DUMMY		Yes	Yes	Yes
INDUSTRY DUMMY		Yes	Yes	Yes
COUNTRY DUMMY		Yes	Yes	Yes
N		408	408	408

*Notes: *,** and *** denote significant at10%, 5% and 1% levels respectively.*

LN_TOBIN'S Q is the natural logarithm of market value measure. LN_ROA, is the natural logarithm of return on assets and LN_ROE is the natural logarithm of return on equity. INDEPENDENCE FACTOR includes independent of the board of directors and independent of the audit committee. FAMILY FACTOR includes family ownership and relatives. BOARD FACTOR includes of board size, board meeting, audit committee size and audit committee meeting. GOVERNMENT FACTOR includes government ownership and government officials on the board. EFFECTIVENESS FACTOR includes audit committee expertise and institutional ownership. EXPERTISE FACTOR includes royal family members on the board and Big 4 audit committee. BOARD COMPOSITION FACTOR includes CEO duality and female directors on the board. LN_GROWTH is the natural logarithm of change in net sales divided by total assets. LN_LEVEVERGE is the natural logarithm of total liabilities divided by total assets. LN_SIZE is the natural logarithm of the total assets.

In relation to the Big-4, prior studies show a positive relationship between Big-4 and firm performance. This is particularly the case in weak investor protection environments where firms which hire one of the Big-4 audit firms have a better performance record [79, 80, 81, 82]. This is because Big-4 audit firms are concerned with their brand and reputation [83, 84, 85]. Another explanation is that royals may use their influence or power to secure the expertise of Big 4 audit firms.

With respect to other factors, namely independence factor, family factor, board factor, government factor, effectiveness factor, board composition factor and control variables (growth, leverage, and firm size), My study fail to find any significance between these variables, firm performance and firm value under GMM regression.

My study first conducted OLS regression and panel data regression. Under the pool OLS regression of model 1, independence factor shows a negative and significant relationship with firm performance while the board factor indicates a negative and significant association with firm value. These results are contrary to the study expectations and also with agency theory. Government factor shows a positive relationship with firm performance and firm value. Expertise factor shows a positive association with firm performance. With regard to control variable, growth and leverage appear to have a significant association with firm performance and firm value. Most of these significant factors disappear with the study's control for endogeneity problem.

7.3 Robustness Test

To check the robustness of the results, the study conducts several additional tests. First, the study runs regression models using a different measurement of firm performance (Adj ROA) and firm value (Adj Tobin's Q). The study runs the main model again using some additional variables such as period, corruption and minority shareholders. These results remain unchanged with these variables but period, corruption and minority shareholders are not statistically significant with firm performance and firm value using the GMM regression approach.

8. DISCUSSION

The study utilises the model that is based on PAC Some point can be highlighted:

The main observations are that the results in the model are inconclusive and there needs to be further study in this area. The results reveal that royal family members on the board and Big-4 have a positive influence on firm performance and firm value. A possible explanation is that under PCA the variance of one variable influences another variable. Thus, this observation indicates that the results from PCA may not give a clear picture. However, if the expectation of the study does not support the finding under the model, the study may tell a more interesting story. According to model, CG factor has a similar impact on long term and short term firm performance. In addition, royal family influence Big4 audit firms to use their expertise to enhance firm performance and firm value.

The independence factor does not have a significant relationship with firm performance and firm value, thus, policymakers should strengthen the role of independent directors through the improvement and restriction of requirements and procedures of nominating independent directors on the board. Independent directors are some of the most important directors on the board as they can be more accountable than an executive [86, 87] due to their independent judgement of board decisions [88, 89].

9. CONCLUSION

This chapter present the results and evidence of the effect of CG on a firm's performance and firm value in GCC countries. A critical glance at the literature review of GCC countries, firm performance and firm value shows that the literature does not adequately consider the uniqueness of an institutional setting such as the presence of royal family members and government officials' members on the board. Additionally, noticeable features are not accounted for in the previous literature, such as a large involvement of relatives and the presence of a female on the board of directors. It is important to understand whether these variables matter or not in this region as this then influences the firm's performance and firm value. Thus, this study focuses on the effect of internal CG of the firm's performance and firm value in five GCC countries. The final sample consists of 220 firms (1,096 firm-year observations) for the fiscal year 2009 to 2013. The main observations are that the results of both models are inconclusive and warranting further investigation. However, if the study looks at the support of findings under these two models, the study may still tell an interesting story. Thus, some corporate governance variables have a different effect on firm performance and firm value. Finally, the study offers some recommendations to policymakers with regard to independent directors from the analysis from the model.

REFERENCES

1. Nenova, T. (2003). The Value of Corporate Voting Rights and Control: A Cross-Country Analysis. *Journal of Financial Economics*, 68(3), 325-351.
2. Harrison, J. R. (1987). The strategic use of corporate board committees. California Management Review, 30(1), 109-125.
3. Ismail, W., Adibah, W., Van Zijl, T., & Dunstan, K. (2010). Earnings quality and the adoption of IFRSbased accounting standards: Evidence from an emerging market. Available at SSRN 1566634
4. Halawi, A., & Davidson, B. (2008). Power Matters: A Survey of GCC Boards. National Investor, Investment Research.
5. Terjesen, S., Sealy, R., & Singh, V. (2009). Women directors on corporate boards: A review and research agenda. Corporate Governance, 17(3), 320-337. http://doi.org/10.1111/j.1467-8683.2009.00742.
6. Epps, R. W., & Cereola, S. J. (2008). Do institutional shareholder services (ISS) corporate governance ratings reflect a company's operating performance?. Critical Perspectives on Accounting, 19(8), 1135-1148.
7. Leng, A. C. A. (2004), 'The impact of corporate governance practices on firms' financial performance', ASEAN Economic Bulletin, Vol. 21, No. 3, pp. 308-18.
8. Tobin, J. (1969). A general equilibrium approach to monetary theory. Journal of money, credit and banking, 1(1), 15-29.

9. Kiel, G. C., & Nicholson, G. J. (2003). Board Composition and Corporate Performance: How the Australian Experience Informs Contrasting Theories of Corporate Governance. Corporate Governance: An International Review, 11(3), 189-205.

10. Weir, C., Laing, D., & McKnight, P. J. (2002). Internal and External Governance Mechanisms: Their Impact on the Performance of Large UK Public Companies. Journal of Business Finance and Accounting, 29(5), 579-611.

11. Ding, Y., Zhang, H. & Zhang, J. (2007) Private versus state ownership and earnings management: evidence from Chinese listed companies. Corporate Governance: An International Review 15: 223-238.

12. Al-Matari, E. M., Al-Swidi, A. K., & Fadzil, F. H. B. (2014). The measurements of firm performance's dimensions. Asian Journal of Finance & Accounting, 6(1), 24-49.

13. Black, B. S., Jang, H. & Kim,W. (2006). 'Does corporate governance predict firms' market values? Evidence from Korea'. Journal of Law, Economics, and Organization, 22 (2): 366-413.

14. Amico, A. (2014). Corporate Governance Enforcement in the Middle East and North Africa. OECD Corporate Governance Working Papers, (15).

15. Baydoun, N. (2013). Corporate governance in five Arabian Gulf countries. Managerial Auditing Journal, 28(1), 7-22.

16. Amico, A. (2012). The role of MENA stock exchanges in corporate governance.

17. IFC, international finance corporation (2008). Family Business Governance Handbook, <http://www.ifc. org/ifcext/corporategovernance.nsf/AttachmentsByTitle/Family+Business_Second_Edition_English+/$FI LE/Englilsh_Fam- ily_Business_Final_2008.pdf>, pp. 23-27.

18. Held, D., & Ulrichsen, K. (Eds.). (2013). The transformation of the Gulf: politics, economics and the global order. Routledge.

19. Nugée, J., & Subacchi, P. (Eds.). (2008). The Gulf Region: A New Hub of Global Financial Power. Chatham House (Formerly Riia).

20. Jensen, M. C., & Meckling, W. H. (1976). Theory of the firm: Managerial behavior, agency costs and ownership structure. *Journal of financial economics*, 3(4), 305-360.

21. Eisenhardt, M. (1986). Agency Theory!: and Assessment Review. Accounting Management Review, 14(1), 57-74.

22. Shabbir, A. & Padgett, C. (2005). 'The UK Code of Corporate Governance: Link between Compliance and Firm Performance', Working Paper, ICMA Centre, available at: http://ssrn.com/abstract=934313.

23. Jebran, K., Chen, S., Tauni, M. Z., & Ahmad, H. (2019). Corporate Governance, ultimate owner, and target cash holdings: evidence from China. SAGE Open, 9(4), 2158244019894293.

24. Byrd, J. W., & Hickman, K. A. (1992). Do outside directors monitor managers?: Evidence from tender offer bids. *Journal of financial economics*, 32(2), 195-221.

25. Al-Musalli, M. A. K., & Ismail, K. N. I. K. (2012). Corporate governance, bank specific characteristics, banking industry characteristics, and intellectual capital (IC) performance of banks in Arab Gulf Cooperation Council (GCC) countries. Asian Academy of Management Journal of Accounting and Finance, 8(1), 115-135.

26. Mahadeo, J. D., Soobaroyen, T., & Hanuman, V. O. (2012). Board composition and financial performance:Uncovering the effects of diversity in an emerging economy. Journal of Business Ethics, 105(3), 375-388.

27. Gupta, M., & Fields, L. P. (2009). Board independence and corporate governance: Evidence from director resignations. Journal of Business Finance & Accounting, 36(1-2), 161-184.

28. Ho, C.A. & Williams, S.M. (2003). International Comparative Analysis of the Association between Board Structure and the efficiency of Value Added by a Firm from its Physical Capital and Intellectual Capital Resources. The International Journal of Accounting, 38, 465-491.

29. La Porta, R., LopezSDeSSilanes, F., & Shleifer, A. (1999). Corporate ownership around the world. The journal of finance, 54(2), 471-451.

30. Cruz, C. C., Gomez-Mejia, L. R., & Becerra, M. (2010). Perceptions of benevolence and the design of agency contracts: CEO-TMT relationships in family firms. Academy of Management Journal, 53(1): 69-89.

31. Kappes, I., & Schmid, T. (2013). The effect of family governance on corporate time horizons. Corporate Governance (Oxford), 21(6), 547-566.

32. McConaughy, D.L., Matthews, C.H. & Fialko, A.S. (2001). Founding-family-controlled firms: performance risk and value. Journal of Small Business Management 39(1): 31- 49.

33. Villalonga, B., & Amit, R. (2006). How do family ownership, control and management affect firm value? *Journal of financial Economics*, 80(2), 385-417.

34. Gupta, N., (2005). Partial privatization and firm performance. Journal of Finance 60 (2), 987-1014.

35. Liu, G. S. & Sun, S. P. (2005). The class of shareholdings and its impacts on corporate governance: A case of state shareholdings composition in Chinese publicly listed companies. Corporate Governance: An International Review, 13: 46-59.

36. Sun, Q. & W. Tong (2003), 'China Share Issue Privatization: The Extent of its Success', *Journal of Financial Economics*, Vol. 70, pp. 182-222.

37. Wei, Z., Xie, F. & Zhang, S. (2005) Ownership structure and firm value in China's privatized firms: 1991-2001, *Journal of Financial* and Quantitative Analysis, 40: 87-108.

38. Larcker, D. F., Richardson, S. a., & Tuna, I. (2007). Corporate Governance, Accounting Outcomes, and Organizational Performance. The Accounting Review, 82(4), 963-1008.

39. Yan, X. & Zhang, Z., (2009). Institutional investors and equity returns: are short-term institutions better informed. The Review of Financial Studies, 22(2), 893-924. http://dx.doi.org/10.1093/revfin/hhl046 Notes

40. Amer, M., Ragab, A., & Shehata, S. (2014). Audit Committee Characteristics and Firm Performance: Evidence from Egyptian Listed Companies. In 6th Annual American Business Research Conference on Sheraton LaGuardia East Hotel, New York, USA.

41. Kipkoech, S. R. (2016). Audit Committee Size, Experience and Firm Financial Performance . Evidence Nairobi Securities Exchange, Kenya, Research Journal of Finance and Accounting. 7(15), 87-95

42. Charumilind, C., Kali, R., Wiwattanakantang, Y., (2006). Connected lending: Thailand before the financial crisis. Journal of Business 79, 181-218.

43. Faccio, M. (2006). Politically connected firms. The American economic review, 96(1), 369-386.

44. Fisman, R. (2001). Estimating the value of political connections. American Economic Review, 91: 1095- 1102.

45. Johnson, S., & T. Mitton, (2003), "Cronyism and Capital Controls: Evidence from Malaysia,"Journal of Financial Economics, 67, 351-382.

46. Leuz, C., & Oberholzer-Gee, F. (2006). Political relationships, global financing, and corporate transparency:Evidence from Indonesia. *Journal of Financial Economics,* 81(2), 411-439.

47. Siegel, J., (2005). Can foreign firms bond themselves effectively by renting US securities laws? *Journal of Financial Economics* 75, 319-359.

48. Van Tendeloo, B. and A. Vanstraelen. (2008). Earnings Management and Audit Quality in Europe: Evidence from the Private Client Segment Market. European Accounting Review 17 (3): 447-469

49. Van Tendeloo, B., & Vanstraelen, A. (2005). Earnings management under German GAAP versus IFRS. European Accounting Review, 14(1), 155-180.

50. Lin, J., & Hwang, M. (2010). Audit Quality, Corporate Governance, and Earnings Management: A MetaAnalysis.i International Journal of Auditing. Vol.10. Pp. 1099-1123.

51. Charles. J., Stanley, C., & Charlotte, H. (2010). The Imp act Of Audit Quality On Earnings Management to Achieve User Reference Points In EPS. Journal of Applied Business Research. Vol. 26 No.1, p19-30

52. Chen, C. J. P., Chen, S., & Su, X. (2005). Profitability Regulation, Earnings Management, and Modified Audit Opinions: Evidences from China. Auditing: A Journal of Practice & Theory. Vol. 20(2), pp 9-30.

53. Adams, R. and Ferreira, D. (2009). Women in the Boardroom and Their Impact on Governance and Performance. *Journal of Financial Economics,* 94(2) 291-309.

54. Falato, A., Kadyrzhanova, D., & Lel, U. (2014). Distracted directors: Does board busyness hurt shareholder value?. *Journal of Financial Economics,* 113(3), 404-426.

55. Field, L., Lowry, M., & Mkrtchyan, A. (2013). Are busy boards detrimental?. *Journal of Financial Economics*, 109(1), 63-82.

56. Smith, N., Smith, V., & Verner, M. (2006). Do women in top management affect firm performance? A panel study of 2,500 Danish firms. International Journal of productivity and Performance management, 55(7), 569-593.

57. Haniffa, R., & Hudaib, M. (2006). Corporate Governance Structure and Performance of Malaysian Listed Companies, 33(October), 1034-1062.

58. Rutledge, R. W., Karim, K. E., & Lu, S. (2016). The effects of board independence and CEO duality on firm performance: evidence from the NASDAQ-100 index with controls for endogeneity. Journal of Applied Business and Economics, 18(2), 49.

59. Baysinger, B. D., & Butler, H. N. (1985). Corporate governance and the board of directors: Performance effects of changes in board composition. Journal of Law, Economics, & Organization, 1(1), 101-124.

60. De Vuyst, V., & Ooghe, H. (2001). Corporate performance and board structure in Belgian companies. Long range planning, 34(3), 383-398

61. Yermack, D. (1996). Higher market valuation of companies with a small board of directors. *Journal of Financial Economics*, 40(2), 185-211.

62. Agrawal, A.& Knoeber, C. R. (1996). Firm performance and mecha- nisms to control agency problems between managers and share- holders. Journal of Financial and Quantitative Analysis, 31: 377-397

63. Beiner, S., Drobetz, W., & Schmid, M. M. (2006). An Integrated Framework of Corporate Governance and Firm Valuation, 12(2), 249-283

64. Henry, D. (2008). Corporate Governance Structure and the Valuation of Australian Firms!: Is There Value in Ticking the Boxes!?, 35(October), 912-942.

65. Gompers, P., Ishii, J., & Metrick, A. (2003). Corporate governance and equity prices. The quarterly journal of economics, 118(1), 107-156.

66. Core, J., Guay, W. & Rusticus, T. (2006) Does Weak Governance Cause Weak Stock Returns? An Examination of Firm Operating Performance and Investors' Expectations, Journal of Finance, 61, 2, 655-687.

67. Cui, T.Q., Evans, E., Wright, S. & Crowe, S., (2008). Have the objectives of the ASX recommendations on good corporate governance been achieved? [Online] Working Paper, Macquarie University. Available from: http://www.newcastle.edu.au/Resources/Faculties/Faculty%20of%20Business%20and%20Law/Seminars/Business%20Seminar%20Series%202007/BusSeminarPaper18092007.pdf

68. Chung, K. H. & Pruitt, S. W. (1994) A simple approximation of Tobin's q, Financial Management, 23, 70-74

69. Copeland, T., & Dolgoff, A. (2011). *Outperform with expectations-based management: a state-of-the-art approach to creating and enhancing shareholder value*. John Wiley & Sons.

70. Jang, S., & Park, K. (2011). Inter-relationship between firm growth and profitability. International Journal of Hospitality Management, 30, 1027-1035.

71. Velnampy, T. (2005). A study on investment appraisal and profitability. Journal of Business Studies, 2(1), 23-35

72. Amato, L. H., & Burson, T. E. (2007). The Effects of firm size on profit rates in the financial services. Journal of Economics and Economic Education Research, 8(1), 67-81.

73. Al-Hussaini, A., & Al-Sultan, W. (2008). DEVELOPMENT OF ENFORCEMENT MECHANISMS FOLLOWING ADOPTION OF INTERNATIONAL ACCOUNTING STANDARDS IN THE GULF CO-OPERATION COUNCIL MEMBER STATES. Journal of International Business Strategy, 8(3).

74. Wang, M. & Huang, M (2014). Which types of institutional investors constrain abnormal accruals?. Corporate Governance: An International Review, 22(1), 43-67.

75. Tabachnick, B. & Fidell, L. (2001) Using Multivari- ate Statistics, 3rd edn. New York: Harper Collins College.

76. Bowerman, B. L., & O'connell, R. T. (1990). *Linear statistical models: An applied approach.* Brooks/Cole.

77. Myers, R. H. (1990). Classical and modern regression with applica- tions (2nd edition). Boston: PWS-Kent.

78. Alghamdi, S. A. (2012). Investigation into Earnings Management Practices and the Role of Corporate Governance and External Audit in Emerging Markets!: Empirical Evidence from Saudi Listed Companies.

79. Choi, J. H., & Wong, T. J. (2007). Auditors' governance functions and legal environments: An international investigation. Contemporary Accounting Research, 24(1), 13-46.

80. Choi, J. H., Kim, J. B., Liu, X., & Simunic, D. A. (2008). Audit pricing, legal liability regimes, and big 4 premiums: Theory and cross-country evidence. Contemporary Accounting Research, 25(1), 55-99.

81. Niskanen, J., Karjalainen, J., Niskanen, M., & Karjalainen, J. (2011). Auditor gender and corporate earnings management behavior in private Finnish firms. Managerial Auditing Journal, 26(9), 778-793.

82. Rodríguez, M. C., & Alegría, S. S. (2012). The value of audit quality in public and private companies: evidence from Spain. Journal of Management & Governance, 16(4), 683-706.

83. Francis, J. R., & Krishnan, J. (1999). Accounting accruals and auditor reporting conservatism. Contemporary Accounting Research, 16(1), 135-165.

84. Kim, H., Hoskisson, R. E., Tihanyi, L., & Hong, J. (2004). The evolution and restructuring of diversified business groups in emerging markets: The lessons from chaebols in Korea. Asia Pacific Journal of Management, 21(1/2), 25-48.

85. Wiwanya, T. & Aim, J. (2008). The relationship between audit committee characteristics, audit firm size and earnings management in quarterly financial reports of companies listed in the stock exchange of Thailand. 8th Global Conference on Business & Economics, Florence Italy, 18-19th October.

86. Fama, E. F. (1980). Agency Problems and the Theory of the Firm. Journal of political economy, 88(2), 288-307

87. Sonnenfeld, J. A. (2002) What Makes Great Boards Great, Harvard Business Review, 106-113.

88. Chhaochharia, V. & Y. Grinstein, (2009). CEO Compensation and Board Structure. Journal of Finance 64 (1):231- 261.

89. Cadbury, A. (1992). Cadbury report: The financial aspects of corporate governance. Tech reprt, HMG, London.

13 Organizational Culture: A Systems Approach

1. INTRODUCTION

Recognition of the powerful influence of culture on organizational performance has been steadily growing for several decades. Numerous books and research papers have been published using a variety of models and methods attempting to assess various dimensions and strength of those dimensions within the organization. There appears to be wide agreement with Schein's definition of organizational culture as a set of beliefs, values, and shared assumptions "invented, discovered, or developed by a given group as it learns to cope with its problems of external adaptation and internal integration—that has worked well enough to be considered... the correct way to perceive, think, and feel in relation to those problems." ([1], p.9). Hofstede suggested that organizational culture consists of core values that are often unconscious and rarely discussable [2]. Both of these descriptions appear throughout the literature on organizational cultures and combined provide a readily recognizable and useful description of organizational culture. Many researchers and authors have demonstrated the power of culture on organizational performance using both qualitative and quantitative methods.

The widely used, "Culture eats strategy for breakfast" has been bantered around in various forms in management writing and thinking for many years with multiple versions attributed to Peter Drucker, Jack Welch, and others, yet despite the widely accepted recognition that culture is a powerful force in determining success or failure of organizational initiatives, executives seemingly fail to take affirmative action in dealing with cultural inhibitors. Nold and Hagelthorn [3] found that in the context of cross-national mergers and acquisitions, 90% of executives acknowledge that culture was a key factor in the success or failure of the venture. Yet, less than 10% took specific actions to address cultural disconnections either in the due diligence or implementation phases of the project. Executives explored financial and operational issues and established wide ranging goals for operations, financial performance, quality, and market penetration yet rarely focused on the culture with the result that nearly 80% of cross-national mergers and acquisitions fail. We continue to ask "why" do executives acknowledge the importance of culture yet apparently bury their heads in the sand when it comes to acting.

We believe that there are many reasons for this apparently illogical behavior. Tom Peters in *In Search for Excellence* [4] and *A Passion for Excellence* [5] provided renewed focus on the old saying that, "What gets measured gets done". Business schools worldwide have perfected curriculum that emphasizes data driven decision making indoctrinating students on methods to measure performance in order to get things done. Just take a good look at the AACSB criteria that emphasizes quantitative research and accreditation criteria that focuses on research, research, more research. Course curricula at both the undergraduate and graduate level focus on data driven decision making which indoctrinates students with the unconscious and rarely discussable belief that executives must base decisions on hard data. Combine that academic conditioning with the overwhelming demand by stakeholders for quantitative proof of performance to earn bonuses, promotions, or recognition and executives shy away from intangibles that are difficult to measure and even more difficult to understand. Human nature is to avoid what you do not understand or feel comfortable with so executives avoid the issue in the absence of a tool to quantify the intangible.

The annual "employee survey" is a common event in many companies which we believe implies that people need fixing rather than the management systems or leadership. The annual "employee survey" is done to try to control mamagers and give executives cover for missing communications and unclear strategies that are always at top of the list of problem areas identified by employees. Rather than an annual exercise of questionable value, diagnostics should be an infrequent feedback tool for organizational development. We propose a methodology to help quantify many key intangibles of organizational culture along with other heretofore invisible dimensions of that drive performance and the ability of organizations to be agile, to rapidly adapt, and change in the VUCA (**V**olatile, **U**ncertain, **C**omplex, and **A**mbiguous) world that characterizes the 21st Century business environment.

2. ORGANIZATIONAL CULTURE AS PART OF A DYNAMIC SYSTEM

Most of the popular instruments used to assess organizational culture use models that view organizational culture as a standalone dimension. Many proposed models such as the Competing Values Framework (CVF) popularized by Kim Cameron and Robert Quinn, the Denison Model, and Schein's layered framework are joined by a host of other models [6, 7, 8]. Popular instruments such as the Organizational Culture Inventory (OCI), Organizational Culture Assessment Instrument (OCAI), the Culture Gap Survey (CGS), Organizational Beliefs Questionnaire (OBQ), the Corporate Culture Survey (CCS), Denison's Organizational Culture Survey, and the Great Place To Work Institute methodology attempt to provide insight into many beliefs and values held by a group of people but largely ignore how the culture interacts with other key elements of the organization [8, 9]. We suggest that viewing culture as a standalone organizational attribute is a major contributing factor to the low success rate of change initiatives that has been estimated at between 20–30% [10].

Since Descartes, the "scientific method" was built on the basic assumption that a system could be broken down into its individual components for analysis then the system could be understood by adding up all of the various sub-components in a linear fashion [11]. The "scientific method" essentially assumes that systems are closed systems in that the components of the system and the system in total exists in isolation and is unaffected by outside forces. Ludwig von Bertalanffy described organizations as dynamic systems where all parts are inextricably connected with each part is dependent on and influenced by the other parts and the external environment, similar to a living organism [12]. Rather than a system being the sum of the parts, the functions of a system are characterized by the complex interactions among all of its components and external forces [13] General systems theory assumes that components of the system and the system itself is open to environmental forces that shape and influence both the components and the system in its entirety. Alfred Kuhn [14] observed that within social systems, like an organization, communication or flow of information and knowledge among the various components of the system and the system as a whole provides the energy for the system. Decisions made by all members that influence or are influenced by the system represent outcomes which can be readily observed. According to Kuhn, "Culture is communicated, learned patterns...and the society [organization] in a collective of people having a common body and process of culture." ([14], p. 154). According to Kuhn, subcultures can only be interpreted when viewed relative to all of the other subcomponents of the system and culture must be viewed as a pattern of behaviors within the system. Therefore, the study of the social interactions that power the system consists of interpreting "communicated, learned patterns common to a relatively large groups [of people]" [p. 157].

With regard to organizational systems, Walonick suggested that healthy organizational systems must change through time in order to remain healthy and productive [11]. However, since organizational systems are open, they are sensitive to changes in the general environment as well as to internal changes. The ability of all parts of the organizational system to anticipate, sense, and adapt to environmental change is a key factor for success. Decisions powered by the flow of information and knowledge throughout the system become observable outcomes by which to evaluate the health of the system (organization). General systems theory forces scholars, executives, and consultants to expand the scope of their investigations to consider how the flow of information and resulting decisions affect all of the subcomponents of the system, the system as a whole, and the general environment [11].

We believe that organizations must be viewed holistically and that effective change initiatives require conscious actions and reactions to all parts of a dynamic system. We believe that in order to improve on the 70–80% failure rate, it is necessary to assess "unconscious and rarely discussable" dimensions of leadership, systems, and culture that permeate all elements of an organization. It is necessary for executives to gain insight into many heretofore unseen dimensions of these key components of every organization in order to form targeted actions to deal with these invisible issues. The question then becomes twofold, what are the critical "unconscious and rarely discussable" dimensions and can they be measured"? After nearly two decades of observation and research, we suggest that the answer is YES!

3. THE PERFORMANCE TRIANGLE MODEL

Our work on The Performance Triangle Model (PTM) for organizational design in a turbulent world emerged from nearly twenty years of observation and research with over 200 organizations worldwide [15, 16]. The PTM shown in Figure 1 describes a dynamic system of culture, leadership, and systems that is powered by people who work in an environment that nurtures healthy relationships, collaboration, and a strong sense of purpose. Culture is a major component of the dynamic system and cannot be effectively changed without recognizing and addressing key elements of the ENTIRE system [14, 11]. Chris Argyris and Donald Schón popularized the concept of "actionable knowledge" as knowledge that is required to support or shape a decision and take action [17]. While teaching university courses we constantly emphasize the need for action and decisive decision making. Knowledge without resulting action is worthless to an organization, so we have developed and validated a diagnostic instrument to assess the strength of multiple dimensions that drive the PTM system [18]. Over the decades, we have observed countless organizations where unseen beliefs and shared assumptions infect large segments of an organization that interfere with knowledge sharing and decision making process like a virus in the human body. These interferences are almost always unknown to senior executives and derail or sabotage the most well-conceived strategic plan or action. In most cases, executives would be wise to address the interferences and eliminate the viruses BEFORE spending valuable energy and resources on change initiatives with a low probability of success. We contend that armed with insight into many "unconscious and rarely discussable" beliefs, values, and shared assumptions embedded within the employee population, executives will be able to take targeted and effective actions to design organizations that will be successful in a VUCA 21st Century environment and dramatically increase the probability of a successful change initiative.

Figure 1. The Performance Triangle Model.

4. QUALITATIVE AND QUANTITATIVE FOUNDATIONS OF THE PERFORMANCE TRIANGLE MODEL

The concept and resulting diagnostic tools for the Performance Triangle emerged and gained definition over nearly 20 years from observations and data gathered from case studies involving over 200 organizations in different industries throughout the world plus results from survey data gathered from a sample of 50 organizations between 2006 and 2011. A unique opportunity in 2014 with a large sample allowed us to subject the diagnostic instrument to independent statistical analysis. Analysis of qualitative and quantitative information from these multiple sources revealed recurring themes and relationships between specific dimensions of organizations that evolved into the Performance Triangle Model and established statistical validity and reliability of our diagnostic instrument.

4.1 Qualitative Origins

After carefully analyzing responses from senior business leaders from case studies over 10 years representing over 100 firms, several trends, recurring themes, and stated concerns began to stand out as significant. Three primary groupings of themes were identified as being essential for success in a dynamic and fluid 21st Century business environment: leadership, systems, and culture.

Several themes revolving around leadership emerged. The need for intense, focused, and rapid leadership and managerial interactions in response to an increasingly fast-paced and complex business environment became apparent. This observation coincided with the fact that an increasing number of employees were hired for their knowledge and not for their physical contributions to work. The trend toward knowledge workers and knowledge economy has been documented by many researchers and authors for decades [19, 20, 21]. Feedback from senior executives and leaders suggested that this changing demographic called for a different leadership style requiring more involvement and engagement with people at all levels both internal and external to their organizations. Creating and maintaining a healthy environment that enables knowledge workers to maximize their unique and valuable abilities required focus of attention and constant energy from leaders and managers throughout the organization.

Several common themes emerged revolving around command and control systems in response to growing organizational complexity and pressure from increasing governmental regulation. Business leaders frequently indicated that traditional command and control systems with traditional tools and methods that were introduced in the industrial 20th Century were becoming increasingly less effective. Complex 21st Century organizational structures required different ways to maintain adequate data and behavioral control while simultaneously empowering operational managers enough authority and flexibility to make effective on-the-spot decisions.

Time also emerged as a recurring theme related to systems in the sense that time is a scarce resource that is non-recoverable once gone. Maximizing efficient use of a leader's or manager's time as well as reducing the time needed to get relevant information into the right decision makers hands when and where it is needed were growing concerns. Feedback from executives consistently indicated concern that decisions were being made based on data and information that was inaccurate or not relevant to the question or that relevant information was received AFTER a decision was made that might have resulted in a different decision if available in a timely manner. Either situation resulted in a flawed or less than optimal management decisions. Time related themes associated with speed, quality, and efficiency of information and knowledge flow enabled by systems were frequent and emphatic.

The third major theme that emerged over this 10-year period was a growing awareness of the hidden potential of intangible, human, factors that shape human behaviors and responses. With increasing frequency business leaders identified the need for shared beliefs, values, and assumptions in the collective minds of organizational members which forms and defines the organization's culture. Growing numbers of leaders identified intangible "unconscious and rarely discussable" dimensions of the culture as a key factor for improving performance, innovation, and unlocking new sources of profitability. Themes involving organizational culture as the unseen force connecting systems and leadership emerged such that organizational culture clearly was a critical factor for success. Successful executives must have insight, a keen understanding, and an appreciation for the power that organizational culture exerts.

Combining and visualizing these three central themes resulted in the emergence of a dynamic triangular system consisting of leadership, systems, and organizational culture which is powered by the unique talents and skills of people. Energy for this people-centric system is transmitted throughout the system by people with a shared sense of purpose with healthy relationships that enable effective collaboration. Superior performance in the VUCA 21st Century demands that organizations harness the vast energy of people with shared values, beliefs, and assumptions within the organization to be successful. Perceptions and opinions are one thing, but business leaders asked what value a theory or model brings to the organization and asked if recommendations emerging from the PTM were based on fact or opinion. In order to answer this important question, it became necessary to subject the emergent themes to statistical analysis using a survey instrument to capture data to test for correlation significance and fit with the PTM.

4.2 Quantitative Analysis: Phase One

4.2.1 The sample

Between 2006 and 2011, responses from PTM surveys from a sample of 50 organizations were compiled identifying relationships among recurring themes that shaped the PTM. The general research question was "Are there relationships between leadership, systems, culture and success"? The hypothesis for each intersection of leadership, culture, systems, and success was that there would be a significant relationship. The survey consisted of 120 questions designed to provide insight into numerous aspects of leadership, systems, culture, and success that were consistently identified as key elements in many case studies. Senior level leaders and managers in these 50 organizations responded to questions asking them to assess the perceived strength of the element within their own organizations using a 9-point Likert-type scale. The sample encompassed a wide array of industries, firm sizes, countries, and ownership forms as identified in Figure 2.

4.2.2 The Themes

Each theme of the survey (leadership, systems, culture, success) was broken down into five elemental factors that were identified as significant in the qualitative phase of the PTM development. Questions were developed for each factor based on observations in the case studies and designed to assess the degree of influence of specific factors within the organization as perceived by the respondent. Figure 3 shows the factors within each theme and the thematic question explored by the factor.

Organizations	50
Participants	895 participants; Range from 3 to 80 per organization with an average of 18 participants per organization
Time Period	2006 through 2011
Industries Surveyed	Financial Services (6); Manufacturing and Construction (7); Consumer Goods and Food (10); Logistics and Energy (3); Media and Tourism (5); Pharmaceuticals and Chemicals (5); Public Service (5); Foundations (2); Professional Services (7)
Firm Size (Number of Employees)	0-99 (13); 100-199 (17); 1,000-9,999 (12); > 10,000 (8)
Country (of origin)	US/Canada (5); Central Europe (24); Middle East/Africa (6); United Kingdom (5); Asia (5); Latin America (2); Australia/New Zealand (3)
Ownership	Public Shareholders (28); Private/Family (15); Public Service (5); Foundations/NGO (2)
Scope (of operations)	Global (10); International (15); Local (25)

Figure 2. Sample Demographics.

Figure 3. Factors and Themes.

The objective of the study was to assess the perceived relative strength of these elements in the organization as a whole. The survey was employed as a diagnostic tool for practical evaluation of the subject organizations and the results shared with the sponsoring executive in each organization. We found that individuals quickly and easily understood data on a 100-point scale or as a percentage. Since the results represent an assessment of the degree or strength of the perception, we found that an association with temperature or percentage to be useful and practical to facilitate understanding with business executives. Therefore, it became necessary for presentation purposes to normalize responses to each factor on a scale of 1 to 100 in order to allow executives to quickly and easily comprehend the intensity of the themes within the organization. Values on the Likert-type scale 1, 2, 3, 4, 5, 6, 7, 8, 9 translated into 0, 12.5, 25, 37.5, 50, 62.5, 75, 87.5, and 100 on the 100-point scale, similar to the Celsius temperature scale. Regardless of the scale, relationships and correlations remain unchanged.

4.2.3 Phase One Survey Results and Interpretation

Analysis of data from responses by senior level managers in 50 organizations with an average of 18 participants in each company suggested the existence of meaningful relationships between the central themes of culture, leadership, systems, and success. Using MINITAB statistical software for statistical analysis, results indicated that the correlations between these relationships are significant providing positive support for the hypotheses and the general research question. Table 1 shows descriptive statistics for individual themes, correlations, and the regression analysis of relationships between themes.

Table 1. Descriptive Statistics, Correlations, and Linear Regression of Relationships (N = 50).

Themes	Mean	Median	Std. Dev.	
Leadership	69.84	69.35	13	
Systems	68.17	68.55	12.31	
Culture	68.97	68.95	14.35	
Success	73.52	72.2	11.49	
Theme	**Leadership**	**Systems**	**Culture**	
Systems	0.694			
Culture	0.551	0.562		
Success	0.509	0.581	0.52	
(Note: $p < .001$ for all results)				
Relationships	**Correlation**	**Y-Intercept**	**Slope**	**F-Value**
Success vs. Culture	0.52	44.8	0.416	17.77
Culture vs. Leadership	0.55	26.4	0.609	30.95
Culture vs. Systems	0.56	24.3	0.655	22.15
Leadership vs. Systems	0.69	19.9	0.733	44.63
Success vs. Leadership	0.51	42.1	0.45	16.81
Success vs. Systems	0.58	36.5	0.543	24.5
(Note: $p < .001$ for all results)				

Table 1 indicates that regression analysis performed on the responses from the sample of 50 firms shows a significant correlation among the themes of the

Performance Triangle Model. The strongest positive correlation in the sample is between systems and leadership giving an early indication that these attributes of the PTM can drive effective decision-making.

4.3 Quantitative Analysis: Phase 2

Qualitative and quantitative study in phase one led to the development and refinement of a diagnostic instrument designed to yield additional insight into many unseen elements of dynamic management systems, structures, and processes, including culture. Making a precise and relevant evaluation of the dynamic management structure of an organization is inherently difficult because of the vagueness, multidimensional nature, and complexity of the phenomenon [22, 23, 24]. Verdú and Gómez-Gras observed that tools developed to evaluate multidimensional organizational systems have rarely been supported by empirical testing [25]. Part of the reason for the lack of empirical testing is that relevant factor analysis requires data from a large sample, typically over 500 participants, during the same time period. All of the cases used to develop the PTM model and diagnostic instrument had less than 500 participants, except one. Application of the diagnostic instrument with a large organization in 2014 provided a unique opportunity for independent statistical testing conducted by faculty with a PhD in statistics at a major university in Germany.

	Total	Electric Utility	Finance	Police	Airport	Community Dvpt.	Parks & Recreation	Information Technology	Water Utility	The Lakeland Center	Fire	Public Works	Other
Executives	38	8	2	2	1	1	2	1	1	2	2	2	14
Supervisors	421	86	15	39	5	17	74	17	47	21	29	50	20
Employees	703	162	23	94	6	34	103	37	75	12	47	65	45
Total	**1162**	**256**	**40**	**135**	**12**	**52**	**179**	**55**	**123**	**35**	**78**	**117**	**79**

Figure 4. Distribution of Sample Participants.

4.3.1 The Sample

The sample consisted of all employees working for a mid-size city government in the southeastern United States. A series of highly publicized scandals in the city resulted in the recommendation by a select committee of citizens for a survey of the culture and morale of the all city employees. The PTM diagnostic tool was selected after comparison to multiple "morale survey's" because the model and diagnostic instrument provided greater depth and insight into the organization as a system and contributors to "morale" as well as the high degree of perception for change. 1,162 employees participated out of a total employee population of 2,400 (48.4% participation rate). Participants were asked to identify the department in which they work and whether they were a top executive (department or assistant department head), supervisor (anyone below department head with supervisory responsibility), and employees (anyone with no supervisory responsibility). Figure 4 shows the distribution of all participants horizontally by management level and vertically by department. Departments with less than ten employees were grouped into "Other" to protect the confidentiality of individual respondents.

4.3.2 Design of the Diagnostic Instrument and Data Gathering

The diagnostic instrument consisted of 55 statements worded to provide insight into the strength of perception by employees pertaining to specific elements and dimensions of the PTM. Participants were asked to rate perceptions on a 9-point Likert type scale ranging from very strongly disagree (1) to very strongly agree (9). Questions were worded such that senior executives were asked to evaluate the strength of the dimension within the departments in their area of responsibility. All other participants were asked to evaluate perceptions within their work group or department. This approach provided visibility into potential disconnects between what executive and employees perceive on the same construct.

Due to the size and diversity of the sample, responses were collected in multiple ways. Responses were captured electronically, transmitted through the internet, and stored on a secured server for analysis and interpretation. With full cooperation of the information technology department, links to the diagnostic instrument were transmitted to executives via email while all other participants were allowed access to the instrument on computers at their workstations. Kiosks were set up and made available to all employees who did not have a permanent workstation. All participants were given time while on the job to participate and several videos were created and transmitted to all participants explaining the reason for the project, how the process works, and to provide assurance of confidentiality. Employees had ten days in May 2014 to participate. At the conclusion of the data gathering window, raw data was transmitted to the independent research team in Germany for analysis.

4.3.3 Test Methodology

Similar to Charbonnier-voirin [26] exploratory factor analysis was performed to assess the validity of the individual dimensions of the system in the PTM with Cronbach's alpha to determine internal reliability of the primary constructs. The factor structure and psychometric qualities of the model were successfully analyzed using SPSS 23.0. Principle Component Analysis (PCA) with varimax rotation with

Kaiser normalization was employed in order to test the dimensionality of the construct. PCA is often used in the development phase of a questionnaire [27]. The purpose of PCA is to retain enough items to characterize the phenomenon. Similar to Roussel [28] items with factor loadings below 0.5 were eliminated from the PCA analysis.

For the PCA the seven primary constructs of the PTM were clustered into three groupings. Effective leadership is strongly influenced by systems that provide timely and relevant information to key decision makers. Conversely, leadership styles strongly influence the design and implementation of systems. Therefore, leadership and systems are grouped into cluster 1. Culture, representing unseen values, beliefs, and shared assumptions is a very strong influence on the behavior of people, leaders, and systems is cluster 2. The entire system is powered by people through relationships, collaboration, purpose and focus therefore multiple people-centric constructs are aggregated into cluster 3.

4.3.4 Results

As seen in Table 2, results of exploratory factor analysis on the specific dimensions of the PTM are all greater than 0.5 with 13 of 20 (65%) factor loadings above 0.70. Factor loadings for dimensions of leadership are particularly high with 4 of 5 above 0.80. The results suggest that the statements used to evaluate the dimensions comprising the PTM have high levels of validity. Those that evaluate dimensions of leadership are particularly strong. Since all of the dimensional items have factor loadings greater than 0.5, all were included in the subsequent PCA analysis.

Table 2. Construct reliability, descriptive statistics, factor analysis and PCA.

Cronbach's alpha for the major constructs of culture, leadership and people were all above 0.80 demonstrating good internal validity. Cronbach's alpha for systems and the connectors of the model (purpose, collaboration, relationships) indicate questionable internal validity. Low alphas for systems and the connectors may partially be due to the few numbers of items in the instrument. Cronbach's alpha for all three clusters is above .81 suggesting strong internal validity.

Results from the PCA analysis shown in Table 1 shows a clear factor structure supporting the major constructs of the model. After six iterations three distinct factors emerged for each of the three clusters. The results reveal that 19 of the 20 the dimensions have factors greater than 0.5 suggesting that the diagnostic is a good fit with the model.

Because of the tight interrelationship of leadership with systems, the dimensions comprising leadership and systems in the model were grouped into cluster 1.

All of the factors are above 0.5 in cluster 1 however leadership and systems are commonly separated in the literature. Further work is advisable to analyze each attribute separately. One possible approach might be to simplify some of items to provide a greater distinction between leadership and systems. Interestingly, three dimensions associated with people in cluster 3 (purpose, awareness, choice) also have factor weightings above 0.5 indicating a possible strong association with leadership and systems.

Cluster 2 is made up of dimensions of culture in the model. All of the factor weightings are greater than 0.5 suggesting that the model is consistent with the literature dedicated to culture. Three (agenda, aspirations, and norms) having factors greater than 0.8 suggesting a particularly strong association or influencing component of organizational culture. Interestingly, two items (tools and purpose) outside of the culture cluster have factor weighting greater than 0.5 suggesting possible relationships with culture.

Cluster 3 aggregates the group of dimensions corresponding to intra- and inner-people-centric dimensions of the model. The only item below 0.5 is awareness, however, 0.495 is only .005 away from the 0.5 threshold therefore awareness is also included and considered relevant. The results are consistent with the literature dedicated to human performance. Interestingly, the people dimension of purpose yields factor weightings above 0.5 in all three clusters suggesting that people in organizations who share a common purpose can have a significant influence in all aspects of the organization and are instrumental in an agile organization.

The overall results offer strong evidence that the components of Performance Triangle Model for organizational systems; culture, leadership, systems, and people when aligned contribute to building agile and successful organizations and that the diagnostic instrument has a good level of validity and reliability [18]. Further, the PTM diagnostic instrument has adequate reliability and validity on which to base recommendations and give executives valuable insight into many intangible "unconscious and rarely discussable" dimensions of the culture that were identified in the qualitative phase of development [18].

5. Practical Implications

After nearly 20 years of research and study by a team of practitioners and academics in Europe and the USA, we are confident that there are many lessons learned and practical implications. Organizational culture is a key factor for success in the VUCA 21st Century business world. Evaluating the underlying "unconscious and rarely discussable" elements or the influence of culture on the performance of an organization must be done holistically by considering how the culture interacts with leadership and systems. Further, since the culture is contained in the shared values, beliefs, and assumptions of the people, power for the organizational system comes from people and linked through shared purpose, relationships, and collaboration. Executives and leaders at all levels must first ask the "right" questions in order to gain insight into those pesky "unconscious and rarely discussable" beliefs, values, and shared assumptions.

5.1 How Do We Measure Success?

In the 20th Century, success was traditionally measured using tangible assets and for-profit companies still measure success by stock price, earnings per share, return on assets, etc. While such financial measures are important, we prefer to define success by attributes of successful organizations that we have observed. By defining success by attributes rather than financial performance or tangible assets, we can include not-for-profit organizations, NGO's, governmental agencies, and private companies in addition to the for-profit companies. We have observed that top tier companies have strong foundations in responsiveness, alignment, capabilities, motivation, and cleverness. The PTM diagnostic assessment tool helps assess the perceived intensity of these dimensions within the employee population in answering the following questions.

Responsiveness – Is the organization flexible and able to react to changes in the environment?

Alignment – Is the direction of the organization clear? Does the structure fit the strategy? Is it shared broadly and are employees aligned to support the strategies?

Capabilities – Does the organization have the competencies and skills needed to deliver on promises?

Motivation – Are employees throughout the organization inspired to perform above and beyond expectations?

Cleverness – Are employees empowered to be creative and use their creativity to meet expectations or demands from clients or customers within boundaries that do not stifle creativity?

We feel that if the answer to these questions is yes, then the organization will likely be successful. Essentially, if people are equipped with proper capabilities, are aligned and motivated to excel, and empowered to use their innate creativity to react to changes; the organization will be successful. Unfortunately, if (for example) well intentioned rules and regulations stifle creativity or if actions in one department interfere with the ability of another department to align with corporate strategy, senior executives will rarely be aware of the condition. Few employees will walk into the CEO's office and say "you are killing me with unnecessary rules" in any organization.

5.2 Culture: The Glue that Binds the Organization

We agree with the assertion that culture has two major components (visible and invisible), underlying beliefs, values, and shared assumptions that shape the collective thoughts that can be observed through decisions, behaviors, and actions of the people in the organization. Culture has a stabilizing effect on the organization and helps people make things meaningful and predictable. Each organization has a unique culture that evolves over years and is reinforced as people absorb, repeat, and pass along what works. There may be an infinite number of dimensions that make up the culture of an organization, but we have identified five attributes that seem to be nearly universal and thrive, unseen, in the minds and actions of employees at all levels of the organization. These five attributes help form a shared context within the organization.

Understanding – Do people in the organization see the same things? Do people understand WHAT it takes to win?

Intent – Do the people in the organization think the same way? Do people share a common idea, view, and direction of the organization? Do people know HOW to play the game to win?

Agenda – Do people do the same things and play a well-coordinated game? Are people moving in the same direction with common goals and objectives and priorities?

Aspirations – Do people aim at the same things? Do people share a common vision and values of the organization to find purpose and drive performance?

Norms – Do people act in the same way? Do people know what gets them ahead, share appropriate boundaries, and do what they say they are going to do?

We have seen many organizations where the answer to one or more or all of these attributes is a resounding NO. In our classes and client workshops, we frequently ask students or clients if they have observed situations where managers or executives clearly have agendas that are more self-serving that supportive of organizational goals and invariably many hands immediately go up. We had a client several years ago where we found that managers and executives believed that rules and boundaries were well known and appropriate. Yet, the overwhelming response from people throughout the organization was that people had conflicting agendas and aspirations and that bending rules to advance their career was an acceptable norm. Our suggestion to the senior leadership of this organization was to spend a year getting everyone on the same page and following the same rules before starting big change initiatives. Today, this governmental organization is functioning demonstrably better and serving the needs of the community much more effectively.

5.3 Leadership: Shaping Vision and Inspiring the Organization

It is commonly accepted that the culture of an organization is shaped from the top of the management hierarchy down. We generally accept this belief however we have observed many organizations where there is a huge disconnect between what top executives THINK is going on and what the rank-and-file employees ACTUALLY believe. It does not matter whether this apparent disconnect is real or imagined, the perception makes it real. Leaders and managers at all levels must recognize that their actions and behaviors are being observed and interpreted by employees through the lenses of their own beliefs and values. Unknowingly, many leaders fail to connect with employees and inadvertently communicate conflicting values and beliefs throughout the organization. Employees will rarely approach the CEO and tell them that "you said (this).... But we actually did (that)... which is it and what is going on?" The result in many cases is that employees are left to develop their own interpretation that, in many cases, are inconsistent with organizational goals. Leadership is a complex and indefinable quality, but we have identified five "unconscious and rarely discussable" leadership attributes that contribute to weakening the culture and performance of the organization.

Sense making – Are managers and employees aware of what is going on? Do we have the capability to quickly turn data into information and make informed decisions?

Strategy conversation – Are the strategies and tactics in the game broadly known and trusted throughout the organization? Does the strategy provide direction and help establish trust and encourage critical thinking among employees throughout the organization?

Performance conversion – Do managers effectively and routinely communicate whether the organization and individuals are on track toward meeting organizational goals? Do managers go beyond traditional performance measurement to translate strategy into objectives and establish a shared agenda?

Contribution dialogue – Do managers help staff make sense of what is going on and find a sense of purpose? Do managers maintain an ongoing conversation with direct reports to reach mutual agreement and focus attention on how employees can make a contribution?

Risk dialogue – Do leaders and managers maintain ongoing conversations with others to define boundaries and establish trust? Do leaders conduct conversations to help people focus on entrepreneurial degree of freedom and on risk limits as boundaries?

In our observations with clients and research we have found that many leaders and managers avoid having personal, face-to-face, discussions of this nature unless forced to do so, typically in the highly structured and stressful annual performance review. Employees will almost never go to the boss and tell them "I have no idea what we are trying to accomplish" or "I don't know if I should do ... (this)... or (that)" until after the fact, when it is too late. Managers typically assume that followers KNOW it. Yet, more time than not, they DO NOT KNOW it. Without continuous dialogue in all of these areas a significant gap between leaders and followers develops that can by highly destructive. We had a client with a new CEO. The client was attempting to respond to declining market share and a host of other internal and external changes. The client was spending large sums of money on consultants who were implementing six-sigma, or lean, or leadership training programs and getting almost nowhere. After conducting a diagnosis of the top managers in the organization it became apparent that there were significant unseen barriers to any kind of change initiative. High level managers had the perception that if they took a risk and the risk did not yield the expected benefits, they would be reprimanded or worse. The new CEO had no idea that this was a shared assumption. This realization explained why the change initiatives, all of which involve risk taking, were unsuccessful. We recommended that the CEO take an extended period to have constructive dialogues with his senior managers to change these underlying beliefs BEFORE starting extensive change projects.

5.4 Systems: Rules, Routines, and Tools that Shape Decisions

Systems are both influenced by and influence the culture and leadership practices that shape the decision-making process. When we talk about systems, we are not just talking about the computerized IT systems but the rules and routines that shape the input and output from the computerized tools. Everyone reading this chapter is familiar with the phrases "garbage in... garbage out" and "what gets measured, gets done" but we contend that such thinking is just scratching the surface of the complex dimension that we call "systems". What managers and employees do with the output from IT systems and how that output shapes decisions and behaviors seems to be rarely considered. Similarly, we have witnessed many examples of systems that were developed in prior decades being used to drive decisions today despite the fact that world and the business environment is dramatically different. We have seen many instances where managers created systems to generate relevant data needed to solve some problem or give the organization an edge... 20 years ago. The problem was solved, partially with the aid of the data, and the company gained an edge over competitors. Sadly, today, those same managers are making decisions using the same data that is no longer relevant because the problem was solved decades ago, and the competitive dynamics have changed significantly. What was relevant and meaningful 20 years ago may not be today, leading to fateful decisions. It therefore becomes imperative for leaders to constantly critically evaluate whether the rules, routines, and tools being used to drive decisions are relevant and shape desired behaviors. We have identified five questions, the answers to which provide insight into "unconscious and rarely discussable" beliefs, values, and shared assumptions that either inhibit or enable the effectiveness of systems.

Information – Do we get relevant information to the right people at the right time to make informed and effective decisions? Does the information provide adequate sensors so that people know what is going on and does the information facilitate immediate action?

Strategy – What game are we playing, is it the right game, and are we all playing the same game? Does the strategy help focus capabilities and provide a sense of purpose for employees throughout the organization?

Implementation – Are expected outcomes clearly defined and consistently applied? Is there rich conversation on expectations that facilitates collaboration throughout the organization?

Beliefs – Do leaders inspire and engage employees throughout the organization to do more than the norm, or minimum expectation? Do leaders practice behaviors that demonstrate a clear vision and values of how things are to be done?

Boundaries – Are the limits or degree of freedom clearly established and known throughout the organization? Do the boundaries provide adequate focus while allowing people to take advantage of opportunities?

Developing and constantly adapting effective rules, routines, and tools that shape effective decision making requires constant inquiry and dialogue with day-to-day decision makers from top to bottom of the organization. Peter Drucker said that "The greatest danger in times of turbulence is not the turbulence; it is to act with yesterday's logic." We have seen countless organizations attempting to adapt to a changing business environment using systems and logic that worked fine.... 20 years ago, ... but is woefully outdated in the 21st Century world. We worked with one company that insisted on using the same metrics and routines that were successful for the first 20 years after the company was founded... in 1964. All of the senior executives had the same profile; first job out of college, mentored by one of the founders, rose through the ranks with their mentor's tutelage, never questioned the metrics or the decision-making process, and believed in their own superiority because of their history. The result is that the decision-making process is not measured in days, or month, but years and the decisions are being made using information that was no longer relevant but since the executives know no other system. The company continues on a downward spiral with no idea on how to go about changing the downward trajectory of the company. People brought in from the outside who introduce new ideas were inevitably ostracized and driven out of the company. New ideas that question the strategy, beliefs, or boundaries were viewed as heresy to be stamped out. Given the intertwined relationship between systems, leadership, culture and the people who power the system it is imperative for executives to constantly ask questions then make adjustments throughout the organization.

5.5 People: The Power for the System

People are complex and difficult to handle yet the underlying beliefs, values, and shared assumptions of people determine the success or failure of all organizations. Virtually every organization on the planet has some public statement along the lines of "people are our greatest asset". Human resources departments in organizations worldwide conduct initiatives intended to shape desired behaviors and improve performance throughout the organization. We subscribe to the theory that culture exists in the minds and personalities of people at multiple levels that can be divided into two general groups: climate and culture. The climate part of organizational culture includes the visible artifacts, behavior patterns, and norms that can be readily observed and can be relatively easily influenced by management through rewards or punitive actions. The culture part is invisible and difficult to assess because it exists in the values, beliefs, and basic assumptions that can only be assessed indirectly. We can observe artifacts and behaviors and draw a conclusion about the underlying beliefs and values, but it is difficult to know for sure what those beliefs and values really are. People can modify behaviors to mask their underlying true beliefs and values. We all know this.

We contend that it is relatively easy to shape behaviors but very difficult to change underlying beliefs and values of people which provides the power to the system that drives success. So, is it possible to identify some of the most critical beliefs, values, and shared assumptions that shape behaviors? If so, can the strength of these dimensions be assessed directly. We suggest that the answer is, yes and yes. The PTM identifies four dimensions of the culture that we believe are key to harnessing the power of people to drive the system and ultimately success of the organization.

Awareness – Are people aware of what is happening around them? Can people sense minute changes in the work environment internally or externally to the organization?

Choice – Are people empowered to use their creativity and make choices to effectively respond to customers, clients, or other people inside and outside of the organization? Do people have the freedom of action within appropriate boundaries?

Trust – Do people view management as credible, fair, and respectful of the needs, concerns, and conditions of employees? Do people have the self-efficacy and confidence to trust in their own decisions and actions?

Focus of attention – Has management created an environment that allows people to focus their skills, abilities, and talents to perform their jobs effectively? Does management create interferences that prevent people from being able to focus their attention of being effective and productive?

Those of us who were involved in sports know how someone or a team can get into a "zone" when everything they do works. A weaker team or player can defeat a stronger team or player when they get hot, and the game becomes easy when every shot goes in or every play works. The game becomes really fun, at least for the team in the "zone". In the workplace, management should strive to create an environment where people get into a state of "flow" where they enjoy what they do, and it seems easy [29]. Yet, Peter Drucker and others have observed that, "So much of what we call management consists of making it difficult for people to work". We have observed countless instances where management inadvertently introduced interferences that prevent awareness, choice, trust, and focus thereby preventing people from getting into a state of "flow". Typically, these interferences are unintended consequences from attempts to control the organization or behaviors of people. Also, typically, people throughout the organization almost never question the "boss" or go to the "boss" and tell him that what he is doing is hurting the people or the organization.

We ran into one of the most extreme, and humorous, example of this in 2016 (the date is important). During a workshop with the executives of a company in Germany our assessment of the people dimensions indicated that there were many interferences that prevented people from being able to focus their attention on doing their jobs. This was a surprise to the CEO who asked his management team for an example whereupon several executives almost immediately named "the Friday gasoline report". The ensuing conversation went something like this:

CEO: WHAT Friday gasoline report?

Executives: The report that every driver in the fleet of vehicles submits Friday morning with how much gasoline they used during the week and how much gasoline is in the tanks for the next week. The report is collected and compiled by supervisors, then managers, then ultimately submitted to your administrative assistant every Friday.

CEO to his administrative assistant: What do you do with the gasoline report?
Administrative assistant: I file it in in the storage room down the hall.
CEO: WHAT storage room down the hall?

The administrative assistant then led the CEO and the executive team to the storage room what was filled, floor to ceiling, with filing cabinets full of Friday gasoline reports dating back to 1942. Gas rationing during World War II made such a report very important and the Friday gasoline report was apparently added to job descriptions and was never questioned over the decades as people came and went. For 74 years, people generated the report that was just filed away and never used for anything. The example of the Friday gasoline report not only illustrates how interferences get into organizations causing employees to lose focus, but it shows how important the interrelationships between people, systems, culture, and leadership really are. For example, regular open and honest dialogue on the relevance of information or contribution dialogue could have identified such an interference decades before 2016. Since 2016, the Friday gasoline report is no longer done, and the storage room has been cleaned out and repurposed. The point of this true story is that until executives become aware of "unconscious and rarely discussable" beliefs, values, and shared assumptions or in this case a routine it is virtually impossible for people to get into a state of flow and become the valuable assets that so many company's champion.

5.6 Purpose, Relationships, and Collaboration: Transferring People Power Throughout the System

People provide the power for the PTM system of culture, leadership, and systems and that power is transmitted and flows throughout the organization when people have a common purpose, healthy relationships, and collaborate effectively. As with a two-wheel bicycle, a person provides the power to make the wheels turn but the system needs a chain to connect the power source (the person) with the wheels; a mechanism that is largely "unconscious and rarely discussable" connects people with the rest of the PTM system. We have identified three such dimensions with the following characteristics.

Purpose – Do people have a strong common and shared sense of higher purpose? Does the purpose that motivates people inspire people to go above and beyond the minimum expectations?

Relationships – Do people have healthy relationships that build trust and agreement among employees and external stakeholders alike? Do the relationships among employees and stakeholders facilitate knowledge sharing and growth?

Collaboration – Do employees and stakeholders share unique knowledge and work together toward common goals to achieve success in their everyday activities? Do people demonstrate trust, creativity, and patience when working together as unexpected events occur?

As with the other dimensions that make up the PTM, what people say they do may not necessarily be true representations of their underlying values, beliefs, and assumptions. Virtually every organization on the planet has published mission and purpose statements with high sounding language that sounds noble and worthy. Argyris and Schön [17, 30] explained the difference between espoused theories (what we say we do) and theories in use (what we actually do) and the difference is all too common. Many times executives or employees are not aware of the apparent disconnect. Unfortunately, we have seen, and I suspect many readers of this chapter have seen, executives and rank and file employees give lip service to the noble statements then take actions that are diametrically opposed to the stated mission or purpose. Employees will rarely confront executives to make them aware of the apparent disconnect. Employees simply conclude that the executive is either a liar or stupid. Either way employees are left to develop their own sense of purpose that many times is NOT what the organization wants.

Similar dynamics emerge with relationships that become toxic, inappropriate, or abusive and senior executives are unaware until a scandal emerges, and HR gets involved ... or worse... the media. Collaboration breaks down and becomes ineffective for an infinite number of reasons like ego, knowledge hoarding, and narcissism and executives wonder "why can't we get things done"? We have observed these and many other interferences that infect an organization like a virus that prevents the power of people from being harnessed. Most of the time executives know or sense that "something isn't right" but they have no idea what or where to begin to make improvements.

5.7 Can Anything be Done ... and if So... What?

We contend that something can and should be done if organizations expect to be successful in the VUCA 21st Century. Readers should have noticed that the definitions for the dimensions of success, culture, leadership, systems, people, and the system drivers are phrased as questions rather than statements. This is done for a reason. The reason is that each largely "unconscious and rarely discussable" dimension has many interpretations that change as the context changes. We want readers and participants in the diagnostic to reflect on how they would answer the question in the context of their specific organization and try to assess the intensity or strength of the perceptions. Armed with observations and data gathered from 220 organizations in 2017, we can identify patterns that differentiate top tier organizations from bottom tier organizations. We gathered data using our statistically validated and reliable diagnostic instrument designed to assess the intensity of participants perceptions of the various dimensions within their organizations then converted the data to a 100-point scale which provides a useful visualization of the temperature (intensity) of the dimension.

Figure 5 offers insight into differences between top and bottom tier companies. What we see are significant separation in scores with the lowest top tier score (focus, 67) is greater than the highest score for bottom tier companies (systems, 58). Additionally, top tier companies have created environment or cultures where people have freedom of choice and collaborate effectively while bottom tier companies are weakest in these areas.

	Bottom Tier		Middle Tier		Top Tier	
1	Systems	58	Trust	68	Choice	79
4	Leadership	57	Choice	66	Trust	77
5	Awareness	57	Purpose	64	Collaboration	76
6	Trust	56	Culture	64	Relationships	75
7	Relationships	55	Relationships	64	Culture	74
8	Culture	53	Focus	63	Purpose	73
9	Purpose	51	Leadership	62	Awareness	73
10	Choice	50	Awareness	62	Leadership	72
11	Focus	50	Systems	61	Systems	68
12	Collaboration	48	Collaboration	58	Focus	67

Figure 5. Comparison of top and bottom tier companies.

Figure 5 also shows that bottom tier companies have cultures that emphasize systems and leadership while top tier companies show leadership and systems toward to bottom. This pattern suggests that bottom tier companies tend to have cultures that emphasize command and control while top tier companies have cultures that take advantage of the power of people. We contend that success in the 21st Century depends on creating a culture and environment where people share their tacit knowledge and collaborate in ways that give organizations a competitive advantage. Also, notice that focus is toward the bottom of both top and bottom tier organizations which leads us to believe that Peter Drucker was right when he observed that "So much of what we call management consists of making it difficult for people to work". Even top companies over manage people and inadvertently introduce interferences that prevent people from attaining a state of flow.

Now that we are aware of these patterns of "unconscious and rarely discussable" dimensions that drive the PTM system, can anything be done to change the perceptions and improve the organization's chance for success? We believe that taking a diagnostic approach to changing the culture and underlying beliefs and shared assumptions that drive success is the key.

Members of our team have been senior executives in the past and spent large sums of money and effort on various initiatives purportedly targeted at changing the environment, or performance, or leadership effectiveness, etc. The result has been, as it is in most organizations, a continuous stream of initiatives that yield limited results, if any. Most organizations employ the "flavor of the month" strategy. Nobody would return to a doctor who started prescribing drugs before listening to your heart, taking your blood pressure, etc. to diagnose the physical problem you are having. Yet, in business, executives do exactly that by trying this, then that, then something else hoping that something will yield results. Typically, the only winners in this strategy are the highly compensated consultants. We suggest that taking a diagnostic approach based on using clinically (or in this statistically) proven assessment instruments will allow the executives to target root causes of unseen and previously unknown interferences that prevent people from maximizing their potential. Instead of patching the problems of the organization with band aids, executives can gain insight into many "unconscious and rarely discussable" beliefs and assumption then initiate actions to address the root problem instead of just stopping the bleeding. In many cases, executives would be more successful in the long run by taking time, maybe a year, to establish trust or engage in deep dialogue with people to seek alignment and common purpose BEFORE launching into some dramatic change initiative. However, little progress can be made until the executives first become aware of hidden interferences and gain insight into the invisible dynamics that are interfering with success. Once executives become aware of what is going on, they can take a comprehensive approach targeting the systems, leadership, AND culture. With investors and stakeholders demanding annual and quarterly results, time is not on the side of the executives. Executives cannot, and should not, blindly try this or that and hope for the best. This strategy would not work on the athletic field but sadly it is the approach that most executives take mostly because there are few alternatives.... Until now.

6. CONCLUSION: WHAT HAVE WE LEARNED?

So, you have suffered through numerous pages of academic research and psychobabble, but have you learned anything that makes you think or question the status quo? We hope the answer is, yes. We hope we made a compelling case for evaluating organizational culture as part of an inextricable interconnected system that drives organizational success. There are many approaches that focus on one or the other key element for organizational success. Six-sigma, lean, Great Places to Work, and leadership training among many others are popular approaches. We contend that they typically fall short because they do not address the organization as a whole. The statistics support this assertion because the vast majority of change initiatives fail to deliver results that meet expectations. We believe that part of the reason is that an organization is a complex and dynamic system so that executives must consider more than just productivity or leadership or culture to bring about permanent change. After nearly two decades of study and observation, we have developed a model that, we believe, touches on the key elements needed for success in the modern world. The Performance Triangle Model is a visual representation of a dynamic system with key focal points in systems, leadership, and culture that is powered by people who have a shared sense of purpose, who have healthy relationships, and who collaborate effectively. Unfortunately, in many organizations "unconscious and rarely discussable" beliefs, values, and shared assumption interfere with the ability of people to attain a state of "flow" that prevents people and the organization from reaching its full potential.

Theories and models are great but ... SO WHAT! What is the value if the theory or model cannot be used to help executives actually make significant change? As former executives, we have focused our efforts on developing a methodology and tools to help executives bring about permanent change in their organizations. We reject the "flavor of the month" approach and propose a diagnostic approach to changing the culture and the organization as a whole. In a VUCA world where both internal and external environments change at a blinding pace, executives do not have the luxury of experimenting and hoping for the best. Organizational success in the 21st Century depends on the ability of organizations to adapt and change .... QUICKLY! We are all familiar with the 5 Why technique to get to the root cause of problems. The key is in asking the "right" questions then taking targeted action after gaining insight into these unseen or unspoken perceptions that abound in the organization.

Figure 6 displays the results from the 18 executives in the sample discussed in Section 4.3 used to validate the diagnostic instrument formatted as a leadership scorecard. Introspective dialogue to answer the questions and understand the underlying causes can help executives be more agile, responsive, effective, and most important... timely ... as they adapt the organization to ever evolving business environments. What unseen forces are interfering with the interactions between systems, leaders, and the culture that prevent the organization from being as successful as possible? This is the most basic question that executives need to ask and gain insight into to maximize success in a VUCA world.

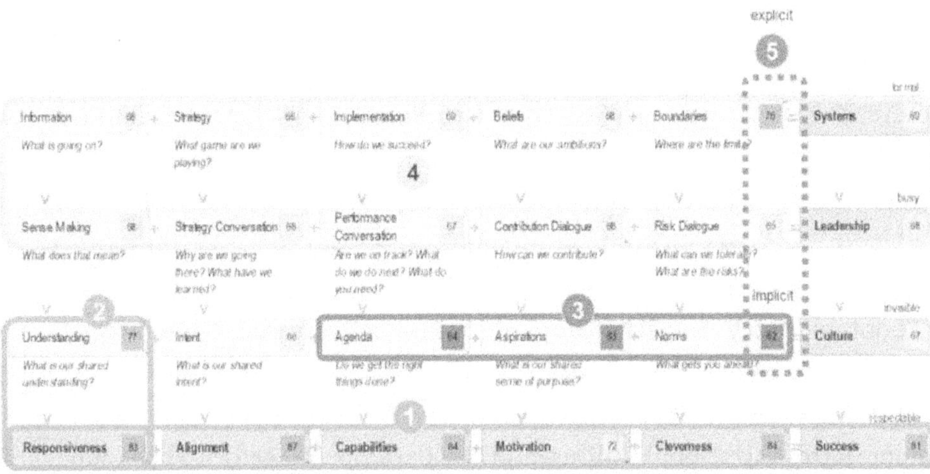

Figure 6. The Leadership Scorecard - 15 Questions to Frame Dialogue.

The results in groups one and two (green) show that the leadership team has a firm understanding if what it takes to be successful. However, grouping four (yellow) suggests that systems and leadership are hindering their ability to be successful. Also, armed with insight gained from several hundred organizations, we can see patterns that tell a story. In this case, the green 76 for boundaries says that these leaders believe they have appropriate rules and procedures that are well understood. However, the red scores in grouping three (red) for agenda, aspirations, and norms indicates that they have differing personal goals and objectives and that it is acceptable to "bend the rules" to advance a career. This "unconscious and rarely discussable" dimension of the culture clearly introduces interferences preventing optimal success. Executives need an assessment tool that quantifies previously "unconscious and rarely discussable" dimensions within their organizations. Then they need to have honest and sometimes uncomfortable dialogue followed by actions to fix the underlying or root causes of interferences preventing organizational success. We believe that a diagnostic approach using a statistically valid and reliable assessment instrument of key elements of organizational success can provide necessary insight to executives to target the root cause of interferences and make permanent changes.

REFERENCES

1. Schein, E. Organizational Culture and Leadership, San Francisco: Jossey-Bass; 1985.
2. Hofstede, G, Neuijen, B, Ohayv, D, Sanders, G. (1990). Measuring organizational cultures: A qualitative and quantitative study across twenty cases, Administrative Science Quarterly, 1990;35; 286-316.
3. Nold. H, Hagelthorn, A. Investigating Business and National Culture during Due-Diligence and its Impact on Multi-National Ventures, Organizational Cultures: An International Journal, 2016:16(2): 1-19. http://ijmoc.cgpublisher.com/product/pub.258/prod.90
4. Peters, T, Waterman, R. In Search of Excellence, New York, NY: Random House; 1982.
5. Peters, T, Austin, N. A Passion for Excellence, New York, NY: Random House; 1985
6. Ilieş, L, Metz, D. The Link between Organizational Culture and Organizational Performance - a Literature Review. Managerial Challenges of the Contemporary Society, 2017;10(1): 35-40. Retrieved from https://search-ebscohost-com.contentproxy.phoenix.edu/login.aspx?direct=true&db=bth&AN=128134886&site=ehost-live&scope=site
7. Taylor, J. Organizational Culture and the Paradox of Performance Management. Public Performance & Management Review, 2014;38(1), 7-22. https://doi-org.contentproxy.phoenix.edu/10.2753/PMR1530-9576380101
8. Sirikrai, S. Measurement of Organizational Culture: A Literature Review, 2006. Available from: www.jba.tbs.tu.ac.th/files/Jba109/Article/JBA109Sajee.pdf

9. Nold, H. Linking knowledge processes with firm performance: Organizational culture. Journal of Intellectual Capital, 2012;13(1): 16-38. https://doi.org/10.1108/14691931211196196

10. Whalen, T. B. Utilizing the social transaction theory of social ontology to understand organizational culture change. Journal of Business & Economics Research(Online),2014;12(1):37-n/a.Retrievedfromhttps://search-proquest-com.contentproxy.phoenix.edu/docview/1477975247?accountid=35812

11. Walonick, D. General Systems Theory (essay). 1993. https://statpac.org/walonick/systems-theory.htm

12. von Bertalanffy, L. General System Theory: Foundations, Development, Applications, New York: George Braziller. 1968.

13. McNeill, D, Freiberger. Fuzzy Logic. New York, NY: Simon & Schuster. 1993.

14. Kuhn, A. The Logic of Social Systems. San Francisco, CA: Jossey-Bass. 1974.

15. Michel, L. The performance triangle: diagnostic mentoring to manage organizations and people for superior performance in turbulent times, London, UK: LID Publishing Ltd. 2013.

16. Nold, H, Michel, L. The Performance Triangle: A Model for Corporate Agility, Leadership and Organizational Development Journal, 2016;37(3):341-356. DOI: http://dx.doi.org/10.1108/LODJ-07-2014-0123

17. Argyris, C, Schön, D. Organizational learning: A theory of action perspective, Reading, Mass: Addison Wesley. 1978.

18. Nold, H, Anzengruber, J, Woelfle, M. Michel, L. Organizational agility – Testing, Validity, and Reliability of a Diagnostic Instrument, Journal of Organizational Psychology, 2018;18(3):104-117.

19. Davenport, T, Prusak, L. Working knowledge: How organizations manage what they know, Boston, MA: Harvard Business School Press. 1998.

20. Drucker, P. Landmarks of Tomorrow, New York, NY: Harper & Row. 1957.

21. Mládková, L. Management of knowledge workers, Economics & Management, 2011;16:826-831.

22. Lin, C, Chiu, H, Chu, P. Agility index in the supply chain, International Journal of Production Economics, 2006;100(2):285-299.

23. Sherehiy, B. Relationships between agility strategy, work organization and workforce agility, University of Louisville. 2008.

24. Tsourveloudis, N, Valvanis, K. On the measurement of enterprise agility, Journal of Intelligent and Robotic Systems, 2002;33(3):329-342.

25. Verdú, A, Gómez-Gras, J. Measuring the organizational responsiveness through managerial flexibility, Journal of Organizational Change Management, 2009;22(6):668-690.

26. Charbonnier-voirin, A. The development and partial testing of the psychometric properties of a measurement scale of organizational agility, M@n@gement, 2011;14(2):120-154.

27. Roussel, P. Rémunération, motivation et satisfaction au travail, Paris, France: Econimica. 1996.

28. Roussel, P. Méthodes de développement d'échelles pour questionnaires d'enquête, In P. Roussel & F. Wacheux (Eds.). Management des Ressources Humaines: Méthods de recherche en sciences humaines et sociales (pp. 245-276), De Boeck: Burxells. 2005.

29. Csikszentmihalyi, M. Finding flow, Psychology Today, 1997;30:46-48.

30. Argyris, C, Schön, D. Theory in practice: Increasing professional effectiveness, San Francisco: Jossey-Bass. 1974.

14 Internationalization and Turkish Manufacturing Firm Performance – Does Managerial Personality Matter?

1. INTRODUCTION

Internationalization and efficiency of business operations have been a matter of great concern in international business by scholars around the world for more than five decades. When expanding operations to global markets, companies have growth opportunities, accumulate knowledge from foreign markets, and help businesses reduce production costs and incur costs due to international environmental uncertainty [1]. However, internationalization also harms firm performance. For example, businesses will face risks and may face failure when expanding internationally [2].

Although there have been many previous empirical studies on internationalization and business performance, the empirical results are often inconsistent due to differences in analytical methods and research. And sometimes contradictions lead to mixed conclusions. Most of these studies are conducted in countries with developed economies, and the research subjects are multinational companies. While many other empirical studies have found a linear relationship between internationalization and business performance of multinationals in the world and Taiwan [3, 4] and including the positive (negative) impact of internationalization on the business performance of emerging market firms [5] and the U.S. market [6], Riahi-Belkaoui [7] is one of the rare scholars who finds a non-linear relationship between the degree of internationalization and the business performance of multinational companies in the large-scale economy (USA).

The role of moderating variables in the relationship between internationalization and business performance has attracted interest, although quite rare since 2006, such as the study by Hsu et al. (two thousand and thirteen). Furthermore, research on the manager's role is scarce.

According to the Uppsala model, Vahlne and Johanson [8] pointed out that managerial competence is an essential key in achieving growth and that managers play a vital role in making decisions on doing business in foreign markets. Upper-echelons theory in organizations has shown that to manage complexity from international markets and ambiguity, the manager's role in decision-making when processing information is vital. Adequate confidence is necessary [9]. Therefore, the study's question is whether or not the positive effect of internationalization on business performance will be enhanced or decreased when moderating the managers' characteristics.

This research will contribute to the literature review of internationalization by threefold: (1) provide additional empirical evidence for the theory of internationalization; (2) highlight with a vital role of personal traits of the managers of the firms; (3) provide a particular research context, i.e., manufacturing enterprises in transition economies.

2. LITERATURE REVIEW

Internationalization is the process by which businesses expand their business to foreign markets. Internationalization is an effective growth strategy for businesses when the domestic market is limited; internationalization helps companies grow their economic scope and scale, and at the same time, helps companies reduce input costs [10]. According to researchers, internationalization is also understood as the process of firms increasing their participation in foreign markets and making strategic decisions to improve international sales [11]. When businesses participate in overseas markets, there will be many benefits, such as increasing knowledge about foreign markets, enhancing competitiveness through gaining practical experience, and exploiting local strategic assets [12].

Expanding business operations to a new market also creates many challenges and increases businesses' costs, particularly regarding the legal liability of "foreigners" when doing business in another market [13]. Besides, to be successful in the international market, companies must understand the market's cultural characteristics to make product innovations suitable for the market. Therefore, for a business to be successful and limit the risks of uncertainty, the complexity and constant volatility of foreign markets depend significantly on the leading executive role.

The business performance shows the firm's ability to use its resources to achieve its goals. Experimental results in the world have also demonstrated that the relationship between internationalization and business performance of enterprises in the period from 1998 to the first three months of 2020 is non-linear (shape The U, the inverted U, the S, and the W), are sometimes linear (forward, inverse) and mixed relationship. Internationalization is also explained in the direction of considering the methods of entering the business's international market, more clarification in the Uppsala model. The Uppsala model, also known as the "internationalization process" theory, was developed from Uppsala University by Johanson and Vahlne [14]. This model explains that the internationalization of a business can be divided into four stages of development: (1) no regular exports, (2) exports through independent representatives, (3) sales branches in foreign markets, and (4) production in international markets. Over the past four decades (from 1977 to 2017), Johanson and Vahlne have repeatedly developed the Uppsala model. The 2017 Uppsala model is their newest model, and the management ability is considered a significant bottleneck in achieving growth [8].

We argue that internationalization is a complicated business strategy and is tied to the business managers' decision to do business. A business manager is a unit of analysis. Upper-Echelon theory refers to groups of people with high social status [15] or top managers of the business, such as CEOs, senior managers, or top management team (board). Hambrick and Mason [16] argued that firm performance is influenced by factors related to the manager's characteristics; personal opinions change the manager's perceptions, and these affect the choice of a firm's business strategy [15]. Many studies use the Upper-Echelon theory to explain a firm's internationalization strategy related to the traits of managers such as experience [17], education level, age [9], gender [18].

Managerial experience. Management experience is measured by the number of years that the manager is working in the current position. As the number of years working increases also means that the number of managers' experience increases, knowledge accumulation during the working time will create experience and motivation for international business expansion [14]. A manager with knowledge accumulated increasingly after years of working in a leadership position creates valuable experiences in dealing with international markets' complexities and uncertainties while overcoming the psychic distance associated with doing business in global markets [19]. These experiences values motivate them to develop strategies and expand their business to new international markets [20]. At the same time, managers' experience also directly affects firms' business results in global markets [21]. Along with the expertise, knowledge of foreign cultures, and the selection of managers' business methods will help businesses eliminate barriers of cultural differences through innovation and innovation product policies and brand promotion to suit each country's culture.

Hypothesis H_1: Managerial experience will positively moderate the relationship between the degree of internationalization and firm performance.

Managers' gender. Turkey is a country with a prosperous transition economy. The Turkish government is always supportive of corporate business; it is trying to reinforce Islamic values, which could hinder women's advancement in society

[22]. Some studies show that Men and Women in Turkey consider women as house workers, suitable for the role of motherhood [23]. Men are represented in most of the leadership roles in Turkey [24], and women are not represented in the senior leadership ranks or the committee director of a business [25].

The empirical studies have shown that male managers bring more benefits to businesses than women [26]. Firms headed by women do not have the majority of the financial resources led by men [27]. Since internationalization is a cost-effective strategy to maintain international relations and strengthen its position in the market, a business with a South manager is more suitable to engage in the process. Next, male managers face less discriminatory barriers and barriers to entry into international markets than Female managers [28]. Simultaneously, ideological stereotypes against women also create doubts from new clients about women's performance and their ability to deliver quality products to international markets on time [29]. All of these make such a significant obstacle to the internationalization process if the manager is a female.

Hypothesis H_2: The female manager will negatively moderate the relationship between internationalization and firm performance (Figure 1).

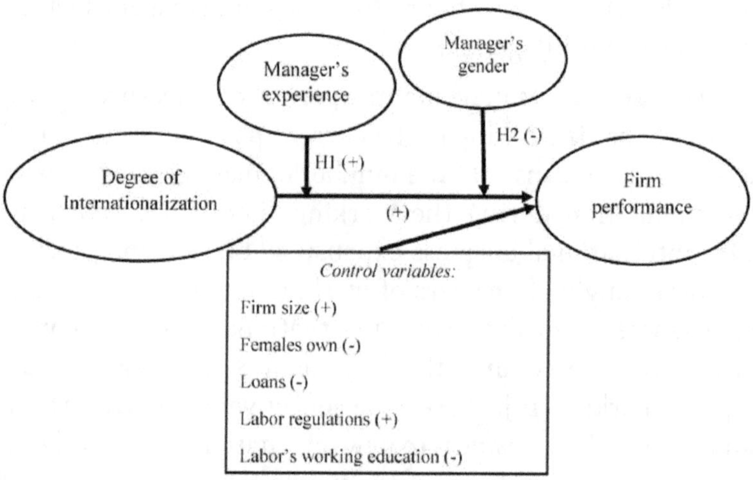

Figure 1. Conceptual model.

3. INTERNATIONALIZATION AND FIRM PERFORMANCE IN TURKEY

Turkey is located in a favourable geographical position for economic development. This is the intersection between two continents (Asia and Europe, most of the territory are in Asia), connecting the Black Sea and the Aegean Sea, so it is easy to cooperate and develop trade with other countries. Thanks to the implementation of drastic measures to reform the economy towards industrialization, the Turkish economy has a huge difference before and after 1980. In 1980, the Turkish economy was moving to the market economy stage. The economic development policy at this time is to industrialize its production towards export. According to the statistics of the Turkish Statistical Institute (wwwdata.tuik.gov.tr), the Gross Domestic Product of Turkey also has a significant increase; GDP in 1980 reached 69 billion USD, 151 billion USD in 1990, 273 billion USD in 2000 and most recently 766.51 billion USD in 2019. It is the strong development since the economic reforms, Turkey now the 6th largest economy in Europe after Germany, the UK, France, Italy, Spain and the 16th largest in the world (according to International Monetary Fund, www.imf.org) and also a member of the G20 (Group major economies).

The current Turkish economy is mainly based on industry and services, develop towards a free market. According to an assessment of the Organization for Economic Cooperation and Development (www.oecd.org), in 2017, Turkey was the country with the third growth rate after China and India; in 2011–2017, the average GDP growth rate reached 6.7%. Industry, service and agriculture accounted for 26%, 64% and 10% respectively in 2013 in the economic structure. Production output has been considered the main driver of Turkish economic growth since the 1960s, including processing and manufacturing industries such as iron and steel production, oil refining. Therefore, one of the most critical sectors of the Turkish economy is the manufacturing and processing industry. In 2010, the Turkish manufacturing and processing industry accounted for 53.4% of the total export value. According to the Turkish Ministry of Industry and Technology (www.sanayi.gov.tr), over the past 20 years, the Turkish manufacturing and processing industry has also contributed a part major in GDP from 15–20%. In 2018, this sector's share of GDP was 19.1%.

According to the Turkish Institute of Statistics, the number of enterprises operating in the manufacturing and processing sectors was 3,221,000. Small and medium enterprises (SMEs) account for 99.8% of all enterprises, with 72.4% of jobs created in 2019. The majority of SMEs are in the commercial sector, with 36.3% of firms operating in the sales sector. Wholesale and retail; 14.4% of businesses in transportation and storage; 12.4% are manufacturing and processing industries. Also, 91.4% of the export turnover of SMEs is the product of manufacturing.

According to the World Bank's survey data, the current internationalization situation through direct-and-indirect exports of manufacturing enterprises in Turkey has significantly decreased. Specifically, in 2008 there were only 320 enterprises over 854 enterprises (accounting for 37.47%) having export activities. In 2013 and 2019, there were 282 exporting firms out of 1055 firms (accounting for 26.73%) and 207 exporting firms over 1036 enterprises (accounting for 20.18%). Many businesses have not engaged in export activities, accounting for more than 87.2% (2175 exporters/2495 processing and manufacturing enterprises). This shows that the difference between enterprises that have export activities and do not have export activities is still quite significant. The decreasing trend in Turkish processing and manufacturing enterprises' export activities may stem from the domestic and international barriers that businesses will face when entering the market.

Barriers for internationalization entry. According to a survey by the World Bank on Turkish enterprises' environment and business performance, many obstacles hinder businesses' internationalization in this country. First, the level of corruption varies considerably between regions in Turkey. The Bribery Depth Index shows that the percentage of 6 legal transactions and interest transactions related to asking for bribes for an average of 1 business in Turkey was %6 in 2008 and %3 in 2013. However, this Bribery Depth index varies significantly from region to region: namely, in East and Southeast Anatolia and the Aegean, it is three times higher than that of other Turkey areas. Consequently, the degree of corruption could exert tremendous financial and cost pressures on small Turkish firms and have limited financial capacity; this itself can interfere with enterprises' export process.

Second, the reliability of power supplies in Turkey is weak. Many Turkish businesses report power outages that account for 5% of their annual sales. Furthermore, there are notable geographical differences. In the Marmara region, power outage losses are only 2% compared with 12% in East and Southeast Anatolia. An increase in the proportion of businesses that own or share generators is also a sign of the country's inadequate electricity supply. Next, companies in Turkey view the tax rate as the biggest obstacle to their current operations, after factors of competition and political instability. According to the World Bank, 455/854 enterprises (accounting for 46.72%) consider the tax rate a factor hindering enterprises' current business activities in 2013 and 2019. Namely, there were 342/1055 enterprises (accounting for 67.58%), and 301/1036 enterprises (accounting for 70.95%) mentioned this factor as a barrier.

Fourth, international trade participation allows businesses to expand, raise business performance standards, import raw materials at lower costs, and access up-to-date technology. However, the transaction also requires firms to deal with customs regulations, and often firms are required to have an export and import license. Delays in export and import customs procedures add costs to the business, disrupt production, and hinder goods' supplies. Finally, most Turkish enterprises are small and medium-sized, so they often face difficulties in accessing finance. This can cause obstacles in the process of expanding operations and reduce the efficiency of business operations. Most SMEs have low equity capital and often have trouble getting bank loans. In Turkey, only 40% of firms had a bank loan or credit line in 2013 compared with 57% in 2008, the use of banking services had a downward trend among firms. The proportion of financial investment financed from banks has decreased from 38% in 2008 to 17% in 2013, and even in 2019.

The Purchasing Managers Index (PMI) measures the economic "health" or efficiency of the manufacturing industry, with data taken from a survey of 400 processing enterprises. Create. The PMI index also shows the level of "excitement" of purchases in the manufacturing sector in 1 month. The monthly changes will reflect the growth or weakening of the manufacturing industry. Index of Industrial Production (IIP) is an index that determines industrial production's growth rate based on production volume. Turkey Manufacturing PMI-Purchasing Managers Index (Turkey Manufacturing PMI-Purchasing Managers Index) is also known as purchasing power management index; According to Markit Economics, this index in Turkey averaged 50.05 points from 2011 to 2020, reaching a peak of 55.70 points (January 2018). This PMI score of>50 indicates that the Turkish economy tends to develop positively, and manufacturing expands production activities. According to the Turkish Institute of Statistics, industrial production of Turkish processing and manufacturing enterprises in the 2008–2018 generally tended to increase gradually, reaching from 124 USD 5 billion (2008) to USD 146.1 billion (2018). This shows that the Turkish manufacturing and processing industry is growing with increasing production over the years and accounting for a relatively high GDP proportion, at the highest level of 19.1% (2018). The lowest is 15.1% (2010).

The two indicators mentioned above have shown that the Turkish economy is developing positively, and the business activities of enterprises in the manufacturing and manufacturing sectors in the domestic market are increasingly expanding and more developed. This also shows that these enterprises' business potential in overseas markets through export is a vast business turnover. Revenue is one of the factors that reflect the business results of an enterprise. According to the Turkish Institute of Statistics, in the period from 2007 to 2018, enterprises' revenue in the Turkish manufacturing and processing sector has many fluctuations, mainly tends to increase gradually and increase from 138.10 thousand billion euros (2007) to 241.20 trillion euros (2018), an increase of about 103.1 trillion euros. According to the Turkish Institute of Statistics, the percentage change in average annual turnover of Turkish manufacturing and manufacturing enterprises also fluctuates with the lowest percentage change of 6.9% (in 2016). The highest is 30.27% (in 2018). In general, the percentage change in annual revenue of businesses is positive.

4. TRAIT CHARACTERISTICS OF THE MANAGERS OF THE FIRMS IN TURKEY

According to the World Bank, the proportion of women's participation in the private sector as owners and employees has decreased significantly since 2008, leading to Turkey suffering from other countries with income levels. In 2013, only

5% of businesses were managed by 1 senior female leader compared with 12% in 2008. The same trend is observed for women-owned businesses, from 41% per year. 2008 decreased to 25% in 2013. The proportion of women among all enterprise workers has also significantly reduced from 25% in 2008 to 22% in 2013. The difference between the proportion of Women and Men in Turkish manufacturing is enormous. This can be traced back to the country's socio-cultural context. More than 98% of the population are Muslims, and women's business role is less important than staying at home and taking care of the house, family, and children.

As a result, most senior leaders in manufacturing and manufacturing in Turkey are men because they have more advantages than women; men have a higher education level than women. Men face fewer business barriers than women at work. A leader's experience is often measured through years of experience in leadership positions in the manufacturing industry. Leadership experience is essential in the business expansion to international markets. According to the World Bank, senior leaders in the manufacturing and manufacturing sector have a relatively high number of years of experience, focusing mainly on 20–30 years of experience. Some businesses are also run by leaders with up to 70 years of experience. Also, many companies are managed by leaders with low years of experience from 2 to 5 years. Differences in the years of leadership experience in companies will also affect domestic and international business strategies, bringing different business operations results and between businesses. Therefore, along with the leader's gender, the leader's experience is also an important factor affecting the company's business process.

5. DATA AND RESEARCH METHOD

5.1 Data

This study uses secondary data sources on Turkey surveyed by the European Bank for Reconstruction and Development (EBRD), the European Investment Bank (EIB), and the World Bank (W.B.) on the business environment and business performance of 4,159 enterprises. In this study, the panel data set are firms are operating in the manufacturing and manufacturing sector of Turkey in 3 survey periods in 2018, January 2013–December 2014 and September 9. 2018 - May 2019. The final sample used for analysis has 789 observations, including 263 processing and manufacturing enterprises.

5.2 Estimation Model

The regression method with Feasible Generalized Least Squares (FGLS) is used to estimate the moderating effects on the relationship between the independent and dependent variables. The multicollinearity phenomenon is not a concern in this study [30] because the correlation coefficients in the Pearson correlation matrix of the variables are all less than 0.8, and the VIF index is below the "threshold" value 10.0. To choose between REM and FEM models, we conducted a Hausman test. Accordingly, with Prob> chi2 = 0.0714 and greater than P-value = 0.05 (accept H0 hypothesis), the REM model is more suitable than the FEM model. Then, the Lagrange test is used to check the heteroskedasticity of the REM model. As a result, it obtains Prob> chibar2 = 0.0000 smaller than P-value = 0.05, so rejecting hypothesis H0 (homogeneous variance), the model exists the heteroscedasticity phenomena with significance level 0.05. To cope with this issue, we use the Feasible Generalized Least Squares (FGLS) method as a method to correct this issue and thus increase the effectiveness of the estimation model.

The estimation model is constructed as follows:

$ROS_{it}=\beta_0 + \beta_1 doi_{it} + \beta_2 firmsize_{it} + \beta_3 femalesown_{it} + \beta_4 applyloans_{it} + \beta_5 laborregu_{it} + \beta_6 eduworkit + \beta_7 expertmit + \beta_8 gendertmit + \beta_9 (doiex)_{it} + \beta_{10} (doige)_{it} + \varepsilon_{it}=$

Dependent variable: ROSit is the Return on sales of Turkish processing and manufacturing firms' business performance at time t.

Independent variable: doiit: a degree of internationalization of the firms.

Control variable: firmsizeit, femalesownit:, applyloansit:,laborreguit: labor regulation, eduworkit: labor's education.

Moderator variables: extmit: managerial experience, gendertmit: lmanager gender.

Interaction terms:

doiexi: the interaction between the degree of internationalization and management experience (measured by multiplying the doi variable and the extm variable),

doigeit: the interaction between the degree of internationalization and the gender of the leader (measured by multiplying the doi variable and the variable gendertm together).

β0: intercept (constant)

βi: are the coefficients representing the marginal impact of factor i in the model, i = 1,...N, where N is the number of firms in the sample; t = 1,... T, where T is the research period.

and εit is the random error of the model (Table 1).

Table 1. Descriptions of variables.

Define	Symbol	Measure	Expected
Dependent variable			
Return on Sales	ROS	The rate of profit on total sales [31]	
Independent variables			
Degree of internationalization	doi	Percentage of export revenue over total revenue: $\frac{\%directexportsales + indirectexportrevenue}{totalrevenue}$ (2) (−) ([31]; [32])	(-)
Moderator variables			
Managerial experience	expertm	Years of experience = years of managers in the manufacturing and processing industry [33]	(+)
Manager gender	gendertm	Manager's gender, 1 = Female, 0 = Male [34]	(+)
Control variables			
Firm size	firm size	Number of employees in the firms 0 is small and medium-sized enterprise (> = 5 to <= 99 employees), 1 is a large-scale enterprise (> = 100 people) [35]	(+)
Females business owners	femalesown	Whether women own the business or not Dummy variable (1 = yes, 0 = no) [26]	(-)
Loans	applyloans	Business with or without a loan Dummy variable (1 = Yes, 0 = no) ([36]; [37])	(-)
Labor regulations	laborregu	Likert-5 levels: "To what extent, labor regulations are an obstacle to business operations." 0: no obstacles 4: extremely obstacles [38, 39]	(+)
Education level of labor	eduwork	Likert-5 levels: "At what level, the education level of labor is an obstacle to the operation of the business." 0: no obstacles till 4: extremely obstacle [38]	(-)

6. RESULTS AND DISCUSSION

Table 2 shows the results of the descriptive statistics of the variables in the research model. The average value of the return on sales of the business (ROS) is %43,412, the maximum value is %100, and the smallest amount is %1994.94-. The degree of internationalization, on average, reaches %0.293, with the highest value being %100 and the lowest %0. Moreover, the average of the managers' experience is about 23 years. Meanwhile, most of the managers are male rather than female (see Table 2).

Table 2. Descriptive statistics.

#	Variable name	Symbol		Number of observations	Mean	Standard deviation	Min	Max
1	Return on Sales (ROS) (%)	ros	789	43,412	34,278	-199,94	100	
2	Degree of Internationa lization (DOI)	doi	789	0,293	0,368	0	100	
3	Managerial experience	expertm	789	23,099	12,047	2	70	
4	Manager's gender	gendertm	789	0,074	0,261	0	1	
5	Firm size	firmsize	789	0,274	0,446	0	1	
6	Females own businesses	femalesown	789	0,313	0,464	0	1	
7	Loans	applyloans	789	0,398	0,490	0	1	
8	Labor regulation	laborregu	789	1,137	1,280	0	4	
9	Education level of labor	eduwork	789	1,572	1,418	0	4	

Source: World Bank Enterprises Survey (2019).

Next, Table 3 presents the correlation matrix between pairs of variables in the model, Table 4 presents the regression results of 3 models Pooled OLS, REM, and FEM. Regression results with FGLS estimates are shown in Table 5.

Table 3. Description of the statistics and correlation table (n = 789).

Variables	Mean	S.D	VIF	1	2	3	4	5	6	7	8	
1. Return on Sales	43,412	34,278		1								
2. Degree of internationalization	0,293	0,368	5,03	-0,021 ns	1							
3. Managerial experience	23,099	12,047	1,68	0,011 ns	0,012 ns	1						
4. Manager's gender	0,074	0,261	2,05	-0,031 ns	0,078*	-0,069*	1					
5. Firm size	0,274	0,446	1,11	0,010 ns	0,257***	0,069*	0,012 ns	1				
6. Female business owner	0,313	0,464	1,16	-0,114**	0,119***	0,058 ns	0,312***	0,143***	1			
7. Loans	0,398	0,490	1,07	-0,165***	0,153***	0,033 ns	-0,011 ns	0,134***	0,104**	1		
8. Labor regulations	1,137	1,280	1,73	0,082*	-0,087*	-0,089*	0,027 ns	-0,032 ns	-0,087*	-0,121***	1	
9. Education level of labor	1,572	1,418	1,70	-0,012 ns	-0,048 ns	-0,024 ns	0,065*	0,037 ns	-0,047 ns	0,012 ns	0,628***	1

*** *$p < 0.001$.*

** *$p < 0.01$.*

* *$p < 0.05$ (ns) $p > 0.10$ (non-significant).*

The value in parentheses is the standard error.

Table 4. Pooled OLS, REM, FEM models.

Variables	Return on sales: ROS		
	Pooled OLS	REM	FEM
Constant	50,51*** (4,011)	49,04*** (3,837)	43,60*** (4,547)
Control variables			
Firm size	2,913 ns (2,834)	3,057 ns (2,880)	4,514 ns (3,857)
Female business owner	-8,170** (3,138)	-7,529** (2,723)	-4,954 ns (3,201)
Loans	-10,19*** (2,665)	-9,378*** (2,513)	-6,213* (3.104)
Labor regulations	2,859* (1,188)	2,190 ns (1,225)	-0,0262 ns (1,533)
Education level of labor	-1,937* (0,984)	-1,251 ns (1,095)	0,864 ns (1,353)
Main effect			
Degree of internationalization	-12,78 ns (8,368)	-10,23 ns (7,167)	-1,285 ns (8,513)
Managerial experience	-0,117 ns (0,127)	-0,092 ns (0,126)	-0,016 ns (0,146)
Manager's gender	10,21 ns (5,860)	11,15 ns (6,400)	14,11 ns (7,428)
Moderator effect			
Degree of internationalization x Managerial experience	0,727* (0,316)	0,621* (0,279)	0,296 ns (0,323)
Degree of internationalization x manager's gender	-25,78 ns (13.998)	-28,43** (10,965)	-35,61** (12,880)
Number of observations	789	789	789
	F(10,778) = 5,04	Wald chi2 (10) = 41,86	F(10, 516) = 1,70
	Prob>F = 0,0000	Prob>chi2 = 0,0000	Prob > F = 0,0776
	R2 = 0.06221	R2 within = 0.0242	R2 within = 0,0319

*** *p < 0.001.*

** *p < 0.01.*

* *p < 0.05, (n.s) p > 0.1 (non. significant).*

The values in parentheses are standard errors.

Table 5. Feasible Generalized Least Squares (FGLS).

Variables	Return on sales: ROS Model 1	Model 2	Model3	Model 4	Model 5
Constant	48,93** (1,391)	47,73*** (2,104)	52,61*** (2,325)	47,72*** (2,077)	51,51*** (2,397)
Control variables					
Firm size	5,959*** (1,445)	5,647*** (1,501)	4,106* (1,632)	4,487** (1,556)	3,443* (1,691)
Female business owners	-6,749*** (1,349)	-6,616*** (1,461)	-6,614*** (1,533)	-6,106*** (1,537)	-6,888*** (1,666)
Loans	-10,22*** (1,256)	-9,354*** (1,502)	-8,897*** (1,523)	-9,901*** (1,544)	-9,560*** (1,613)
Labor regulation	3,460*** (0,643)	3,770*** (0,686)	3,835*** (0,686)	3,422*** (0.683)	3,401*** (0,728)
Education level of labor	-2,347*** (0,530)	-2,605*** (0,555)	-2,436*** (0,598)	-2,376*** (0,554)	-2,245*** (0,629)
Main effects					
Degree of internationalization		-1,534 ns (1,900)	-16,54*** (4,202)	1,792 ns (2,087)	-9,588* (4,632)
Managerial experience		0,064 ns (0,579)	-0,138 ns (0,077)	0,057 ns (0,058)	-0,096 ns (0,079)
Manager's gender		-0,933 ns (3,144)	-0,885 ns (2,855)	10,75* (4,981)	9,963* (4,899)
Moderator effects					
Degree of internationalization × Managerial experience			0,647*** (0,167)		0,476** (0,177)
Degree of internationalization × Manager's gender				-24,65*** (6,616)	-21,21** (6,837)
Number of observations	789	789	789	789	789
Wald chi2	191,24***	177,08***	178,64***	176,59***	149,12***

*** $p < 0.001$.

** $p < 0.01$.

* $p < 0.05$, (ns) $p > 0.10$ (non. significant).

The value in parentheses is standard error.

Model 5 in Table 5 includes all the main variables in the research model, the value Prob> chi0.000 = 2 shows the suitability of the model with actual data at %99 confidence level. All variables in model 5 are statistically significant, except for the variable of managerial experience (β0.096- = 7). There are 4 variables positively correlated with the return on sale (ROS) including: firm size (β3,443 = 1), labor regulations (β3,401 = 4), manager's gender (β9,963 = 8), the interaction between the degree of internationalization and managerial experience (β0.476 = 7). They are statistically significant at %5 ,%0.1 ,%5, and %1. Nevertheless, the remaining variables have a negatively correlated with the return on sales (ROS): business owner is Female (β6,888- = 2), loan (β9,560- = 3), labor level (β2,245- = 5), the degree of internationalization (β9,588- = 6), the interaction between the degree of internationalization and the manager's gender (β21.21- = 10) and all have statistical significance at %5 ,%0.1, and %1 level.

According to model 5, there is a negative relationship between internationalization and firm performance, but it is insignificant. This connection is contrary to expectation. Internationalization is a risky process, and firms have to burden additional costs in which these costs exceed the benefits that the business achieves, leading to a decline in the firm performance. In the early internationalization stage, the costs incurred will also increase because firms often focus on market exploration, enhancing knowledge learning, and experience in international markets [14]. At the same time, companies have to deal with obstacles and cost barriers such as the cost of the liability of "foreigners" [13]; the costs of adapting to cultures and institutions in different countries [1]; corporate governance and administration costs [40]; shipping costs and tariffs [1].

Model 5 in Table 5 shows the interaction of internationalization level and leader experience (variable doiex) positively correlated. This result implies that the relationship between the degree of internationalization and the firm's business performance is strengthened as the managers' years of working experience increase. Therefore, hypothesis H_1 has been accepted. Experience in management positions helps leaders gain knowledge and confidence in managing and managing businesses. Those things create the motivation for leaders to develop products and expand business activities to international markets; the manager's experience also assists them in coping with the complexities and uncertainties of global markets; and directly affects the business performance of firms in international markets. Also, managers can use their experience to interact with partners in foreign markets better, contribute to building trust and enhancing the reputation and image of the business in mind and thereby providing to the elimination of barriers of distance (cultural, social and geographical) in the process of expanding cross-border business activities.

Model 5 shows that the interaction between the degree of internationalization and the manager's gender is negatively correlated with firm performance. The hypothesis H_2 is hence supported. Hence, the relationship between the degree of internationalization and the firm's business performance will decline when the firm has a female manager, in contrast, a male manager will contribute to enhancing the positive effects of internationalization on the business performance. It can be explained that male managers are more successful than female leaders because, unlike women, men are not typically more focused on aspects such as risk reduction and risk aversion, and resilience, and higher risk tolerance [41].

7. CONCLUSION

Internationalization plays a vital role as an increasingly necessary and valuable business strategy [42]. This strategy is even more relevant and essential for firms in a transition economy like Turkey. This study used Moderated Multiple Regression analysis (MMR) with the feasible general least-squares estimation (FGLS) method to find empirical evidence to support the hypotheses. Namely, the degree of internationalization has a more substantial positive influence on firm performance if the managers are males and have more managerial experience. The relationship between the degree of internationalization and firm performance may vary depending on the firms' managerial characteristics. Therefore, firms may carefully consider the managers' traits before deciding to expand the market in the global context.

The results show several important governance implications for corporate boards and managers who aspire to become senior managers in an international environment. First, to have a better performance, firms or executive boards of the firms may be better able to choose males and have much experience than females and have less experience operating the internationalization process. Second, female managers may better improve their international management experience to cope with additional transaction costs in foreign countries such as the "newness" and the "liability of foreignness."

This study goes without limitations. First, this result is limited to manufacturing firms, so that it is difficult to generalize to various business sectors. Second, the number of female managers may depend on a particular culture, region, and the whole country, but the data shows inadequate. Future research should extend the scope of research space and time (phases of internationalization); consider the managers' characteristics such as functional experience, education, age, and marital status, concurrent rights in the business, foreign language ability, and cultural contexts. Third, research in the future may pay attention to the influence of top managers' characteristics without considering how other corporate board members affect the relationship between the degree of internationalization and business performance. Finally, scholars may use diversified indices to measure firm performance.

REFERENCES

1. Contractor, F. J., V. Kumar. & S. K. Kundu. (2007), 'Nature of the relationship between international expansion and performance: The case of emerging market firms', Journal of World Business, 42(4), 401-417

2. Benito-Osorio, D., A. Colino., L. Á. Guerras-Martín & J. Á. Zúniga-Vicente (2016), 'The international diversification-performance link in Spain: Does firm size really matter?', International Business Review, 1248, 11

3. Hsu, C.-C (2006), 'Internationalization and performance: the S-curve hypothesis and product diversity effect', Multinational Business Review, 14(2), 29 - 46

4. Lin, W.-T., Y. Liu. & K.-Y. Cheng (2011), 'The internationalization and performance of a firm: Moderating effect of a firm's behavior', Journal of International Management, 17, 83-95

5. Cuervo-Cazurra, A., L. Ciravegna., M. Melgarejo. & L. Lopez (2018), 'Home country uncertainty and the internationalization-performance relationship: Building an uncertainty management capability', Journal of World Business, https://doi.org/10.1016/j.jwb.2017.11.002

6. Tashman, P., V. Marano. & J. Babin (2019), 'Firm-specific assets and the internationalization–performance relationship in the U.S. movie studio industry', International Business Review, 28, 785-795

7. Riahi-Belkaoui, A (1998), 'The effects of the degree of internationalization on firm performance', International Business Review, 7, 315-321

8. Vahlne, J.-E. & J. Johanson (2017), 'From internationalization to evolution: The Uppsala model at 40 years', Journal of International Business Studies. DOI: 10.1057/s41267-017-0107-7

9. Herrmann, P. & D. K. Datta (2005), 'Relationships between top management team characteristics and international diversification: An empirical investigation', British Journal of Management, 16(1), 69-78

10. Dunning, J. H (1988), 'The eclectic paradigm of international production: A restatement and some possible extension', Journal of International Business Studies, 19(1), 1-32.

11. George, G., J. Wiklund. & S. A. Zahra (2005), 'Ownership and the internationalization of small firms', Journal of Management, 31(2), 210-233

12. Ghoshal, S. and C. A. Bartlett (1990), 'The multinational corporation as an interorganizational network', Academy of Management Review, 15(4), 603-625.

13. Hymer, S (1976), *The international operations of national firms: A study of direct investment,* Boston, MA: MIT Press

14. Johanson, J. & J.-E. Vahlne (1977), 'The internationalization process of the firm-a model of knowledged development and increasing foreign market commitments', Journal of International Business Studies, 23-32

15. Hambrick, D. C (2007), 'Upper echelons theory: an update', Academy of Management Review, 32(2), 334-343.

16. Hambrick, D. & P. A. Mason (1984), 'Upper echelons: The organization as a reflection of its top managers', Academy of Management Review, 9(2), 193-206

17. Cavusgil, S., G. Kinight. & J. Riesenberger (2012), *International Business*, Pearson Education, NJ.

18. Ho, S. S. M., A. Y. Li., K. Tam. & F. Zhang (2015), 'CEO gender, ethical leadership, and accounting conservatism', Journal of Business Ethics, 127(2), 351-370

19. Johanson, J. & J.-E. Vahlne (2009), 'The Uppsala internationalization process model revisited: From liability of foreignness to liability of outsidership', Journal of International Business Studies, 40, 1411-1431

20. Tihayi, L., A. E. Ellstrand., C. M. Daily & D. R. Dalton (2000), 'Composition of the top management team and firm international diversification', Journal of Management, 26(6), 1157-1177

21. Athanassiou, N. & D. Nigh (2000), 'Internationalization, tacit knowledge and the top management teams of MNCs,' Journal of International Business Studies, 31(3), 471-487

22. Burke, R. J., M. Koyuncu., P. Singh., N. Alayoglu. & K. Koyuncu (2012), 'Gender differences in work experiences and work outcomes among Turkish managers and professionals,' Gender in Management: An International Journal, 27 (1), 23-35

23. Kabasakal, H., Aycan, Z. & Farakas, F (2004), *Women in management in Turkey,* in Davidson, M.J. and Burke, R.J. (Eds), Women in Management Worldwide: Facts, Figures and Analysis, Gower, Aldershot.

24. Kabasakal, H., Aycan, Z., Farakas, F. & Moden, C (2011), Women in management in Turkey, in Davidson, M.J. and Burke, R.J. (Eds), Women in Management Worldwide: Progress and Prospects, Gower, Aldershopt

25. Broadbridge, A (2010), 'Women at the top in British retailing: plus ca change?', The Service Journal, 30, 1-25

26. Fairlie, R. W. & A. M. Robb (2009), 'Gender differences in business performance: evidence from the characteristics of business owners survey', Small Bus Econ, 33, 375-395

27. Williams, D.A (2013), 'Gender and the internationalization of SMEs', Journal of International Business Research, 133 – 146.

28. Brush, C.G., N. M. Carter., E. Gatewood., P. G. Greene. & M. M. Hart (2004),*Clearing the Hurdles: Women Building High Growth Businesses, Prentice* Hall Financial Times, New York. 304 pp

29. Fernando, W. A. J. A (2005), Gender subordination and women entrepreneurship, *Master's thesis*, Dublin Metropolitan University of Ireland, Dublin

30. Hair, J. F., W. C. Black., B. J. Babin., R. E. Anderson & R. L. Tatham (2006), '*Multivariate data analysis* (6th ed)', Upper Saddle River: Pearson/Prentice Hall. 899pp

31. Xiao, S. S., I. Jeong., J. J. Moon., C. C. Chung. & J. Chung (2013), 'Internationalization and performance of firms in China: Moderating effects of governance structure and the degree of centralized control', Journal of International Management, 19, 118-137

32. Gashi, P., I. Hashi. & G. Pugh (2014), 'Export behavior of SMEs in transition countries', Small Business Economics, 42(2), 407-435

33. Johanson, J. & J.-E. Vahlne (1990), 'The mechanism of internationalization', International Marketing Review, 7(4), 11-24

34. Bathula, H (2008), Board characteristics and firm performance: Evidence from New Zealand, AUT University, pp.128

35. Cerrato, D., M. Piva (2012), 'The internationalization of small and medium-sized enterprises: The effect of family management, human capital, and foreign ownership', Journal of Management & Governance, 16(4), 617-644

36. Hibbert, E (2000), The Globalization of Markets-How Can SMEs Compete?, *Marketing Discussion Papers,* Business School, Middlesex University.

37. Erdogan, A. I (2015), 'Which SMEs perceive access to finance as an obstacle to their operation? Evidence from Turkey', Journal of Economic and Social Development, 2(2), 13-19.

38. Baykal, N. A., & Gunes, E. (2004). Effectiveness of SMEs in Turkish economy and agricultural industry sector. International Journal of Management and Enterprise Development, 1(4), 359-374.

39. Almeida, R., & Carneiro, P. (2009). Enforcement of labor regulation and firm size. Journal of comparative Economics, 37(1), 28-46.

40. Contractor, J. F., S. K. Kundu. & C.-C. Hsu (2003), 'A three-stage theory of international expansion: The link between multi-nationality and performance in the service sector', Journal of International Business Studies, 34(1), 5-18

41. Maden, C (2015), 'A gendered lens on entrepreneurship: Women entrepreneurship in Turkey', Gender in Management: *An International Journal,* 30(4), 312-331

42. Hsu, W.-T., H.-L. Chen. & C.-Y. Cheng (2013), 'Internationalization and firm performance of SMEs: The moderating effects of CEO attributes', Journal of World Business, 48, 1-12

15 Accounting Quality and Its Challenges in 21st Century

1. INTRODUCTION

The quality of financial accounting mainly determined its value. The central concept's accounting quality is that accounting information is better than other accounting information for business communication intended to convey. Accounting quality is very attractive to participants in the financial reporting supply chain for that reason. For example, better quality accounting can result in a lower cost of capital or equity for a reporting entity. For an investor and creditor, better accounting quality can translate into a firm's adaptability, scalability, growth opportunities, a low-risk firm, and a more profitable capital allocation. Meanwhile, this chapter shows that the quality of financial accounting had other areas, which is government accounting. It focuses on the quality of accounting information produced by government units (agents) that political and behavioural aspects dominate this quality.

The quality of accounting is an endurable issue that will never end to be investigated. Many aspects act as proxies for accounting quality, such as earnings quality, audit quality or earning management [1, 2, 3, 4, 5, 6, 7]. Those previous studies have investigated the determining factors, both in organisations, governments and politics or its consequences. Until now, the research focuses more on financial issues, specifically in the stock market, price, or return. For example, in the context of earning quality determining factor, more researchers discuss corporate governance mechanism, unsystematic risk, type of ownership or source of investment, managerial ability, and corporate social responsibility [8, 9, 10, 11, 12, 13, 14, 15]. The impact of board diligence and audit committee attributes is negative. Foreign ownership contributes to financial reporting quality, but audit quality has a significant effect [16].

Accounting quality following applicable standards is closely related to financial information's usefulness to the users', especially in supporting user decision making. We could highlight this usefulness aspect not only from a financial side but also from a behavioural part. In other words, this paper presents an idea uniqueness that behavioural factors, including political hegemony, bureaucracy ratcheting, cognitive distortion and standard-setting, influence the future accounting quality.

Accounting information results from a process involving many parties, either from the preparers (public or private) or parties who can guarantee the quality of the accounting information presented. Thus, the behavioural meaning of accounting quality is an important issue to be researched as well.

2. BRIEF OF THE ACCOUNTING QUALITY

The previous literature has revealed that although the concept of accounting quality is often employed in scientific discussions, that there is no single, widely accepted, or specific definition in terms of "accounting quality." The quality of accounting is a broad concept that has a series of diverse measurable attributes. Practically, definitions of accounting quality vary significantly across individuals, projects, and organisations. Recall from Renata [17] highlights that accounting quality-related research has gained interest until now.

The previous study [1, 18, 19] showed that the qualitative characteristics of financial information (according to US GAAP or IFRS requirements) or quality of financial statements (financial reporting) defines accounting quality. Such as, Hribar et al. [1] defines accounting quality as the extent to which accounting information accurately reflects the company's current operating performance, helps predict future performance, and helps assess firm value. Callen et al. [20] define accounting quality as the precision with which financial reports convey information to equity investors about the firm's expected cash flows. Poor accounting quality is likely associated with uncertainty about stock valuation parameters and incomplete information. It then could lead the users of financial accounting information adversely.

The previous research mostly linked accounting quality with better-earning quality, better earnings management, more timely loss recognition, higher firm value, and a lower cost of capital or cost of equity [2, 3, 14, 18]. Hribar et al. [1] state three broad accounting quality areas related to research are 1) the accounting quality analysis in the context of accounting harmonisation; 2) analysis of firm-specific factors influencing accounting quality and its consequences; 3) assessment of how institutional factors impact changes in accounting quality which is often dedicated to IFRS adoption. Although there are many accounting quality definitions, those all ultimately act the one purpose: to enable people to make value judgments regarding accounting information. Therefore, someone that measures the quality of accounting information will create the value judgments themselves.

3. CONSTRAINTS AND CHALLENGES TO PROVIDE QUALIFIED INFORMATION

Being measure accounting quality, the researcher has used many approaches and developed new methods continually. They are usually determined to expect measures of accounting quality directly from the financial statement or report. For example, the measurement of accounting quality used to detect the earning management is the Beneish model's "M-Score" [9], computed from eight variables. The quantitative accounting metrics based its measured, that is, sales in receivables days.

Another measurement in terms of earning quality is accrual and deferral manipulations [5, 7, 21]. Meanwhile, the information other than the financial information or an entity report may base the measurement of accounting quality, such as the fee companies should pay to the external auditors or forecasts made by securities analysts to forecast the return. Thus, in most previous research, the accounting quality measurement is based on the history, archival data, or financial approach. Meanwhile, we know that the financial statements or report is the result of the accounting system process. Therefore, many parties are involved in this process to have better accounting quality, which behavioural perspective can also do.

In the current study example, the government's decline in audit quality changes the audit opinion on financial statements due to political hegemony, particularly in the financial statement audit process. From the auditor's side, the cognitive distortion influences the quality of their judgment, representing audit quality. Then, the study predicts that accountability can mitigate this chaotic cognitive [22, 23]. Meanwhile, the quality of government financial reports also was disturbed by the bureaucracy ratcheting. Audit on financial statements is an essential tool to reduce information asymmetry or maintain accounting quality. So, to get or improve financial performance or quality financial reports, it must be supported by audit quality, including the auditors' credibility and reliability.

Audit quality is a critical issue because the auditor's competence, independence, integrity, performance, and reputation are at stake in these auditing activities related to the findings of the audit opinions. As a result of the accounting system process, assessing the accounting system weaknesses found in the audit is an achievement of the auditor's competence. Meanwhile, the disclosure of anomalies in the results of the assessment system is an indicator in measuring the triumph of auditor independence. Thus, audit quality is part of the opinion quality produced by the auditor's consideration as an individual, which is affected by his competence Watkins et al., [24], including the skills and adequacy of the knowledge, experience, education, and cognition of the auditor as a requirement to carry out a professional and qualified audit. A high-quality auditor effectively ensures the credibility of financial information.

3.1 Political Hegemony

Political hegemony plays a substantial role in developing countries. However, the role of the government is not vital enough to control all units or agents under it because it does not yet have maturity. In other words, the central government in developing countries are usually annexed by an imperium or superstructure. The process of annexation generally is that superstructure controls governance processes. For example, the superstructure governed the auditing process of the financial statement of government units. This process is conducted by the Audit Supreme Board (ASB) of developing countries until its implementation. However, this process could be on performativity due to superstructure influencing. In other words, the audits carried out and the audit outputs, even though they are processed, still produce low quality because the auditors are annexed. Therefore, the auditor behaves in performativity in the annexed audit process, which is unlikely to produce high-quality audited financial statements. This subsection presents in Figure 1 as follows.

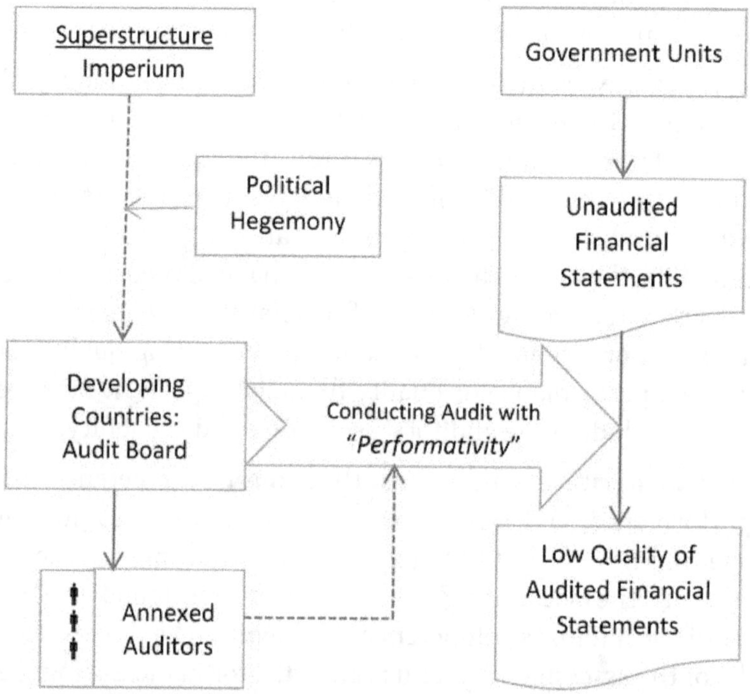

Figure 1. Role of political hegemony in auditing process.

The term hegemony was first introduced by Gramsci et al. in 1971 [1] in his book "Selection from Prison Notebooks". There are three aspects of Gramsci's theory of hegemony. First, Croce's alleged influence over the latter is rejected, favouring equal concern with the whole generation of Italian intellectuals, not just Croce. Second, philosophy plays an essential role in Gramsci's theory of hegemony because it provides a fundamental critique of common sense and false consciousness. Third, the intellectual needs for a new hegemony are organic and involve traditional intellectuals in complex new formations [2]. Finally, the concept of hegemony is straightforward, which means that political leadership is based on the consent of the led, the agreement guaranteed by the diffusion and popularisation of the worldview of the ruling class [3]. Thus, we can refer to hegemony as the domination of one group over another, often supported by norms and legitimating ideas. Related terms hegemon is used to identify the actor, group, class, or state that exercises hegemonic power or is responsible for spreading hegemonic ideas.

Gramsci had identified the dominant role mode as a ruling class and was interested in explaining how concrete institutional forms and material relations of production became prominent. The supremacy of class and the subsequent reproduction of the associated mode of production can be obtained by brute domination or coercion. However, Gramsci's central observation is that in advanced capitalist societies, the preservation of the ruling class is achieved through consensus, mainly through intellectual and moral leadership. Gramsci also shows how hegemony requires the articulation and distribution of popular ideas beyond narrow class interests through the concept of national popularity.

Regarding audit quality as one of the accounting qualities dimensions, in the recent study, Sumiyana et al. [4] investigated political hegemony as a determinant of audit quality in public accounting. This chapter defined a political hegemony as equivalent to (as if) existed direction from the superstructure. Political hegemony can affect auditor independence and then the quality of audited financial statements. The authors highlighted that research could investigate political hegemony with auditors' organisational and political skills [25, 26, 27]. One form of organisational skills is establishing communication and relationships between supervisors and subordinates to achieve and improve performance and organisational capacity [28]. Meanwhile, political skill is defined as a person's ability to understand other parties and, with his skills, can influence the thoughts and actions of others to follow his wishes [26]. Political hegemony applies to the auditor if he acts with direction, and in the context of government auditors, they accept influence by consensus and without coercion [29, 30, 31].

This study shows that organisational and political skills, as proxies for political hegemony, affect audit quality. These results confirmed that annexed auditors desire quality audits in their work regarding organisational and political skills. This chapter demonstrates that the political hegemony of the highest leadership, implemented through the mass media, affects the auditors' cognition as subordinates. Directions or requests by the highest leadership are followed by attendants obediently. Furthermore, this study concludes that the mass media is a tool the ruling elite can convey their wishes.

If political hegemony is associated with audit quality, which requires the auditor to have competent and independent requirements, the following consequence will be decreased audit quality. This decline in audit quality includes changes in audit opinion on financial statements due to political hegemony, especially in auditing financial statements. This study enhances the understanding of how political hegemony, supported by imperium, the psychological ruling class, and spheres of influence substantially erode the constitutive role of auditors, giving rise to concerns about the value of taxpayers' money and the effectiveness and efficiency of the public sector.

This chapter provides evidence that the audit findings of the Indonesia Audit Supreme Board (IASB) were not followed up with further investigation or by the court. The first example is the land acquisition for the Sumberwaras Hospital, for which IASB identified a loss to the local government of IDR 199 billion [32]. Supposedly, the IASB proceeded with its audit finding to the court, but the case was stalled. This chapter suggests that the imperium influenced this discontinuation because this land acquisition decision-maker was close to the state power. In other words, with its sphere of influence, the imperium affected the termination of further investigations. Another law agency stated that conflicting codes of conduct in Indonesian business law ended this process. In the second example, IASB found evidence of underlying accounting data showing that the Indonesian Ministry of Religion transferred project funds to personal bank accounts of government officials [33]. The IASB stated that the evidence of the audit findings had high validity supported by evidence of transactions it had attached. However, the IASB still issued an unqualified opinion on the financial statements of the Ministry of Religion, which should not have been possible because these transactions violated internal control procedures. Moreover, many personnel in the ministry acknowledged transfers of money into their personal bank accounts for political reasons.

The third example in this subsection shows an absence of follow-up to the IASB audit findings, specifically in the case of the Audit Results Report (ARR) on the Financial Statement (FS) of the Jakarta Provincial Government for the 2013 fiscal year [34, 35]. This ARR recorded a local (provincial) government loss of IDR 85.36 billion, a revenue shortfall of IDR 95.01 billion and wasteful budget spending of IDR 23.13 billion. However, the audit findings indicated the absence of accountability for the province's financial management and issued an adverse opinion for its financial statements. The criminal investigation agency never followed up on this ARR. The IASB report was published, and then there was no follow-up.

This chapter infers that those managerial policies of government bureaucrats involve committing systemic violations of regulations that affect the quality of accounting information. These bureaucratic policies indicate that the quality of government accounting information in developing countries is deficient. The authors complement this evidence with many cases that have been dismissed without continuing the process through the courts. The dismissal of cases without clarity indicates that the influence of the dominant superstructure is most likely regulating and controlling the handling of cases. This study concedes that the superstructure is invisible, but the legal process is always at a standstill at a certain point without a solution. These dismissals of cases are also eliminated from the news later. However, this chapter noted that so many lawsuits being terminated is evidence of how political hegemony works.

3.2 Bureaucrat Behaviours in Budget Ratcheting

Financial statement quality would still be ongoing for 21st because the behaviour of bureaucrats in developing countries is not yet mature, engaged, and ready enough to optimise both individual and organisational self. Budget ratcheting is usually the orientation of bureaucrats' behaviour in developing countries. In short, government bureaucrats in developing countries always choose the maximal budget to measure activity and performance. On the other hand, the central government of developing countries has set the same policy to improve with various blocked grant systems continually. The authors defined that government agents who always choose the maximum and continuously increase cause bureaucrats' ratchet behaviour. Moreover, these agents apply mechanistic regulations from the central government whose budget size must be improved. Furthermore, budget ratcheting dominates the low quality of the governments' financial statements. Shorten the explanation; this subsection presents Figure 2 as follows.

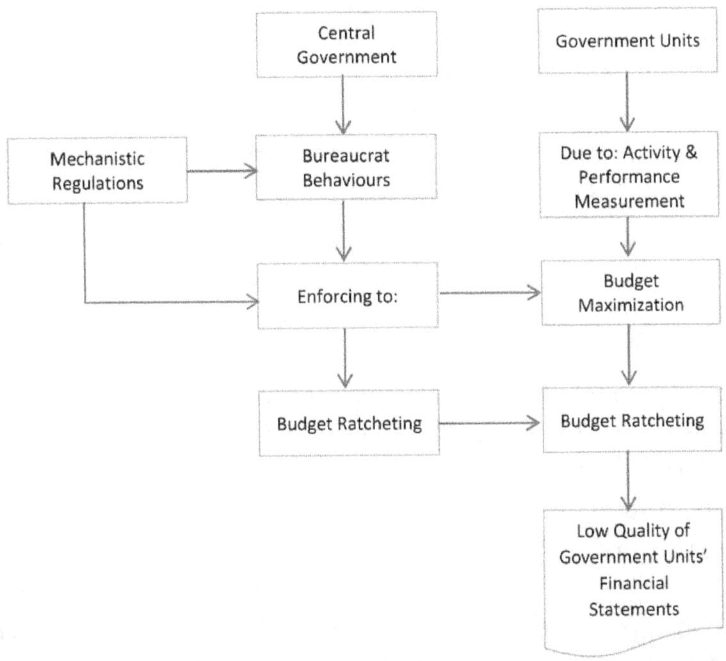

Figure 2. Flow of budget ratcheting in governmental accounting.

The qualified financial information depends on the quality of its regulation, standards and procedures applied to the accounting system [33]. However, the accounting system's implementation could be the technical and political practice in the government, which is low on the political agenda because politicians based their decisions primarily on budget. On the other hand, the existing system is deemed appropriate to meet information needs so that there is no strong impetus for further changes [36]. Thus, in governmental accounting, the budget has a central position. Regarding the budget, one of the behavioural problems is ratcheting. Qualified governmental accounting is impossible to achieve when bureaucrats run ratchets. Commonly, ratcheting occurs when over-spending at the last year's expenditures (exceeding those budgeted) lead to more significant absolute changes in current budgeted expenses than underspending with a similar magnitude. Ratcheting refers to the use of past performance to set higher future targets.

The ratchet effect refers to the motivational implications of ratcheting as agents reduce their effort to avoid further raising future targets [37]. With ratchet behaviour as praxis, the accounting information is more of a description of the desires of the bureaucrats rather than solely for public service. Bureaucratic ratchet praxis gets more support than before when there is no underlying to produce quality accounting. In governmental accounting, there is no analysis of profit or the relationship between revenue and expenses. Therefore, rachet praxis can appear both budget-maximising and budget-minimising behaviour and for both self-interest and non-self-interest reasons. The praxis of these bureaucrats is driven by their characteristics and the problems they face: regulatory-wide regimes, organisational expedience, Undecidability, and Commodification [38, 39]. These four components then become the source of performativity for the subsequent bureaucratic praxis behaviour.

In the public choice literature, bureaucrat ratchets are associated with Niskanen's presumption behaviour of budget maximised. He argues that bureaucrats are self-interested individuals who try to maximise their utility through larger budgets. Economic literature calls it the Leviathan model of government [40, 41]. According to this model, first, the government will grow and increase its power if it is not carefully checked by law [42]. Second, the budget maximiser is pursued because the bureau is a monopoly producer of goods and services demanded by sponsors. Many studies used Niskanen's theory in empirical research [43, 44, 45, 46, 47]. However, this presumption of the budget maximiser [48] still received much criticism in recent years. The authors considered that Niskanen's theory is that a bureaucrat oversimplifies behaviour. The motivations of bureaucrats are too varied to be captured under a budget-maximiser straightforward [49].

A study by Bowling et al. [50] uses a typology of bureaucrats [38] to offer a budget manager–budget maximiser continuum. Budget-maximising bureaucrats are more likely to be advocates and aggrandises (Climber) types, while Altruists (Statesman) or Abider (Conserver) types tend not [50]. The presumption of budget maximiser offers a more plausible theoretical basis for budget maximisation than self-interest for bureaucrats in the spirit of Public Service Motivation (PSM) [51]. Budget maximiser relates in part to the characteristics of bureaucrats. For example, Budget-Minimizer behaviour occurs in bureaucrats who are professional or career-oriented [52]. Several surveys in The American State Administrators Project (ASAP) show a preference for the Budget-Minimizer. Budget-Minimizer does not mean lowering the budget but more a tendency not to increase the budget. Several factors in the emergence of a budget minimiser are the influence of ideology in Partisanship. Partisanship in the republican party will partly use a budget minimiser compared to the democratic party [53]. However, the overall results of the reported survey of agency chiefs [50] using ASAP data still show the behaviour of bureaucrats to increase budgets. Then, why do bureaucrats generally behave to increase the budget?

A recent study was conducted to highlight the phenomenon of ratchet behaviour in public budgeting. This study offers a new insight that budget rachets are bureaucratic praxis. Praxis is the diverting process of bureaucrats' awareness about the constraints they experience and making them explicit in practice [54, 55, 56]. This study is in the Indonesian context compared to the American state. There are differences in state tax collection, government spending, and citizens' resistance between the United States and Indonesia. In the United States, society has reached a point where society can no longer bear taxes (tax revolt). Meanwhile, in Indonesia, such conditions have not occurred. However, there is a similarity that the two countries also continue to experience growth in spending.

This study has interviewed 24 local government officials and internal government auditors. This study found at least four reasons related to the bureaucrats' characteristics for what bureaucrats carry out ratchet praxis. First, the applicable regulatory-wide regime may shape the bureaucratic cognition of decentralised regulatory practices in Indonesia. Second, local governments can get discretionary grants such as block grants. They are a dominant source of regional income but result in chaotic or confusing performance [57]. They also design blurs discretion and creates pseudo accountability. Third, local governments face a mismatch between revenue and expenditure responsibilities to local governments [58]. The Indonesian Government practices covering regional budgets when there are regional fiscal difficulties. This policy means that the government has a low commitment to local bureaucrats. This study notes that these two conditions encourage district and provincial governments to get budgetary slack [59].

Second, organisational expedience causes officials to focus too much on achieving goals at the expense of established rules or norms [60]. In dealing with regional problems, regional heads may make expenditure budgets, not under central regulations. This study shows that the policy actions of district and provincial bureaucrats in the regulatory regime can be called selective attention syndrome [61]. Third, the undecidability budget, which is a local government budget that certainty cannot determine. This study defines that the budget amount determines what can be decided in a specific form. Many local governments face budget undecidability by creating budget slacks to pursue security in their budget execution [62]. Fourth, Commodification means that after autonomy and decentralisation, the budget executor initiates regional economic development. People demand fiscal independence and decentralise physical infrastructures such as roads, bridges, markets, and tourist attractions. This study notes a change in the role of local government from administration to business management [63, 64, 65]. As a result, local governments rely on funds from the Government of Indonesia and always ask for additional budgets.

At the central government level, this study identifies a continuous increase in the central government budget. This condition means that government budget growth always occurs in national scope budgeting for government agencies, not a zero-sum game [66, 67, 68]. The bureaucrats are more focused on their respective institutions. However, it becomes a zero-sum game at the national level in a centralised country. An increase in budget revenues at one ministry, agency, or regional government will reduce the budget or hinder budget increases at other ones. Bureaucrats have different characteristics than their private counterparts. The disconnection between bureaucrats' efforts and the rewards they receive makes researching bureaucratic behaviour a challenge. It seems complicated to generalise the behaviour of bureaucrats in increasing budgeting.

The government budget is a viewpoint of allocated funds contested by most of the existing government agencies. So at least, it can be concluded. First, the practices of the tendency of budget-maximiser and self-interest behaviour are not as strong a motivator as they have been believed. Previous studies on federal officials have also shown similar results [69]; second, budgets keep moving up. The opinion that is still valid regarding the budget ratchet is that the growth in government spending is stable although relatively small compared to the increase in budgets during the Great Depression, World War I and World War II [70]. According to Holcombe, the best estimate for the twenty-first century is probably the steady growth of government, but not shrinking. Thus, the era of excellent governance will still be ongoing [70]. Instead of bureaucrats' practices as budget maximisers driven by self-interest, this article suggests that budget ratcheting is related to bureaucratic praxis. It will reflect politics, budgeting institutions, program implementations and different budget control systems in each country and performativity for bureaucrats to behave.

This chapter provides evidence that bureaucrats always choose ratchet budgeting in an emerging country, Indonesia. The first example: the preference for adding more local government programs with only 30 regional apparatus organisations running between 150 and 600 programs, so they do not focus on regional priorities [71]. Second, local government bureaucrats also often create budgetary programs that are not directly related to their performance. For example, awards night events are budgeted more than two billion for the prizes and the event itself [72]. The third is unimagined budgetary programs, such as recruiting social-media influencers, disbursing IDR 5 billion more than the COVID-19 research budget [73]. The latest is that expenses for official travel by bureaucrats are also expenditures for target fulfilment of budgetary ratcheting. This chapter noted that the official travel budget for a local government unit could spend more than IDR 514 billion [74].

The four examples show that the accounting activities of local governments in an emerging country are frequently out of control. Consequently, local governments' accounting information can never reflect the reality of their budgetary programs. A further consequence is that many expenditures and disguised activity targets burden the quality of accounting information. Therefore, this chapter infers that the quality of (local and central) governments' accounting information does not display the causality of effort-accomplishment. Furthermore, the authors show that, in all budgetary processes for government activities, accomplishments are in the budgetary rachets that are not deterministically related to actual output. Meanwhile, the efforts continually increase to maintain the safety margin of budgetary programs. Moreover, the motives of state civil officials' behaviour support these disguised efforts in all objectives. Finally, the relationship between the efforts and accomplishments implies the low quality of government accounting information.

3.3 Auditors' and Users' Cognitive Distortion

This section explains that financial statements are hard to achieve in high quality. We show that preparers, auditors, and users have embedded cognitive distortions, such as parataxic distortion, denial, psychological projection, and transference. As a result, even high-quality financial statements can be perceived as low by users and vice versa. Likewise, financial statement preparers who treat standards strictly have believed that the prepared financial statements are of high quality but is quiet and vice versa. Consequently, high-quality financial statements produce poor quality because the preparers, auditors, and users are in cognitive distortions. This cognitive condition results in the quality of accounting information being never-ending and durable for the 21st century. Shorten the explanation; this subsection presents Figure 3 as follows.

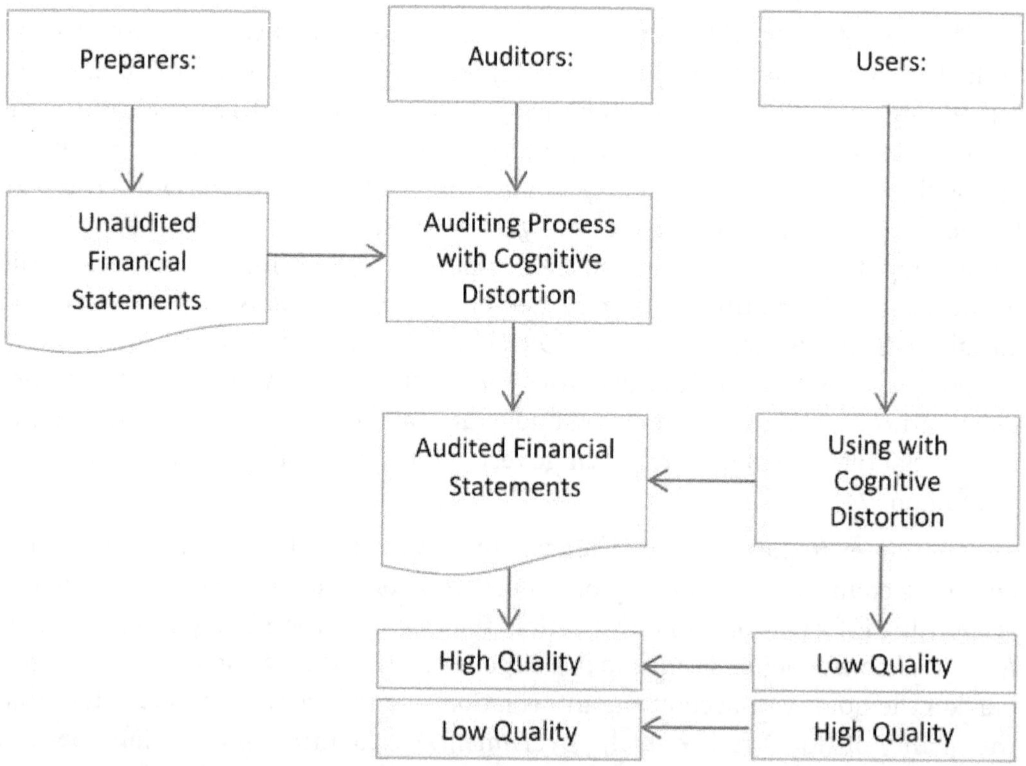

Figure 3. The problem of auditors' & users' cognitive distortion.

A cognitive distortion is a deviated thought that occurs due to the reversal of a fact during information evaluation activities. For example, individuals with an initial preference weigh minor negative (disagreement) than positive (agreement) that has the desired impact on supporting their choice. In addition, individuals tend to be more optimistic when assessing the character of relevant information, whether it is favourable or unfavourable information, related to decisions [75]. Regarding the audit process, the affirmative process in auditor cognitive distortion occurs during evaluating evidence [76, 77]. Meanwhile, the auditor's judgment on decision-making (JDM) depends on the individual situational conditions [78]. This chapter also argues that the financial statement users did what auditors were on JDM.

Bonner [79] suggests that predispositions influence JDM in individuals, including knowledge, skills, emotions, cognition, and other psychological dispositions. To carry out audit considerations, the auditor needs and sorts out information following his preferences and assignments. Bedard & Biggs [80] exemplify protocol analysis (verbal reports) in analytical review studies. When the auditor reviews analytically, a sequential and interactive diagnostic process involves representing mental models, formulating hypotheses, searching for information, and evaluating hypotheses before assessing the client's internal control is made [81, 82, 83, 84, 85]. Furthermore, Rybowiak et al. [86] stated that cognitive and attitudinal predispositions influence current behaviour to be easily controlled in various situations. So, the predisposition to auditor cognitive distortion can be controlled by situational factors. Finally, the authors show that the users of financial statements utilise information on the financial statements with cognitive and attitudinal predispositions that influence their current behaviour.

Previous auditing research found distorted judgment and decision making based on the human tendency to generate systematic errors due to cognitive factors rather than evidence. Distortions tend to arise in auditors who already understand and are familiar with assignments because of individual self-protection mechanisms based on their experience [87]. When auditors are psychologically committed to a given position, they selectively select information and seek evidence supporting previous predispositions [77]. Information seeking helps auditors' preferences [80, 88], and they tend to search excessively for information that supports their initial beliefs or predispositions [89]. This chapter also argues that the users of financial statements did too. The authors comprehend that the users of financial statements in utilising financial statements in their successively previous predisposition.

A study has investigated the relationship between auditors' cognitive distortion and their decision quality as an indicator of audit quality. Previous research revealed the ties between cognitive distortions and individual behaviour from the aspect of psychological [90], in the context of Auditing [91] and accounting [92]. Rybowiak et al. [86] explained that the predisposition of cognitive and attitudinal distortions affects auditor behaviour in various situations. Thus, cognitive distortion becomes an antecedent that influences and is relevant to dysfunctional behaviour. In this chapter, cognitive distortion is defined as when the auditor's interests unconsciously lead to a systematic process of making wrong decisions. As a result, auditors predispose to cognitive distortions that result in dysfunctional behaviour [93, 94, 95, 96, 97, 98, 99, 100, 101, 102, 103, 104, 105]. We argue that the users of financial statements having their leading process in utilising the contents of financial statements.

Defence mechanisms are the auditor's strategy in maintaining self-image and reputation. In this study, four predisposing indicators of cognitive distortion were identified as psychological deviations in the taxonomy of defence mechanisms, namely: parataxic distortion, denial, psychological projection, and transference [87, 106, 107, 108, 109] refers to the research of Nelson et al., [110]; Pickerd et al., [111]; and Sweeney et al., [112] related to the audit process. Defence mechanisms reflect the existence of cognitive control outside of the awareness of the function of defence mechanisms as protection of one's integrity from excessive fear [106]. Parataxic distortion as the attachment of a false perception of others based on delusions [87, 109, 113, 114]. Auditors experience cognitive distortions in the form of attachment distortion due to long [115, 116, 117] and tied [118] engagements. We show that the users of financial statements were probably in parataxic distortion, denial, psychological projection, and transference due to their defence mechanism.

Furthermore, denial is a habit of dealing with problems interpreted as threats even though they are trivial [119, 120, 121]. There are incidents when auditors have difficulty forecasting, experience challenging uncertainties, complex, subjective, and estimative material misstatements that open opportunities for errors to occur, then they avoid them. The habit of avoiding this problem makes the auditor perform non-optimal analyses, such as estimation errors and assessments of materiality, risk, internal control, and audit evidence that impact inappropriate decision-making considerations [93]. Moreover, Buckner & Carroll [122], Harms et al. [123]; and Payne [124] defines psychological projection as thoughts, motivations, needs, and feelings that cannot be accepted as they are because they do not match the attributes of others. Psychological projection tends to make someone look down on others. This projection is a way to maintain a self-image because of the perceived threat or fear. According to their cognitive distortions, the auditors prefer client management preferences to senior choices due to economic factors [117, 125]. The authors inferred that the users, such as auditors, of financial statements have the psychological projection used to avoid threat and fear and maintain their self-preferences.

Lastly, transference is a person's current feelings, impulses, fantasies, and defences that are not by the truth [109, 126, 127, 128]. Andersen & Berk [129] describe transference as the activation and application of representations of others, leading to inference and memory representations, evaluations, affect, motivation, expectations and self-change. For example, auditors who identify with clients are distorted and oriented to act in their interests [130, 131]. This variation in defence mechanisms depends on the interaction between developing a person's level of cognitive maturity and the characteristics of the situation at hand [132]. Thus, this research analyses the different levels of cognitive distortion from denial to parataxic distortion related to cognitive complexity defence in dysfunctional auditor decisions. Moreover, this chapter revealed that the users of financial statements were on transference because of their complexity in distorted cognition. Then, this research showed that accountability could mitigate this auditor's cognitive distortion based on the cognitive-behavioural theory.

This chapter finally presents an argumentation that could reduce auditors' and users' cognitive distortions. We raise accountability when it means the pressure to anticipate because of the justification of one's judgments and decisions against other parties [133, 134]. Accountability pressure is the ability to respond to other parties. Accountability is a mechanism to show that the previously established standards are relevant to fulfilling obligations, duties, expectations, and additional burdens. Organisations can use and condition accountability pressures as situational factors to mitigate cognitive distortions that support dysfunctional considerations that impact audit outcome decisions. Accountability pressure is a mechanism organisations use to control and direct employees [133, 134, 135]. Previous research has shown the effect of accountability pressures on decision considerations in various professions, including professional accountants, tax practitioners, the medical work and corporate accountants [112, 135, 136, 137, 138, 139].

This section provides evidence of the cognitive distortions of executive officers that probably affect the quality of accounting information. Accounting policies and discretionaries follow adverse hazards because of the defence mechanism to carry out the executive officers' agenda. First, two members of the board of directors of Garuda Indonesia refused to sign the 2018 annual report, which is a parataxic distortion. This refusal was due to irregularities in the Annual Income Statement. The discrepancy lies in the cooperation between Garuda Indonesia and PT Mahata Aero Teknologi (a subsidiary firm) worth USD 239.94 million, which is a long-term receivable but was recorded by Garuda Indonesia executive officers as realised revenue. This designation resulted in Garuda Indonesia recording a profit of USD 809,850 in the 2018 annual report. Therefore, Garuda Indonesia would have recorded a loss if this long-term contract operation was not included [140]. The second example is the executive officers' defence mechanism with a transference. PLN Co., Ltd. (the leading electricity company in Indonesia) recorded a loss due to the difference in the dollar exchange rate on the date of the financial statement issued, which was December 31, 2019. PLN published its financial statements and used the dollar exchange rate used on March 31, 2020, without recognising foreign exchange losses [141].

In the third example, Jiwasraya Insurance Company published errors and irregularities in recognising profits in its Financial Statements. Since 2006, the company had consistently recorded a profit. However, the accounting earnings were false due to accounting engineering or window dressing, where in fact, the company had suffered losses. These losses arose from a managerial error in making an investment decision recorded the losses as deferred charges at the end of the year. In addition, Jiwasraya Insurance Company in 2017 realised a profit of IDR 360.3 billion and got the auditor's adverse opinion because an existing fraud of IDR 7.7 trillion was treated without adjustment for that current year [142]. The fourth example is the psychological projection distortion occurring in Pertamina with the COVID-19 pandemic. This company experienced real impacts: a decrease in oil demand, Indonesian rupiah depreciation, and very sharp fluctuations in crude oil prices in the first semester of 2020 and recorded losses of IDR 11.13 trillion. These losses greatly affected Pertamina's financial performance, impacting executive officers who did not recognise these losses in the first semester. These CEOs published firms' profits with optimistic behaviours as the year ended (the second semester), although changing swiftly to double or triple net income was an impossibility [143].

3.4 International Accounting Standard (IAS) and Accounting Quality

Ideally, accounting quality could increase because of changes in the financial reporting system contemporaneous with firms' adoption of IAS, for example, more rigorous enforcement. Thus, we can predict that accounting values or amounts based on IAS are higher than those found on domestic standards. In addition, the worldwide adoption of IFRS (as one of IAS) by public interest companies drives accounting harmonisation. There have also been considerable efforts to achieve international convergence of accounting standards by reducing cross-country differences in accounting practice.

Ebaid [144] investigated the implementation of IAS and its relationship to the accounting quality in code-law countries in Egypt. This study reveals that accounting quality, as measured by earnings management, has decreased in the post-adoption period compared to the pre-adoption period. IFRS is set up to provide high-quality financial reporting. However, this cannot be achieved solely by a regulatory requirement to follow. Even if IFRS are higher quality standards, the institutional features of the Egyptian market could eliminate any improvement in accounting quality arising from adopting IFRS. Firms are applying IAS exhibit less earning smoothing, less managing earnings towards a target, more timely recognition of losses, and a higher association of accounting numbers with share prices and returns. IAS firms have a higher accounting quality between the pre- and post-adoption periods [145].

Accounting standards also are expected to act as a mediator of conflicts of interest between investors and managers. As the role of the mediator, this mediation must be able to reconcile financial reports and the role of efficient contracts from accounting information or how to determine the amount of socially correct information (right). This paper referred to the genuine motivation of the International Accounting Standards Committee (IASC). International accounting standards and the International Accounting Standards Board (IASB) aims to produce high-quality financial reporting. Thus the IASC and IASB issue principles-based standards and take steps that provide alternative accounting opportunities and require a better measure reflecting the economic position and performance [145]. However, differences in accounting quality would remain lasting due to IFRS adoption. Meanwhile, accounting quality is an influential function of the firm's overall institutional setting, including the legal and political system of the country in which the firm resides [19]. In the end, this paper inferred that the objectives of international standard-setting could not be achieved due to differences in each country's context and regulations.

4. CONCLUSIONS

The purpose of presenting the financial reports is to provide how general-purpose financial information must be compared with the entity's previous financial statements and other entities' financial statements. The general-purpose financial statements provide information about the entities' financial position, income statement, and cash flow statement. These statements are then useful for various users in making and evaluating decisions about resource allocation. General-purpose financial reporting aims to provide valuable information for decision making and demonstrate the entities' managerial accountability and responsibility for the resources entrusted to these firms.

Users of financial reports vary widely, such as shareholders, creditors, suppliers, the media, or the public. The demands of the report users mainly drive the presentation of financial reports that are useful for decision making. However, the challenge to produce quality financial reports is quite heavy many factors determining it. The users, especially the public, generally do not utilise financial statement information to make decisions. For example, in the public sector, people tend to use information about the government services they receive. The implication is that the auditor's role in assessing the fairness of the presentation of financial statements is also less than optimal.

Moreover, the audit report on financial statements can also be distorted by the auditor's cognition and political hegemony, reducing audit quality. Another weakness is the attitude of the legislators, who tend to use budget information rather than financial reports as a medium for oversight of the government. Meanwhile, the budget discussed by the top executive officers and legislative is made to be carried out by ratcheting. In this case, finally, financial reports are more of a means of control from the central government to its subordinate agencies rather than presenting quality information to other users. This condition will vary significantly in each government, depending on the government system, budgeting system, demands for public accountability. The implication is the diversity of the application of accounting standards.

Finally, in the spirit of ease to compare the financial report among entities across countries, the facts revealed that accounting harmonisation is not easy to realise. Instead of this phenomenon, the financial statement among entities across countries must adapt to their condition. The other aspect, as an endurable issue in accounting research, the following study can investigate the accounting quality in various aspects. For example, to determine the earnings management activities carried out by managers, a mixed-method subsequent can carry out. It can predict using archival data related to management abilities or a behavioural perspective related to moral ethics or a manager's cognitive bias.

5. FUTURE RESEARCH

The audit should be held as a contract by engaging external auditors to further research government financial statements. This method is expected to exclude the ongoing political hegemony. The IASB's auditors are part of the state civil apparatus immune from being fired, constantly under political hegemony and performativity. The state civil apparatus staffing system makes them behave in a "take it easy" way. Furthermore, this chapter raises the issue of terminating political hegemony if the IASB could implement an artificial intelligent-based auditing system. Indonesia must build an autonomous system, i.e., by applying machine learning, artificial neural networks, etc. In line with this system, an AI (artificial intelligence)-based audit [146, 147] frames all computer systems-based audit procedures and analyses so that auditors are not influenced and affected by subjective norms [148]. With AI-compliant results, in the end, the results are communicated, and there is no longer any chance for justification due to political hegemony.

As for the budgetary ratchet perspective, future research should associate with performance measurements, and what applies is likely the relationship between administrative law and business administration. Furthermore, future research should emphasise bureaucrat behavioural orientation that lets the budgetary rachet become a defence mechanism. The related concepts that could be examined for future research are the transformation of controller behaviours whose efforts and accomplishments are not directly associated with bureaucrat performance. Such a study could also focus on the budgetary system used with a multi-year perspective, not an annual cut-off system. Furthermore, the bureaucrat performance measurement would be based on a managerial-based process rather than an output-based process.

As for future research on cognitive distortion, a motive described in positive accounting theory will affect the cognitive distortion of defence mechanisms. Moral hazards such as altruism, self-interest, selfishness, and political will are dominant and support executive officers' cognitive distortion. This chapter noted that research related to dysfunctional behaviour and cognitive distortions are extensive. Many previous studies have investigated the characteristics illustrating the deficiency of Positive Accounting Theory (PAT) as a comprehensive, contextual, and holistic analysis of accounting policy in organisations. Positive research is blamed for failing to recognise the socially constitutive character of academic knowledge and its underlying value predispositions. In devising an alternative, Chabrak [149] introduces hermeneuticphenomenology. It is a new framework that offers the possibility of exploring and constructing a new understanding of an organisation's accounting policy to preserve its holistic and casuistic character on the epistemological level.

Kahneman et al. [150] state that there are biases in managerial decision making. Heuristics can often lead to systematic bias [151]. Bias judgment and decision-making are human tendencies to make systematic errors based on cognitive factors rather than evidence. For example, people make predictable irrational choices when choosing between alternatives, often producing the same repeatedly deviations. According to Bazerman and Moore [152], general bias can be attributed to and categorised in their radiating heuristics. Furthermore, Kahneman et al. [150] explain that the human brain's irrationality often influences individuals' decisions that they and others around them fail to anticipate. Thus, errors and irregularities resulting from the cognitive bias prevent the making of sound decisions. What is more, even when executive officers have accumulated a lot of work experience and knowledge, they are still subject to that bias and, in some instances, even more so than inexperienced executives.

REFERENCES

1. P. Hribar, T. Kravet, and R. Wilson, "A new measure of accounting quality," *Rev. Account. Stud.,* vol. 19, no., pp. 506-538, 2014, doi: 10.1007/s11142-013-9253-8.

2. H. Ngoc DANG, C. Duc PHAM, T. Xuan NGUYEN, and H. Thi Thanh NGUYEN, "Effects of Corporate Governance and Earning Quality on Listed Vietnamese Firm Value," J. Asian Finance., vol. 7, no. 4, pp. 71-80, 2020, doi: 10.13106/jafeb.2020.vol7.no4.71.

3. N. Bhattacharya, F. Ecker, M. Olsson, and K. Schipper, "Direct and Mediated Associations among Earnings Quality, Information Asymmetry, and the Cost of Equity," *Source Account. Rev.,* vol. 87, no. 2, pp. 449-482, 2012, DOI: 10.2308/accr-10200.

4. M. D. Beneish, "The Detection of Earnings Manipulation," *Financ. Anal.* J., vol. 55, no. 5, pp. 24-36, 1999.

5. P. Dechow, W. Ge, and C. Schrand, "Understanding earnings quality: A review of the proxies, their determinants and their consequences," J. Account. Econ., vol. 50, no. 2-3, pp. 344-401, Dec. 2010, doi: 10.1016/j.jacceco.2010.09.001.

6. J. Arquilla and A. W. Marshall, "Ethics and Information Warfare," in Strategic Appraisal, 1st ed., Z. M. Khalilzad and J. P. White, Eds. RAND Corporation, 1999, pp. 379-402.

7. S. P. Kothari, A. J. Leone, and C. E. Wasley, "Performance matched discretionary accrual measures," J. Account. Econ., vol. 39, no. 1, pp. 163-197, Feb. 2005, doi: 10.1016/j.jacceco.2004.11.002.

8. M. Liu, Y. Shi, C. Wilson, and Z. Wu, "Does family involvement explain why corporate social responsibility affects earnings management?" J. Bus. Res., vol. 75, pp. 8-16, Jun. 2017, doi: 10.1016/j.jbusres.2017.02.001.

9. Y. Kim, M. S. Park, and B. Wier, "Is Earnings Quality Associated with Corporate Social Responsibility?," *Source Account. Rev.*, vol. 87, no. 3, pp. 761-796, 2012, doi: 10.2308/accr-10209.

10. F. Heidarpoor and F. S. Shahrivar, "Unsystematic risk and internal control quality impact on the earning quality by using volatility profits index in tehran stock exchange," *Indian J. Sci. Technol.*, vol. 8, no. 11, 2015, doi: 10.17485/ijst/2015/v8i11/71800.

11. S. Setin and E. Murwaningsari, "The effect of Managerial Ability towards Earning Quality with Audit Committee as Moderating Variable," ABRM, 2018. Accessed: Mar. 31, 2021. [Online]. Available: www.jbrmr.com.

12. J. N. Myers, L. A. Myers, and T. C. Omer, "Exploring the Term of the Auditor-Client Relationship and the Quality of Earnings: A Case for Mandatory Auditor Rotation?," *Account. Rev.*, vol. 78, no. 3, pp. 779-799, 2003.

13. M. Moshtagh, J. Mirlashari, H. Rafiey, A. Azin, and R. Farnam, "Human identity versus gender identity: The perception of sexual addiction among Iranian women," Health Care Women Int., vol. 38, no. 7, pp. 732-752, 2017, doi: 10.1080/07399332.2017.1322594.

14. J. Francis, D. Nanda, and P. Olsson, "Voluntary Disclosure, Earnings Quality, and Cost of Capital," Source *J.* Account. Res., vol. 46, no. 1, pp. 53-99, 2008, doi: 10.1111/j.l475-679X.2008.00267.x.

15. J. Francis, A. H. Huang, S. Rajgopal, and A. Y. Zang, "CEO reputation and earnings quality," *Contemp. Account. Res.*, vol. 25, no. 1, pp. 109-147, 2008, doi: 10.1506/car.25.1.4.

16. F. Almaqtari, A. A. Hashed, M. Shamim, and W. M. Al-ahdal, "Impact of corporate governance mechanisms on financial reporting quality: a study of Indian GAAP and Indian Accounting Standards," Probl. Perspect. Manag., vol. 18, no. 4, pp. 1-13, 2020, doi: 10.21511/ppm.18(4).2020.01.

17. R. Legenzova, "A Concept of Accounting Quality from Accounting Harmonisation Perspective," Econ. Bus., vol. 28, no. 1, pp. 33-37, Apr. 2016, doi: 10.1515/eb-2016-0005.

18. M. E. Barth, W. R. Landsman, and M. H. Lang, "International accounting standards and accounting quality," *J. Account. Res.*, vol. 46, no. 3, pp. 467-498, Jun. 2008, doi: 10.1111/j.1475-679X.2008.00287.x.

19. N. S. Soderstrom and K. J. Sun, "IFRS adoption and accounting quality: A review," Eur. Account. Rev., vol. 16, no. 4, pp. 675-702, 2007, doi: 10.1080/09638180701706732.

20. J. L. Callen, M. Khan, and H. Lu, "Accounting quality, stock price delay, and future stock returns," *Contemp. Account. Res.*, vol. 30, no. 1, pp. 269-295, Mar. 2013, doi: 10.1111/j.1911-3846.2011.01154.x.

21. P. M. Dechow and I. D. Dichev, "The quality of accruals and earnings: The role of accrual estimation errors," in Accounting Review, Mar. 2002, vol. 77, no. SUPPL., pp. 35-59, DOI: 10.2308/accr.2002.77.s-1.35.

22. S. Sumiyana and S. Sriwidharmanely, "Mitigating the harmful effects of technostress: inducing chaos theory in an experimental setting," *Behav. Inf. Technol.*, vol. 39, no. 10, pp. 1079-1093, Jul. 2020, doi: 10.1080/0144929X.2019.1641229.

23. S. Sumiyana and S. Sriwidharmanely, "The Chaotic Behaviour of ICT Users," in Chaotic System, IntechOpen, 2020, p. 20.

24. Watkins, A. L., Hillison, W., & Morecroft, S. E. Audit quality: Asynthesis of theory and empirical evidence. Journal of Accounting Literature. 2004. 23, 153-193. ISSN 0737-4607

25. H. Mintzberg, "The Organization as Political Arena," *J. Manag. Stud.*, vol. 22, no. 2, pp. 133-154, Mar. 1985, doi: 10.1111/j.1467-6486.1985.tb00069.x.

26. G. R. Ferris, P. L. Perrewé, and C. Douglas, "Social Effectiveness in Organisations: Construct Validity and Research Directions," J. Leadersh. Organ. Stud., vol. 9, no. 1, pp. 49-63, Aug. 2002, doi: 10.1177/107179190200900104.

27. A. H. Kimura, "Understanding Fukushima: Nuclear impacts, risk perceptions and organic farming in a feminist political ecology perspective," in *The International Handbook of Political Ecology*, Edward Elgar Publishing Ltd., 2015, pp. 260-273.

28. G. Lăzăroiu, "Work Motivation and Organisational Behavior," Contemp. Readings Law Soc. Justice, vol. VII, no. 2, pp. 66-75, 2015.

29. M. Clark, *Antonio Gramsci and the revolution that failed.* Yale University Press, 1977.

30. John J. Mearsheimer, "The Future of the American Pacifier," Foreign Aff., vol. 80, pp. 46-61, Jul. 2001, doi: 10.4324/9781315251943-10.

31. T. Rogers, D. P. Green, J. Ternovski, and C. Ferrerosa Young, "Social pressure and voting: A field experiment conducted in a high-salience election," Elect. Stud., vol. 46, pp. 87-100, Apr. 2017, doi: 10.1016/j.electstud.2017.02.004.

32. A. Rudi, "Menurut BPK, Ini 6 Penyimpangan dalam Pembelian Lahan RS Sumber Waras," *Kompas.com,* 2016. https://megapolitan.kompas.com/read/2016/04/13/15314101/Menurut.BPK.Ini.6.Penyimpangan.dalam.Pembelian.Lahan.RS.Sumber.Waras. (accessed Aug. 29, 2021).

33. M. R. Priyasmoro, "Evaluasi APBD, Kemenkeu Temukan Pemborosan Pemerintah Daerah," Liputan6.com, 2020. https://bisnis.tempo.co/read/1036107/evaluasi-apbd-kemenkeu-temukan-pemborosan-pemerintah-daerah (accessed Aug. 29, 2021).

34. BPK Perwakilan Provinsi DKI Jakarta, "Hasil Pemeriksaan BPK atas LK Pemerintah Provinsi DKI Jakarta TA 2013," 2014. https://jakarta.bpk.go.id/hasil-pemeriksaan-bpk-atas-lk-pemerintah-provinsi-dki-jakarta-ta-2013/ (accessed Aug. 29, 2021).

35. A. M. Keteng, "BPK Temukan Potensi Kerugian APBD DKI 2013, Ahok: Ini Kado Ultah - News Liputan6.com," Liputan6.com, 2014. https://www.liputan6.com/news/read/2066253/bpk-temukan-potensi-kerugian-apbd-dki-2013-ahok-ini-kado-ultah (accessed Aug. 29, 2021).

36. I. Brusca, E. Caperchione, S. Cohen, and F. M. Rossi, "Comparing Accounting Systems in Europe," in Public Sector Accounting and Auditing in Europe: The Challenge of Harmonization, I. Brusca, E. Caperchione, S. Cohen, and F. M. Rossi, Eds. New York: Palgrave Macmillan, 2015.

37. C. Aranda, J. Arellano, and A. Davila, "Ratcheting and The Role of Relative Target Setting," Account. Rev., vol. 89, no. 4, pp. 1197-1226, Jul. 2014, doi: 10.2308/accr-50733.

38. A. Downs, "A Theory of Bureaucracy," Am. Econ. Rev., vol. 55, no. 1, pp. 439-446, 1965.

39. A. Downs, "Inside Bureaucracy." Little Brown Company, Boston, 1967.

40. G. Brennan and J. M. Buchanan, "Towards A Tax Constitution For Leviathan," J. Public Econ., vol. 8, pp. 255-273, 1977.

41. G. Brennan and J. M. Buchanan, "Tax Instruments As Constraints On The Disposition Of Public Revenues," J. Public Econ., vol. 9, no. December 1977, pp. 301-318, 1978.

42. W. B. Alfonso, "Leviathan or Flypaper: Examining the Fungibility of Earmarked Local Sales Taxes for Transportation," Public Budg. Finance., vol. 35, no. 3, pp. 1-23, 2015.

43. A. Blais and S. Dion, "Are Bureaucrats Budget Maximizers? The Niskanen Model & Its Critics," Polity, vol. 22, no. 4, pp. 655-674, 1990.

44. J. C. Garand, C. T. Parkhurst, and R. J. Seoud, "Bureaucrats, Policy Attitudes, and Political Behavior: Extension of the Bureau Voting Model of Government Growth," J. Public Adm. Res. Theory, vol. 1, no. 2, pp. 177-212, 1991.

45. T. M. Lee and E. Plummer, "Budget Adjustments in Response to Spending Variances: Evidence of Ratcheting of Local Government Expenditures," J. Manag. *Account. Res.*, vol. 19, pp. 137-167, 2007, doi: 10.2308/jmar.2007.19.1.137.

46. S. B. Megdal, "The Determination of Local Public Expenditures and the Principal and Agent Relation : A Case Study," Public Choice, vol. 40, no. 1, pp. 71-87, 1983.

47. A. Rolle, "An Empirical Discussion of Public School Districts As Budget-Maximising Agencies," J. Educ. Finance., vol. 29, no. Spring, pp. 277-298, 2004.

48. W. A. Niskanen, Bureaucracy and Representative Government. Chicago: Aldine, Atherton, 1971.

49. L. Sigelman, "The Bureaucrat as Budget Maximizer: An Assumption Examined," Public Budg. Finance., vol. 6, no. 1, pp. 50-59, 1986.

50. C. J. Bowling, C.-L. Cho, and D. S. Wright, "Establishing a Continuum from Minimising to Maximizing Bureaucrats," Public Adm. Rev., vol. 64, no. 4, pp. 489-499, 2004.

51. D. P. Moynihan, "Does Public Service Motivation Lead to Budget Maximization? Evidence from an Experiment," Int. Public Manag. J., vol. 16, no. 2, pp. 179-196, 2013.

52. J. E. Ryu, C. J. Bowling, C. L. Cho, and D. S. Wright, "Effects of Administrators' Aspirations, Political Principals' Priorities, and Interest Groups' Influence on State Agency Budget Requests," Public Budg. Finance., vol. 27, no. 2, pp. 22-49, 2007.

53. T. Arapis and C. Bowling, "From maximising to minimising: A national study of state bureaucrats and their budget preferences," J. Public Adm. Res. Theory, vol. 30, no. 1, pp. 144-160, 2020, doi: 10.1093/jopart/muz011.

54. A. Feenberg, The Philosophy of Praxis. Marx, Lukács, and The Frankfurt School, no. October 2013. 2019.

55. W. M. Foster and E. Wiebe, "Praxis Makes Perfect: Recovering the Ethical Promise of Critical Management Studies," J. Bus. Ethics, vol. 94, no. SUPPL. 2, pp. 271-283, 2010.

56. R. P. Nielsen, "Organization Ethics from a Perspective of Praxis," Bus. Ethics Q., vol. 3, no. 2, pp. 131-151, 2018.

57. B. Brodjonegoro and J. Martinez-Vazquez, "An Analysis of Indonesia's Transfer System: Recent Performance and Future Prospects," in *Reforming Intergovernmental Fiscal Relations and the Rebuilding of Indonesia: The 'Big Bang'* Program and its Economic Consequences, J. Martinez-Vazquez, S. M. Indrawati, and J. Alm, Eds. Cheltenham Glos: Edward Elgar Publishing, 2005.

58. J. Alm, R. H. Aten, and R. Bahl, "Can Indonesia Decentralise successfully? Plans, Problems and Prospects," Bull. Indonesia. Econ. Stud., vol. 37, no. 1, pp. 83-102, 2001, doi: 10.1080/000749101300046537 To.

59. J. Kornai, "The Soft Budget Constraint," Kyklos, vol. 39, no. 1, pp. 3-30, 1986.

60. J. M. Parks, L. Ma, and D. G. Gallagher, "Elasticity in the 'Rules of the Game: Exploring Organisational Expedience," Hum. Relations, vol. 63, no. 5, pp. 701-730, 2010.

61. C. Hood, H. Rothstein, and R. Baldwin, The Government of Risk: Understanding Risk Regulation Regimes. Oxford: Oxford University Press, 2001.

62. N. Jackson and P. Carter, Rethinking Organisational Behaviour. A Poststructuralist Framework, Second. Pearson Education Limited, 2007.

63. S. Lawrence and U. Sharma, "Commodification of Education and Academic Labour - Using the Balanced Scorecard in a University Setting," *Crit. Perspect. Account.*, vol. 13, no. 5-6, pp. 661-677, 2002.

64. A. Mounier and P. Tangchuang, "Quality Issues of Education in Thailand," in Education in Thailand: An Old Elephant in Search of a New Mahout, Singapore: Springer, 2018, pp. 477-499.

65. P. Smith, Cultural Theory: An Introduction, vol. 27, no. 2. Oxford, UK: Blackwell Publishing, 2001.

66. B. F. Burke, "Altruism, Accountability, and Transparency: Cooperative Aspirations in Contemporary State-Level Budgeting," J. Public Budgeting, Account. Finance. Manag., vol. 18, no. 2, pp. 197-222, 2006.

67. N. C. Dometrius and D. S. Wright, "Governors, Legislatures, and State Budgets across Time," Polit. Res. Q., vol. 63, no. 4, pp. 783-795, 2010.

68. D. Goodman and E. J. Clynch, "Budgetary Decision Making by Executive and Legislative Budget Analysts: The Impact of Political Cues and Analytical Information," Public Budg. Finance., 2004.

69. J. Dolan, "The Budget-Minimizing Bureaucrat? Empirical evidence from the Senior Executive Service," Public Adm. Rev., vol. 62, no. 1, pp. 42-50, 2002.

70. R. G. Holcombe, "Government Growth in the Twenty-First Century," Public Choice, vol. 124, no. 1/2, pp. 95-114, 2005.

71. Vindry Florentin, "Evaluasi APBD, Kemenkeu Temukan Pemborosan Pemerintah Daerah - Bisnis Tempo.co," Tempo.co, 2017. https://bisnis.tempo.co/read/1036107/evaluasi-apbd-kemenkeu-temukan-pemborosan-pemerintah-daerah (accessed Aug. 29, 2021).

72. L. H. Wiwoho, "Pemborosan Anggaran Masih Terjadi," *Kompas.com,* 2016. https://nasional.kompas.com/read/2016/02/09/15030051/Pemborosan.Anggaran.Masih.Terjadi?page=all (accessed Aug. 29, 2021).

73. C. Iswinarno and N. Ardiansyah, "Influencer Diguyur Miliaran Rupiah, PKS: Pemerintah Cuma Pentingkan Citra," suara.com, 2020. https://www.suara.com/news/2020/08/21/123812/influencer-diguyur-miliaran-rupiah-pks-pemerintah-cuma-pentingkan-citra (accessed Aug. 29, 2021).

74. B. Rahmat, "FITRA Riau: Pemborosan Rp 1,3 Triliun pada Rencana APBD Riau Tahun 2017," Tribunnews, 2017. https://m.tribunnews.com/regional/2017/01/19/fitra-riau-pemborosan-rp-13-triliun-pada-rencana-apbd-riau-tahun-2017?page=all (accessed Aug. 29, 2021).

75. J. E. Russo, M. G. Meloy, and T. J. Wilks, "predecisional distortion of information by auditors and salespersons," Manage. Sci., vol. 46, no. 1, pp. 13-27, 2000, doi: 10.1287/mnsc.46.1.13.15127.

76. H. R. Arkes and C. Blumer, "The psychology of sunk cost," Organ. Behav. Hum. Decis. Process., vol. 35, no. 1, pp. 124-140, 1985, doi: 10.1016/0749-5978(85)90049-4.

77. D. Frey, "Recent research on selective exposure to information," Adv. Exp. Soc. Psychol., vol. 19, no. C, pp. 41-80, 1986, doi: 10.1016/S0065-2601(08)60212-9.

78. M. Nelson and H. T. Tan, "Judgment and decision making research in auditing: A task, person, and interpersonal interaction perspective," Auditing, vol. 24, no. SUPPL., pp. 41-71, 2005, DOI: 10.2308/aud.2005.24.supplement.41.

79. S. E. Bonner, "Judgment and Decision Making Research in Accounting," 1999.

80. J. C. Bedard and S. F. Biggs, "Pattern Recognition, Hypotheses Generation, and Auditor Performance in an Analytical Task," Account. Rev., vol. 66, no. 3, pp. 622-642, 1991.

81. J. R. Cohen, G. Krishnamoorthy, and A. M. Wright, "Evidence on the effect of financial and nonfinancial trends on analytical review," Auditing, vol. 19, no. 1, pp. 26-48, 2000, DOI: 10.2308/aud.2000.19.1.27.

82. D. E. Hirst, L. Koonce, and S. Venkataraman, "Management earnings forecasts: A review and framework," Account. Horizons, vol. 22, no. 3, pp. 315-338, 2008, doi: 10.2308/acch.2008.22.3.315.

83. D. E. Hirst and L. Koonce, "Audit analytical procedures: A field investigation," Contemp. *Account. Res.,* vol. 13, no. 2, pp. 457-486, 1996, doi: 10.1111/j.1911-3846.1996.tb00511.x.

84. L. Koonce and M. G. LIPE, "Earnings Trend and Performance Relative to Benchmarks: How Consistency Influences Their Joint Use," J. *Account. Res.,* vol. 48, no. 4, pp. 859-884, 2010, doi: 10.1111/j.1475-679X.2010.00377.x.

85. W. F. Wright, "Discussion of A cognitive characterisation of audit analytical review," Audit. A J. Pract. Theory, vol. 12, no. Supplement, p. 79, 1993.

86. V. Rybowiak, H. Garst, M. Frese, and B. Batinic, "Error Orientation Questionnaire (EOQ): Reliability, validity, and different language equivalence," J. Organ. Behav., vol. 20, no. 4, pp. 527-547, 1999, doi: 10.1002/(SICI)1099-1379(199907)20:4<527::AID-JOB886>3.0.CO;2-G.

87. S. Freud, "How past relationships," vol. 13, no. 12, pp. 608-609, 2000.

88. J. Kennedy, "Debiasing Audit Judgment with Accountability : A Framework and Experimental Results Author (s): Jane Kennedy Published by : Wiley on behalf of Accounting Research Center, Booth School of Business, University of Chicago Stable URL : http://www.jstor.or," J. *Account. Res.,* vol. 31, no. 2, pp. 231-245, 1993.

89. Raymond S. Nickerson, "Confirmation bias: a ubiquitous phenomenon in many guises," Rev. Gen. Psychol., vol. 2, no. 2, pp. 175-220, 1998.

90. A. H. Eagly and S. Chaiken, "The advantages of an inclusive definition of attitude," Soc. Cogn., vol. 25, no. 5, pp. 582-602, 2007, doi: 10.1521/soco.2007.25.5.582.

91. T. L. N. Emerson, S. J. Conroy, and C. W. Stanley, "Ethical attitudes of accountants: Recent evidence from a practitioners' survey," J. Bus. Ethics, vol. 71, no. 1, pp. 73-87, 2007, doi: 10.1007/s10551-006-9125-2.

92. J. Shaftel and T. L. Shaftel, "The Influence of Effective Teaching in Accounting on Student Attitudes, Behavior, and Performance," Issues Account. Educ., vol. 20, no. 3, pp. 231-246, 2005, doi: 10.2308/iace.2005.20.3.231.

93. M. T. Bradshaw and K. Peterson, "The Interactive Role of Difficulty and Incentives in Explaining the Annual Earnings Forecast Walkdown," vol. 91, no. 4, pp. 995-1021, 2016, doi: 10.2308/accr-51398.

94. J. L. Brown, S. Farrington, and G. B. Sprinkle, "Biased self-assessments, feedback, and employees ' compensation plan choices," Accounting, Organ. Soc., vol. 54, pp. 45-59, 2016, doi: 10.1016/j.aos.2016.08.003.

95. R. N. Schmidt, "The Effects of Auditors' Accessibility to "Tone at the Top" Knowledge on Audit Judgments," vol. 26, no. 2, pp. 73-96, 2014, DOI: 10.2308/bria-50824.

96. J. E. Shipman, Q. T. Swanquist, and R. L. Whited, "Propensity Score Matching in Accounting Research," vol. 92, no. 1, pp. 213-244, 2017, doi: 10.2308/accr-51449.

97. K. T. Trotman, "Design Issues in Audit JDM Experiments," vol. 192, no. August, pp. 181-192, 2001.

98. T. D. Carpenter, J. L. Reimers, and R. College, "Professional Skepticism: The Effects of a Partner's Influence and the Level of Fraud Indicators on Auditors' Fraud Judgments and Actions," vol. 25, no. 2, pp. 45-69, 2013, DOI: 10.2308/bria-50468.

99. M. Donle, "Organizational Error Climate and Auditors' Predispositions toward Handling Errors," Behav. Res. Account., vol. 23, no. 2, pp. 69-92, 2011, doi: 10.2308/bria-10061.

100. T. Jeffrey, "Predecisional distortion of evidence as a consequence of real-time audit review," 2002.

101. S. E. Kaplan, K. R. Pope, and J. A. Samuels, "Intentions to Report Fraud to a Manager," vol. 27, no. 2, pp. 77-94, 2015, doi: 10.2308/bria-51126.

102. W. R. Knechel, G. V Krishnan, M. Pevzner, L. B. Shefchik, and U. K. Velury, "Audit Quality: Insights from the Academic Literature," vol. 32, no. April 2012, pp. 385-421, 2013, DOI: 10.2308/ajpt-50350.

103. G. Liu, "Gathering Evidence through Enquiry :" Behav. Res. Account., vol. 24, no. 2, pp. 153-175, 2012, doi: 10.2308/bria-10271.

104. B. Pierce and B. Sweeney, "Perceived Adverse Consequences of Quality Threatening Behaviour in Audit Firms," international J. Audit., vol. 39, pp. 19-39, 2006.

105. D. Satava, C. Caldwell, L. Richards, D. Satava, and L. Richards, "Ethics and the Auditing Culture : the Foundation Rethinking and Auditing of Accounting," vol. 64, no. 3, pp. 271-284, 2011, doi: 10.1007/sl0551-005-0556-y.

106. P. Cramer, "Defense Mechanisms : 40 Years of Empirical Research," no. August, pp. 37-41, 2014, doi: 10.1080/00223891.2014.947997.

107. S. J. Harrington, "A test of a person - Issue contingent model of ethical decision making in organisations," J. Bus. Ethics, vol. 16, no. 4, pp. 363-375, 1997, doi: 10.1023/A:1017900615637.

108. Z. S. Yadin, "Analysing the Patient's First Name in the Search for Identity," *Contemp. Psychoanal.,* vol. 52, no. 4, pp. 547-577, 2016, doi: 10.1080/00107530.2016.1235461.

109. E. Singer, "Transference and Parataxic Distortion," vol. 7530, no. June, 1993, doi: 10.1080/00107530.1993.10746818.

110. M. W. Nelson, C. A. Proell, and A. E. Randel, "Team-Oriented Leadership and Auditors' Willingness to Raise Audit Issues," vol. 91, no. 6, pp. 1781-1805, 2016, doi: 10.2308/accr-51399.

111. J. S. Pickerd, S. L. Summers, and D. A. Wood, "An Examination of How Entry-Level Staff Auditors Respond to Tone at the Top `-vis Tone at the Bottom vis-a," vol. 27, no. 1, pp. 79-98, 2015, doi: 10.2308/bria-50918.

112. B. Sweeney, D. Arnold, and B. Pierce, "The impact of perceived ethical culture of the firm and demographic variables on auditors' ethical evaluation and intention to act decisions," J. Bus. Ethics, vol. 93, no. 4, pp. 531-551, 2010, doi: 10.1007/s10551-009-0237-3.

113. J. J. Geller, "Parataxic Distortions in the Initial Stages of Group Relationships," vol. 7284, 2015, doi: 10.1080/00207284.1962.11508231.

114. C. H. Shubs, "Transference Issues Concerning Victims of Violent Crime and Other Traumatic Incidents of Adulthood," Psychoanal. Psychol., vol. 25, no. 1, pp. 122-141, 2008, doi: 10.1037/0736-9735.25.1.122.

115. M. Barrett, D. J. Cooper, and K. Jamal, "Globalization and the coordinating of work in multinational audits," Accounting, Organ. Soc., vol. 30, no. 1, pp. 1-24, 2005, doi: 10.1016/j.aos.2004.02.002.

116. M. Willekens and H. Vander Bauwhede, "Auditor Reporting Conservatism as a Defence Mechanism against Increased post-Enron Litigation Risk," no. January 2004, 2014.

117. E. M. Bamber and V. M. Iyer, "Auditors' identification with their clients and its effect on auditors' objectivity," Auditing, vol. 26, no. 2, pp. 1-24, 2007, DOI: 10.2308/aud.2007.26.2.1.

118. M. J. Meyer, J. T. Rigsby, and J. Boone, "The impact of auditor-client relationships on the reversal of first-time audit qualifications," Manag. Audit. J., vol. 22, no. 1, pp. 53-79, 2007, doi: 10.1108/02686900710715648.

119. P. M. Fernbach, Y. Hagmayer, and S. A. Sloman, "Effort denial in self-deception," Organ. Behav. Hum. Decis. Process., vol. 123, no. 1, pp. 1-8, 2014, doi: 10.1016/j.obhdp.2013.10.013.

120. J. Friedrichs, "Useful lies: The twisted rationality of denial," Philos. Psychol., vol. 27, no. 2, pp. 212-234, 2014, doi: 10.1080/09515089.2012.724354.

121. E. Trunnell and W. E. Holt, "The Concept of Denial and Disavowal," *J. Am. Psychoanal. Assoc.*, vol. 22, no. 4, pp. 769-784, 1974.

122. R. L. Buckner and D. C. Carroll, "Self-projection and the brain," vol. 11, no. 2, 2006, doi: 10.1016/j.tics.2006.11.004.

123. P. D. Harms, A. J. Vanhove, and F. Luthans, "Positive Projections and Health : An Initial Validation of the Implicit Psychological Capital Health Measure Positive Projections and Health :" 2017, DOI: 10.1111/apps.12077.

124. B. K. Payne, "Stereotypes Focus Defensive Projection," vol. 1, 2005, DOI: 10.1177/0146167205285556.

125. C. M. Stefaniak, R. W. Houston, and R. M. Cornell, "The effects of employer and client identification on internal and external auditors' evaluations of internal control deficiencies," Auditing, vol. 31, no. 1, pp. 39-56, 2012, DOI: 10.2308/ajpt-10179.

126. S. M. Andersen, R. Tuskeviciute, and E. Przybylinski, "Coherent variability: The self with significant others in memory and context," Soc. Cogn., vol. 35, no. 2, pp. 107-123, 2017, doi: 10.1521/soco.2017.35.2.107.

127. S. M. Andersen and J. S. Thorpe, "An IF-THEN theory of personality: Significant others and the relational self," J. Res. Pers., vol. 43, no. 2, pp. 163-170, 2009, doi: 10.1016/j.jrp.2008.12.040.

128. T. J. Perfect and L. J. Harris, "Adult age differences in unconscious transference : Source confusion or identity blending ?" vol. 31, no. 4, pp. 570-580, 2003.

129. S. M. Andersen and M. S. Berk, "Transference in Everyday Experience : Implications of Experimental Research for Relevant Clinical Phenomena," vol. 2, no. 1, pp. 81-120, 1998.

130. J. Svanberg, P. Öhman, and P. E. Neidermeyer, "Auditor objectivity as a function of auditor negotiation self-efficacy beliefs," Adv. Account., vol. 44, no. January, pp. 121-131, 2019, doi: 10.1016/j.adiac.2018.10.001.

131. J. Svanberg and P. Ohman, "Auditors ' identification with their clients : Effects on audit quality," vol. 47, 2015, doi: 10.1016/j.bar.2014.08.003.

132. S. Dawood and A. Pincus, "Contemporary integrative interpersonal theory of personality," no. June, 2018.

133. A. P. Brief, J. M. Dukerich, and L. I. Doran, "Resolving Ethical Dilemmas in Management: Experimental Investigations of Values, Accountability, and Choice," J. Appl. Soc. Psychol., vol. 21, no. 5, pp. 380-396, Mar. 1991, doi: 10.1111/j.1559-1816.1991.tb00526.x.

134. F. T. DeZoort and A. T. Lord, "A Review and Synthesis of Pressure Effects Research in Accounting," J. Account. Lit., vol. 16, pp. 28-85, 1997, Accessed: Oct. 26, 2018. [Online]. Available: https://search.proquest.com/openview/8e9eb137bf01a22e74892170d5ca251d/1?pq-origsite=gscholar&cbl=31366&casa_token=l95Z2uomsssAAAAA:O8V_VTb_gJwxZUQbEBQWvkiqTpQRdgFpt9aEYhl5Cd ffaP2KFQosX9U A7noVIhzyaSXjHBpZIw.

135. Y. F. Gong, S. Kim, and N. Harding, "Elevating professional scepticism an exploratory study into the impact of accountability pressure and knowledge of the superior's preferences," Manag. Audit. J., vol. 29, no. 8, pp. 674-694, Aug. 2014, doi: 10.1108/MAJ-08-2013-0914.

136. H. F. Buchan, "Ethical Decision Making in the Public Accounting Profession : An Extension of Ajzen ' s Theory of Planned Behavior," J. Bus. Ethics, vol. 61, pp. 165-181, 2005, doi: 10.1007/s10551-005-0277-2.

137. M. Ann, D. Stephen, and J. E. Blanton, "Social Cognitive Theory : The Antecedents and Effects of Ethical Climate Fit on Organizational Attitudes of Corporate Accounting Professionals — A Reflection of Client Narcissism and Fraud Attitude Risk," J. Bus. Ethics, pp. 453-467, 2015, doi: 10.1007/s10551-014-2210-z.

138. M. Mansouri and J. I. A. Rowney, "The Dilemma of Accountability for Professionals: A Challenge for Mainstream Management Theories," J. Bus. Ethics, vol. 123, no. 1, pp. 45-56, 2014, doi: 10.1007/s10551-013-1788-x.

139. A. Musbah, C. J. Cowton, and D. Tyfa, "The Role of Individual Variables, Organisational Variables and Moral Intensity Dimensions in Libyan Management Accountants' Ethical Decision Making," J. Bus. Ethics, vol. 134, no. 3, pp. 335-358, 2016, doi: 10.1007/s10551-014-2421-3.

140. T. D. Komalasari, "PT Garuda Indonesia Tercatat Raih Laba, Sebenarnya Mengalami Kerugian," Pikiranrakyat.com, 2019. https://www.pikiran-rakyat.com/ekonomi/pr-01314448/pt-garuda-indonesia-tercatat-raih-laba-sebenarnya-mengalami-kerugian (accessed Aug. 29, 2021).

141. A. Martin and Sukmana, "Dicecar DPR soal Rugi Rp 38 Triliun, Ini Kata Bos PLN Halaman all - *Kompas.com,*" Kompas.com, 2020. https://money.kompas.com/read/2020/06/25/160606426/dicecar-dpr-soal-rugi-rp-38-triliun-ini-kata-bos-pln?page=all (accessed Aug. 29, 2021).

142. C. Akbar, "Kerugian Jiwasraya Lebih dari Rp 10T Akibat Salah Investasi Saham," Tempo.co, 2020. https://bisnis.tempo.co/read/1292772/kerugian-jiwasraya-lebih-dari-rp-10t-akibat-salah-investasi-saham (accessed Aug. 29, 2021).

143. Daryono and C. Umam, "Pertamina Rugi Rp 11,327 Triliun: Pernyataan Ahok Disorot hingga Tanggapan Pengamat Migas," Tribunnews.com, 2020. https://www.tribunnews.com/bisnis/2020/08/26/pertamina-rugi-rp-11327-triliun-pernyataan-ahok-disorot-hingga-tanggapan-pengamat-migas?page=3 (accessed Aug. 29, 2021).

144. I. E. S. Ebaid, "International accounting standards and accounting quality in code-law countries: The case of Egypt," J. Financ. Regul. Compliance, vol. 24, no. 1, pp. 41-59, Feb. 2016, doi: 10.1108/JFRC-12-2011-0047.

145.M. E. Barth, W. R. Landsman, and M. H. Lang, "International accounting standards and accounting quality," J. *Account. Res.*, vol. 46, no. 3, pp. 467-498, 2008, doi: 10.1111/j.1475-679X.2008.00287.x.

146. J. Kokina and T. H. Davenport, "The Emergence of Artificial Intelligence: How Automation is Changing Auditing," Emerg. Technol. Account., vol. 14, no. 1, pp. 115-122, 2017, doi: 10.2308/jeta-51730.

147. K. Omoteso, "The application of artificial intelligence in auditing: Looking back to the future," Expert Syst. with Appl. J., vol. 39, pp. 8490-8495, 2012, doi: 10.1016/j.eswa.2012.01.098.

148. I. Munoko, H. L. Brown-Liburd, and M. Vasarhelyi, "The Ethical Implications of Using Artificial Intelligence in Auditing," J. Bus. Ethics, vol. 167, no. 2, pp. 209-234, Nov. 2020, doi: 10.1007/S10551-019-04407-1.

149. N. Chabrak, "The politics of transcendence: hermeneutic phenomenology and accounting policy," *Crit. Perspect. Account.*, vol. 16, no. 6, pp. 701-716, Aug. 2005, doi: 10.1016/J.CPA.2004.03.003.

150. D. Kahneman, D. Lovallo, and O. Sibony, "The Big Idea: Before You Make That Big Decision," Harv. Bus. Rev., vol. 89, no. 6, pp. 50-60, 2011.

151. J. S. Hammond, R. L. Keeney, and H. Raiffa, "The Hidden Traps in Decision Making," *Harv. Bus. Rev.*, vol. 76, no. 5, pp. 47-58, 1998, Accessed: Aug. 31, 2021. [Online]. Available: www.hbr.org.

152. M. H. Bazerman and D. A. Moore, *Judgmental in Managerial Decision Making.* 2013.

Index

www.ingramcontent.com/pod-product-compliance
Lightning Source LLC
LaVergne TN
LVHW062112200926
848484LV00007B/1647